2nd Edition

Social Policy & Social Work

An Introduction

Jo Cunningham
& Steve Cunningham

SAGE | LearningMatters

SAGE | **Learning**Matters

Learning Matters
An imprint of SAGE Publications Ltd
1 Oliver's Yard
55 City Road
London EC1Y 1SP

SAGE Publications Inc.
2455 Teller Road
Thousand Oaks, California 91320

SAGE Publications India Pvt Ltd
B 1/I 1 Mohan Cooperative Industrial Area
Mathura Road
New Delhi 110 044

SAGE Publications Asia-Pacific Pte Ltd
3 Church Street
#10-04 Samsung Hub
Singapore 049483

Editor: Kate Keers
Production controller: Chris Marke
Project management: Deer Park Productions
Marketing manager: Camille Richmond
Cover design: Wendy Scott
Typeset by: C&M Digitals (P) Ltd, Chennai, India
Printed by: CPI Group (UK) Ltd, Croydon, CR0 4YY

First published in 2012.
Second edition published in 2017.

Library of Congress Control Number: 2017936985

British Library Cataloguing in Publication Data

A catalogue record for this book is available from
the British Library.

ISBN 978-1-4739-1654-8
ISBN 978-1-4739-1655-5 (pbk)

At SAGE we take sustainability seriously. Most of our products are printed in the UK using FSC papers and boards.
When we print overseas we ensure sustainable papers are used as measured by the PREPS grading system.
We undertake an annual audit to monitor our sustainability.

Contents

About the authors

Jo Cunningham is the Head of the School of Social Work, Care and Community at the University of Central Lancashire. She has been centrally involved in the management and teaching of social work education for the past eighteen years. Before commencing her academic career, Jo was a social worker in the area of children and families. Her research interests include childhood accidents, child death, asylum policy, and more recently the policy and practice context surrounding sex workers.

Steve Cunningham is a Senior Lecturer in Social Policy at the University of Central Lancashire. He has taught Social Policy at both undergraduate and postgraduate level for more than twenty years. His research interests are focused on welfare history, poverty and social security, the sociology of welfare, asylum and immigration policy, child labour and children's rights. Steve is the author of numerous publications in these areas.

Series editors' preface

We have witnessed significant changes and shocks in recent years. These have resulted in numerous challenges for the wider world, and for all four countries of the UK. These include political shifts to the 'popular' Right, a growing antipathy to care and support, and dealing with lies and 'alternative truths' in our daily lives. Alongside this, is the need to address the impact of an increasingly ageing population with its attendant social care needs and working with the financial implications that such a changing demography brings. At the other end of the lifespan the need for high quality childcare, welfare and safeguarding services has been highlighted as society develops and responds to the changing complexion. As demand rises so do the costs and the unquestioned assumption that austerity measures are necessary continues to create tensions in services, policies and expectations.

Migration has developed as a global phenomenon and we now live and work with the implications of international issues in our everyday and local lives. Often these issues influence how we construct our social services and determine what services we need to offer. It is likely that as a social worker you will work with a diverse range of people throughout your career, many of whom have experienced significant, even traumatic, events that require a professional and caring response. As well as working with individuals, however, you may be required to respond to the needs of a particular community disadvantaged by world events or excluded within local communities because of assumptions made about them.

The importance of high quality social work education remains if we are adequately to address the complexities of modern life. We should continually strive for excellence in education as this allows us to focus clearly on what knowledge it is useful to engage with when learning to be a social worker. Questioning everything, especially from a position of knowledge is central to social work.

The books in this series respond to the agendas driven by changes brought about by professional bodies, governments and disciplinary reviews. They aim to build on and offer introductory texts based on up-to-date knowledge and to help communicate this in an accessible way, so preparing the ground for future study and for encouraging good practice as you develop your social work career. The books are written by people passionate about social work and social services and aim to instil that passion in others. The current text represents an up-to-date edition of a key book in the series. It introduces you to core legislation and some of diverse ways in which law is interpreted in, for and by social work practice. The complexities of the law are presented in a clear, accessible way that sets the scene for exploring more specialised areas of law affecting practice.

Professor Jonathan Parker

Introduction

Most social policy textbooks begin by acknowledging the difficulties associated with defining social policy. The need to define the discipline stems partly from the fact that many students are encountering social policy for the first time and are often unclear as to the issues and debates that lie at its heart. One of the problems we face is that social policy is not taught as a distinct academic subject in secondary or further education. Consequently, students are often naturally quite apprehensive when first encountering it at university. Their anxieties are sometimes compounded by the fact that they may not be enrolled on a distinct 'social policy' course and are wondering why, as students on social work, nursing, or other welfare-related courses, they are being 'forced' to engage with a discipline that they have not 'signed up' to. As lecturers who have taught social policy for many years, we are well aware of this reaction. However, many, indeed the vast majority of, students have already been introduced to a range of social policy-related issues and debates prior to attending university – for instance, at secondary schools in their citizenship classes, or in sociology, politics, general studies or health and social care courses at college. In addition, of course, you will all have come across and been touched by social policies in your daily lives and this will have given you at least some knowledge about the issues and debates covered by the subject. Indeed, it is frequently an interest in social policy-related issues that leads individuals to apply for social work, health, social care and social science courses in the first place. Hence, although many students have rarely studied social policy as a distinct academic discipline, we find that they are, sometimes unwittingly, already familiar with the much of the terrain that it covers. Indeed, when we ask students directly what they think social policy 'is', they are, without too much prompting, able to identify a range of themes, issues and debates that do relate to the study of social policy.

So if you are approaching this text feeling unclear as to what social policy is, or are questioning the relevance of the discipline to your course, then please do not panic. Firstly, you can rest assured that you are not alone. Many of your peers who are encountering the discipline for the first time will be experiencing similar anxieties. Secondly, we can reassure you that you will doubtlessly be underestimating the amount of knowledge about the discipline that you already possess. Thirdly, we are confident that having read this text you will understand the relevance of social policy to social work and welfare-related practice. Finally, we hope that the book will stimulate your interest in the discipline, and you come to see your social policy studies as not only a central, but also an enjoyable, engaging aspect of your professional education. Certainly, our own experiences suggest that once exposed to social policy, students are often keen to pursue this element of their studies further.

With this in mind, we are delighted to have been given the opportunity to update this textbook. It seems remarkable to us that almost four years has now passed since the publication of the first edition. Clearly much has happened in the intervening period. On a professional level, in 2014, we published a second edition of our other Learning Matters book, *Sociology and Social Work* (Cunningham and Cunningham, 2014). It was while we were working on the finishing touches to that text that our publisher asked us if we would be interested in writing a second edition of our *Social Policy* book, which, of course, we were. The original *Social Policy* text was positively received by social work students, both at our own university and elsewhere, and we are pleased to be given the chance to publish a second edition.

Since 2012, much has happened, politically, economically and in the spheres of social policy and social work practice and education, which leads us to believe that a second edition is necessary. For example, in 2012 the political, economic and social welfare landscape was very different to that which prevails today. At the time of publication, the country was governed by a Conservative/Liberal Democrat Coalition government, which had set out a radical agenda for reforming welfare. As part of its austerity programme, it committed itself to an unprecedented level of public expenditure cuts, slashing spending on welfare programmes, at a time when social need was at its greatest for decades. Much of the first edition of the book was written before the full impact of these measures had been realised. While we were able to predict the ideological trajectory of the Coalition's social policies, we could only hypothesise about the impact of planned public expenditure cuts and welfare reforms on policy and practice. Four years on, we are now in a better position to assess the impact. Of course, we also witnessed the election of a majority Conservative administration in May 2015. This government made it clear that it wished to press ahead with the Coalition's austerity agenda, reducing the scope of state provision still further. As we will show, it has also expressed a desire to reform social work training and practice. Another notable political event occurred in September 2015, when Jeremy Corbyn won the Labour leadership contest after members of the party embraced his radical alternative to the Conservative's austerity agenda. At the time of writing, Corbyn remains leader of the Labour Party, despite an attempt to unseat him in September 2016. As if this was not enough political turbulence, in the aftermath of the 'Brexit' vote we saw the resignation of the Prime Minister, David Cameron, and his replacement by Theresa May. Then, in June 2017, May called a surprise, snap General Election, seeking to increase her Parliamentary majority. Although ostensibly dominated by Brexit, as with all national elections, the outcome of this campaign had fundamental implications for the trajectory of domestic social policy. In short, the UK's political compass has been fundamentally recalibrated since 2012, pointing to new directions and possibilities for social policy and social work.

The ideological climate has changed too. As insecurity, poverty and exclusion have increased, 'behavioural', 'pathological' interpretations for economic and social problems have re-emerged with a vengeance. Of course, as we showed in the first edition of this book, the UK has a long, undistinguished history of holding vulnerable people morally culpable for their fate, blaming them for the circumstances within which they find themselves. Welfare recipients, in particular, have always been treated with suspicion, accused of being 'irresponsible' or 'feckless'. However, the intensity and ferocity of such accusations have gathered at an unprecedented pace, largely encouraged by senior ministers. Although 'social justice' and even 'compassion' have occasionally been invoked by ministers to justify their welfare reforms, their variants of 'social justice' and 'compassion' are tainted with 'neo-liberalism' (see Chapter 5 for a discussion of neo-liberalism). Reducing the incomes of welfare recipients has thus been presented as a 'caring', 'morally invigorating' exercise; it constitutes part of a 'responsibilisation' process that will, ultimately, improve the quality of the lives of those who are temporarily and 'necessarily' plunged into hardship. Hence, David Cameron, the former Prime Minister, described the £26,000 benefit cap as part of the Coalition's *moral mission* to bring *new hope and responsibility* to those *trapped in a cycle of dependency*. It was *about giving new purpose, new opportunity, new hope – and yes, new responsibility to people who had previously been written off with no chance* (Bingham and Dominiczak, 2014, p1). The principle of 'fairness' was also cited as justification for implementing the benefit cap. Here is Iain Duncan Smith (2014), then the Coalition's Minister for the Department for Work and Pensions:

> *Before we implemented the cap, it was possible for people to receive, in some cases, almost twice as much in benefits as the average weekly wage. This system wasn't fair on hardworking taxpayers, paying out ever-increasing amounts to sustain others in lifestyles they could barely dream of affording themselves. But importantly it has not been fair on benefit recipients themselves. How many of us here would want to live trapped in a system where it was more worthwhile sitting on benefits than going to work.*

For some, this ideological shift represents little more than a 'smokescreen'; it is part of a conscious strategy to provide justification for harsh, politically motivated cuts to welfare. Thus, Owen Jones (2013) argues that the *daily diet of poison* administered by Coalition ministers was *the culmination of a systematic campaign by the Tories and their media allies to turn large sections of the population against each other. 'Strivers' versus 'skivers' and 'shirkers'; sinister images of the workshy and feckless with their curtains drawn.* For others, including ministers themselves, the rolling back of social provision is a progressive, altruistically motivated exercise, designed to liberate the poor from the shackles of a stifling, dependency-inducing welfare state. What is not in doubt is that, since the first edition of this book was published, social policy has taken a distinct, rightward, neo-liberal twist and, moreover, this trajectory has continued since the election of a majority Conservative government in May 2015.

The social work profession has not been immune to the rightward, ideological shift that has taken place over the previous four years, and nor have service users themselves. On a practice level, the local authority budget cuts imposed by the Coalition have left local authority social service departments starved of funds. Again, when the first edition of this text was published, the full scale of this reduction in expenditure was not known. However, we now know that between 2010/11 and 2014/15, local authorities experienced a 27 per cent reduction in their spending power, with those authorities in the most disadvantaged areas being the hardest hit (Hastings et al., 2015). As we will show in Chapter 1, more cuts to local authority budgets are planned. Staffing levels have inevitably suffered, increasing the already heavy pressures social workers face in meeting the needs of service users. At the same time, local authorities have been forced to respond to expenditure reductions by cutting service user provision. Hence, despite a backdrop of growing demand for social care among the over-65s, between 2009/10 and 2012/13, there was a 26 per cent reduction in the number of older people receiving publicly funded support in the community (Ismail et al., 2014). As Lymbery (2014, p367) argues, the *effect of financial cuts means that there is substantially less money to respond to people's needs, despite the demographic changes that indicate there will be an increasing number of vulnerable older people in society.* As we demonstrate throughout this text, other service user groups have faced similar reductions in services, and the quality of provision has deteriorated as a consequence. A Care Quality Commission report, published in September 2015, found that 41 per cent of the community-based adult social care services, hospice services and residential social care services it inspected in the previous 12 months were inadequate or required improvement (Boffey, 2015). We examine the impact of austerity measures on services and service users in greater detail in the next chapter. As we will see, the evidence suggests that the welfare cuts introduced as part of the government's austerity initiatives have impacted negatively on health, psychological and social well-being (Hastings et al., 2015).

Meanwhile, the social work profession has itself been targeted by ministers, who have expressed a desire to see the development of a less social science-based, more 'judgemental', skills-focused form of social work education and practice. As we explained in the previous edition, this is not a particularly novel development (see also Cunningham and Cunningham, 2014). Social work academics have always faced accusations that the education they provide to students is too 'theoretical', and geared more towards encouraging them to 'change society' rather than initiating positive change in the lives of the service users they ought to be representing. Traditionally such sentiments have mainly been the preserve of right-wing commentators and right-leaning, tabloid newspapers, but they are now just as likely to be expressed by senior government figures and officials. As we show in this updated book, the level of intensity of the criticism the profession has faced is quite unique, as is the apparent determination among ministers to push through fundamental reforms to social work education and practice. The development of a number of short, intensive, skills-focused qualifying courses is one example of this tendency. So too was the government's decision to withdraw funding from the College of Social Work (CSW), which had been created to represent the profession. Its Professional Capability of Framework's commitment to embedding an understanding of social justice across all aspects of social work training had never sat comfortably with Coalition and Conservative ministers, many of whom felt that this diverted students from 'core', 'practice-related' activities and learning. The CSW's tendency to criticise welfare cuts and the impact of government policy on social work and service users also contributed to a strained relationship between it and senior government figures.

As this brief discussion of just a few recent developments illustrates, a great deal has occurred in the social policy arena in the relatively short time since the first edition of this book was published in 2012. In a way, this serves to highlight the fact that social policies are rapidly moving, forever evolving and changing, heading in one direction, before diverting off once again in another. All these changes might seem disorientating to the social policy novice. However, it is possible to make sense of them, to develop an understanding of the constantly changing social policy terrain and to identify patterns, trends and influences. Indeed, this is precisely what social policy as an academic subject seeks to achieve, and the changing nature of social policies should not deter you from engaging with the discipline. In fact, quite the opposite; it is the dynamic, fluid nature of social policy that makes it such an exciting and topical subject to study and teach. Of course, this means that, as academics, we can never rest on our laurels! There are always new strategies, initiatives, policy proposals or pieces of legislation for us to scrutinise and dissect.

Exciting and engaging though your social policy studies will be, this is not the principal reason why the subject forms such a key component of your professional social work education. Hopefully, you can already see from our brief discussion above how social policies influence the environment within which social work education and practice takes place. As Ray Jones has recently argued, *Our work is shaped by the powerbrokers in Westminster and what we do is dictated by what they say* (European Union News, 2016). Hence, the current government's vision of a skills-based form of social work education, largely devoid of references to social justice, political structures and social policy, certainly has the potential to fundamentally transform the nature of social work, but not necessarily for the better. It could lead to a more judgemental, oppressive, disempowering form of practice that fails to appreciate the constraints that impose themselves upon the lives of service users. A failure to understand the wider social, economic and political environment within which social work practice operates may also blind practitioners to the impact that problems like poverty, inequality and discrimination have on family dynamics, physical and mental well-being and, more generally, opportunities for service users to secure 'inclusion'. As we show in Chapter 2, the absence of a critical, social science component to social work education in the nineteenth century led to the development of a harsh, 'judgemental' form of social work practice. In short, as practitioners, in order to advocate effectively on behalf of service users, you need to have an appreciation of the origins of their marginalisation, exclusion or vulnerabilities, many of which often lie 'without' rather than 'within'. In addition, the absence of a specific social policy dimension to your social work education would mean your entering the world of social work without any conception of the difficulties and obstacles you will face in putting your values into practice. Sadly, the ideals of social work – its desire to improve the lives of marginalised, vulnerable individuals and to empower service users, enabling them to achieve their full potential – have to operate in a less than ideal world, and it is important that you, as students, are aware of the policy and resource constraints that you will face in practice.

That said, we would not want to give the impression that your social policy studies will be directed solely towards informing you about *obstacles* to good practice. It is crucial to understand that social policy research has a positive role to play in drawing our attention to national and international policy developments that promote good practice and improve the social and economic well-being of the groups of people that social workers engage with. It can and does point to new, exciting possibilities which have the potential to help create a more conducive environment for social work practice and initiate real, positive change in the lives of service users.

Structure of the book

Chapter 1 of the book introduces you to the discipline of social policy. As well as examining the historical development of the subject in higher education, it discusses the links between the academic subject of social policy and social work education. The chapter also explains in greater detail how and why social policy can make an important contribution to your professional studies. We do so by assessing how recent public expenditure cuts have impacted upon service users and the ability of social workers to meet the needs of vulnerable people.

Chapter 2 adopts a historical approach and looks at the development of social policy and social work in the nineteenth century. It is often assumed that social policy and social work developments have, historically, been motivated primarily by humanitarian sentiment. However, such interpretations are partial, and fail to acknowledge the complex range of factors, concerns and forces that have shaped, and continue to shape, policy and practice. Our aim in this chapter, therefore, is to provide you with a broad historical perspective, examining the respective influence of 'care' and 'control' concerns in framing nineteenth-century welfare developments. We also seek to draw your attention to the relevance of historical inquiry to helping us understand policy developments today.

Many social policy and social work textbooks include some discussion of the importance of political ideologies. Often, they contain brief chapters on the topic, which seek to summarise what the key principles of the different ideological positions are. However, although helpful, the student is frequently left with an inadequate understanding of how different political ideologies have, historically, shaped social policy and social work. The discussion is sometimes overly theoretical and somewhat detached from the policy-making process itself. In this book we deviate slightly from the 'norm' in that we locate our discussion of ideologies in four chapters – Chapters 3, 4, 5 and 6, which examine the historical development of the post-war welfare state. The advantage of this approach is that it helps illustrate how different ideological perspectives have exercised different levels of influence on social policy and social work developments at different times in British history. Hence, we chart a timeline of influence for different political ideologies, examining the extent to which each has influenced policy and practice. The main perspectives to be examined are social democracy (Chapter 4), neo-liberalism (Chapter 5) and Marxism (Chapter 6). These are important chapters of the book, and the theoretical perspectives examined here will re-emerge in subsequent chapters of the text where we assess the political and ideological principles that have shaped specific social policies.

The remainder of the text is devoted to an analysis of how social policies impact upon citizens at different stages in their life course. The next four chapters therefore contain separate discussions on children, young people, adults and older adults. Chapter 7 examines how children have been at the forefront of social policy and social work practice developments over the past decade. Within social work, the inquiry into the death of Victoria Climbié and more recently the Baby Peter Connelly case have placed a very public spotlight on social workers' attempts to safeguard children. However, our aim in this chapter is to show how an over-concentration on the issues of 'neglect' and 'child protection' can serve to divert attention away from the pressing need to address other factors that can impinge upon the life chances of vulnerable children, such as poverty, poor educational opportunities and health inequalities.

Young people have always been the subject of social policy and social work interventions. Chapter 8 will consider how policy initiatives contribute to and are in turn influenced by wider 'moral panics' about young people. We examine the growing evidence of youth exclusion in Britain today and question the effectiveness of recent policies. The chapter provides a broad assessment of the overall trajectory of policy, critically analysing the assumptions and concerns that have shaped it. As a case study, we analyse the coalition government's response to young people's involvement in the series of riots that swept across England in 2011.

In their practice, social workers provide advice and assistance to a number of different groups of adult service users. Recent policy, in many cases shaped by user movements themselves, has focused upon the need to empower adult service users, by giving them more control over the services they receive. This is clearly a development to be welcomed, though concerns have been expressed about the direction of what has become known as the 'personalisation agenda'. Chapter 9 will provide a critical analysis of the potential of such initiatives.

Working with and providing services to older people can constitute a significant part of a social worker's role. As is the case with working-age adult services, the focus of some recent initiatives has been geared towards empowering service users, by providing them with the means to make decisions about their own lives. As well as examining these policies, Chapter 10 will also consider a range of other social policy developments that can contribute to or impinge upon the economic and social well-being of older people. In short, it will assess the relative ease with which older people are able to access the citizenship rights that other sections of the population take for granted, such as a decent income, appropriate housing and adequate access to health and social care services.

Finally, we hope that this book will help you appreciate the relevance of social policy to your studies. Certainly, the social work profession itself has acknowledged the importance of social policy to social work. As the draft QAA (2016) Benchmark Statements for Social Work indicate: *Within the UK there are different traditions of social welfare (influenced by legislation, historical development and social attitudes) and these have shaped both social work education and practice.* Social work graduates, it states, must be equipped to *think critically about the complex social, legal, economic, political and cultural contexts in which social work practice is located*, and be able to comprehend the issues and trends in modern public and social policy and their relationship to contemporary practice and service delivery in social work. As social policy and social work academics, we passionately support these statements and have structured the book in a way that we believe will go some way to assisting you to meet these objectives.

Part one

The historical and theoretical context

1: Social policy and social work

(Continued)

The chapter will also introduce you to the following academic standards which are set out in the 2016 QAA social work benchmark statements:

4   Defining principles
5.2   Social work theory
5.3   Values and ethics
5.4   Service users and carers
5.5   The nature of social work practice
5.13   Analysis and synthesis
5.16   Skills in working with others
5.17   Skills in personal and professional development
6.2   Teaching learning and assessment
7.3   Knowledge and understanding
7.4   Subject-specific and other skills

Introduction

The discipline of social policy has a long been seen as a crucial element of social work education. Its links with social work training can be traced back to the early twentieth century, when concerns were raised about the overly moralistic training provided to social workers by the Charity Organisation Society (COS), which located the blame for poverty, squalor and other social ills in the 'inadequate' social habits of the poor. Attempts to promote the development of a broader social policy-based social work curriculum, which sought to acknowledge the wider structural causes of disadvantage, were, we will show, prompted by a desire to provide social workers with a more critical awareness of the causes of economic and social ills. The historical perspective we provide in this chapter will help you understand the development of the links between social policy and social work. However, we also want to stress the contemporary resonance of social policy to your social work studies. Hence, towards the end of the chapter we examine some recent, important social policy developments, in particular the cuts in welfare spending that have been introduced since 2010. As well as assessing the impact of these upon service users, we will examine their implications for social work practice.

The origins of social policy

The origins of social policy as an academic discipline can be traced back to the early twentieth century, when a Department of Social Science and Administration (DSSA) was established at the London School of Economics (LSE) in 1912. The initial aims of this embryonic version of the subject were narrowly vocational and its syllabus was geared mainly towards meeting the perceived training needs of untrained voluntary social workers. *It is intended*, stated its syllabus for 1912, *for those who wish to prepare themselves to engage in the many forms of social and charitable effort* (Titmuss, 1966, p15).

Before this, social work training had been undertaken by the COS at the LSE's School of Sociology. We will look in more detail at the work of the COS in Chapter 2; however, for now it is just worth noting that its 'social policy' courses had contained an overtly moral undertone. In keeping with the prevailing philosophies of the day, as well as the COS's own moralistic philosophy, students were taught that poverty, squalor and other social and economic evils were a result of the ignorance or inappropriate behaviour of the poor. As Jones (1983) argues, at the core of the COS's provision was the notion that poverty and destitution were a consequence of a lack of morality or foresight rather than a lack of material resources. Accordingly, its courses focused upon the benefits of self-help and thrift, while bemoaning the idleness, profligacy and drinking habits of the 'lower orders'.

Those involved in creating the new DSSA, including the Fabian socialist Sydney Webb, were at least partly motivated by recognition of the failings of the COS's methods (Attlee, 1920). They felt that governments could and should intervene to promote citizens' welfare. In the context of the times, this was understandable. This was, after all, a period when the pioneering poverty surveys of Charles Booth and Seebohm Rowntree were laying bare the depths of urban squalor and poverty, provoking the consciences of politicians and social reformers. The failure of the COS's provision to acknowledge, as these exhaustive poverty surveys had done, the structural determinants of social problems was seen as a fundamental weakness and one which the new DSSA would seek to address. As Clement Attlee (1920, pp144–5), an early appointee to the Department's teaching staff, put it: *The days are, it is to be hoped, past when people without any qualifications other than a good heart and the means of obtaining money plunged straight into social work without any consideration of . . . what the effect of their actions were going to have, with the result that they only increased the evils they tried to prevent.* Or as Richard Titmuss (1973, p48), a leading post-war social policy scholar, frankly stated, there was a general sense of *dissatisfaction with the existing methods of training upper-middle-class girls in the technique of instructing the poor how to manage their poverty.*

That said, pathological, behavioural interpretations for social problems continued to find expression in the new DSSA's early social policy provision, which, like that of its predecessor, had a tendency towards the adoption of an overtly moralistic tone. *Academically speaking*, Titmuss acknowledged, *it was not perhaps a very respectable affair in those days.* Students continued to be seen as 'moral entrepreneurs', who would utilise their missionary zeal to put the 'lower orders' back onto the 'straight and narrow'. As Titmuss explains, *If poverty was a matter of ignorance then it was the moral duty of one class in society to teach another class how to live, and to lead them, through sanitation, soap and thrift to a better station in life* (pp18–19). Hence, for the princely sum of ten shillings and six pence, students enrolling in the DSSA could undertake a six-lecture course on *The Household Economics of the Hardworking Poor*, whereupon they would be taught how the working population bought their food, stored and cooked it. There was no recognition here of the fact that large sections of the labouring poor were simply unable to afford a healthy diet, and that it was this, and not 'ignorance' as to 'correct' eating habits, that lay at the heart of the nutritional problems they faced. Another course, taught by the renowned eugenicist Karl Pearson, focused upon the links between drink, alcoholism and infant mortality, while remaining silent on the impact that poverty, squalor and poor sanitation had upon premature infant death. As director of an influential national eugenicist organisation which viewed health, ability, crime and much else besides as 'inborn traits', immune to the influence of social reform, Pearson was perhaps hardly the best choice lecturer for a social policy course. Thus provision at the DSSA, initially at least, continued to be shaped by more than the 'faint whiff' of individualistic, behavioural interpretations of social problems.

The quality of teaching did improve, though. Under the tutelage of a more radical generation of lecturers, such as RH Tawney, TH Marshall and Clement Attlee, a more progressive curriculum emerged, one which encouraged those intending to work with poor, marginalised individuals and families to understand the social and economic constraints that shaped their lives. Titmuss (1966, p18), an LSE student at the time, recalls being mesmerised by an inaugural lecture given by Tawney, a new appointee to the department in 1913:

> *The problem of poverty, he said, is not a problem of individual character and waywardness, but a problem of economic and industrial organisation. It had to be studied at its sources and only secondly in its manifestations.*

The appointment of Clement Attlee to the department in 1915 represented another significant milestone. His views of social work training, expressed in his 1920 book, *The social worker*, could not be further removed from those of the COS. Attlee used his book to condemn the COS's approach to social work education, accusing it of encouraging the adoption of *harsh and tactless methods*:

> *. . . a general assumption is made that all applicants are frauds unless they prove themselves otherwise, and this induces an attitude in the COS workers that is profoundly galling to the ordinary applicant, and is apt to bias those who receive their training from the Society.* (Attlee, 1920, p65)

COS workers, Attlee argued, had *a tendency to clothe themselves in the filthy rags of their own righteousness*, and their *lack of sympathy makes their charity a hard and unlovely thing*. Attlee emphasised the need for social work students to be provided with a much broader, political education, which, when taught alongside their practical vocational studies, would better equip them to assist the people they would be working with. Rather than 'blaming' individuals for their predicaments, social workers should, he insisted, empower service users, and indeed even campaign for progressive social and economic change. Attlee argued that the social worker should be a *social investigator*, a *pioneer* and indeed an *agitator, who has some clear conception of what society he wishes to see produced.* Those of you with a rudimentary grasp of political and social history may be aware of the future role Clement Attlee would play in transforming Britain's economic and social landscape, as the leader of the most radical, reforming, progressive government Britain has ever seen. For as the Labour Prime Minister between 1945 and 1951, Attlee presided over the introduction of the array of welfare services and programmes which we now know as the welfare state.

The reforming impulses of those such as Attlee, Tawney and Marshall did influence social work training at the LSE. By 1923, it was offering a two or three year course to welfare workers, which, as well as providing practical welfare work experience, offered *a theoretical grounding in economics, social history, local government social and political philosophy, industrial legislation and 'current problems'* (Lloyd, 1923, p3). Similar social administration courses (social policy courses in all but name) also emerged in other universities across the UK, including Bristol, Birmingham, Leeds, Liverpool, Edinburgh and Glasgow (Attlee, 1920). This trend towards the incorporation of a greater 'social policy' element in social work training was prompted by a desire to move beyond individualised, pathological explanations for human misery, and to understand the wider structural causes of disadvantage that were largely beyond the control of poverty-stricken families. As we shall see in Chapter 2, social work 'in practice' prior to the Second World War (and indeed after 1945) may not always have lived up to these laudable ideals, but this shift in thinking did nonetheless represent an important change in attitudes to social work training.

The development of social policy after 1945

The huge expansion of welfare services after the Second World War undoubtedly contributed to the further development of social policy as an academic discipline. As new publicly funded services grew and absorbed more workers, so too did the demand for social policy courses and the discipline became established in higher education institutions across the UK. Initially, with a few notable exceptions, it developed on a somewhat narrow, relatively vocational basis, sometimes doing little more than providing welfare workers with descriptive information about the institutions they were employed in, as well as the legislation – or policy – that shaped their practice. However, as Brown (1983, p93) points out, social policy gradually developed into a *more lively and critical subject*, which began to ask more penetrating questions about the origins, values and shape of welfare provision:

> *A new generation . . . looked at the services and asked: how far had they succeeded – and how far had they failed? Who had benefited from them? Whose interests did they serve? What had influenced their operation and determined their outcomes?*

At the forefront of this shift were academics such as Peter Townsend and Richard Titmuss, who, as Brown notes, ensured that the discipline developed *an overriding interest in the actual impact of social policies on individuals* (p94). The scope of the discipline thus became much broader, theoretical and critical, analysing the extent to which the post-war welfare state had succeeded in achieving its aims. Instead of simply describing social service structures, policy and legislation, social policy courses focused upon evaluating the ethos and principles that underpinned welfare, as well as assessing its impact on the social and economic well-being of citizens. The notion that social policies were motivated by altruistic, benevolent intentions – that they were, to quote one academic, *a good deed in a naughty world* (Donnison, cited in Brown, 1983, p95) – began to be challenged, as evidence of the failure of the post-war welfare state to respond to citizens' needs emerged. Indeed, as we show in Chapter 4, by the late 1960s social policy academics were drawing attention to the disciplinary, controlling functions that welfare policies, including those related to social work, could perform. As Chris Jones (2011) points out, attempts to infuse this more radical social science perspective into social work education were not always welcomed by a social work profession that, in some cases, was still wedded to a conservative, vocationally orientated form of training. However, in the context of the civil rights campaigns and protest movements of the late 1960s, it was a perspective that many social work students themselves welcomed. Many had become disillusioned about the failure of their professional courses to tap into the critical and challenging insights provided by social policy/social science literature. Jones recalls his experiences of social work training around this time:

> *I remember all the professional lecturers promulgated views of poverty as though they were manifestations of pathological personalities and inadequate mothering; of how the well-functioning family with the mother at the hearth was the ideal and how clients were both devious and childlike. It really was so much stuff and nonsense and a million light years away from what we were discovering about class inequalities and the reproduction of poverty and disadvantage under capitalism.* (p30)

Social policy today

So what does social policy as an academic subject focus upon today? As Brown (1969, p12) states, *whatever are generally accepted as social problems, together with the complex human needs that underlie them, must be the first area of study* for the social policy student. Basically, at the core of social policy lies an evaluation of societal responses to social problems such as poverty, social exclusion, unemployment, homelessness, crime, health and education inequalities. Hence, the subject seeks to develop an understanding of the 'very real' policy issues and debates that affect people's life chances and opportunities. In this sense it is a dynamic and constantly moving discipline, at the cutting edge of policy debates which ultimately determine government and non-governmental responses to issues like child poverty and neglect, pension provision, asylum and immigration, as well as health, education and social service reform. However, it is perhaps the subject's dynamism, fluidity and breadth which make it somewhat difficult to define precisely. Because social problems and societal responses to them change and evolve, it is impossible to give a once and for all definition of 'social policy', or to provide a definitive list of the issues that it covers.

Traditionally, the curricula of social policy courses in the post-1945 period were geared towards analysing the way the 'big' publicly funded and publicly provided forms of welfare provision, such as social security, health, education, housing and social service, or social work provision, had responded to human need. In part, this reflected the context within which social policy as an academic discipline 'took off' in higher education after 1945. As we have already explained, this period was characterised by a dramatic expansion of state welfare, and a growing demand from public sector welfare agencies and workers for information about the problems that their organisations dealt with. In addition, at that time the state was the 'main' provider of welfare. Governments of all political complexions accepted responsibility for tackling economic and social ills, and social policy academics inevitably focused their attention on analysing the outcomes of public sector interventions.

However, from the late 1970s onwards governments have sought to reduce the state's role in the organisation and delivery of welfare provision, encouraging the development of a voluntary and private sector of welfare. We will examine the ideological principles that influenced this shift in Chapter 5, but for our purposes here it is sufficient to simply point out that today the state is no longer the sole monopoly provider of welfare services, and a whole range of non-statutory organisations, as well as individuals and families themselves, are now involved in its delivery. Moreover, within public welfare agencies – including social service departments – market-led reforms have changed the nature of provision, profoundly altering its shape and organisation. This drive to reform and reduce the scope of state welfare has accelerated recently, as Coalition and Conservative governments have imposed drastic cuts to public expenditure (see Chapter 5). Hence, we are now faced with a much more 'plural', diverse welfare landscape than we were thirty or so years ago, involving a more fluid mix of state, private and voluntary sector interventions. In response to these changes in the way social policies are funded, organised and delivered, the academic discipline of social policy has inevitably had to adjust its focus, and its gaze now spans a much broader, plural, eclectic field of welfare provision. So although the study of the 'public sector' still looms large in social policy courses, social policy curricula also seek to impart an understanding of the role played by private and voluntary sector organisations, as well as individuals and families, in meeting citizens' needs. Again, the intention is not simply to describe the changes that have occurred. Our aim is to critically analyse social policies and trends and assess their impact upon citizens' social and economic conditions.

In developing this critical analysis, new tools, methods and theoretical paradigms have been embraced by social policy academics. 'Traditional' social policy research, epitomised by its focus on particular services and problems, retains a strong hold on the discipline, though this has been accompanied by a more analytical approach, involving broader questions about the 'functions' of welfare and the role of the state. As we have already hinted, from the 1960s onwards, the 'social conscience thesis' – the notion that social policies are necessarily motivated by benevolent intentions – was challenged, and the search for alternative interpretations has led social policy scholars to focus upon the ideological influences that underpin welfare interventions. In doing so, social policy has shown a much greater willingness to draw from other disciplines, such as political science, sociology and economics. As Wilding (1983) argues, the marrying of the 'traditional' social policy approach with this newer 'theoretical' approach is a positive development; it represents a maturing of the subject and is in accordance with the aims and ideals of the subject's early pioneers.

The relevance of social policy to social work

Hopefully, our brief summary of the development of social policy will have given you an appreciation of the historical links between social policy and social work. In order to help you understand its relevance further, we will consider the consequences of some recent social policy developments, in particular the cuts to welfare spending that have been implemented since 2010. As we will show, these have had an impact upon the economic and social well-being of vulnerable people, while at the same time constraining the options and resources available to social workers. In this sense, our discussion here will help reinforce the importance of including a social policy dimension in your social work training.

An analysis of the impact of the Coalition's public expenditure cuts on service users and the social work role

In October 2010, George Osborne, the Coalition's Conservative Chancellor of the Exchequer, announced £18 billion of cuts to welfare spending. He made it clear that welfare benefits (social security) would be affected as well as local authority social care budgets. The Coalition argued this was a necessary part of its deficit reduction strategy, but many politicians and commentators claimed that the speed and intensity of the cuts were unnecessary and would create severe harm and hardship. The Labour Party, for example, proposed a more phased, moderate strategy of public expenditure cuts, while others argued that the deficit could be tackled through other mechanisms, such as tax increases or a clampdown on tax evasion by major corporations and wealthy individuals. In short, political alternatives were proposed, which if pursued may have led to different social policy outcomes. However, the Coalition decided to press ahead with its rapid programme of cuts to welfare spending, which one commentator has described as *one of the most radically regressive and destructive economic experiments the UK has ever seen* (O'Hara, 2015, p1). Moreover, the incoming Conservative administration announced further cuts to public expenditure in November 2015. When combined, the Coalition and Conservative cuts will amount to an unprecedented £42 billion (14 per cent)

back on what is provided in care packages and reduced spending on preventative care (2015, p11). In 2006, 53 per cent of English councils funded the social care of service users with 'moderate needs', but by 2013/14 this had reduced to only 15 per cent, the remainder providing support only to those with 'substantial' or 'critical' needs (UNISON, 2015). As Chapter 9 shows, many local authorities had already begun to ration care in this way prior to the Coalition's cuts, but this process has greatly accelerated since October 2010. In 2014, the Local Government Association (LGA, 2014) surveyed Directors of Social Services, with a view to ascertaining their experiences of the impact of the Coalition's public expenditure cuts. Of those surveyed, 60 per cent admitted that reducing the numbers of service users receiving care had been a 'medium' or 'high' priority for them when it came to devising strategies for coping with the cuts. In addition, 34 per cent admitted that cutting personal budgets for service users had also been targeted as a 'medium' or 'high' priority. One survey conducted by the British Association of Social Workers (BASW) in April 2011 found that three-quarters of social workers had reported that changes to qualifying criteria had resulted in their service users being denied provision that they previously had access to:

> *Services are being restricted to critical cases only, preventative services are being shelved and, overnight, people are being expected to find alternative ways of getting their needs met.* (BASW, 2011)

As well as introducing 'formal' mechanisms of restricting eligibility thresholds, it seems that some local authorities have responded to the cuts by utilising other, more dubious 'informal' methods of denying access to key services. Many social workers, for example, have reported being placed under pressure by managers to reassess service users and reduce their category of need in order to artificially restrict support. A *Community Care* survey completed in May 2011 found that more than half of all children's social workers had been pressurised to downgrade children from 'child protection plans' to 'child-in-need plans', thus reducing entitlement to support. Disturbingly, 40 per cent of respondents said they had also been pressured into prematurely returning accommodated children to birth parents in order to save money (Cooper, 2011).

Since 2011, this trend appears to have continued. A 2013 *Community Care* survey found that 80 per cent of social workers felt that child protection thresholds had increased in the previous twelve months. More recently, in a 2015 survey of 1,000 social workers, 71 per cent expressed anxiety about rising child protection thresholds, with many linking this trend to growing budgetary concerns within local authorities. Naomi's comments were typical of those of many of the survey's participants: *When you're speaking to other professionals they'll say 'You accepted a case just like this two years ago, what has happened? Why aren't you pushing this through?'* For Naomi, the answer was clear; the changing thresholds were *an obvious repercussion of funding cuts . . . It {now} has to be really extreme before it is seen as a child protection issue, because of issues around money basically* (Stevenson, 2015).

Even children who meet the new, tightened child protection thresholds are increasingly experiencing difficulties in accessing much needed support, a trend that the NSPCC (2016) has described as 'alarming'. Its survey of support for children and young people who have experienced abuse found that 98 per cent of welfare professionals felt that there was insufficient therapeutic support for abused children. A further 97 per cent felt that there was not enough child and adolescent mental health service support. In both cases, the situation was reported to have deteriorated since the onset of public expenditure cuts in 2010:

> *Professionals with experience or awareness of referring children to therapeutic services said that it had got harder to access these services in the last five years, both for {abused} children with diagnosable mental health problems (78%) and children who may not have diagnosable mental health problems (87%).*

Other cuts in funding for social care projects and local services

As well as tightening thresholds for care, local authorities have also cut funding for certain key services. The discussion below illustrates how such cuts have impacted on two particular groups of service users – older adults and disabled children – through the reduction or withdrawal of funding from key services and benefits.

Older service users

Age UK estimate that public spending on older people has fallen significantly over the past decade, from £8.26 billion in 2005/06 to just £6.31 billion in 2015/16. This has inevitably had an impact upon the availability and quality of social care for older citizens. Hence, during the same period the numbers receiving support from local authority social service departments fell from 1.2 million to 377,000 (Mortimer and Green, 2015). In 2013/14 alone, more than 42,300 fewer older people received local authority-funded social care than had been the case in 2012/13, a 4.7 per cent reduction. As the Care Quality Commission (2015, p21) note, these trends need to be set in the context of an ageing population and hence a *growing need* for social care services. In order to achieve these savings, councils have been forced to increase the costs of services such as day care and meals on wheels and close day care centres and residential care homes. Age UK has identified the following responses to the cuts:

- Local authority funding for home care support, which enables older people to remain in their homes and live independent, fulfilling lives, was cut by 19.4 per cent between 2010/11 and 2013/14, meaning that 65,380 fewer older people received help with funding their home care needs.

- The need for local authorities to prioritise the care of those with the most severe needs also led to funding cuts for those with more moderate needs, undermining efforts to adopt more preventative approaches that may have delayed or negated the need for more serious intervention. Hence, only 9.1 per cent of recipients of funding received funding for support for two hours or less in 2013/14, compared to 13.8 per cent in 2010/11.

- Community-based services for older citizens have also been affected by cuts in funding. Between 2010/11 and 2013/14, spending on meals on wheels reduced by 47 per cent (from £42.1 million to £22.3 million). The numbers receiving this support fell from 75,885 to just 29,605 during the same period.

- Local authority spending on day-care support also plummeted by 30 per cent between 2010/11 and 2013/14, leading to a fall in the number of people over the age of 65 accessing such assistance from 95,145 to 35,845. Clearly, cuts to local authority commissioned day care services can have a debilitating effect on the ability of older citizens to live rewarding, active and independent lives.

- Cuts to local authority funding also mean that older people assessed as being capable of making some contribution towards the costs of their care are now having to pay more than ever before. In 2005/06, the average contribution was £1,590 per year. By 2013/14, this had risen to £2,563, a real terms increase of more than £1,000.

It is important to emphasise that levels of need among older adults have not diminished. Indeed, demand is intensifying. In 2013/14, local authority adult social care services received 2.16 million contacts from new clients, a 4 per cent increase on the previous year (Local Government Association, 2014). Age UK estimate that over one million older citizens have at least one unmet care need (such as managing medication, cooking, eating, shopping or washing), a number that has increased by over a quarter since 2010/11 (Mortimer and Green, 2015). Despite this, as we have shown, the level of funding available to meet these growing needs has reduced. Again, what this helps illustrate is the extent to which national social policies have a very tangible impact both upon the life chances of service users as well as on the ability of social services to meet their needs. Like other agencies that advocate on behalf of older people, Age UK has expressed real concern at the impact of these cuts on the lives of older service users:

> The numbers of older people in England are steadily growing, and the proportion with long-term conditions is growing faster still, but . . . spending on social care has fallen quite spectacularly over the last five years . . . Unless there is significant change to the funding of our health and care system for older people . . . we look to the future with considerable foreboding. Indeed . . . if an older person asked us today how confident we were that their health and care needs will be met well in the future we would be whistling in the dark if we gave a wholly reassuring answer. That is something about which we should all be profoundly concerned and which the Government must change. (Mortimer and Green, 2015, pp51–2)

Disabled children

A number of studies have drawn attention to the negative impact of cuts to local authority funding upon the welfare of disabled children and their families. A 2014 survey of 134 paediatricians, doctors and other medical and non-medical child care professionals who work with disabled children highlighted the difficulties that such families had experienced. Local authority support for voluntary services for disabled children, it was reported, had been decimated, leading to the closure of many highly valued, long-standing programmes that provided invaluable assistance to families. However, the highest levels of concern were expressed over the impact of austerity on statutory services for disabled children. These are just some of the comments made by practitioners who participated in the survey:

- *Social care for these children is awful and getting worse due to lack of resources. Very little respite or help. Lack of action when Child Protection issues arise, all because they {social services} are so short staffed.*

- *Social care have increased the threshold to accept cases for child protection and disability.*

- *The worst area {to be affected by cuts} in my opinion is children's social care. It's very difficult to get and keep an allocated social worker. Respite care packages have been withdrawn pending reassessment and then not reinstated. Parents have expressed concerns about poor quality respite care from private agencies and withdrawn children as a result: 'They just park him/her in front of video games, instead of taking them out and doing activities, I might as well just do that myself.'*

- *In some areas the children and disability social work service has been disbanded with children being picked up (or often not) by staff with no specialist knowledge of disability.*

- *Thresholds for social work children with disability teams becoming involved have increased over last few years, and social work resource worker posts in child development centres withdrawn.*

- *Many {colleagues} reported reduced support for families from social care, reduced short breaks/respite and reduced support with transport to appointments.*

(British Academy of Childhood Disability, 2015)

In the light of further planned cuts to local authority funding, respondents to the survey did not foresee the situation improving. Indeed, they predicted further delays in diagnosis for conditions where early intervention was crucial; increased use of emergency services and hospital admissions; higher levels of behavioural, emotional and mental health issues; more compulsory detention; and even higher levels of premature death.

Of course, this deterioration in local authority funded provision for families with disabled children needs to be considered alongside the impact of other austerity measures, particularly cuts to benefit support. One survey into the finances of more than 3,500 UK families with disabled children found that the government's welfare reforms had both hindered their children's access to key services and contributed to a significant decline in their living standards. Of those families surveyed, 33 per cent said that they were financially worse off as a result of benefit changes, with almost half of these losing out by £1,560 per year. In addition, 60 per cent foresaw a worsening of their financial situation in the next 12 months. Regarding the impact of this on access to services, 36 per cent of parents said that growing levels of hardship had restricted their ability to ensure that their children accessed much needed specialist equipment, therapies and even hospital visits. Families with disabled children were finding it increasingly difficult to meet their very basic needs. The numbers reporting that they were forced to go without food had grown from 14 per cent in 2010 to 33 per cent in 2015. Likewise, the numbers stating that they had had to go without heating had increased from 16 per cent in 2008 to 33 per cent in 2015. Eighty-four per cent of families had cut back on days out or leisure time, 65 per cent on clothes and 40 per cent on spending on cars and fuel. More than one in five parents surveyed admitted that 'going without' had negatively impacted upon their disabled child's health, while almost half stated that their own health had suffered (Contact a Family, 2014).

The Office of the Children's Commissioner for England (OCC) is tasked with monitoring the impact of social policy upon children's rights, life chances and opportunities. It has expressed grave concerns over the impact of austerity on the lives of disabled children. The OCC's assessment of the impact of welfare and tax changes between 2010 and 2015 concluded that families with disabled children have disproportionately borne the brunt of austerity. *Compared with families as a whole . . . families with disabled children are hit harder by the cuts under all disability definition* (OCC, 2013, p53). According to the OCC, the Coalition government's welfare reforms had potentially breached Article 2 of the United Convention on the Rights of the Child (UNCRC), which stipulates that policy should be non-discriminatory in terms of its impact on children, and Article 23, which provides disabled children with the right to special care and assistance (OCC, 2013; Reed and Elson, 2014). These serious allegations formed the basis of a damning joint submission by all the UK's Children's Commissioners (2015, p34) to the UN Committee on the Rights of the Child (CRC), the body responsible for periodically monitoring whether the UK is abiding by its commitments as a signatory to the UNCRC.

> *Across the UK, changes to welfare benefits have had a disproportionate impact on children with disabilities. These children are already much more likely to be living in poverty. As a result of tax and benefit reforms announced in 2010, CCE {Children's Commissioner for England} has highlighted retrogression in the realisation of disabled children's rights. Government spending decisions made since 2010 have had a disproportionate impact on children with disabilities and their families.*

The CRC's concluding observations on the UK's record on children's rights was published in July 2016. Its report raised serious concerns about the UK's compliance with its commitments under the UNCRC towards disabled children. Child poverty, it noted, *remains high* and *disproportionately affects children with disabilities*. Coalition and Conservative welfare reforms came under particular criticism, with the committee demanding *a comprehensive assessment of the cumulative impact of the full range of social security and tax credit reforms introduced between 2010 and 2016 on . . . children with disabilities* (CRC, 2016, pp16–17).

The CRC is not the only UN human rights body to take an interest in the impact of austerity on disabled children in the UK. By late 2015, the UN Committee on the Rights of Persons with Disabilities (UNCRPD) and the UN Committee on the Covenant of Economic, Social and Cultural Rights had both announced inquiries that would look into alleged violations of disability rights (Elgot, 2015). In the case of the UNCRPD, whose role it is to assess whether or not states are meeting their commitments under the UN Convention on the Rights of Persons with Disabilities, this was the first time the committee had ever felt the need to initiate such an inquiry, a deeply embarrassing decision for the government (Butler, 2015). Published in November 2016, the UNCRPD report provided a damning indictment of the impact of Coalition and Conservative welfare reforms on disabled children. All aspects of disabled children's lives had been detrimentally affected, including *financial income, provision of social care, inclusion in society, independence, quality of life, well-being, housing . . . mobility and mental health*. In an unprecedented judgement, the committee concluded that *there was reliable evidence that the threshold of grave or systematic violations of the rights of persons with disabilities has been met in the State party* (UNCRPD, 2016, p14).

Implications of the public expenditure cuts for the social work profession

Research has consistently shown that many of those who have chosen to enter the social work profession have done so out of a strong sense of social justice, or a more general desire to support and empower vulnerable groups (Hackett et al., 2003; Stevens et al., 2010). It indicates a clear desire among social workers to help address social problems; they want to 'help people'; to 'protect vulnerable groups'; to 'combat discrimination'; and to 'enable people to reach their full potential'. Clearly, the policy developments we have discussed will have an impact upon the ability of social workers (and indeed yourselves) to fulfil these objectives and to perform their roles effectively. In the activity below, we want you to consider the potential implications of the reductions in funding we have outlined for the social work profession itself.

Activity 1.2

- International evidence suggests that the well-being and long-term commitment of practitioners to the profession can be shaped by social policies that impact upon their ability to undertake their roles (Shier and Graham, 2015). What impact might the current social policy environment have had upon morale within the social work profession in the UK? If you are on placement, you might already have had a 'hint' as to what its impact has been.
- How would you personally feel about having to implement the cuts imposed by the government?

Comment

All the evidence suggests that the cuts to local authority welfare budgets have had a direct impact upon the culture of social work teams, constraining and circumscribing the welfare-related decisions that they are able to make. Social workers, it seems, are being pressured into engaging in practices that they themselves know conflict with the needs of their service users, as well as their professional social work value base.

Perhaps the most obvious and predictable impact of the cuts has been on staffing numbers, as evidenced by a survey of 1,571 social work practitioners conducted by the BASW in 2015. Sixty per cent of respondents reported that their teams had experienced cuts to administrative support posts in 2014/15; 38 per cent reported cuts in key managerial positions, while 35 per cent reported that their teams had been subjected to cuts in the numbers of front-line social workers. In short, significant staffing reductions had been made across all levels of social work practice. Inevitably, service provision had suffered as a consequence. Eighty-nine per cent of social work practitioners whose teams had experienced cuts to administrative posts believed that this had a negative impact, with practitioners now being forced to undertake even more administrative duties, leaving them less time to use their expertise with service users. Reductions in the numbers of front-line social workers in teams were reported to have had a particularly damaging affect, with 88 per cent of respondents admitting that these has restricted their ability to perform their roles effectively. The following comments practitioners made were illustrative of the deep concerns among social workers about the impact of the cuts:

- *Service cuts mean that existing roles are meant to take on the work from roles that have been deleted on top of their usual work.* (Children and Families' Social Worker, Midlands)
- *The front-line staffing has been cut enormously having an impact on my team. We are always on duty and never have time to attend competently to individual cases.* (Adults' Services Senior Social Worker, East Anglia)
- *Due to significant cuts and staff shortages which affect all key front-line services, partnership/collaborative working is worse than ever with every service defending and deflecting work away.* (Approved Mental Health Practitioner, Midlands)
- *Budget cuts in front-line services will have a detrimental impact on service delivery. The current demand on front-line services is extremely high – we cannot meet service demand alongside cuts being made. Local government seem to have no idea about the pressures in front-line children's services.* (Head of Service, East Anglia)

(Continued)

(Continued)

- *Financial implications/statistics seem to take over your social work values. It is all about saving money and putting in services adequately and working on the next case. There is no real attention to the quality of social work; instead it is all about quantity.* (Adults' Social Worker, Midlands)

(Munro and Liquid Personnel, 2015, p6)

Working under such financial constraints and pressures, means that quality, face-to-face work with service users has become increasingly difficult. Almost seven out of ten respondents felt that they were not spending sufficient time working directly with the vulnerable children and adults whom they were required to protect. Around half (46 per cent) stated that their caseloads were either 'unmanageable' or 'totally unmanageable', while two-thirds said that their caseloads had become heavier in the previous twelve months, as local authority cuts to services had gathered pace. Again, social workers expressed their concerns at the impact of this on their ability to perform their roles effectively:

- *The team is really struggling to do everything that is required. It means that less serious cases are not being dealt with properly and a lot of our interventions are when there is a crisis. Working in these conditions is difficult and heart-breaking for our team who want to have the time to help each child to the best of our abilities but unfortunately time does not allow.* (Children's Social Worker, South East)
- *The caseloads can be overwhelming and I feel the service users do not get the quality time when I go out to assess. There is always that feeling of rushing through to meet the deadlines and this is a big challenge.* (Adults' Social Worker, Midlands)

(Munro and Liquid Personnel, 2015, p18)

Such working conditions inevitably lead to higher levels of frustration and stress among social workers. Almost three-quarters of respondents (72 per cent) said that they find the conflicts between the needs of service users and meeting the financial and other demands of their organisations stressful. Morale has inevitably suffered as a result and almost half of practitioners described levels in their teams as either low or very low. As one children and families social worker from the Midlands disturbingly admitted: *Many of my colleagues and staff feel that we are a Baby P or Daniel Pelka waiting to happen* (Munro and Liquid Personnel, 2015, p11).

What conclusions can we draw from this discussion of post-2010 spending cuts about the nature of social policy and its relevance to you as a future social worker? What it does highlight is that the wider social policy environment has a profound impact not only upon the welfare of service users, but also upon the ability of social workers to perform their roles effectively. In this sense, it is crucial to understand that social work does not operate in a 'vacuum'; indeed, it is far more susceptible to the ideological whims of politicians than most other professions. What our discussion here has also shown is that social policies are often motivated by intentions that are often other than 'progressive'. In this specific instance, the desire to reduce public expenditure and reassure financial markets has been given primacy over the welfare needs of service users. In subsequent chapters we will interrogate more critically the rationale that has been advanced by the Coalition and Conservative governments to justify their austerity agendas. Have, as ministers have suggested, the cuts represented a 'fair' and absolutely 'necessary' series of reforms which are crucial in order to secure the economic and social well-being of the nation? Or, as O'Hara (2015, pxx) argues, are such claims part of an elaborate, well-articulated fallacy, intended to disguise an ideologically influenced strategy to fundamentally reform the welfare state?

In this chapter, though, our intention has merely been to encourage you to recognise the importance for you, as a future social worker, to have an understanding of the dynamics of social policy. Hopefully, you can now see how this will provide you with a crucial insight into the causes of some of the difficulties that affect the service users you will be working with, and the barriers you might face in supporting them.

Of course, it is not our intention here to present an unduly negative picture of social work today, or to reduce your levels of enthusiasm and motivation to become qualified social workers. As Eileen Munro acknowledges, *despite many challenges, there is still great work being done by practitioners throughout the UK*. It is also easy to detect abundant evidence of high levels of resilience and motivation among practitioners, who, despite the growing financial constraints and obstacles they face, continue to engage in life-changing social work with service users. However, the working conditions that practitioners are increasingly expected to endure *are* dysfunctional and *do* inhibit truly emancipatory social work (Munro and Liquid Personnel, 2015, p25). Likewise, the ability of today's practitioners to initiate positive change in the lives of vulnerable children and adults *is* constrained by a wider social policy environment that has impacted negatively on the groups of people that use social work services. In this chapter we have assessed the impact of policy on just two groups of service users – older adults and disabled children. Subsequent chapters examine how social policy developments have impacted upon the ability of other groups to achieve fulfilling, inclusive lives.

Chapter summary

Throughout this chapter we have emphasised the relevance of social policy to social work education. As we have shown, the two have a long-standing historical connection. Indeed, the origins of social policy can be traced back to the pioneering work of those such as Attlee, Tawney and Marshall, who sought to transform social work training by

(Continued)

(Continued)

infusing within the curriculum an appreciation of the social, economic and political constraints that shape the lives of service users. However, an appreciation of such constraints is no less important today than it was at the beginning of the twentieth century. As our discussion of the post-2010 cuts to welfare spending illustrates, the wider political and social policy environment frequently does constrain and impede the implementation of what can be broadly defined as core social work values. As future social workers and welfare practitioners you will often face obstacles in putting your motivations, aims and values into practice, and an appreciation of the dynamics of social policy can help you understand the extent to which this is the case.

Further reading

For those of you who are interested in a 'first-hand', historical account of attempts to promote a social policy dimension in social work education, Clement Attlee's *The Social Worker* is an interesting and worthwhile read:

Attlee, CR (1920) *The Social Worker.* London: G Bell & Sons.

If you are interested in a more thorough, wide-ranging introduction to social policy than we can provide in this short chapter, you may find the following texts useful. While not written with the specific needs of social workers in mind, they contain an appropriate mix of theoretical and issue-based social policy analysis:

Alcock, P and May, M (2014) *Social Policy in Britain*, 4th edition. Basingstoke: Palgrave Macmillan.

Alcock, P, May, M and Wright, S (2012) *A Student's Companion to Social Policy*, 4th edition. Chichester: Wiley & Sons.

Bochel, H, Bochel, C, Page, R and Sykes, R (2009) *Social Policy.* Harlow: Pearson Education.

Dean, H (2012) *Social Policy*, 2nd edition. Cambridge: Polity Press.

For an excellent analysis of the impact of austerity on poorer, vulnerable sections of the community, see:

O'Hara, M (2015) *Austerity Bites: A Journey to the Sharp End of Cuts in the UK.* Bristol: Policy Press.

2: The development of social policy and social work in the nineteenth century

---

Achieving a social work degree

This chapter will help you to meet the following capabilities from the Professional Capabilities Framework:

- **Values and ethics** – apply social work ethical principles and values to guide professional practice.
- **Rights, justice and economic well-being** – advance human rights and promote social justice and economic well-being.
- **Knowledge** – apply knowledge of social sciences, law and social work practice theory.
- **Critical reflection and analysis** – apply critical reflection and analysis to inform and provide a rationale for professional decision-making.

The chapter will also introduce you to the following academic standards which are set out in the 2016 QAA social work benchmark statements:

4	**Defining principles**
5.1	**Subject knowledge and understanding**
5	**Social work theory**
5.3	**Values and ethics**
5.11	**Manage problem-solving activities**
5.13	**Analysis and synthesis**
5.16	**Skills in working with others**
6	**Teaching learning and assessment**
7.3	**Knowledge and understanding**

Introduction

The study of history in the twenty-first century has become something of a form of popular entertainment. Supermarkets now stock a multitude of 'history' magazines catering for a range of diverse tastes, from the family historian to the more serious academic historian. Mainstream, terrestrial television channels have responded to this growing interest in history and their schedules are liberally peppered with history-themed documentaries and dramas. Indeed, there are now numerous television channels which are devoted solely to the broadcast of history-related material. As two people who share a passion for history, we welcome such developments and can see the appeal of studying history for its own sake – simply because it is interesting! However, there are other reasons why you, as a current or future social worker, should take an interest in history. For example, a knowledge of specific periods of history can help inform us of how we got to where we are today, assisting us to understand not just the past, but also the present. Indeed, as we will see, academics and politicians often make reference to the past when interpreting more recent and indeed future social policy and social work developments. This chapter examines a period of history that is often seen as being crucial in terms of the development of social policy and social work, covering the decades from the early nineteenth century to the early twentieth century. The chapter is interspersed with activities designed to encourage you to think about the links between past and current debates over policy and practice.

The origins of the welfare state: care or control?

When contemplating the origins of the welfare state and the development of social work in Britain, there is a tendency to assume that the primary driving force has been humanitarian concern. It is often assumed that charities, social reformers and legislators were motivated primarily by a strong sense of social responsibility, and that as previously hidden social evils were exposed in the nineteenth century, philanthropists, charities and governments moved to stamp them out. Some historians do subscribe to this interpretation of history. Society, from this perspective, became increasingly sensitive to the needs of the poor, and as social evils were exposed, the harsh excesses of Victorian Britain were gradually curbed by progressive, charitable and state intervention.

This perception, that welfare has historically been about 'helping' the poor, also frequently shapes people's views of social policies in Britain today. Governments, it is often thought, provide welfare services, such as the National Health Service, free education, social security, as well the range of services provided by social workers, for altruistic reasons. They are moved, primarily, by a sense of social justice and a desire to 'assist' the less well off. Indeed, many of our students tell us that this is precisely the reason why they themselves were motivated to become social workers or other welfare practitioners. They want to 'help' and 'empower' disadvantaged groups and make a positive difference to the lives of people who experience difficulties. In a sense, it is pleasing for us to know that many of our students are motivated to join what they see as caring professions by a strong sense of social justice and altruism. However, social policies and social work have, historically, not simply been designed to dispense 'care'. The welfare state has performed, and continues to perform, other functions and in this chapter we want to encourage you to think critically about both the origins of social policy and social work and the nature of social policy and social work today. In particular, we want to draw your attention to the extent to which both have also been shaped as much by a desire to discipline, control or modify the behaviour of disadvantaged groups as they have by humanitarianism. We begin our historical analysis by looking at one of the most influential pieces of social policy legislation to find its way onto the statute books in the nineteenth century, the 1834 Poor Law Amendment Act (PLA Act). However, before looking at the main elements of the PLA Act, it is perhaps first worth giving some consideration to the key features of the system that it replaced.

The old Poor Law

Prior to 1834, families or individuals seeking welfare assistance were dealt with under a locally administered system of 'relief', often known as the 'old' Poor Law. The types and levels of assistance offered varied by region, but by the end of the eighteenth century local parishes tended to provide assistance to able-bodied people via what was referred to as the 'allowance system' (also sometimes called 'outdoor relief'). With the allowance system support would be provided in the community (hence outdoor relief), and there would be no expectation that those seeking assistance would be punished for their predicament by being confined to a workhouse. The support provided included 'doles' (cash payments to unemployed labourers), payments in kind (such as food or tools for work) and wage subsidies, all of which would often be adjusted to take into account the cost of living and size of families. While these systems of support were hardly generous (they were intended to provide only the most basic standard of living), they were influenced primarily by benevolence and humanitarianism, and a genuine desire to prevent the incomes of families falling below subsistence levels (Fraser, 2009). The relief was administered by autonomous local committees of parish overseers who would inquire into families' circumstances before agreeing to give assistance. In some respects, this investigation was an early nineteenth-century equivalent of a needs assessment conducted by social workers today. If evidence of genuine need was found then some assistance would usually be provided. Of course, it goes without saying that cases deemed to be manifestly 'undeserving' would be refused or any support provided made conditional. Moreover, because parish overseers had a good degree of autonomy, practices varied across the country and some parishes adopted a harsher approach than others. However, overall the system is said to have been administered in a relatively humane way (Rose, 1971).

Criticisms of the old Poor Law

By the beginning of the nineteenth century this system of providing relief had become the subject of searching criticism. The old Poor Law had always had its critics, many of whom had long felt that it was too generous and laxly administered. Support, some had argued, was too readily available and this encouraged idleness and fraud. Rather than relying upon their own industry and hard work, individuals and families were choosing the 'easy' option of parish relief. In many respects, the arguments marshalled against the old Poor Law mirrored those used today by right-wing, neo-liberal critics of the welfare state. In short, welfare was said to have a morally corrupting effect, sapping independence and thrift, creating a dependent population, unable, or unwilling, to look after itself. Moreover, because the support provided under the allowance system varied according to family size, it was also said to have encouraged improvident marriages and a rapid growth of the population among 'undesirable' sections of the community who could ill afford to maintain themselves. Thomas Malthus, an influential political philosopher and opponent of the old Poor Law, expressed deep concern at the messages that this sent out to uneducated, 'feckless' sections of the community. There was, he stated, *no occasion for them to put any sort of restraint on their inclinations, or exercise any degree of prudence in the affairs of marriage; because the parish is bound to provide for all that are born* (Malthus, 1973, p66). Put crudely, critics such as Malthus argued that the system provided perverse incentives for 'worthless' paupers to breed more paupers, who would themselves become a burden and charge on the community. Again, we see here parallels with critiques of the welfare state today, particularly the often made claim that teenagers get pregnant 'just to jump the housing queue'.

The old Poor Law under pressure

The ideas of those such as Malthus had, before 1834, already influenced parish overseers in some parts of the country, and in these areas individuals and families requesting assistance were forced to enter a workhouse. The intention was to stigmatise relief in order to deter all but the most desperate from applying for support, and to force individuals to take responsibility for themselves and their families. In reality, there was little evidence of fraud or abuse of the allowance system in these areas. Indeed, the stigmatisation and punishment that occurred in some parishes seems to have been motivated primarily by a desire to cut the costs of supporting the poor, as opposed to any actual proof that they were not in genuine need. However, as the national cost of the old Poor Law grew (it had increased from £4.07 million in 1802/03 to £7 million by 1831), such claims were given added credence. Despite the fact that the vast bulk of requests for assistance were due to factors beyond the individual's control (such as chronically low wages, bad harvests and trade fluctuations, or sometimes desertion or widowhood), the ideological climate had changed. Influential opinion began to embrace the views of prominent critics of the old Poor Law, such as Malthus, who had long bemoaned its 'insidious' effects.

The Poor Law Report of 1834

It was in such a context that in 1832 a Royal Commission on the Poor Laws was tasked with the responsibility of producing proposals for radical reform. Its recommendations, published in 1834, were infused with the Malthusian idea that indiscriminate, lavish levels of support were encouraging laziness and fecklessness. The Commission's report was primarily the work of two men – Nassau Senior and Edwin Chadwick – who, evidence suggests, had preconceived views about what needed to be done. Before commencing the writing of the report, both were already convinced that the old Poor Law created and exacerbated the problems that it was supposed to cure, and accordingly they only selected evidence which supported their preconceived views. Hence, the report has been described by one influential historian as *in essence a piece of propaganda to support a predetermined case* (Fraser, 2009, p43). The report certainly makes interesting reading and it is packed full of 'evidence' which suggests that outdoor relief morally corrupted the poor, encouraging a whole range of dysfunctional, fraudulent patterns of behaviour. Relief, it was argued, was *mischievous and ruinous*, and corruptive of manners, character and civility. It was also accused of encouraging crime and disorder. Idle labourers were said to be *loitering about during the day, engaged in idle games . . . or else consuming their time in sleep, that they may be more ready and active in the hours of darkness.* In addition, in language similar to that used today to condemn 'benefit cheats', the authors of the report argued that it was *utterly impossible to prevent considerable fraud*, claiming that even genuine cases were induced into indolent habits:

> *From the preceding evidence it will be seen how zealous must be the agency, and how intense the vigilance, to prevent fraudulent claims crowding in under such a system of relief. But it would require even greater vigilance to prevent the bona fide claimants degenerating into imposters; and it is an aphorism amongst the parish officers that 'cases which are good today are bad tomorrow, unless they are incessantly watched'. A person obtains relief on the ground of sickness; when he has become capable of moderate work, he is tempted, by the enjoyment of subsistence without labour, to conceal his convalescence and fraudulently extend the period of relief.* (Poor Law Report, cited in Checkland and Checkland, 1974, p148 and pp116–19)

Activity 2.1

- Can you see any links between the concerns outlined in the Poor Law Report and debates that occur today about the nature and impact of welfare on recipients?
- What are your views on the claims that are often made today about the 'extensive' nature of benefit fraud?

(Continued)

(Continued)

- How significant a problem is benefit fraud today, compared with other, related problems, such as non-take-up of benefit?
- As a social worker you will be working with a whole range of vulnerable people, many of whom will be dependent upon some form of welfare. Do you think the attention devoted to the benefit fraud debate might impact upon their self-imagery and their experiences of the welfare system? Might it discourage them from applying to benefits to which they are entitled?

Comment

Many of the comments made in the 1834 Poor Law Report about the 'corrupting' nature of relief do have a contemporary resonance. Similar claims about the extensive nature of benefit fraud are made on a daily basis in the media today. The benefit system, we are told, is laxly administered, too generous and rife with abuse. This message is conveyed to us on a daily basis in lavishly funded benefit fraud campaigns, newspaper articles and television programmes. We are now regularly exposed to a diet of television documentary series dedicated to dramatically exposing the 'cheats' and 'liars' that take us, the unsuspecting public, for a ride. Frequently, stories of the 'sinners', that is the deviant, criminal scroungers, are juxtaposed with the narratives of the 'saints', the honest, law-abiding, genuinely needy claimants who lose out due to the actions of fraudsters. Through exposure to such popular representations of benefit fraud, our anger towards 'benefit cheats' is amplified, and it is hardly surprising, therefore, that most of us feel that this is a major issue that needs to be tackled.

Just how extensive is benefit fraud, though? More specifically, how significant a problem is fraud compared with a related social problem, such as non-take-up of benefits? Certainly, the amount of money lost through benefit fraud each year is not insignificant. Indeed, the estimated £1,100 million that was lost through tax credit and benefit fraud in 2013/14 (Department for Work and Pensions, 2015) is a significant sum that could otherwise be spent on good causes, such as reducing pensioner or child poverty. However, this loss does need to be placed in context. During the same period, £1,400 million was saved to the Exchequer as a result of underpayment of benefit. As Table 2.1 illustrates, a further sum of between £13,900 million and £22,610 million was saved through people not claiming benefits that they were entitled to.

Why does so much money remain unclaimed? Some have argued that the disproportionate emphasis that has been placed upon fraud itself discourages people from making legitimate claims. As the Child Poverty Action Group (2009) has argued, *fraud is a demonstrably small problem and overestimating its extent . . . may discourage genuine claimants from claiming for fear of being thought fraudulent* (cited in House of Commons Library, 2009). The evidence

Table 2.1   Income-related benefits: estimates of non-take-up 2013/14

Benefit	Entitled not claiming (%)	Amount unclaimed
Income Support	19–23	£2,430–£3,250
Pensions Credit	36–39	£2,480–£3,260
Housing Benefit	18–21	£3,160–£4,100
Council Tax Benefit (09/10)	31–38	£2,340–£3,200
Jobseeker's Allowance	39–45	£1,990–£2,620
Child Tax Credit (12/13))	12	£1,500–£2,480
Working Tax Credit (12/13)	34	£2,500–£3,700
Total		£13,900–£22,610

(Department for Work and Pensions, 2015; HM Revenue and Customs, 2014).

suggests that this may particularly be the case for pensioners, many of whom fail to claim their Income Support entitlements under the Pension Credit. The claiming process for the Pension Credit is extremely complicated, and fears about the consequences of omitting crucial pieces of information are reinforced by anti-fraud campaigns (such as the Department for Work and Pensions *No ifs, No buts* fraud campaign), which emphasise the message that fraudsters will be prosecuted irrespective of their motives. Coupled with the stigma associated with having to respond to detailed, complex questions about personal finances and relationships, the overwhelming emphasis placed upon fraud acts as a deterrent to legitimate Pension Credit claims.

A number of commentators have sought to explain why so much emphasis is placed upon the issue of fraud in both media and political commentaries. Some, such as Golding and Middleton (1981), Cook (1989), Tunley (2011) and Jones (2011) argue that the motives are very similar to those of yesteryear – as in the past, the intention is to discredit welfare provision, reinforce personal responsibility and justify the retrenchment of welfare entitlements. At the same time, the real issues, such as the poverty created by the non-take-up of welfare, are obscured by the 'scroungerphobia' generated by sensationalist reporting and political commentaries on the issue. This provides the rationale for politicians to justify retrenching welfare entitlements, even during periods of recession, when such policies would otherwise be seen as unpalatable. Golding and Middleton (1981) argue that it has always been thus, and they detect a remarkable level of continuity in past and current debates about the issue.

The Poor Law Amendment Act 1834

Despite the methodological flaws associated with the Poor Law Report of 1834, the solutions it offered were enthusiastically embraced by the political elite, and legislators set about devising a new Poor Law, which would discipline and control the poor, forcing them to make every effort to support themselves independently. The new Poor Law, which was introduced with the passage of the 1834 Poor Law Amendment Act, aimed to deter people from applying for support by making the receipt of welfare as uncomfortable and stigmatising as possible. Three basic principles underpinned the new Poor Law. These were less eligibility, the workhouse test and centralisation.

Less eligibility

The Poor Law Report had argued that in order to deter bogus, unnecessary applications for relief, the position of those receiving support needed to be made considerably worse (*less eligible*) than that of even the lowest paid independent labourer. As the report stated, *let the labourer find that the parish is the hardest taskmaster and the worst paymaster he can find, and thus induce him to make his application to the parish his last and not his first resource.* Of course, at a time when the average age of death for labourers was in the mid-20s, it would, in practical terms, be difficult to reduce the condition of recipients considerably lower than that of the lowest paid independent labourer, without literally starving them to death. As EP Thompson (1972, p295) argues, at a time when many of those in work barely earned enough to live on, even the most inventive state would have found it difficult to create institutions which simulated conditions worse than those endured by large sections of the working poor. Such conditions were, though, created in the form of the dreaded workhouse. Henceforth this would be the means of putting the principle of less eligibility into effect.

The Workhouse Test

The PLA Act envisaged that all outdoor relief would be abolished and that the provision of support would be conditional upon recipients and their families entering a workhouse. The workhouse regime would be strict, drab, monotonous and intentionally cruel and degrading. The objective was to make workhouses places of dread and as prison-like as possible, thus guaranteeing that the position of those claiming relief would be 'less eligible' (worse) than the lowest paid independent labourers. Inmates would be separated from relatives, be forced to wear uniforms, be fed rudimentary, often inadequate unappetising diets (see our comments on the Andover workhouse below), and be required to engage in monotonous, meaningless arduous labour. They would be made to feel like moral failures and it would be made clear that the cause and solution to their destitution lay in their own hands, not that of the community. The workhouse regime, therefore, would ensure that only the most desperate – those genuinely utterly destitute and incapable of supporting themselves – would contemplate applying to the parish for relief. As one of the Assistant Commissioners tasked with overseeing the new Poor Law stated, *our object . . . is to establish therein a discipline, so severe and repulsive as to make them a terror to the poor and prevent them from entering* (Thompson, 1972, p295). The 'offer' of the workhouse to those seeking help would be a 'self-acting test' (hence *workhouse test*) of genuine destitution, since fear generated by the prospect of entering the workhouse would ensure that only those truly desperate would be prepared to accept it. According to Friedrich Engels, the Poor Law authorities were largely successful in this aim. *Can any one wonder*, wrote Friedrich Engels eleven years after the passage of the Act, *that the poor decline to accept public relief under these conditions? That they starve rather than enter these bastilles?* (Engels, 1845).

Centralisation and uniformity

It was also proposed that the new system would have a centralised form of administration in the form of a new, national Poor Law Commission, which would ensure there would not be any variations in practice. In summary, all areas would be expected to operate the new Poor Law in a uniform, equally harsh manner.

The 'new' Poor Law in practice

The Poor Law Amendment Act was implemented across the country, and many areas built new workhouses or used old ones to incarcerate those claiming public relief. The extent to which the 'workhouse test' was fully implemented is still a matter of debate among historians. Certainly, many areas ignored the efforts of the Poor Law Commission to encourage them to adhere to the 'spirit of 1834' (Fraser, 2009). However, in many others it was vigorously applied, and in those districts paupers in receipt of relief were often subjected to the most punishing, brutal and repressive regimes. The appalling conditions found in the Andover workhouse in 1845 (described below in a *Times* newspaper report), where starving inmates were found desperately gnawing on bones (including human bones), almost beggars belief:

> *Notwithstanding the horrors and atrocities to which the Poor Law has given birth, we could not have believed it possible that the measure . . . could have led to anything so utterly revolting as the facts stated . . . to have occurred in the union workhouse at Andover . . . It appears from the investigation that has taken place into this truly shocking affair, that the paupers are employed in crushing bones collected from various sources, including frequently the bones of horses as well as other animals and occasionally some from churchyards . . . and that while so employed they were engaged in quarrelling with each other for the bones, in extracting marrow from them, and in gnawing off the meat from the extremities.(The Times, 14 August 1845)*

A subsequent government inquiry confirmed these and other atrocities. It was found that the 'master' of the workhouse had acted as a dictatorial tyrant, bullying, intimidating and physically and emotionally assaulting inmates. He and his wife frequently denied paupers medical treatment, and food meant for inmates would be fed to the master's pigs, leaving paupers to scavenge from the bones they were supposed to be crushing to create fertiliser. This workhouse master made Dickens's fictional Bumble the Beadle (the workhouse master in *Oliver Twist*) seem almost tame by comparison. Andover, therefore, truly was a Dickensian workhouse of the worst kind. That said, while it was perhaps at the extreme end of the spectrum, such conditions were certainly not the exception in a system that encouraged contemptible treatment of the poor. As *The Times* (18 August 1845) argued, the practices uncovered were extreme and technically illegal, but were *within the spirit and tendency of the law.*

In the light of what we have told you about the Poor Law Amendment Act, you may find it somewhat strange to find that its architects claimed they were genuinely interested in the welfare of the poor. The savage discipline of the workhouse may have seemed cruel, but it was, they argued, ultimately in the interests of recipients of public relief. As Fraser (2009, p47) has put it, its supporters claimed to be *acting like the loving parent inflicting sharp, painful punishment on the miscreant child – being cruel to be kind.* In the long term, paupers, like children, would benefit from short-term chastisement, learning from their errors and, once the crutch of relief was removed, they would learn to stand on their own two feet.

The Poor Law, the Charity Organisation Society and early social work

Clearly, the values and assumptions that shaped the PLA Act are far removed from those that underpin today's social work value base. However, this was not always the case. Indeed, as we hinted in Chapter 1, the values infused throughout the new Poor Law shaped and influenced embryonic social work, in the form of the Charity Organisation Society (COS). The COS, which was formed in 1869, was not, as its title may suggest, created with the aim of freely dispensing welfare to the poor. On the contrary, its leading figures, many of whom were deeply imbued with the Poor Law values and principles, were driven by the belief that too much indiscriminate charitable alms-giving was sapping initiative and self-help. Hence, at the COS's 1886 annual meeting, the Bishop of London described many charities as, *very little more than the refuge of imposters, who have failed elsewhere to get assistance* (cited in Evans, 1978, p208). The notion that 'crafty beggars' were taking advantage of the charitable assistance available was reflected in the original title of the COS, that is the *Society for Organising Charitable Relief and Repressing Mendacity.* The word 'mendacity' is rarely used today, but in layman's terms it means deception, lies, dishonesty and deceit.

The COS saw itself as the voluntary equivalent of the Poor Law authorities, and its mission was very much the same – to prevent abuse of charity, force individuals to take responsibility for their actions, and rely upon their own efforts and industry. Was there any evidence that charitable support was rife with fraud? Certainly, by 1869, a multitude of charitable organisations had emerged to cope with the distress and need that the new Poor Law failed, or refused, to meet. In London alone, there were well over 1,000 charities with a combined income of somewhere in the region of £8 million, almost the equivalent to the amount spent on Poor Law relief (Mooney, 1998, p68). However, there was little real evidence that haphazard, overly sentimental charitable assistance was encouraging improvidence or fraud.

Nonetheless, the COS's aim was to encourage as many charities as possible to adopt the same rigorous methods of individual case investigation as itself. Like its own caseworkers, other charities should seek to identify the 'deserving' and turn away the 'undeserving', leaving the latter to the vagaries of the Poor Law.

The establishment of the COS was, in short, an attempt to control and coordinate charitable activity and ensure that assistance was only provided to the truly 'deserving', in a way that would restore the spirit of independence, hard work and thrift. Its activities, therefore, were directed as much towards attempts to remoralise, regulate and control the behaviour of the poor, as they were to relieving their distress. The underlying philosophy was similar to that of the Poor Law and the assumption was that poverty, in most circumstances, was the result of avoidable personal failing and could be avoided through hard work and foresight. As one contributor to the Charity Organisation Review stated in 1881:

> There can be no doubt that the poverty of the working classes of England is due, not to their circumstances (which are more favourable than those of any other working population in Europe); but to their own improvident habits and thriftlessness. If they are ever to be more prosperous, it must be through self-denial, temperance and fore-thought.
> (Cited in Jones, 1976, p2)

The COS's interpretations for poverty, therefore, rarely acknowledged the structural problems that afflicted the working population, and poverty of 'spirit' rather than material poverty was seen as the main cause of social ills. To dispense charity to the indigent and morally culpable, and to provide for those who had chosen not to save for predictable, temporary shortfalls in income, would, the COS insisted, be to reward improvident habits and fecklessness. It argued that such individuals should have no access to charity, and be forced to endure the discipline and rigours of the workhouse. Charitable provision should only be used to meet the exceptional, temporary needs of the genuinely 'deserving' poor who could be expected to show improvement. Theirs was, therefore, a particularly harsh approach. According to TH Marshall (1967, p167), its philosophy was *reactionary* and *morally repugnant to the modern mind*. As he points out, the 'hopeless' cases that were turned away included not only the 'idlers', the 'drunken' and the 'immoral', but also those affected by social problems over which they had no control, and those with physical or learning disabilities, the very groups who we today would deem most in need of welfare and social work services. The extent to which the COS was successful in persuading other charities to adopt an equally stern approach is a matter of debate, and our focus on the COS here is not intended to detract from the radicalism that infused the work of individuals and organisations who were motivated by more progressive intentions (see Ferguson and Woodward, 2009; Cree and Myers, 2008). However, the COS was certainly influential in London and a number of other major cities, such as Birmingham, Liverpool and Manchester (Pierson, 2012). Moreover, it also played a crucial part in shaping the national policy agenda, and it is often credited with developing the 'casework' method of investigation that social workers still use today.

The COS and the development of the 'casework' approach

Leading figures within the COS were insistent that charity should not be dispensed without a systematic investigation into the worth, merits and circumstances of each case. To this end, it pioneered the casework method of dispensing welfare that in some respects would be familiar to today's social workers. Before agreeing to provide assistance, no stone would be left unturned in the caseworker's attempts to ascertain the applicant's 'worthiness'. Visitors would seek to establish whether applicants were truly destitute by looking for evidence to suggest they were capable of supporting themselves. Homes would also be checked for evidence of 'indolence' or 'vice', with particular attention being paid to cleanliness of the environment and its inhabitants. A dirty home and dirty children would be seen as evidence of moral culpability and support might be refused on that basis alone. The possibility that the unkempt circumstances of people's homes may have been a result of chronic overcrowding, poverty and other factors beyond the control of individuals or families would rarely be considered, and the roots of distress were invariably located in their personal history or behaviour. As Helen Bosanquet, a leading member of the COS, commented in 1902:

> *If the narrow home makes family life impossible, it is because the family is already weak; where the deeper relations are strong they find a way either to ignore or control the difficulties arising from want of space.* (Cited in Jones, 1976, p3)

Octavia Hill, another leading COS figure, had made much the same point in 1884. She argued that although workers' houses were often *badly built and arranged*, they were *tenfold worse because of the tenants' habits. Transplant them tomorrow to healthy and commodious houses*, she stated, *and they would pollute and destroy them* (cited in Jones, 1976, p3).

Activity 2.2

In an attempt to rescue the poor from their own 'depravity', Octavia Hill began to establish and manage a number of housing settlements, offering low-cost housing for poor 'deserving' families. Her legacy to social policy and social work has been a matter of considerable debate ever since. Some have described her as a heroine of the Victorian age, a philanthropist who devoted her professional life to improving the lives and homes of the poor. As Young and Ashton (1956, p. 115) wrote, *Octavia Hill has sometimes been called the grandmother of modern social work, because her influence and her principles permeated all the later nineteenth-century thought.* Others, however, have been less complimentary, highlighting Hill's dogmatic opposition to the development of publicly funded welfare schemes, as well as her authoritarian treatment of her own housing tenants. There can be little doubt that her views on both public and charitable welfare were shaped by her enthusiastic embrace of COS philosophy.

These same, deeply moralistic values infused the administration of her housing settlements. The rent would not be the only cost of residence, and those prepared to become tenants would face curfews and a strict regime of intensive supervision. Regular inspections and instructional visits would be made by Hill's lady rent collectors, who would advise on cleanliness and moral rectitude. Hill was clearly seeking to do much more than provide housing to her tenants. Moral re-education was the broader aim, a strategy which was clearly based upon the missionary zeal underpinning the COS's broader philosophy. She acted as an all-seeing, omnipresent ruler and those refusing to abide by the instructions of her lady visitors were promptly evicted.

Social care or social control? Family intervention projects today

As we have seen, Hill's treatment of her tenants was shaped as much by a desire to regulate, modify and control their behaviour as it was to provide them with housing support. In this task we want you to think about the assumptions that underpin recent initiatives based upon intensive family intervention. After reading the extract below taken from a report published by Tony Blair's Labour government on its family intervention project (FIP) initiative, try answering the questions that follow:

> In some communities there are a small number of highly problematic families that account for a disproportionate amount of anti-social behaviour. Although much has been done to tackle these problem families, it is clear that we need to go further, for their sake and the sake of the wider community . . . Based on evidence, we now know that this small number of families need an intensive, persistent and, if necessary, coercive approach. The Respect programme will establish a national network of family intervention projects . . . This will ensure that the destructive behaviour which is so often passed from generation to generation, blighting not only these families but entire communities, is effectively tackled for the first time . . . Family intervention projects use intensive tailored action with supervision and clear sanctions to improve the behaviour of persistently anti-social households. A key worker 'grips' the family, the causes of their poor behaviour and the agencies involved with them, to deliver a more co-ordinated response.
>
> There are three distinct models of intervention which can be applied:
>
> - Intensive outreach programmes to families in their own homes . . .
> - Intensive outreach programmes to families in dispersed accommodation. Families are provided with a non-secure tenancy by the project. Staff visit and provide/ refer to structured individual and family sessions to work with the family on a range of issues identified as causing their anti-social behaviour. If the family complies with interventions and behaviour improves sufficiently then the tenancy can be made secure.
>
> (Continued)

(Continued)

- **Intensive support programme in supervised accommodation.** *Families in this type of provision receive 24-hour support and supervision from staff provided by the project. Families are likely to be involved in many structured sessions complemented by daily unstructured observation. If the family complies with interventions and behaviour improves sufficiently then they will be able to move into one of the above . . .*

(Respect, 2006, pp2–5)

1. Can you see any links between the methods adopted by Hill in her 'housing settlements' and the intentions of the Labour government's FIPs?
2. To what extent were Labour's FIPs based upon behavioural, pathological interpretations for disadvantage?

Comment

While family intervention was clearly not a novel phenomenon within social work and social policy, FIPs were a relatively new development, forming a key part of Labour's 'Think Family' approach to social exclusion. Delivered by a combination of local authorities and voluntary agencies, its FIP programme involved intensive levels of both outreach and residential-based family intervention and supervision, backed up in many cases with coercive powers to discipline families who failed to modify what was often considered to be their own 'destructive' behaviour. Sanctions, such as eviction and even the threat of removal of children from families, were seen as integral to the success of FIPS.

While the precise nature of FIPs varied – some were shaped by a more progressive, welfare-focused ethos than others – the ideological inspiration for the programme was clearly discernible. Hence, as with Hill's interventions, the location of intervention with FIPs was set at a family rather than a societal level, and there was an implicit assumption that families themselves were responsible for their own, and indeed their community's exclusion (Parr, 2011). In fact, Labour ministers made no attempt to disguise the behavioural assumptions that would underpin the government's FIP strategy. Announcing an expansion of FIP initiatives, the then Home Secretary, John Reid, boldly stated that *By tackling bad parenting we are tackling child disadvantage and social exclusion* (Doward, 2010).

Before Labour left office, it envisaged that all local authorities would embrace FIPS by 2011, and that 20,000 families would be enrolled on them by then. Labour ultimately lost the General Election in 2010, but FIPs continued to form a key part of the Coalition government's social policy agenda, and by March 2012 around 10,000 families had participated on them. This was after David Cameron had announced in 2010 that he would like the initiative intensified and extended to encompass tens of thousands of what he described as 'troubled' families (Welshman, 2013).

Announced in the week following the riots that swept across the UK in August 2011, David Cameron's Troubled Families Programme (TFP) aimed to 'turn around' the lives of 120,000 families who, it was claimed, were gripped by a *culture of disruption and irresponsibility that cascades through generations*. These families were, Cameron insisted, *the source of a large proportion of the problems in our society*, costing the taxpayer up to £9 billion per year. Cameron's interpretation for the 'dysfunctional' behavioural characteristics of these families focused upon the 'morally corrupting' influence of a 'broken' welfare system. In this respect, the assumptions that underpinned the TFP were very similar to those that shaped the Poor Law Amendment Act. Troubled families were the victims of an excess of unthinking, impersonal, corrupting welfare; they had *been subjected to a sort of compassionate cruelty . . . smothered in welfare yet never able to escape* (Cameron, 2011).

Activity 2.3

We examine the TFP in greater detail in Chapter 8, where we focus upon government responses to youth exclusion. Here, though, we would like to pause for a moment to consider the assumptions that underpin the programme:

1. Theresa May's Conservative government committed to extending Cameron's TFP. Take a look (below) at the rationale advanced to justify the programme, which is drawn from a key TFP document. Do you detect any similarities between this strategy and Labour's FIP sanctioning approach?
2. Thinking about the wider ideological impact of these programmes, can you see any dangers in focusing so directly and publicly on what are perceived to be the 'problematic', 'destructive' patterns of behaviour of such a small number of families?

Troubled families are those that have problems and often cause problems to the community around them, putting high costs on the public sector . . . Through family intervention, families and their problems are 'gripped' . . . An authoritative and challenging approach with families to create the 'wake up' moment . . . can be vital if there is to be any realistic prospect of change. Families are sometimes labelled 'too hard to engage', 'hard to reach', 'declining a service' and 'refusing to engage'. No troubled family should be left 'in trouble' without there being consequences for them if they do not accept help on offer from family intervention. Good family intervention operates within a system where the agencies and its leaders will relentlessly challenge families and use sanctions where necessary to encourage them to take help . . .

(Continued)

(Continued)

Sanctions or the threat of sanctions might include:

- *Parenting Orders*

- *Action by housing providers to address anti-social behaviour and nuisance (demoted tenancies or housing injunctions)*

- *Sanctions relating to poor school attendance (prosecution or fines for non-attendance, or the threat of exclusion)*

- *Criminal justice system actions (pre-court actions such as Anti-social Behaviour Contracts or final warnings, or court orders such as supervision orders or curfews)*

- *Actions around safeguarding children (child protection interventions, backed by the ultimate threat of action to remove children if they are at significant risk).*

Evidence shows that the threat of sanctions such as loss of tenancy 'concentrates the mind' of families and is a key mechanism for bringing about change.

(Department for Communities and Local Government, 2012, pp9 and 28)

Comment

Ministers responsible for both FIPs and the TFP have claimed that the projects have been an enormous success, yet there is little empirical evidence to support their conclusions. The evaluations of FIPS, for example, tended to be based upon the subjective views of project staff, who had a vested interested in amplifying their success rate. Nor did many of the FIP evaluations use 'control groups' to assess whether other kinds of intervention would be any more successful than FIPs. In fact, a re-analysis of FIP evaluations concluded that their success rate had been greatly exaggerated (Gregg, 2010). Likewise, as we show in Chapter 8, ministerial claims that the TFP has a 99 per cent success rate in 'turning around' the lives of the 120,000 families that were targeted have been greeted with incredulity by social policy analysts (Department for Communities and Local Government, 2015). As Crossley (2015) argues, no social policy can expect to achieve such a high success rate and the government's claims are, quite simply, too good to be true. In fact, closer inspection shows that the threshold used to determine whether or not a family has been 'turned around' is notoriously low – for instance, the participation of one family member on the Government's Work Programme for the unemployed is seen as an indicator of a family being 'turned around'. Ministers have also adopted a 'light touch' approach to auditing outcomes, in a way which allows local authorities to inflate their success rates under the TFP (Cunningham and Cunningham, 2014).

Just as importantly, of course, when assessing the wider ideological impact of these types of family intervention, we should not underestimate their potential to tap into popular stereotypes, reinforcing negative societal perceptions of vulnerable families by portraying their exclusion as pathological. Of course, this may well be an intentional outcome of the programme, but it is not without consequences. As Garrett (2007) and Welshman (2013) argue there is a danger that the narrow focus within these programmes upon family pathology and biological metaphors (such as generational transmission of 'dysfunction' and the 'pollution' of the wider community), has acted as an 'ideological smokescreen', disguising the 'structural' causes of family troubles. It evokes nineteenth-century, Poor Law imagery, and can lead to the scapegoating of small, vulnerable sections of the population for problems that have wider, societal origins. A number of practitioner groups have warned of the dangers this poses to different categories of service users. Drugscope and Adfam (2012, p7) are concerned that the TFP programme will serve to *reinforce the public opinion, often fuelled by the media, that there exist a number of badly behaved 'problem families' which constitute an irreversible drain on society and are categorically different from the rest of us*. It points out that the inevitable stigma that this generates could make it difficult to elicit support for meaningful, progressive work with vulnerable individuals and groups. Disability rights organisations have made much the same point. They argue that this initiative, coupled with more general rhetorical assaults upon the 'integrity' of claimants of disability benefits, has had the effect of demonising disabled people who are reliant upon welfare. Richard Hawkes, SCOPE's chief executive, has accused ministers of irresponsibly *playing directly into a media narrative about the need to weed out scroungers. Our polling,* he argued, *shows that this narrative has coincided with attitudes towards disabled people getting worse. Disabled people tell us that increasingly people don't believe that they are disabled and suddenly feel empowered to question their entitlement to support* (cited in Walker, 2012). In the light of these comments, it is easy to see how the ideological fallout caused by the behavioural focus of this kind of family intervention has the potential to impact upon *all* poor or vulnerable citizens and not just those families directly affected. Newspaper headlines surrounding these initiatives, such as the *Daily Mail*'s '500,000 Problem Families Cost Us £30 billion a year' (Stevens, 2015, p14) and the *Express*'s '£200m Blitz on the Families that Shame Britain' (Rockett, 2014, p28), do seem to suggest that such fears are not unfounded. In summary then, there can be little doubt that current discourses surrounding 'family intervention' have much in common with the Poor Law and COS casework approaches, focusing the blame for societal ills on families themselves. As Welshman (2013, p227) argues, such interpretations *have once again provided a convenient, if simplistic, explanation for social problems at a time of economic recession and deep cuts in public spending.*

The COS and its 'casework'

Before providing support, the COS's caseworkers would make detailed inquiries into the character of individuals. Poor Law officials, saving clubs, trade unions, the local clergy, landlords, employers, previous employers, neighbours and relatives would be contacted in an attempt to ascertain an applicant's true character. Once again, if there was a suggestion of impropriety, assistance would be refused, despite the fact that poor references may have been the result of personal grudges rather than accurate character assessments. Perhaps not surprisingly, many of those who came into contact with the COS's caseworkers resented their inquisitive, stigmatising methods of investigation, and many were deterred from applying for much needed assistance. This clearly happened in at least one of the unsuccessful applications for COS support outlined in Table 2.2 (Case 4). These cases, taken from the records of the Fulham and Hammersmith District of the COS, illustrate the sort

Table 2.2 Rejected COS applications

Date	Assistance requested	Decision
Case 1 14/01/80		*Labourer out of work for four weeks with young family, applicant earns well in summer and if he was more careful he would not require charity . . . referred to Poor Law.*
Case 2 20/01/80	Arrears of rent	*Lodging house keeper with nine children (mostly grown up); she drinks, home dirty and there was a large piece of beef on the fire when I visited . . . ineligible.*
Case 3 8/2/80	Temporary	*Bricklayer with young family out of work for seven weeks due to weather; RO says he is drunken lazy man but will give some bread for children; bad references from everyone; house dirty . . . undeserving.*
Case 4 16/2/80	Temporary	*Pregnant 35-year-old cook has been deserted by husband but does not give references, by 21/2/80, the applicant declines any help as she did not think so many enquiries would be made of her . . . ineligible.*
Case 5 7/4/80		*Plumber with five children deserts his family and absconds to America; wife cannot account for his going away as they have always lived on the most affectionate terms . . . referred to Poor Law.*
Case 6 14/5/80	To be started hawking	*47-year-old carman with family out of work for nine months due to illness. Mixed recommendations, RO says family are dirty, lazy, and encouraged eldest son to cohabit; children do not attend school; home dirty . . . undeserving.*
Case 7 -/7/80		*56-year-old governess (formerly employed by Lord Alfred Churchill) . . . Former landlady says applicant used to tell neighbours that landlady was trying to poison her. Lord Alfred Churchill says she was highly gifted but he had to part with her as she appeared strange in manner. When visited by agent she was busy painting a likeness on a piece of china of Mr Plimsoll, late MP for Derby, and it was certainly beautifully done. She admits she was in a lunatic asylum for four years . . . refer to Poor Law.*
Case 8 3/8/80	To get son into blind school	*38-year-old widow with three sons, two of them blind. Good references, and children are indeed blind, but when women went before the [Poor Law] Guardians and they asked her questions she became so abusive she was ordered out of the room . . . undeserving.*

Adapted from Whelan (2001, pp101–36).

of reasons for which families were turned down. As you can see, explicit moral judgements were made about the 'worth' of each candidate.

When assistance *was* provided by the COS, it was not given unconditionally, and caseworkers would engage in further interventions with the families concerned. Hence, material assistance would be accompanied by strict moral guidance and supervision, designed to ensure future self-reliance and independence. Indeed, for the COS, this casework element was the most crucial part of the assistance given, because it offered its visitors the opportunity to rehabilitate and treat the 'moral failings' that had contributed to destitution in the first place. As CS Loch, a leading COS figure, stated in 1910, *Treatment would take the place of mere relief. The 'applicant' would become a supervised class, treated in connection with the home* (cited in Jones, 1976, p9).

The COS under threat and the emergence of the interventionist state

From the 1880s onwards, the assumptions that shaped the COS's work were increasingly challenged, and governments began to make tentative steps towards ameliorating some of the terrible social conditions that had previously been largely ignored. Indeed, the period 1870–1920 is often seen as heralding the beginnings of the 'interventionist state', when governments began to actively intervene to promote citizens' welfare. Over this 50-year period, a host of social policies were introduced, including free compulsory education, improved housing legislation, unemployment and health insurance and old age pensions. Legislation prohibiting child neglect was introduced, as were a range of other measures intended to promote child welfare, such as free school meals and medical inspection of school children. Indeed, many historians identify this era, and particularly the years of the reforming Liberal administration between 1906 and 1914, with the origins of the British welfare state (Fraser, 2009). Of course, as the social investigations of Charles Booth and Seebohm Rowntree vividly illustrated, these reforms were by no means adequate to meet need. They either used stigmatising means tests to target only the very poor, or failed to provide universal coverage (in the case of unemployment and health insurance). Nonetheless, the measures introduced did represent an acknowledgement that the state had a responsibility to look after the welfare of citizens, a recognition that had previously been largely absent.

In assessing this shift to a more interventionist stance, few historians now believe that legislators were motivated primarily by humanitarian concern. For example, the extent of poverty, and the problems caused by low wages, unemployment, under-employment, child labour, poor housing and inadequate sanitation had already previously been well docur   ʳed by commissions of inquiry, yet little had been done to alleviate them. Hence it seems unlikely that politicians were influenced by the sudden exposure of what, in fact, w acknowledged economic and social evils. More important, it seems, were contemʳ concerns over the impact of physical deterioration upon national efficiency. In the light of the economic and military competition from abroad that Britain faced at the end of the nineteenth century, it was becoming increasingly evident that the state could no longer ignore the appalling conditions experienced by the mass of the working population. By now, Britain's position as the foremost workshop of the world and its place as the leading world economic and military power were under severe pressure, due to competition from Germany and the United States (Hall, 1984). The ill-fated Boer War campaign (1899–1902) in South Africa, where huge numbers of potential British recruits were unfit for military service, also provided a wake-up call to the political establishment. In Leeds, for instance, 47.5 per cent of volunteers were found to be unfit, whereas in Manchester 8,000 out of 11,000 (72.7 per cent) did not meet the relatively low standard of fitness required for service (Johnston, 1909). In 1904 William Taylor, the Army Medical Services Director General, bluntly told a Royal Commission on Physical Deterioration that up to 60 per cent of all recruits were *unfit for military service on account of defective physique. Is it not true*, he asked, *that the whole labouring population of the land are at present living under conditions which make it impossible that they should rear the next generation to be sufficiently virile to supply more than two out of five men for the purposes of either peace or war?* (Taylor, 1904, p96).

By the end of the nineteenth century, therefore, an ill-educated, overworked, stunted, poorly housed and ill-fed population had become an economic and military liability, and there was a need to follow the example of other countries, in particular Germany, which had already introduced a raft of social legislation. In fact, leading Liberal politicians who were responsible for many of the early twentieth-century measures of social reform were perfectly open about their motives for legislating, drawing attention to the economic benefits of social reform. Rather than harming economic progress and encouraging dependency, progressive social legislation could, they insisted, contribute to the creation of a healthier, better educated population, promote efficiency and foster the emergence of a more able, independent citizenry.

Reformers also felt that social policy could be used as a 'ransom' to prevent newly enfranchised workers from turning to the revolutionary creeds of the emerging socialist political associations and parties. Certainly, Britain's political landscape had changed by the end of the nineteenth century. The franchise had been extended and by 1884 around 66 per cent of adult males in England and Wales were entitled to vote. New, radical political parties and movements had emerged to cater for this new electoral constituency, and they assailed the electorate with specifically working-class propaganda. As Hall (1984) notes, with the emergence of the Socialist League, the Fabian Society and the Social Democratic Federation, the 1880s saw the movement towards independent working-class political representation. Later, in 1893, the Independent Labour Party was formed, and this was followed by the foundation of the Labour Representation Committee in 1900, which subsequently became the Labour Party. In the 1906 General Election 53 Labour MPs were returned to Parliament. At the same time new, more general, industrial trade unions emerged, which had at their heads a much more radical style of leadership. Many, such as John Burns, Ben Tillett and Tom Mann, were themselves socialists, and by the turn of the century were campaigning for increased state intervention. With the extension of the franchise, these new forms of political and industrial representation posed a significant electoral threat to the established political parties, and their demands could no longer be ignored (Thane, 1996). Conservative and Liberal governments, concerned about the working population's steady development towards political independency, are said to have seen social welfare legislation as an anecdote to socialism, as something that would help to 'spike the socialist guns' (Mishra, 1977). To an extent then, sheer political expediency also forced otherwise reluctant politicians to recognise and act upon the demands of the labour movement to a far greater extent than before (Fraser, 2009; Gilbert, 1973).

The COS's response to state intervention

How did the COS respond to this growing propensity to introduce social reform? Perhaps not surprisingly, it was at the forefront of those opposed to government intervention, including the principle of free school meals for necessitous children, old age pensions, municipal housing, Poor Law reform and initiatives designed to provide work for the unemployed (Jones, 1976, 1983). The position of its more orthodox stalwarts had hardly changed since its inception, and its leadership warned of the morally corrupting impact of state welfare on recipients, claiming it would deter self-help and promote dependence. The following comments were made by CS Loch, one of the COS's more prominent figures, in 1906, and they can be read as a response to the growing tendency for governments to intervene to ameliorate poor social conditions:

> *The individual should provide against hunger, nakedness, and want of shelter; the father against these things both for himself and his family. The ordinary contingencies of life, which fall within the range of ordinary foresight, should for the individual's sake, and for society's sake, be met by the efforts of the individual.* (Cited in Jones, 1976, p4)

Ultimately, the COS was unable to prevent many of the social reforms that it opposed from being enacted, but it did exert considerable influence in shaping the way many social policies were implemented. This is because its charity social workers were used extensively by local authorities to administer relief under schemes such as those of medical and food assistance to children. According to Jones (1973), this was a particularly successful strategy, which allowed the COS to ensure that its principles continued to underpin most aspects of relief work.

The COS and the development of social work training

The COS's development of social work education at the beginning of the twentieth century was discussed briefly in Chapter 1. Its involvement in social work training also represented an attempt to ensure that its underlying philosophy would continue to be enshrined in both policy and practice. It is in such a context, Jones (1976) argues that the COS established its School of Sociology in London in 1903. It was, he states, shaped by a *desire to reassert their claims of expertise in all the fields of social relief.* As the following comments, made by EJ Urwick, the first Director of the School, illustrate, at a time when the COS's philosophy was increasingly questioned, its efforts to formalise social work training did indeed seem to represent an attempt to reinvigorate and renew a message that seemed to many to be out of tune with the times:

> *The terms in which our truths are expressed often belong to a past age; have we not all been at times uneasily conscious that the mere appeal to fundamental principles of self-help, independence, thrift and the like, has lost much of its force, and that these principles must be recast, brought into new connections with current thinking, clothed in new language? For it is unquestionably true that the new generation is receptive enough, but, as always, demands a new preparation for its food.*

This was, then, a sophisticated attempt to ensure that the COS continued to play a decisive role in the future of welfare administration, constituting *an essential part of its strategy to extend its hegemony over the entire field of relief policies* (Jones, 1976, p19). The COS would, through its social work training programmes at the School of Sociology, seek to inoculate its practitioners from the corrupting influences of collectivist thinking and, to quote one of its central council members, to *create a definite public opinion* upon the subjects with which it was concerned. According to CS Loch, the School had the potential to achieve much *more than Parliament or preaching, or books, or pamphleteering* ever could (cited in Jones, 1976, pp14, 20).

At the same time, the COS would use the School of Sociology to disguise the moral basis of its arguments and provide academic credence to its claims about the behavioural causes of social problems. In this respect, Jones cites Helen Bosanquet's attempts to explain destitution in terms of the individual's psychological malfunctioning. Dismissing social and economic explanations, she insisted that it was due primarily to their parents' failure to teach them *progressive interests*, such as thrift and self-help, at a key stage in their psychological development. Such theories, Jones argues, gave a cloak of academic and scientific respectability to the COS's insistence that it was the individual and not society that should be the object of rehabilitation. The whole aim of the project was, according to Jones, to *mobilise and organise its 'theoretical' works for the purpose of producing an enlarged cadre of trained social workers, who, it hoped, would* come *to have a major determining influence on social reform developments* (p20). Ultimately, the COS failed to stem the tide of reform, and as we will show in Chapter 4, the twentieth century saw the development of what we now recognise as the welfare state. However, the continued influence of the COS's moralistic casework approach to social policy and practice continues to be the subject of much debate and disagreement among academics today.

The legacy of the Poor Law and the COS on social policy and social work today

As we explained in the previous chapter, much has occurred in the spheres of social policy and social work since the early twentieth century. However, the period examined in this chapter is crucially important, and not just to those of us with an interest in social and political history. This is because commentators and politicians often refer back to late nineteenth/early twentieth-century developments as evidence to support their assertions about the nature of social policy and social work today. More importantly, proposals for the future development of policy and services are also often justified with reference to developments that occurred during this period (see Chapter 5). The 'lessons' to be learned from this crucial phase of history differ, depending upon the ideological predisposition of the commentators or politicians. However, the fact that it is universally seen as such a key era makes it important that you, as a future social worker, have a grasp of some of the key developments and debates that occurred.

Chapter summary

One of our aims in this chapter has been to inform you of some of the key developments and debates that took place in what is widely regarded as a key period in the history of social policy and social work. In doing so, we wanted to highlight some of the continuities in nineteenth- and twenty-first-century debates about administering welfare. As we saw, a theme that pervaded nineteenth-century policy and practice was the need to restore independence and self-sufficiency, influenced by the notion that moral culpability and not wider structural constraints were the cause of the problems that individuals and families faced. Some of the modern-day case studies that we looked at – for instance our discussions of benefit fraud, FIPs and the TFP – show that such assumptions do, to an extent, continue to influence policy and practice today.

Our other main aim in this chapter has been to draw your attention to the relevance and importance of understanding historical debates about social policy and social work. You should now be able to appreciate their significance, and see that they have very real, immediate, policy-making relevance to social policy and social work in the twenty-first century. Academics and politicians do often refer to the past when justifying policies in the present and, in order to be in a position to assess the claims they make, it is crucial that you have an adequate understanding of the period examined in this chapter. We hope that this chapter has stimulated your interest in history, and that you will consult some of the texts we have indicated below for further reading.

Further reading

If you are interested in reading a good general history of the welfare state, then we would recommend:

Fraser, D (2009) *The Evolution of the British Welfare State*, 3rd edition. Basingstoke: Palgrave Macmillan.

For the Poor Law, the following book combines some useful discussion of the topic together with a wealth of original documents:

Rose, ME (1971) *The English Poor Law, 1780–1930.* Newton Abbott: David & Charles.

For those of you who want to learn more about the activities of the COS, there are a couple of texts that we would recommend. For a positive interpretation of its activities, written from a neo-liberal perspective, see:

Whelan, R (2001) *Helping the Poor: Friendly Visiting, Dole Charities and Dole Queues.* London: Civitas.

For a more critical perspective see:

Jones, C (1983) *State Social Work and the Working Class.* London: Routledge.

The following book documents the influence of pathological 'family-focused' explanations for social problems on the shape of policy and practice from the nineteenth century onwards:

Welshman, J (2013) *Underclass: A History of the Excluded since 1880*, 2nd edition. London: Bloomsbury.

Finally, John Pierson's analysis of the history and context of social work looks in greater depth at some of the themes covered in this chapter:

Pierson, J (2011) *Understanding Social Work: History and Context.* Maidenhead: Open University Press.

3: Ideology, social policy and social work

Achieving a social work degree

This chapter will help you to meet the following capabilities from the Professional Capabilities Framework:

- **Values and ethics** – apply social work ethical principles and values to guide professional practice.
- **Diversity** – recognise diversity and apply anti-discriminatory and anti-oppressive principles in practice.
- **Rights, justice and economic well-being** – advance human rights and promote social justice and economic well-being.
- **Knowledge** – apply knowledge of social sciences, law and social work practice theory.
- **Critical reflection and analysis** – apply critical reflection and analysis to inform and provide a rationale for professional decision-making.

The chapter will also introduce you to the following academic standards which are set out in the 2016 QAA social work benchmark statements:

4   **Defining principles**
5.2   **Social work theory**
5.3   **Values and ethics**
5.4   **Service users and carers**
5.6   **The organisation and delivery of social work services**
5.13   **Analysis and synthesis**
5.16   **Skills in working with others**
6.4   **Learning methods**
7.3   **Knowledge and understanding**

Introduction

From past experience of teaching social policy, it has become evident that the word 'ideology' can generate a certain amount of apprehension among students. Students, perhaps naturally, gravitate towards topics and issues that they feel are more attention-grabbing, topical and relevant to their interests, studies and future chosen careers. As future welfare and social workers, many of you will doubtlessly feel that an understanding of the detail of how social policy affects particular groups of service users is more important to you than an appreciation of ideology, a concept that possibly succeeds only in sending shivers down your spine! Hence you may feel tempted to skip the rest of this section of the book and jump straight into the next section, which contains chapters on children, young people, adults and older people. Needless to say, we would implore you not to do so, because we are firmly of the belief that it is crucial for you to have a basic grasp of at least some of the main political ideologies that have shaped the views of politicians, academics and commentators on social policy and social work issues. This chapter introduces you to the concept of ideology. The next three chapters are devoted to an analysis of how different ideological perspectives have influenced the development of social policy.

Ideology and welfare

As an incentive to encourage you to engage with our discussion of the merits of different ideological perspectives (and read this section of the book!), we list below a few 'benefits' that you will derive from gaining a basic understanding of some of the main ideologies of welfare.

- It will help you work out one of the most confusing, unfathomable quandaries that many students new to social policy and social work face.

When writing an essay, you may have wondered why different academics and politicians who are discussing exactly the same issue seem to interpret it in very different, contradictory ways. Let us take the welfare state, the very subject of social policy. Some academics and politicians argue that we need to spend more on welfare, in order to more effectively tackle problems such as child and pensioner poverty, and to provide wider opportunities for vulnerable groups to secure 'inclusion' in society. Here, the solution to the difficulties faced by certain individuals and groups can be overcome by expanding and improving services. Others, however, argue precisely the opposite. They claim that the welfare state is already too generous, and that rather than 'solving' social problems it actually creates them by locking recipients into a state of passive dependency. The solution to social ills from this perspective is to cut welfare and contract service provision, forcing individuals to take more responsibility for their own welfare. Our students often find it odd that equally intelligent, esteemed, authoritative commentators on social policy issues can disagree so profoundly over such a fundamental point. An understanding of the ideologies of welfare will help you understand why such major disagreements occur.

- You will be able to impress your friends with your powers of prediction.

Unfortunately, we cannot provide you with the powers to predict this week's lottery numbers, football scores or winning horses, but we can help you foresee how certain politicians and academics will interpret and respond to particular economic and social problems.

- It will help you work out your own ideological predisposition.

As Heywood (1998, p1) points out, *All people are political thinkers. Whether they know it or not, people use political ideas and concepts whenever they express their opinions or speak their mind.* You may not realise it, but your views and ideas on particular issues are likely to have been shaped by one or more of the ideological perspectives we discuss in the chapters included in this section of the book. Are you a social democrat, a neo-liberal, a Marxist, or a combination of all three? Read on, and you decide . . .

What is a political ideology?

David McLennan (1986) has described ideology *as the most elusive concept in the whole of the social sciences.* Although this might not be a great starting point for our discussion of ideology, it does sum the concept up quite well, and partly explains the confusion that tends to surround it. One of the problems is that the term, 'ideology', has tended to mean different things to different people.

Ideology and ruling-class interests

For some, the term 'ideology' is seen to refer to the ideas of the ruling class. From this perspective, dominant groups seek to propagate a particular set of values (or ideology) that reflect their own interests, while at the same time justifying their dominance and rule over subordinate groups. In this sense, a ruling-class ideology seeks to 'reconcile the oppressed to their oppression' and is used to perpetuate a misleading and false view of the world. Karl Marx, a leading nineteenth-century political philosopher, used the term in this conspiratorial way to describe how ideology was subtly used by dominant groups to create 'false class consciousness' and to disguise from the working population the fact that their interests lay in the overthrow of the ruling classes. Ideology, therefore, was seen to act as a mystifying smokescreen, a vehicle through which the ruling class sought to promote and protect its interests, while 'tricking' the population into thinking that their rulers were concerned about the well-being of all the people.

Competing ideologies

However, since Marx's death in 1883, the term 'ideology' has lost some of this conspiratorial taint, and in much of the literature you will find reference to ideologies, rather than one ruling-class ideology. It is now generally acknowledged that there are different, competing interpretations of the world, some of which may reflect the interests of dominant groups and the rich, but others of which might not. We use the term 'ideologies' in this sense to refer to rival, alternative sets of values and ideas that influence the way we think about events and issues. The three ideologies we intend to focus upon in this section of the book are social democracy, neo-liberalism and Marxism. Other 'ideologies of welfare' and theoretical approaches could have been chosen, and some of these – such as feminism, anti-racism and postmodernism – are referred to in other sections. However, as George and Wilding (1994, p7) point out, social democracy, neo-liberalism and Marxism are *major ideologies of welfare* and merit a detailed analysis in their own right. As we will show, each of these three ideologies is based upon very different sets of assumptions and values. Each offers competing explanations for and solutions to the social problems that you as welfare professionals will be responding to. However, before moving on to look at these ideologies, it is perhaps worth emphasising the link between political action and ideology.

Ideology and politics

Those who stress the importance of ideologies argue that politicians are motivated by much more than a simple desire to win popular support, elections and power, and that their political ideas and views have more deep-rooted, traceable ideological roots. This is, of course, not to suggest that elections are not of considerable importance to politicians. Clearly, the aim of most politicians is to govern and without election victories they are confined to the wilderness of opposition. Nor is it to imply that politicians do not occasionally deviate from their ideological allegiances when particular circumstances demand a more pragmatic approach. However, politicians are motivated by particular sets of values and ideas – ideologies – which shape their convictions about what needs to be done once power is achieved. In recent years, Conservative politicians are said to have been influenced by neo-liberal ideology, whereas the ideas and policies of Labour and Liberal Democrat politicians are traditionally said to have been influenced by variants of social democratic ideology. As we will show, these two ideologies contain very different values and sets of assumptions about a whole range of issues that are of importance to you as students of social policy and social work, such as:

- the causes and solutions to economic and social problems experienced by service users;
- the role of the state (or governments) in securing the needs of citizens and supporting vulnerable people;
- the role of the welfare state and social work in meeting the needs of service users.

Activity 3.1

The issues that we have listed above lie at the heart of debates about the nature of social policy and social work in the UK and they are the subject of much ideological disagreement.

In order to illustrate this point, we would like you to take time to explore how your own ideological preferences may differ from those of your student peers by discussing your views on each of the issues listed. We suggest that you put all sharpened instruments to one side because we predict a lively debate!

Comment

As part of the above activity, you have presumably discovered your fellow students possess widely divergent views. This is hardly surprising. You probably each come from different family, social class and educational backgrounds; you may read different newspapers, watch different television programmes and have very diverse interests and hobbies. Some of you may have taken an active interest in politics and welfare-related issues, while others will not have done so. The point is, the contributions you and others made to the discussion will have reflected these influences, which themselves will have helped shape your value base or, to put it another way, your own ideological predisposition. In short, despite what you may think, you are not a disinterested, objective analyst of the world around you, and your ideological disposition shapes the way you interpret the world and respond to particular issues.

Activity 3.2

In this activity, we want you to try to ascertain where you stand ideologically. In Table 3.1 we provide you with a summary of social democratic, neo-liberal and Marxist standpoints on each of the issues you discussed in the previous activity. It is a necessarily brief and somewhat simplistic summary of the three approaches (we look at each in more detail later), but it is sufficient for the purposes of this activity. Have a look at the table and try to identify whether you are of a social democratic, neo-liberal or Marxist disposition.

Comment

When we have tried this activity with our own students, we find that most tend to opt for a 'pick and mix' approach that draws from elements of each of the

(Continued)

(Continued)

Table 3.1 Summary of welfare ideologies

	Social democratic perspective	Neo-liberal perspective	Marxist perspective
The causes and solutions to economic and social problems experienced by service users.	The economic and social problems experienced by service users result, primarily, from structural factors which are beyond their control, such as unemployment, poverty, poor educational opportunities, low wages and discrimination. Solutions lie in targeted interventions designed to address the root causes of these problems.	Well-meaning, but morally degenerative interventions have caused the problems they were designed to solve. Overgenerous welfare and an overbearing 'Nanny State' have inculcated a range of dysfunctional patterns of behaviour, encouraging 'dependency', destroying self-help and voluntarism. Solutions lie in the reduction of state support and the promotion of self-help.	Capitalism is the root cause of economic and social ills. It is an economic system based upon greed, exploitation and an insatiable thirst for profit. Businesses rely on the fear of poverty to compel workers to engage in low-waged, exploitative labour. Until it is abolished genuine, fundamental social and economic improvement is impossible.
The role of the state (or governments) in securing the needs of citizens and supporting vulnerable people.	Tackling the causes of economic and social ills is primarily the state's responsibility. Its economic and social policies should be geared towards expanding opportunities so as to ensure that all are able to achieve their potential. It should also seek to eradicate the 'barriers' that prevent marginalised social groups from accessing 'inclusion'.	It is not the state's responsibility to seek to secure the economic/social needs of individuals. It should merely seek to create an environment whereby individuals can secure their own welfare needs through work, or in a private 'welfare market'. Those unable/unwilling to look after themselves should rely primarily on voluntary/charitable provision.	The state in capitalist societies is not a neutral entity that objectively and compassionately responds to the needs of citizens. On the contrary, it always ultimately acts in the interests of business. Social policies are, in reality, geared towards meeting economic needs of business rather than the welfare needs of citizens.
The role of the welfare state and social work in meeting the needs of service users.	The welfare state has a crucial, positive role to play in mitigating the difficulties experienced by service users. The postwar welfare state is seen as a hugely positive development, and one which should be celebrated and extended. Benefits should be improved and eligibility should be widened in a way that enhances people's opportunities to secure 'inclusion'. Social work has a crucial role to play in enabling service users, and in helping to meet their needs.	State welfare has 'seduced' service users into a state of passive dependency, and it needs to be drastically curtailed. A very basic safety net can be provided, but benefits should be cut, means-tested and eligibility tightened. Social workers should cease being politically correct, sentimental 'do-gooders' and should concentrate on 'correcting' dysfunctional behaviour, instilling appropriate norms and values, and stimulating self-help, hard work and thrift.	The welfare state (and social work) perform contradictory roles. On the one hand, they mitigate suffering, but on the other, they benefit capitalism. Welfare services that genuinely promote well-being should be welcomed, but the limitations of reform must be acknowledged. Social workers should seek to reduce suffering in the 'here and now', but they also have a 'political' role to play in fighting for a better society.

ideological perspectives. Some, for example, tend to agree that social problems are largely a result of factors which are beyond the control of individuals and families (a social democratic view), while also being sympathetic to the notion that 'generous' levels of welfare erode individual initiative and encourage idleness and dependency (a neo-liberal view). This apparently contradictory position is hardly surprising. On the one hand, research shows that many social work students are motivated to study social work out of a sense of social justice and a concern to help vulnerable service users (Hackett et al., 2003). Hence, aspects of social-democratic approaches to welfare do appeal to them. On the other hand, as we saw in Chapter 2, 'behavioural' interpretations for social problems have a long historical pedigree and they still feature prominently in media and political commentaries. Our students have clearly been exposed to this particular welfare discourse, and it is inevitable that this too will shape their views of welfare and welfare recipients. In this sense, it is not uncommon for people to hold a mixture of views on welfare-related issues.

However, unlike many of our students (and possibly you), many politicians and academics tend to gravitate towards one or other of the political ideologies we have briefly outlined above. Their ideological allegiances are often more fundamental and deep rooted, and there is a tendency for them to be either 'left-wing', 'centrist' or 'right-wing'.

Research summary

The left–right political continuum

Political ideologies are also sometimes located on what has been referred to as a 'left/right' continuum. In its most simplistic form, the continuum can be visualised as a straight line, with ideologies located at particular points on the line depending upon how 'left-wing', 'centrist' or 'right-wing' they are. The usage of a continuum has been criticised for being an imprecise indicator of political allegiances, but the fact that it is so commonly used means that it is worth devoting some attention to outlining its key features.

In terms of its origins, the 'left–right continuum' can be traced to the years preceding the French Revolution, when the aristocracy and those supporting the king sat to his right, while their opponents, or those considered more radical, sat on the left. In more recent times, 'left-wing' ideologies are seen to be those that are critical of capitalism and believe that it needs to be reformed, or even abolished, with the aim of creating a more equal, fair, socially just society. They therefore tend to advocate varying degrees of economic and social change in order to reduce

(Continued)

(Continued)

economic and social inequality. Put simply, the more stringent the criticism of capitalism is, the more 'left-wing' an ideology is perceived to be. Social democracy, therefore, is often described as a 'centre-left' political ideology, because although it is critical of the injustices generated by capitalism, it believes it is possible to gradually 'tame' it through piecemeal social and economic reform. By contrast, Marxism is portrayed as a 'left-wing' ideology, because its critique of capitalism is more fundamental. As we have seen, Marxists believe capitalism is incapable of reform and must be abolished. In the UK, the Labour Party has traditionally espoused 'social democratic' values, and hence is often referred to as a 'centre-left' party. As we shall see in subsequent chapters, it is said to have moved 'rightward' in recent years, though the election of Jeremy Corbyn in September 2015 was thought to have heralded a 'leftward' shift.

'Right-wing' ideologies are those which reaffirm their support for the existing state of affairs and, in particular, capitalism. They tend to be supportive of free markets, as well as the notion that individuals should be responsible for meeting their own economic and social needs. In this sense, 'right-wing' ideologies have become associated with a defence of the status quo and support for tradition, privilege and inequality. As with the ideologies of the 'left', the more stringent and extreme the defence of the existing state of affairs is, the more 'right-wing' an ideology is said to be. Neo-liberalism is considered to be a right-wing ideology. It is fundamentally opposed to state intervention in economic and social affairs and promotes individualism, markets and free enterprise. Inequality is seen to be a natural outcome of effort and hard work and it is argued that government attempts to promote equality will reduce incentives to work and harm entrepreneurship, and promote dependency and idleness. In the UK, the Conservative Party has become associated with neo-liberal values, particularly since 1979. Since then, its economic and social policies have shifted 'rightward' and it is now widely seen to have embraced an orthodox neo-liberal political stance.

The overarching influence of ideologies on the way politicians interpret and respond to welfare-related issues should not be underestimated. Indeed, it is frequently their dogged belief in a particular ideological framework that influenced them to pursue political careers. Hence, they are not neutral observers of all that is around them, and their values and attitudes – their ideological predispositions – condition and shape the way they interpret and respond to welfare-related issues. These ideologies provide structure, or a 'lens' through which they view and understand social problems, providing them with a moral framework, a map or point of reference which guides them in certain directions rather than others. Indeed, in the world of politics, ideologies can have an almost religious quality for some individuals, and the principles that underpin particular ideological perspectives become almost like articles of faith to their adherents. The former Conservative Prime Minister, Margaret Thatcher, for example, is said to have been particularly ideologically driven, in that she showed a determination to maintain an orthodox neo-liberal position on welfare policy. In this sense, there was a direct link between neo-liberal ideology and the responses of successive Conservative governments to the shape and delivery of social policy and social work. The Conservative-dominated coalition that governed the UK between 2010 and 2015 is also said to have been influenced by neo-liberalism, and a distinct neo-liberal tone could be detected in the post-2015 welfare reforms implemented by Theresa May's Conservative government. Similarly, social democracy is also said to have shaped policy and practice for considerable periods in the UK's history. For instance, the period 1945 to the mid-1970s is said to have been characterised by something of a political consensus over social democratic values and ideas, whereby politicians of all political parties tended to accept the basic assumptions underpinning social democracy. The next chapter is devoted to an analysis of the emergence of social democratic ideas and the development of this 'social democratic consensus'.

Chapter summary

In this chapter, we have sought to introduce you to the concept of 'ideology', and to encourage you to think about your own ideological predisposition. We have also provided a brief summary of three ideological perspectives – social democracy, neo-liberalism and Marxism – each of which has influenced the way commentators, academics and politicians react to social problems and welfare-related issues. The following three chapters provide a more detailed outline of each of these three ideological approaches, assessing the relative influence of each on the development of social policy and social work practice.

Further reading

The following texts provide a good introduction to debates about the links between ideology and welfare:

George, V and Wilding, P (1994) *Welfare and Ideology.* London: Harvester Wheatsheaf.

Lavalette, M and Pratt, A (2006) *Social Policy: Concepts, Theories and Issues.* London: Sage.

Lister, R (2010) *Understanding Theories and Concepts in Social Policy.* Bristol: Policy Press.

For a discussion of feminist and anti-racist perspectives on welfare see:

Williams, F (1989) *Social Policy: A Critical Introduction.* Cambridge: Polity Press.

4: Social democracy and the development of social policy and social work after 1945

Achieving a social work degree

This chapter will help you to meet the following capabilities from the Professional Capabilities Framework:

- **Values and ethics** – apply social work ethical principles and values to guide professional practice.
- **Rights, justice and economic well-being** – advance human rights and promote social justice and economic well-being.
- **Knowledge** – apply knowledge of social sciences, law and social work practice theory.
- **Critical reflection and analysis** – apply critical reflection and analysis to inform and provide a rationale for professional decision-making.
- **Contexts and organisations** – engage with, inform and adapt to changing contexts that shape practice. Operate effectively within own organisational frameworks and contribute to the development of services and organisations. Operate effectively within multi-agency and inter-professional settings.

The chapter will also introduce you to the following academic standards which are set out in the 2016 QAA social work benchmark statements:

4	**Defining principles**
5.2	**Social work theory**
5.3	**Values and ethics**
5.4	**Service users and carers**

Introduction

This chapter begins by discussing the emerging influence of more interventionist, collectivist, progressive ideals on social policy at the end of the nineteenth century. It then goes on to examine the growing influence of social democratic principles and, in particular, the way they shaped the development of the welfare state after the Second World War. This is the first of three chapters looking at how the three ideological perspectives we outlined in Chapter 3 have shaped welfare developments. As we stated in the Introduction to the book, we hope this historical, chronological approach to discussing our three ideological approaches will help you understand how each has exercised different levels of influence on social policy and social work at different times in British history.

Social democracy and welfare

As we explained in Chapter 2, throughout much of the nineteenth century British governments did little to address many of the social evils that accompanied the Industrial Revolution. They pursued a strategy based upon 'classical liberalism'. A key principle of classical liberalism was that of the minimal state. Individuals and manufacturers, it was argued, were best left to pursue their own self-interests without interference from governments, and it was not seen as the state's place to promote economic and social well-being. Social problems like unemployment, poverty, ill-health and insanitary housing were seen as having individual, behavioural causes – they were the result of 'thriftlessness', 'idleness' and 'drunkenness'. 'Laissez-faire' (leave alone) became the key defining principle of this era and, as we illustrated, this was reflected in nineteenth-century social policy and social work practice, which sought to modify the behaviour of the poor rather than relieve their distress.

The origins of social democratic ideology can be traced back to the latter quarter of the nineteenth century, when a new, emerging group of political philosophers, activists and organisations began to question prevailing classical liberal economic and political orthodoxies. They challenged the notion that individuals were necessarily responsible for their own misfortunes, drawing attention to evidence pointing to the wider structural, economic causes of social ills. The pioneering poverty surveys of Charles Booth in London and Seebohm Rowntree in York, which proved that poverty was extensive and largely beyond the control of individuals, provided plenty of ammunition with which to mount an assault on the assumptions underpinning classical liberalism. As Fraser (2009, p137) argues, *Together these surveys provided the compelling statistical justification for a more collectivist policy. Such a policy would have to take account of the growing acceptance that much poverty was the consequence of complex economic and social factors beyond the control of the individual.* Governments, it was increasingly argued, had a moral responsibility to intervene to assist people to overcome problems that were not of their making, and create conditions which would enable all citizens to achieve their full potential. Within social work, the challenge to COS methods of working with the poor was led by people such as Clement Attlee, RH Tawney and TH Marshall, all of whom were passionate advocates of this 'new' way of thinking.

Many of those leading the challenge against classical liberalism, including Attlee, Tawney and Marshall, were influenced by socialism. They felt that collectivist social reform could be used as the means of not only alleviating the economic and social problems created by capitalism, but also as a mechanism of replacing unregulated capitalism with a fairer economic and social system, based upon the principles of equality and egalitarianism. Some socialists favoured a policy of violent revolutionary upheaval, but the most influential among them, within the Fabian Society, the Labour Representation Committee and later the Labour Party, believed that it was possible to reform society gradually, within the existing parliamentary system. Herein lies the beginnings of social democracy, that is the attempt to transform society and create a more progressive, equal economic and social order through democratic, parliamentary means.

The creation of the Labour Party in 1906 was part of this social democratic strategy. It represented an attempt to secure the election of representatives of the working class to Parliament so as to begin the process of securing the gradual reform of capitalism through the use of the democratic process. In Chapter 2, we discussed some of the social reforms that were introduced at the beginning of the twentieth century partly as a result of the challenge to the central tenets of classical liberalism. However, despite some progress, the period before 1939 continued to be largely characterised by an ideology of non-intervention. As RH Tawney, a key advocate of social democracy, pointed out, prior to this social policies were only reluctantly introduced, never sufficiently catering for the widespread unmet need that existed. They were designed more to 'manage' and 'preserve' unacceptable economic and social inequalities rather than to 'challenge' and 'eradicate' them. To cite Tawney (1964, p219), social policies *crept piecemeal into apologetic existence, as low grade palliatives designed at once to . . . conceal the realities of poverty.*

Tawney's *Equality*

Tawney's classic text *Equality*, first published in 1931, provided an eloquent and compelling case for the adoption of social democratic ideas. Written during a period of economic depression, mass unemployment and widespread poverty, it set out a very different ideological path to that pursued at the time. By and large, governments of the period maintained a largely laissez-faire attitude to economic and social problems. Wages and unemployment benefits were in many cases insufficient to meet subsistence needs, secondary education was available to only a privileged minority and health care was a commodity that millions could not afford to purchase. Governments, Tawney argued, should adopt a radically different approach, and seek to intervene in the economy and welfare sphere in order to create a more equal, fair society, where opportunity would depend upon aptitude and not ability to pay. Tawney set out a moral case for such intervention, appealing to common humanity and decency, but he also emphasised the economic and political benefits that would accrue from the adoption of a progressive welfare agenda. There was, for example, a pressing economic need (as well as a moral one) to improve the lamentable standard of schooling in Britain, which, prior to the Second World War, allowed roughly 80 per cent of children to leave school at 14 with no secondary education or formal qualifications whatsoever. As Tawney (1964, p146) argued, apart from any other consideration, *the mere economic loss involved in withholding from four-fifths of British children the educational opportunities required to develop their powers is extremely serious. The nation,* he insisted, *has not such a plethora of ability at its command that it can afford to leave uncultivated, or undercultivated, the larger proportion of that which it possesses.* Similarly, there was both a moral and an economic case for providing free health care for citizens. Unnecessary sickness, he pointed out, accounted for the equivalent of the loss of 12 months' work of 560,000 persons, and cost the nation around £100 million. Hence, a national health service would not only enhance the life chances and opportunities of working-class people who at the time could not afford health care, it would also improve the health and economic efficiency of the community as a whole. Finally, Tawney also maintained that such 'civilising' policies would also serve to strengthen democracy itself. In the 1938 edition to his book he wrote that *democracy is unstable . . . as long as it remains a political system and nothing more, instead of being, as it should be, not only a government but a type of society* (p30). Creating a fairer, more equal type of society, where all had the opportunity to achieve their full potential would add legitimacy to the British democracy, avoiding a repetition of events in 1930s Germany where resentment of mass unemployment and poverty had generated disillusionment with democracy and propelled Hitler to power.

Activity 4.1

Although the origins of the welfare state can be traced to the early twentieth century, substantive, genuinely progressive social reforms were not introduced on a large scale until after the Second World War.

- Why do you think the Second World War was such a catalyst for change in terms of the development of the welfare state?
- Social policy historians have cited the Blitz, rationing and the evacuation programme as important factors contributing to a radical change in thinking on welfare. Why might this have been the case?

The triumph of social democracy: the Second World War and the development of the welfare state

Many historians of the welfare state see the Second World War as a catalyst in the emergence of widespread support for the principles underpinning social democratic thought, and of the development of the welfare state. In interpreting these two trends, historians have pointed to how the peculiar circumstances of war fundamentally altered people's perceptions of what governments could and should do to tackle social and economic problems. As Derek Fraser (2009) argues, the Second World War was *perhaps the first 'people's war', wholly dependent on the efforts and support of the whole population, not just the military prowess of the professional army.* Even more so than the 1914–18 conflict, it was reliant upon the efforts and sacrifices of the whole of the country, not just those involved in direct combat. Indeed, Titmuss (1950), one of the most influential writers on the post-war welfare state, estimated that the number of British civilians injured by enemy bombing raids was approximately the same as the number of British soldiers wounded fighting in all theatres of war. The very nature of this led to a feeling of 'shared sacrifice' and generated a momentum for social improvement after the war. As Paul Addison (1994, p130), another influential historian, points out, *The war effort . . . hurled together people of different social backgrounds in a series of massive upheavals caused by bombing, conscription and the migration of workers . . . The war effected a quiet revolution.*

A number of other developments occurred which also helped convince people of the merits of the social democratic case for government intervention. For instance, in the inter-war years, it was commonplace for politicians to claim that chronic unemployment was a result of the existence of a sizeable number of 'unemployables', who were unwilling or incapable of work. The 'solutions' that were proposed ranged from cutting welfare support in order to stimulate the 'lazy' and 'feckless', to the compulsory sterilisation of the 'residuum'. The war served to shatter this myth, because within a year unemployment had been all but eradicated. This showed that unemployment was a problem of lack of opportunity rather than motivation or ability. This realisation strengthened social democratic arguments for the development of a proactive response to unemployment after the war, based upon governments providing people with genuine opportunities to work, rather than reducing benefits in a misguided attempt to incentivise the so-called 'idle'. The war years also saw the creation of an embryonic national health service, a development prompted by concern about levels of wartime casualties, but one that had been strongly resisted by governments before 1939. For the first time, free hospital care was provided to all British citizens on the basis of need, and again this reinforced the social democratic case for governments to accept responsibility for the health of citizens after the cessation of hostilities. Rationing also served an important precedent. It constituted a state guarantee for all citizens to be provided with access to a healthy, nutritious diet, a commitment previous governments had never been prepared to make (Addison, 1994). The experiences of the wartime evacuation programme, which involved hundreds of thousands of children being uprooted from poor, disadvantaged areas at risk of bombing and relocated in more affluent rural areas, was another significant development. As Fraser (2009, p210) argues, it *was part of the process by which British society came to know itself, as the unkempt, ill clothed, undernourished and often incontinent children of bombed cities acted as messengers carrying the evidence of the deprivation of working-class life into rural homes.* Many of those who hosted evacuated children were genuinely appalled at the condition in which they arrived, and this did lead to much soul searching, and support for ameliorative measures to be introduced to combat the evils identified. Each of these developments and trends helped strengthen support for egalitarian policies and state intervention – key principles of social democratic ideology – both during and after the war. People began to question why, if governments could use their powers of intervention to secure these achievements amid the chaos and destruction of war, was it not possible to do the same in peacetime? It was within such a context, in December 1942, that one of the most important social policy documents in British history, the Beveridge Report, was published.

The Beveridge Report

The Beveridge Report, the brainchild of the civil servant Sir William Beveridge, was published on 2 December 1942. Beveridge had been tasked with producing recommendations on how to improve Britain's uncoordinated system of social service provision, but nobody, least of all the coalition government which commissioned the report, could have predicted the popular response to it. Arguably, never before or since has an official government report been greeted with such public enthusiasm or acclaim, or generated such a high degree of optimism. On its first day of publication 70,000 copies flew off the shelves of newsagents and booksellers, and altogether some 635,000 copies were sold.

When one considers what the Beveridge Report promised, it is easy to understand why it was so popular, and also why it has come to be seen as a classic social democratic blueprint. Basically, Beveridge argued that any post-war government should, as a matter of urgency, seek to use its powers of intervention to abolish what he referred to as the *five giant evils* that had characterised inter-war Britain.

- **Want.** By Want, Beveridge meant poverty. Poverty, he argued, was largely due to circumstances beyond the individual's control, caused by *an involuntary interruption or loss of earning power or the failure to relate income during earning to the size of family* (Beveridge, 1942, p7). Governments should, he insisted, accept their responsibility for eradicating poverty, by introducing a comprehensive system of social security (pensions, family allowances, unemployment insurance).

- **Disease.** *Restoration of a sick person to health is*, Beveridge argued, *a duty of the State.* The pre-war system of British health care was wholly inadequate to meet need, leaving millions responsible for the unaffordable costs of their own health-care provision.

Beveridge's report stated that governments should introduce *a health service providing full preventative and curative treatment of every kind to every citizen without exceptions, without remuneration limit and without an economic barrier at any point to delay recourse to it* (Beveridge, 1942, pp159, 162).

- **Ignorance**. In calling for the eradication of ignorance, Beveridge drew attention to the wasted talent that resulted from a system that compelled 80 per cent of children to leave school at 14 without any formal academic qualifications at all. There was, he insisted, a need for *an immense programme of building schools, training and employment of teachers . . . to fit opportunity to young ability wherever it is found.*

- **Squalor** had created bad conditions of life for a large part of our population and needed to be the subject of a planned attack by government. The war, Beveridge (1944, p257) argued, *will leave a yawning gap* in provision which the state must ensure is *filled without delay by building more homes.*

- **Idleness.** By idleness, Beveridge meant involuntary unemployment. If governments could create conditions conducive to full employment amid the chaos and destruction of war, there was, he insisted, no reason why the same could not be achieved in peacetime. *We cure unemployment through hate of Hitler*, he wrote, *so we ought to cure it through hate of . . . a needless scandal and wasting sore* (Beveridge, 1944, pp254–5).

Beveridge was well aware of the criticisms that his proposals for a massive increase in government responsibility for welfare would face from those still steeped in classical liberal traditions. *There are some,* he wrote, who may think his proposals were *inconsistent with initiative, adventure, personal responsibility.* However, he argued that there was *no economic or moral justification* for why Britain should not seek to tackle the five giant evils he had identified. *A revolutionary moment in the world's history is*, he insisted, *a time for revolutions, not for patching* (p6).

Critiques of the Beveridge Report

As we have already hinted, the levels of public support for the report were extraordinary. However, the reaction to the Beveridge Report was not one of universal acclaim. For example, senior figures within the Conservative Party were ideologically opposed to such a wide extension of state intervention. In addition, some feminist writers accused the Beveridge Report of failing to provide adequately for the social security needs of women.

Political opposition to the Beveridge Report

Although the Beveridge Report was welcomed by the Labour Party, which unsurprisingly welcomed the social democratic tone of its proposals, many Conservatives, including the Prime Minister Winston Churchill, were distinctly unimpressed with its recommendations for widespread government intervention and social reform. The Conservative Party's largely critical reaction to the Beveridge Report provides us with a good example of how a commitment to a particular ideological framework can shape the way politicians respond to particular social problems and issues. Many within the Conservative Party continued to be steeped in classical liberal traditions, believing in minimal state intervention and self-help, and this structured their response to the report. The ideological climate had changed as a result of the 'peculiar conditions' of war, but because the bulk of the Conservative Party remained wedded to classical liberal ideals, it failed to tap into this wholesale shift in the political environment.

The Conservatives' lukewarm response to the Beveridge Report was to prove to be a monumental political misjudgement and it would cost the party dear at the general election in 1945. For despite having the great wartime leader, Winston Churchill, as their figurehead, they were to suffer a humiliating landslide election defeat. Churchill was beaten at the polls by the leader of the Labour Party and former social worker Clement Attlee. His Labour Party took office, and immediately set about implementing what we now know as the welfare state. In the light of their crushing electoral defeat and the popular support for the welfare state that emerged after 1945, most Conservatives came to accept the notion that the state had a responsibility for securing citizens' welfare. Hence, the period between 1945 and the mid-1970s has come to be seen as one characterised by a 'social democratic consensus', particularly over welfare-related issues. There were, of course, exceptions to the consensus, and some Conservatives continued to cling on to their classical liberal allegiances, but to varying degrees, both Conservative and Labour governments pursued interventionist policies designed to reduce inequalities and extend opportunity.

Feminist critiques of the Beveridge Report

In a much-cited pamphlet written on behalf of the Women's Freedom League, Elizabeth Abbott and Katherine Bompas (1943) drew attention to the 'gendered' nature of Beveridge's proposals and its failure to acknowledge women's own individual social security requirements. *At present*, they wrote, *the Plan is mainly a man's plan for a man* (p20). As a number of more recent feminist social policy analysts have pointed out, Abbott and Bompas were right to suggest that the Beveridge Report was influenced by a pervasive 'ideology of motherhood' (Williams, 1989). The assumptions that marriage provided women with a 'meal ticket for life' and that a women's place was in the home did underpin the Beveridge Report. Consequently, it was assumed that most married women would not need any individual entitlement to social security in their own right.

As Timmins (1996) points out, the idea that a woman's place was in the home and that women would and should return to the domestic sphere following the end of hostilities did seem to run contrary to contemporary developments, not least the fact that an additional 1.8 million women had entered industry alone between 1939 and 1943. In addition to this, many women had joined the armed services or undertook other work, trends that dramatically altered women's roles, status and indeed aspirations. Beveridge was not unaware of these trends, but he regarded them merely as a temporary aberration, assuming that once the war was over, the 'equilibrium' would be restored and women would return to performing their 'vital' household duties. For Beveridge, married women's unpaid work in the home was crucially important if the next generation of workers were to be socialised and reared effectively, and his proposals for social insurance were explicitly designed to reinforce 'traditional' gender roles. Hence, most married women were treated as dependents of their husbands, ineligible for social insurance related benefits (such as sickness benefits and pensions) in their own right, and if they did work they were in most cases only entitled to lower rates of support in times of need. As Williams points out, it is for this reason that Beveridge has since been seen as the *arch villain in much feminist writing* concerning the welfare state, with one such feminist commentator referring to his report as *one of the most crudely ideological documents of its kind ever written* (Wilson, cited in Williams, 1989, pp124–5).

It is not just the fact that Beveridge failed to acknowledge the possibility that married women's aspirations may have changed as a result of their experiences during the war that perturbs feminists today. Just as objectionable, they argue, was his failure to predict post-war social trends – such as an increased divorce rate and growing numbers of lone parents – which meant that marriage could no longer be relied upon as a principal means of economic security for women. Consequently, as we will see, those women who subsequently failed to conform to the 'traditional' family norm were, at best, forced to negotiate a social security system that was ill-suited to their needs, and at worst, subjected to discrimination and harassment. More serious still, the gendered assumptions underpinning the Beveridge Report are said to have had a *remarkably enduring influence* on social policy. According to Colwill (1994), *for many women the principles and assumptions around which welfare provision is constructed remain as intrusive, objectionable and oppressive as ever they were.*

More recently, some commentators have sought to defend Beveridge from his feminist detractors, claiming that he was a product 'of his time' and that he could not have predicted the far-reaching changes in family formation that would occur after the war. As Timmins (1996, p54) argues, *if he failed to foresee radical changes to come then that foresight was denied to many others.* For those such as Timmins, the real blame for the failure to adapt the post-war welfare state to changing social trends lies not with Beveridge but with post-war politicians who lived through those very changes. However, putting the question of culpability to one side, there is a general consensus that the gendered nature of Beveridge's proposals continues to shape the way in which many women today experience the social security system.

Children's education and welfare during the Second World War

During the war, full employment, rationing and the increased availability of free medical care certainly improved the lives of millions of citizens. As we have seen, these precedents showed that the state could use its powers to enhance the 'common welfare' of its people, and in doing so they contributed to the groundswell of support for the Beveridge Report's optimistic, compelling blueprint for the eradication of economic and social ills. However, the trajectory of wartime social policy developments was uneven and by no means uniformly positive, particularly in relation to children's education and welfare. Certainly, children benefited from improvements in nutrition wrought by rationing, but in certain other respects, wartime developments could be said to have hindered both their education and their well-being. Indeed, a recognition that children should be 'compensated' for this hindrance contributed to already existing pressures for the state to take greater responsibility for improving their education and welfare after the war.

Children's education was undoubtedly one of the casualties of war, as schooling was severely disrupted by bombing, the evacuation programme and the exodus of good, experienced teachers from schools into the armed forces. In many agricultural areas, this disruption was exacerbated by the wholesale withdrawal of children from school in order to help with harvests, a practice that severely impacted upon their education. Educational historiographies of the Second World War rarely mention this relatively widespread practice, which was formally sanctioned by the wartime coalition government, but illegal, exploitative child labour was rife in certain parts of the country, as unscrupulous farmers used the wartime emergency as an opportunity to substitute adult workers for cheaper, more compliant children (see Cunningham, 2002). It was partly a recognition of the educational sacrifices made by children during the war that led to the passage of one of *the* major pieces of wartime social legislation – the 1944 Education Act. However, the passage of this landmark piece of legislation, which raised the school leaving age to 15 and provided all children with access to *some form* of secondary education, should not be allowed to detract from the negative impact that the war had upon children's educational experiences.

With hindsight, we also now know that children's experiences of the evacuation programme were not entirely positive. While the problems uncovered by evacuation may have helped illuminate the need to improve children's welfare after the war, there was a 'darker' side to the programme. For example, little or no screening was undertaken to ensure that families receiving child evacuees were suitable foster parents, and many of the 1.5 million children evacuated during the Second World War faced neglect, as well as emotional, physical and sexual abuse at the hands of their hosts. Indeed, oral histories of the period seem to uncover as many tales of woe as they do affection, and for many hosts, evacuee children were little more than an economic resource (Waugh et al., 2007; Welshman, 2010). As Welshman (2010, p206) notes, *as many of the evacuated children found to their cost, they were only too welcome as unpaid servants and scapegoats, as were their money and ration books*. He recounts the experiences of seven-year-old Mary-Rose Benton, who was evacuated from Margate in 1940 and billeted with the 'Newbold' family in Stafford. Separated from her two brothers who were billeted elsewhere, Mary-Rose was subjected to arbitrary vicious beatings and deliberate, wilful neglect:

> *Mrs Newbold had absolute power over Mary-Rose, and it corrupted her absolutely. At some point she began to starve the girl. Mary-Rose would be given one slice of bread for breakfast, or nothing at all; her food was set on the plate separately, always a smaller portion than for the others . . . It was not because of rationing; the other children had enough. Mary-Rose began to get painful cramps in her stomach, went to bed hungry, and began to scavenge for food. She took cabbage leaves through the allotment fence, ate berries and leaves, and picked up discarded sweets and chewing-gum.* (Welshman, 2010, p207)

Mary-Rose's neglect continued for two years, until she returned to live with her mother. Sadly, her experiences were far from unique. One survey of former child evacuees estimates that almost half (46.9 per cent) suffered some form of abuse (Waugh et al., 2007). At the time, though, few concerns were raised about the treatment of evacuee children. While contemporary reports did identify symptoms of psychological distress among them, such as bedwetting, tearfulness, anxiety and desperate homesickness, this was invariably seen to be a product of the process of separation, rather than emotional or physical abuse, as a problem of 'attachment' rather than anything more sinister (Welshman, 2010). With hindsight, the failure to identify or acknowledge the experiences of those such as Mary-Rose seems remarkable, especially in the light of the emphasis that was being placed upon social reconstruction at the time and, in particular, the need to prioritise children's welfare after the war.

However, the abuse faced by 'separated' children would very soon be placed at the forefront of the nation's, and indeed the world's, attention when Dennis O'Neill, a 12-year-old boy, was brutally tortured and killed at the hands of his foster parents. As Abrams (2012) notes, this case was significant for two reasons. Firstly, it highlighted the palpable failure of the state to protect children who had been entrusted into its care. Secondly, the findings of the two inquiries that were set up in the wake of Dennis' death – the Monkton Inquiry and the Curtis Committee – reinforced already existing pressures for the state to do much more to protect the welfare of citizens, in this specific case vulnerable children in its care.

Dennis O'Neill was not an evacuee. Along with his siblings, he had been removed from his parents in May 1940 on the grounds of neglect and entrusted into the care of Newport County Borough Council. The Council had initially 'boarded out' Dennis and his brother Terence to two sets of foster parents in Herefordshire, but in June 1944 Dennis was placed with the Gough family, at their farm near Minsterley in Shropshire. He was initially alone, but was joined by Terence a month later. As the following statement made by the prosecution during the trial of the foster parents, Reginald and Esther Gough, illustrates, thereafter the boys faced appalling levels of abuse:

> *He {Dennis} was undernourished and practically starved. No fat was found on him, and you will see the pictures – they are the most revolting pictures I have ever seen – showing signs on his back that he had been unmercifully beaten and signs on his chest where he*

had been assaulted. It is clear that he had been assaulted by the man with his fist. The pathologist is of the opinion that the actual cause of death was probably the assault which caused the chest injuries, the boy at that time being in an emaciated and weak state of health. The prosecution alleges that both of these prisoners contributed to his death, the woman by her semi-starvation of the boy and the man by the beating and assault upon him . . . Dennis was so hungry that he used to crawl to the cattle and suck their teats . . . With regard to the actual physical violence, Terence says that every night to start with they were thrashed on their hands . . . On the Saturday before his death Dennis . . . was thrashed for biting a swede . . . Terence also says that on the Sunday night while Dennis was naked he was thrashed by Gough with a thin stick and that bits broke off the stick until it became too short. He was then thrashed with another stick until his legs were all blue and swollen . . . On the morning of the day on which Dennis died Terence says he remembers Mr Gough pummelling Dennis. (Guardian, 1945a)

The trial's proceedings were reported extensively in the national and world press. The sense of outrage and shock generated by the trial was unprecedented, comparable to that which followed in the wake of the more recent Maria Colwell, Victoria Climbié and Baby Peter Connelly cases. The judge's pre-sentencing comments encapsulated the nation's collective feeling of horror at the circumstances surrounding Dennis's death; *You have shown a beastly cruelty,* he told Reginald Gough, *and you have killed, partly by slow and partly by swift means, a boy whom you knew to be in your power . . . Your behaviour has, I think, rightly shocked the world; and shocked England (Guardian,* 1945b).

The jury took just twenty minutes to find Reginald Gough guilty of manslaughter and his wife, Esther Gough, of neglect. He was sentenced to six years penal servitude, while his wife received a six-month prison sentence. Although the jury itself was not asked to make any judgement as to the culpability of welfare agencies in contributing to Dennis' death, as the following editorial in the *Daily Mail* (1945) illustrates, it soon became clear that the child welfare system itself was also in the 'dock':

The jury, as the judge rightly said, were not concerned with the system under which the death of the little boy could come about. But it is very much the concern of the rest of us . . . It is obvious that defects in the system helped to encompass the death of Dennis O'Neill.

This conclusion was reinforced by the Monkton Inquiry (1945), which was tasked with investigating the tragic circumstances surrounding Dennis's death.

An even more damning indictment of the child protection system would follow one year later, with the publication of the Curtis Committee's (1946) report into the care of the 124,900 looked-after children across England and Wales. The inquiry was not prompted by the death of Dennis O'Neill, but his case had raised the profile of the Committee's work and its findings were eagerly awaited. The standards of 'care' described in the report make sober reading. The worst levels of neglect were experienced by the 6,500 children who were 'accommodated' in what the committee accurately described as *forbidding* workhouses, which were entirely unsuitable for the care of children. Often, children were placed in workhouses as an emergency, interim measure, while more suitable accommodation was sought, but they frequently found themselves confined in them for months. These *large gaunt looking buildings with dark stairways and corridors, high windows . . . bare boards and draughts* were oppressive, soulless Dickensian institutions, whose original purpose had been to strike fear in the 'feckless' poor (see Chapter 2). Their remit had changed somewhat by 1946, by which time they tended to be repositories for the destitute sick and aged who had no other means of support, but they were no more suitable for housing vulnerable, separated children than they were in their original guise. The stigma and austerity of the workhouse regime was as strong as ever, and for those lone, neglected, bewildered children who were placed in these adult institutions, it must have been a truly terrifying experience. Few attempts were made by the poorly trained, ill-equipped workhouse staff to assuage children's anxieties, to cater for their complex needs or even provide them with the opportunity to attend school. As the Curtis Committee (1946, p45) found, children *were left to the casual kindness of aged inmates or to the indifferent attention of busy staff to whom they were nothing but an additional burden*. In one section of its report, the Committee described its visit to one workhouse nursery, which housed 32 children:

> *In the children's ward was an eight year old mentally defective girl, who sat most of the day on a chair commode, because, the nurses said, 'she was happy that way'. She could not use her arms or legs. There were two babies with rickets clothed in cotton frocks, cotton vests and dilapidated napkins, no more than discoloured cotton rags. The smell in this room was dreadful. A premature baby lay in the opposite ward alone . . . The day room was large and bare and empty of all toys . . . They slept in . . . corrugated hutment in old broken black iron cots . . . The mattresses were fouled and stained . . . The children wore ankle length calico or flannelette frocks and petticoats and had no knickers. Their clothes were not clean. Most of them had lost their shoes; those who possessed shoes had either taken them off to play or were wearing them tied to their feet with dirty string. Their . . . bodies in some cases were washed and stained.* (Curtis Committee, 1946, p40)

These conditions were by no means unique to workhouse establishments. The Curtis Committee's report documented a hitherto 'hidden' world of neglect, which, to varying degrees, was a characteristic feature of *all* forms of accommodation used to house looked-after children. The quality of provision in public assistance children's homes, which catered for 16,900 separated children, was frequently equally oppressive as that found in workhouses. These often overcrowded, understaffed, dilapidated homes were little more than 'holding units' for their child occupants, offering little in the way of 'care'. One such home, which was far from untypical, could suitably accommodate 256 children, but it actually housed 385, around one-fifth of whom were forced to share a bed. Infection and sickness was rife in this and other similar overcrowded, unsuitable, understaffed children's homes. The Committee's overall conclusions provided a damning indictment of the child protection system in England and Wales. Almost the entire system was characterised by *dirt and dreariness, drabness and over-regimentation*. Individual children were seen as *merely one of a large crowd* and few attempts were made to ascertain or meet their complex needs. In many cases, this was the result of wilful neglect. In other instances, staff simply lacked the skills, education and training needed to perform such a role. As the Committee noted, there was a *widespread and deplorable shortage of the right kind of staff, personally qualified and trained to provide the child with a substitute for a home background. The result*, the Committee concluded, was *a lack of personal interest in and affection for the children which we found shocking* (p134).

The Curtis Committee also drew attention to the failure of the state to effectively monitor and regulate standards of care. This left all children, irrespective of where they were housed, at risk of neglect and abuse. The absence of oversight, the Committee noted, meant that there was a *danger, even in an organisation or under an authority with an enlightened policy, that individuals in charge of groups of children may develop harsh or repressive tendencies or false ideas of discipline, and that the children in their care may suffer without the knowledge of the central authority* (Curtis Committee, 1946, pp133–4).

One newspaper described the Committee's findings as *the greatest scandal of modern times*:

> *They discovered that the days of Oliver Twist are not dead. On the contrary, cruelties and neglect persist in every class of accommodation, from the reception of young children newly taken from their homes to the time when, ill-educated and broken in spirit, they are sent out to face a world in which they have no friends.* (Smith, 1946a, p1)

The *Guardian*'s coverage of the report concurred with this assessment: *what stands out most vividly from this detailed and patient report is the description of some of the places where children whose birthright is a normal, happy life are leading lives of great misery* (*Guardian*, 1946a, p4). The Committee's report, the *Guardian* noted, *points to slackness by local authorities, it tells of institutions, wretchedly equipped and badly staffed, where conditions reminiscent of the days of Dickens still prevail* (*Guardian*, 1946b, p4).

At a time when the state was committing itself to securing the economic and social well-being of citizens, the lamentable, casual disregard for the welfare of children in its care uncovered by the Curtis Committee illuminated the fundamental shortcomings that had hitherto characterised social service provision. The consequences of the 'old', non-interventionist, laissez-faire approach to welfare could not have been laid more bare; a failure of government oversight and intervention had led to the scandalous neglect of tens of thousands of the country's most vulnerable children. In this respect, the Curtis Committee, along with the tragic death of Dennis O'Neil, provided impetus to the already existing clamour for the introduction of progressive, social democratically inspired social reconstruction.

'Never had it so good?' The impact of post-war social policy during the period of the social democratic consensus

There can be little doubt that the commitment post-war governments made to maintaining full employment, improving the nation's social services, and reducing social and economic inequality via the welfare state contributed to significant overall improvements in economic and social well-being. The 1950s and 1960s were decades of relatively full employment, and hence one of the primary causes of poverty in the inter-war years – unemployment – had been effectively removed. Health care and secondary education were now free to all, and better social security and housing provision helped alleviate some of the chronic levels of poverty and destitution that were a feature of inter-war Britain. In relation to social services, Attlee's Labour government passed the 1948 Children Act, which sought to eliminate the abuses uncovered by the Curtis Committee. Following the passage of the Act, new children's departments were created. Headed by a qualified children's officer, the intention was to infuse social work with children with a more welfare-focused ethos (Pierson, 2011). In 1964, in the introduction to the fourth edition of RH Tawney's *Equality,* Richard Titmuss asked whether, in the light of these successes, the aims of social democracy had become redundant and outdated. *Have we in Britain*, he wrote, *reached such an equalitarian position that further substantial measures of collective redistribution are not called for, economically and morally?* (in Tawney, 1964, p15).

Certainly, many contemporary politicians and academics believed that the welfare state had largely achieved its aims, and that there was little need for measures to further reduce social class inequalities. As the Conservative Prime Minister, Harold Macmillan, famously said, it seemed as if the British population had *never had it so good.* Even leading social democratic intellectuals felt confident enough to proclaim that capitalism had been fundamentally transformed. According to CAR Crosland, author of the key 1956 social democratic text, *The Future of Socialism*, it was now manifestly inaccurate to call Britain a capitalist society. Capitalism, if not completely transformed, had been irreversibly greatly modified. Such optimistic assessments of the impact of the welfare state were reinforced by the findings of Seebohm Rowntree's third survey of poverty in York, published in 1951, which concluded that full employment and the welfare state had largely succeeded in eradicating subsistence poverty. His 1936 survey of York had found that nearly two persons in every 11 were in poverty, but by 1951 this had apparently fallen to two in every 118. As *The Times* (15 October 1951, p7) pointed out, it seemed that a *remarkable improvement – no less than the virtual abolition of the sheerest want – has been brought about.* Similar claims concerning the abolition of poverty and the creation of an 'affluent society' continued into the 1960s.

Activity 4.2

In this activity, we want you to try to think about the imagery you associate with the 1960s. What feelings does that decade conjure up in your imaginations? Do you associate it with positive or negative developments?

Comment

When we ask our students about the 1960s, they almost uniformly associate it with positive imagery, linking it to technological breakthroughs (landing men on the Moon), positive changes in popular culture, sexual liberation and progressive civil rights campaigns. This image of the 1960s seems to be in tune with how many of us think of the decade today. We tend to link it with great technological advancement, economic growth, prosperity and conspicuous consumption. This was, after all, the decade of the Beatles, the Rolling Stones, civil rights protests, the hippy movement and, dare we say it, 'free love'. Even Preston North End (the preferred football team of one of the authors of this text) was a half-decent side in the 1960s, only narrowly being beaten by West Ham United in the 1964 FA Cup final! All this seems to point to a 'rosy' period of affluence and prosperity, and support for the notion that the objectives of social democracy – a more fair, equal and socially just society – had been achieved.

There can be little doubt that the material conditions of the working population in Britain did improve in post-war Britain as a result of the welfare state and full employment (Lowe, 1993). Certainly, when one compares social and economic conditions in post-war Britain with those of the 1930s, there had been huge gains. However, in the 1960s doubts began to emerge about claims that the five giant evils identified by Beveridge in 1942 had been conquered. A new, radical group of social policy academics began to draw attention to failings in welfare provision. Inequalities of wealth, income and power were, they argued, as firmly entrenched in the 1960s as they had been before the Second World War. Moreover, there were significant flaws and gaps in provision, which meant that many vulnerable people were not receiving the assistance they were entitled to and desperately needed. In addition, social work itself came under close scrutiny, as it became clear that pre-war, moralistic assumptions about the culpability of the poor remained remarkably resistant to change within social work practice, frustrating the adoption of a more progressive approach.

The rediscovery of poverty

In 1965 Brian Abel Smith and Peter Townsend published a study entitled *The Poor and the Poorest* (Abel Smith and Townsend, 1965), which succeeded in shattering the comfortable assumption that poverty was 'a thing of the past'. Their definition of poverty differed from the subsistence-level definitions which had traditionally been adopted in poverty studies, most recently in Rowntree's 1951 York inquiry. Abel Smith and Townsend argued that previous poverty research had placed too much emphasis upon assessing incomes needed to maintain subsistence, whereas more attention needed to be devoted to assessing relative needs. *People*, Townsend (1962, p221) argued, *are poverty-stricken when their income, even if adequate for survival, falls markedly behind that of the community.* Abel Smith and Townsend (1965) redefined poverty using National Assistance levels (the then equivalent of Income Support) as an indication of an 'acceptable' standard of living. They argued that anyone with an income on or below 140 per cent of National Assistance levels could be seen as living on the margins of poverty. In redefining poverty they rediscovered it, finding that the numbers living in or on the margins of poverty had increased from 2.5 million people (7.8 per cent) in 1953/4 to 7.5 million people (14.2 per cent) in 1960 – 41 per cent of those in poverty were in work, but not earning enough to bring their incomes up to National Assistance levels. Three million older people and one in seven children were also found to be in poverty.

Research summary

Lone parenthood and poverty in the 1960s

Many of the children Abel Smith and Townsend found in poverty were living in lone-parent families, and to an extent they can be seen as victims of the 'gendered' nature of Britain's welfare system, which continued to see women as dependents rather than citizens with their own social security needs. By 1961, there were 325,000 'fatherless' families in Britain, but because they failed to conform to the traditional family norm, their needs were not catered for. Indeed, as one contemporary study showed, when they did seek assistance they often faced a hostile, harsh process that was geared more towards stigmatising 'deviant' lone parents than it was providing them with even a modicum of support (Marsden, 1969). Hence for lone parents the claiming of means-tested support continued to be mired with the stigma of the Poor Law, and officials seemed to go out of their way to 'discipline' lone parents, making the claiming process as arduous and uncomfortable as possible. Mothers of illegitimate children were particularly targeted, but irrespective of the causes of 'fatherlessness', lone parents were constantly under suspicion and monitored in order to ensure they were not cohabiting with a male partner. Marsden's (1969) study found that almost 40 per cent of lone parents were failing to claim their benefit entitlements, which was hardly surprising given the treatment they received when attempting to do so.

The Poor and the Poorest was received sympathetically by the press and public. *There is,* acknowledged *The Times, concrete levels of evidence available that, at the lowest levels of wages, workers have not in fact shared in material affluence that is popularly supposed.* The Child Poverty Action

Group was formed in the wake of the report's publication, and it called for the introduction of more generous family allowances, and for a more concerted effort to ensure people entitled to benefits (particularly pensioners and lone parents) received them. The screening of Ken Loach's hard-hitting docudrama *Cathy Come Home* less than a year later served to reinforce doubts about the success of the post-war welfare state.

Activity 4.3

If you can, try to obtain a copy of *Cathy Come Home*. Watching this film will help to give you an appreciation of the questions that were increasingly being asked about the nature of welfare provision in the mid-1960s. The film sensationally drew attention to the fact that more than 5,000 children were removed from parents each year, not through fear of neglect, but simply because their parents did not have access to adequate housing provision. It also highlighted the stigmatising, moralistic tone that continued to underpin welfare provision at the time (a theme we expand upon below). *Cathy Come Home* was watched by more than 12 million viewers, and repeated less than a week after its first broadcast due to popular demand. It is fair to say that its impact was significant. As *The Times* (3 December 1966, p9) noted, *the public conscience finds it unacceptable that, in a relatively wealthy society, so much bad housing is allowed to stand, that so many people live in unhealthy hovels, that so many live in hopeless overcrowding.*

Social work during the social democratic era

There can be little doubt that the standard and level of provision of social work services improved after 1945, and that the social democratic era did coincide with a somewhat more progressive form of practice. Prior to 1939, many state and voluntary social work agencies would have railed against the idea that the causes of the problems faced by the poor were out of their own control. Likewise, the mere notion that state and voluntary welfare workers should show empathy towards such individuals and families, and devote considerable efforts to restoring and rehabilitating them, would have been seen as something of an anathema. On the contrary, throughout the 1920s and 1930s, the chronic poor were often described as a 'social problem group', written off as hereditary 'low grade defectives' incapable of rehabilitation. As we have seen, in instances where the state intervened to remove children from this 'social problem group', their welfare needs would be largely ignored. Often confined to soulless, uncaring institutions, their 'care', such as it was, constituted little more than a period of emotionally traumatic 'containment', after which they would be cast, largely unprepared and unsupported, into a society that they were ill-prepared to cope with. The post-1945 period was to see the adoption of a somewhat more progressive approach, and cases that would previously have been ignored by social workers were now deemed worthy of intervention. As one prominent figure in the Family Welfare Association, the new name for the Charity Organisation Society, acknowledged in 1950:

> *In the past, the families who today we are trying to treat with special concern and are calling problem families were probably written off as poor law cases or feckless and unhelpful.* (Cited in Jones, 1983, p39)

However, individualist interpretations of social problems proved hard for some of those engaged in social work practice to shake off. For although the 'levelling effect' of the Second World War had led to considerable support for the notion that the state should accept responsibility for securing the welfare of its citizens, certain developments also served to reinforce behavioural, pathological interpretations of social problems. Earlier we discussed the 'progressive' impact the evacuation programme had in changing attitudes towards social reform. However, evacuation also served to reinforce pathological interpretations for social problems. For example, public and professional opinion was not wholly sympathetic towards the parents of the often poorly clad, incontinent, malnourished evacuees. Indeed, there was a general feeling that much of the poverty could have been avoided if only parents of the evacuees had acted more responsibly and brought their children up more effectively. Bad parenting, or more often than not 'bad mothering', was frequently seen to lie at the heart of the evacuees' problems. Mothers were, according to one account, invariably *dirty, verminous, idle and extravagant.* They *could not hold a needle and did not know the rudiments of cooking and housecraft* and *had no control over their children who were untrained and animal in their habits.* Many of the mothers were *foul mouthed, bullying and abusive, given to drinking and frequenting public houses, insanitary in their habits and loose in their morals* (Women's Group on Public Welfare, 1943, p3). Such anecdotal accounts of irresponsible parenting were widely reported in the press, adding credence to the notion that feckless parents were morally culpable for the condition of many of the child evacuees.

Many of the more lurid allegations made against working-class parents were baseless, and showed no appreciation of the poverty and deprivation that families had been forced to endure before the war (Macnicol, 1986). Nonetheless, they did help generate an inaccurate but pervasive image of morally culpable, irresponsible working-class parents. Accordingly, it was increasingly felt that improved welfare provision alone would not deliver the cure to the problems uncovered by evacuation and that any solution must involve a process of 're-moralisation' and reform of the working-class family. As Macnicol (1987) points out, what emerged was a discourse centred on the 'problem family', where emphasis was placed on the need for social workers to treat 'curable' poor socialisation, immorality and lack of social skills. So, while intervention was to be different, and to an extent more humane than previously, as the following extract from the wartime *Our Towns* report, conducted by the Women's Group on Public Welfare (1943, ppxiii–xiv) illustrates, the language used to describe those suffering from a range of social problems was depressingly similar:

> *The . . . submerged tenth . . . still exists in our towns like a hidden sore, poor, dirty and crude in its habits, an intolerable degrading burden to decent people forced by poverty to neighbour with it. Within this group are the problem families, always on the edge of pauperism and crime, riddled with mental and physical defects, in and out of the Courts for child neglect, a menace to their community, of which the gravity is out of all proportion to their numbers . . . Next to the problem families come those which may be described as grey rather than black; they are dirty and unwholesome in their habits through lack of personal discipline and social standard.*

The authors of this report, an influential group of leading voluntary social work professionals, were prepared to acknowledge a link between what they referred to as *the dark side of town life* and poverty (p103). In this sense they were at least partly in tune with the social democratic mood of the times. However, they saw *the problem of improving social conditions as one of education as much as of environment,* arguing that *more effort should be made to rouse and strengthen the human will . . . for decent living* (pxiv). Thus they continued to emphasise behavioural interpretations of the difficulties besetting what they referred to as *problem families.* Other voluntary social work organisations, such as the Family Service Units, which by the late 1950s could be found in a number of English cities, adopted a similar approach. They too often utilised disparaging language to describe 'problem families', but also believed that rehabilitation was possible through treatment and casework (Welshman, 1999). Their intensive family casework with 'problem families' would sometimes involve up to three supervisory visits each day, with treatment directed mainly at correcting the behavioural faults of the parents, usually the mother (Starkey, 1998). This blaming of mothers was to prove a common, recurring theme in post-war social policy and social work, and often it was they who were held responsible for the problems associated with families experiencing chronic difficulties. As Starkey (1998, p543) argues, *The caricature of the typical 'problem mother' of a typical 'problem family', current in the late 1940s and 1950s, became firmly fixed in the minds of public health workers, social workers, housing managers and educationists as the central feature of an easily identifiable social nuisance.* Even the Archbishop of Canterbury accorded with this view, claiming in 1953 that the neglect of children in problem families was a result of *the heedlessness, the shiftlessness, the carelessness and ignorance of their mother,* and not the family's poor financial circumstances (cited in Starkey, 1998, p544).

As Welshman (1999) and Starkey (1998) note, voluntary organisations were hugely influential in terms of the development of social work after 1945, both in terms of their links to leading academics and policy-makers, but also the direct social work they performed for and alongside local authorities. Statutory social work was fragmented, uncoordinated and still very much in its infancy, and hence there was a continued reliance upon voluntary sector agencies, many of which continued to be steeped in pre-war attitudes and prejudices (Lowe, 1993). As late as 1959, the Younghusband Report estimated that there were only around 3,000 social workers employed by local authorities, and the vast majority of these (89 per cent) had no qualifications in social science or professional social work (cited in Hansard, 17 February, 1960, Vol. 221, c.). According to Eileen Younghusband (1978, p22), training was not considered a priority by local authority welfare departments. More important, she suggests, were the perceived virtues of *taking a firm line, standing no nonsense and not allowing people to get away with it.* Moralistic judgements about the causes of family difficulties therefore prevailed in the statutory and voluntary sectors. The job of the social worker, it seemed, was to supervise and control service users, and few attempts were made to include people in discussions that affected their lives. As late as the mid-1950s, some senior social service officials were still of the view that their main role was to *ensure that people do as they are told and to make them realise that they will be punished if they don't* (cited in Younghusband, 1978, p23). Medical Officers of Health, who also had a key role in shaping and delivering social work to vulnerable families (through the health visitors, home helps and other welfare workers they employed), also uncritically embraced the discourse of the 'problem family'. Indeed, as Starkey has shown, a number of Medical Officers of Health continued to believe social problems were a result of defective genetic inheritance, and feared that 'unfit', genetically determined weaknesses would be passed on to succeeding generations. For this reason, many local authority health departments would seek to target their family planning services at 'problem families', a policy that was supported by central government. Hence, in 1968, the government's Chief Medical Officer called for such services to be targeted at families characterised by *squalor, ill-health, an inability to cope and limited intelligence* (cited in Welshman, 1999, p468).

Of course, by no means all social and welfare workers subscribed to such claims, and by the 1960s academics and social workers had begun to question the validity of 'problem family' discourses. The publication of Barbara Wootton's (1959) *Social Science and Social Pathology* represented a challenge to moralising approaches, which, she argued, failed to identify the structural origins of service user difficulties. She was particularly critical of contemporary casework methods, which concentrated upon psychological maladjustment rather than material need. *Always plumbing the depths of her client's personality*, Wootton wrote, *the social worker all too easily ignores the glaring evils on the surrounding surface* (p286). Modern social work had, she argued, found it difficult to divest itself of the moralistic, individualised casework approach, and was still in the habit of *confusing economic difficulties with personal failure or misconduct* (p291). There was a need, Wootton insisted, to *put the social back in social work*; for social workers to reject pathological interpretations, and to acknowledge and address the poverty and deprivation that continued to structure the lives of those suffering from a multitude of social problems.

It is partly because of the continued emphasis on family pathology, that Jones (1983, p40) has questioned whether or not the development of social work during the period of the social democratic consensus constituted a gain for working-class users of services. *A clear cut and unambiguous answer*, he concludes, *is not possible*, though he does identify a difference between the more progressive approach adopted by qualified statutory social workers in children's departments and the more 'traditional' practice found in other areas of the welfare state. Lowe (1993, p263) agrees, describing the 1940s and 1950s as a *far from heroic period* for the personal social services, when the implementation of a more humane policy was impeded by *the persistence of pre-war attitudes and institutions*. It was not until the publication of the Seebohm Report, which led to the introduction of social service departments and greater coordination and professionalism within social work, that more progressive attitudes would begin to prevail within policy and practice.

The emergence of more progressive thinking within social work should be seen in the context of the more general realisation that the welfare state had not succeeded in achieving its aims. In 1962, Peter Townsend published *The Last Refuge*, an exhaustive survey of conditions experienced by older people living in residential institutions. In painstaking detail, Townsend (1964) documented a broken, uncaring system, which differed little from that which existed under the nineteenth-century Poor Law. The Poor Law may have been formally abolished in 1948, but its spirit was very much alive and well in the former Victorian workhouses that now housed up to 30,000 elderly citizens. These institutions had changed little in terms of either their physical appearance or their austere, 'less eligibility' ethos. They were, Townsend noted, *as forbidding and inhospitable as they were originally intended to be and . . . totally unadaptable to modern ways of living*. On entering these cold, damp, unwelcoming institutions, husbands and wives would face a humiliating, heartless regime. They would be separated from each other, required to wear institutional clothing, their personal possessions were forbidden and their privacy and dignity were fragrantly disregarded. This unnecessarily punitive regime conditioned the working practices and attitudes of the staff working within it. Indeed, Townsend described the general outlook of half of all matrons and wardens that he interviewed as overtly *unsympathetic or needlessly authoritarian*. Outside these institutions, Townsend did find *some* evidence of good practice in elderly care, but this was confined to a relatively small number of voluntary sector residential care homes. For the most part, *all* provision – local authority, voluntary and private sector – was lamentably poor. Townsend was himself a passionate social democrat, yet his study provided a damning indictment of the quality of residential care provision during the era of the 'classic' welfare state.

Inquiries into the quality of care provided in mental health institutions also served to reinforce the perception that the 'classic' welfare state had failed to protect vulnerable service users. For example, in 1969 horrific conditions were uncovered at the Ely and Farleigh mental health hospitals, prompting widespread concern about the abuse suffered by patients in mental health institutions. At Ely, *Patients were knocked about, there was an unduly casual attitude to sudden death . . . and there was pilfering of the food by staff* (*The Times*, 29 March 1969, p3). Meanwhile, at Farleigh, it was said to be *an everyday practice to punch people about* and casually increase the dosage of drugs to patients to keep them quiet (*The Times*, 12 August 1969, p2). The revelations prompted the Labour government's Health Minister, Dick Crossman, to visit a number of institutions under his jurisdiction and he was reported to have been *subdued and shaken* by what he witnessed. Following one such visit, he told one of his colleagues, *I am responsible for the worst kind of Dickensian, Victorian loony bin* (cited in Timmins, 1996, p259).

Within social work, the general sense of malaise that began to surround the 'classic' welfare state manifested itself in the emergence of a new, more radical group of social workers, who began to question psychological, pathological explanations for the difficulties faced by service users (Butler and Drakeford, 2005). The focus instead moved towards combating the structural problems that contributed to individual and family difficulties through higher levels of welfare spending, community work and welfare rights approaches. We therefore began to see the emergence of what has become known as the *radical social work* tradition, a trend accelerated by the growing influence of left-wing (particularly Marxist) ideas, as well as organisational changes to social work which helped generate a collective sense of identity (Ferguson and Woodward, 2009). However, the emergence of radical social work coincided with the growing strength of right-wing, neo-liberal critiques of welfare, which were also challenging the assumptions that underpinned the post-war 'social democratic' consensus.

Chapter summary

In this chapter we have examined how social democratic principles shaped the development of the post-war welfare state. As we explained, out of the ashes of war grew a new sense of social purpose, and a determination to use state intervention to eradicate the social and economic problems that had beset pre-war Britain. Never again, it was thought, would Britain be stalked by the giant evils of Want, Idleness, Squalor, Disease and Ignorance. The 'social democratic settlement' that characterised Britain's political landscape between 1945 and the 1970s undoubtedly brought enormous benefits to British citizens. As Lowe (1993, p294) argues, there was *by any historic standard, a dramatic and sustained improvement in the rate of economic growth, the absolute living standards of the poor, the standards of health, the attainment of educational qualifications, the quality of housing and the care of traditionally neglected groups.* With hindsight, Townsend agrees with Lowe's assessment of the 'classic' post-war welfare state. Despite being a contemporary critic of its failure to provide sufficient protection to citizens, in retrospect, he felt that the 1960s were, in some respects, a 'golden era' for welfare. *I have to say,* he admitted, *that I now look back at the 1960s and think 'my goodness, we used to criticise', I know, but we didn't realise at the time that 'we'd never had it so good', in the phrase that Harold Macmillan used, both in terms of economic prosperity and in terms of national acceptance of minimum citizen rights* (BBC, 1998).

However, post-war Britain was no 'New Jerusalem' and it continued to be beset by a range of economic and social problems. Moreover, the welfare state itself – including social work – never fully managed to rid itself of the legacy of the Poor Law, and often welfare continued to be dispensed in a grudging, judgemental, stigmatising way. As we have already indicated, by the end of the period examined in this chapter, calls were being made for governments to reaffirm their commitment to a genuinely social demo-cratic project and to redouble their efforts to address the nation's economic and social ills. These calls, though, had to compete with two alternative, competing 'solutions' to the crisis affecting social democracy, both of which were based upon radically different ideological principles. The next two chapters look at each of these in turn. Chapter 5 focuses upon the challenge posed by neo-liberal critiques of welfare, and Chapter 6 examines the influence of Marxist perspectives on social policy and social work.

Further reading

For a couple of classic texts written from within the social democratic tradition, we would recommend:

Tawney, RH (1964) *Equality.* London: George Allen & Unwin.

Crosland, CAR (2006) *The Future of Socialism: 50th Anniversary Edition.* London: Constable & Robinson.

The latest version of Rodney Lowe's well known text provides a good, thorough analysis of the post-war welfare state:

Lowe, R (2004) *The Welfare State in Britain Since 1945.* London: Palgrave Macmillan.

Barbara Wootton's now classic book constitutes an excellent contemporary critique of the nature of social work in the 1950s:

Wootton, B (1959) *Social Science and Social Pathology.* London: George Allen & Unwin.

For an analysis of the continued influence of behavioural pathological interpretations of economic and social problems during the period of the social democratic welfare state see:

Welshman, J (2013) *Underclass: A History of the Excluded, 1880–2000,* 2nd edition. London: Hambledon Continuum.

5: Neo-liberalism and the development of social policy and social work after 1979

Achieving a social work degree

This chapter will help you to meet the following capabilities from the Professional Capabilities Framework:

- **Professionalism** – identify and behave as a professional social worker, committed to professional development.
- **Values and ethics** – apply social work ethical principles and values to guide professional practice.
- **Rights, justice and economic well-being** – advance human rights and promote social justice and economic well-being.
- **Knowledge** – apply knowledge of social sciences, law and social work practice theory.
- **Critical reflection and analysis** – apply critical reflection and analysis to inform and provide a rationale for professional decision-making.
- **Contexts and organisations** – engage with, inform and adapt to changing contexts that shape practice. Operate effectively within own organisational frameworks and contribute to the development of services and organisations. Operate effectively within multi-agency and inter-professional settings.

The chapter will also introduce you to the following academic standards which are set out in the 2016 QAA social work benchmark statements:

4   **Defining principles**
5.2   **Social work theory**
5.3   **Values and ethics**

Introduction

The realisation that all was not well with the welfare state led social democrats to call for more funding for welfare and for the implementation of better, more progressive provision. However, in the light of the apparent failings of post-war social policy, social democratic values themselves were increasingly challenged. In particular, the general feeling of malaise that surrounded social welfare served to reinvigorate the critiques of social democratic values generated by those on the 'right' of the political spectrum. These critics, who included many prominent figures within the Conservative Party, were seeking to rehabilitate classical liberal values of individualism and self-help and utilise them to explain the problems that seemed to be besetting Britain. They claimed that too much rather than too little welfare lay at the heart of the nation's economic and social ills, and the country needed welfare retrenchment rather than expansion. The term that is most commonly used to describe this new, emerging ideology is neo-liberalism. In the discussion below, we examine the key themes of neo-liberal critiques of state welfare and consider their influence upon policy and practice.

Neo-liberalism

Neo-liberalism is most commonly associated with the economic and social policies pursued by Conservative governments between 1979 and 1997, but attempts to promote neo-liberal values and ideas began well before 1979. Indeed, the principles underpinning social democracy had been subjected to a sustained ideological attack since the inception of the welfare state, yet the 'crisis in welfare' described in the previous chapter gave neo-liberalism a renewed vigour and resonance. The political 'right' saw this as a gilt-edged opportunity to undermine support for welfare and to advance their proposals to roll back the frontiers of the state. Neo-liberals argued that the economic and social problems the country faced were the result of benevolent but misguided attempts on the part of government to 'help' the poor. The post-war welfare state, with its range of free benefits and services, had sapped individual initiative, creating a state of 'helpless dependency'. Rather than relying upon their own efforts and initiative in the workplace, and making provision for their own welfare needs, people were choosing the 'easy' life of welfare. The 'Nanny State' was providing a seductive feather bed, luring people into a life of fecklessness, fraud and deceit.

become seduced by perverse left-wing ideologies. They were too willing to *abuse their power and authority to urge or condone anti-social behaviour either on political grounds – against an 'unjust society', against 'authority' – or as 'liberation from the trammels of the outmoded family'* (cited in *The Times*, 21 October 1974). They had become one of the principal causes of social ills rather than one of the solutions, too prepared to excuse deviant behaviour and unwilling to use their powers to discipline dysfunctional individuals and families. For those such as Joseph, social work needed to go back to its Victorian basics, to rediscover its role in controlling recalcitrant families and individuals and restoring moral discipline.

Keith Joseph's critical comments about the nature of social work formed part of a wider, orchestrated political and media attack on the profession. This was partly prompted by a number of widely publicised child abuse scandals, which undermined support for social workers (Butler and Drakeford, 2011). To a certain extent, it also represented a backlash against the radical social work movement (see Chapter 6 for a discussion of radical social work). However, it should also be seen as part of a wider strategy being waged by neo-liberals within the Conservative Party to chip away at the social democratic consensus and weaken popular support for the principle of state welfare generally. If welfare professionals could be portrayed as ideological zealots, more interested in attacking liberal democracy and initiating political change than the welfare of those they were supposed to be serving, then it would be easier to persuade the electorate of the merits of cutting services and provision. In this sense, it is worth acknowledging that social workers were not the only welfare professionals to be attacked by neo-liberals. Those employed in other areas of the welfare state – doctors, nurses, teachers – received the same hostile treatment, as did the services within which they worked. Then, as is often the case now, such claims were embraced by a sympathetic right-wing press, which utilised its sensationalist powers of persuasion to reinforce neo-liberal critiques of welfare.

From critique to policy

From the 1970s onwards, neo-liberalism provided an increasingly influential critique of the post-war social democratic welfare state. However, as well as criticising existing welfare practices, its adherents also sought to provide an alternative future for welfare, one which would be based upon the key neo-liberal principles of minimal government intervention, self-help and the supremacy of the private market. Neo-liberals argued that the solution to the country's social and economic problems was for the state to withdraw from providing most forms of welfare. The considerable reductions in national insurance and taxation generated by this would leave citizens with the income needed to make provision for their own social security, education, health and social care needs in the private market. *Legislation and state interference*, wrote Rhodes Boyson, *should be cut back and limited to a requirement that all should insure against ill-health, misfortune and old age* (1971, cited in Butterworth and Holman, 1975, p386). Boyson was but one of countless prominent contemporary thinkers and politicians seeking to influence the future direction of social policy within an increasingly confident Conservative Party, and each shared a common ideological trajectory. State assistance, it was argued, should be maintained at a basic minimal level, designed merely to provide for the most needy, leaving all others to purchase their own care needs:

> *It is not the job of the Conservatives to run an indiscriminate, improvident welfare state . . . Our aim must be to increase personal independence, to spread private insurance, and to encourage true charity – by individuals not by institutions financed by involuntary taxes . . . The Conservatives must actively work for the welfare state to wither away as personal prosperity and independent provision take its place.* (Boyson, 1978, p123)

The promotion of the virtues of private welfare was a key feature of the neo-liberal approach to welfare. State services were dismissed as unnecessarily costly, inefficient and overly bureaucratic. In the absence of any effective competition, welfare providers – for instance, the NHS, or local authority social service departments – had no incentive to cut costs and seek efficiency gains. They were, neo-liberals alleged, self-serving fiefdoms, more concerned with their own size, status and prestige than the welfare of those they were intended to serve. State welfare was also said to deny choice, enforcing a one-size-fits-all model, which was insensitive to service users' needs (Harris, 1971).

By contrast, neo-liberals argued that a competitive, private welfare market would lead to greater cost efficiencies and contribute to improved standards of provision. The need for providers of health, education, social care and other services to remain financially solvent would force them to keep a constant watch on costs and efficiency, driving down the overall expenditure on welfare. Meanwhile, competition for business would drive up standards of provision, as packages of care would need to be attractive to newly enfranchised welfare 'consumers'. In this ideal-type private welfare system, power would thus be transferred from the welfare agency to the consumer – that is to the patient, the pupil and the residential care service user, who could choose from a wealth of individually tailored packages of care best suited to their needs and desires. As well as empowering service users, such a system would be morally beneficial, promoting initiative, self-reliance and personal character. It appears to be a 'win-win' situation.

Neo-liberal welfare

Despite vigorously promoting private welfare, neo-liberals did accept (and continue to accept) the need for some limited, minimal form of welfare, but they maintain that this should be restricted to providing a very limited form of security. We outline some of the key features that might characterise an 'ideal-type' neo-liberal public welfare system below.

It should be based upon needs and not rights

Neo-liberals are deeply sceptical of universal, as-of-right benefits and services, and believe they should be replaced by means-tested welfare based upon strict eligibility criteria. This should be designed to restore incentives to work and to deter dysfunctional patterns of behaviour that are said to contribute to social and moral breakdown. It should, therefore, be proactive in weeding out what David Marsland (1996, p187), a prominent neo-liberal academic, refers to as *impulsive, profligate and irresponsible* individuals. Nor, argues Marsland, should it *be shy of making positive use of shame and stigma, where it is appropriate, to encourage people to shift into self-reliance.* This would help ensure that only the genuinely needy and destitute would seek assistance.

The assistance given should be temporary and conditional

Neo-liberals argue that unconditional welfare has an inevitable tendency to corrupt and should be avoided. Receipt of public support – whether housing, health care or income maintenance – should be dependent upon good character and the performance of obligations and duties. Hence, recipients of unemployment benefits should be expected to engage in useful work or training in return for any assistance given. It may even be necessary to link access to other publicly funded welfare services, such as health care, and to character, as is the case in some states in the United States. (In the US, access to means-tested publicly funded health care for families who have no private health care insurance can be denied on grounds of character.)

It should be delivered by voluntary or private organisations rather than state agencies

Although neo-liberals accept the validity of some limited form of public welfare provision, they tend to argue that the state's role should be restricted to funding and regulating the delivery of services, and not providing them. Large-scale state welfare agencies should be broken up, and private and voluntary organisations should deliver services currently provided by government. Their preference would be for these agencies to be locally based, so as to enable an intimate knowledge of the reputations and characters of potential recipients, and a more effective monitoring and control of those receiving assistance. There would be little, if any, role for social workers in this ideal-type neo-liberal public welfare system. For those such as Marsland (1996, p188), *the dangerous temptations of social work should be avoided altogether*, or at the very least there would need to be a radical overhaul of social work training and practice:

> *There should be a decisive shift away from the current emphasis on rights to education in the practical skills required to help people to help themselves and to the inculcation of values appropriate in a free society . . . The prevailing attitudes of social and welfare workers, in particular their simplistic and exaggerated conception of rights and their impertinently anti-democratic commitments to liberating their clients from oppression, are a major impediment to genuine welfare.*

Thus, rather than social workers, there should be a reliance on the private and voluntary sectors. According to Marsland (1996, p179), the latter are more *committed to individualist rather than collective principles – and as such, better attuned to the . . . fundamental mission of restoring those in need of help to self reliance.* Robert Whelan (2001), another neo-liberal academic, makes a similar set of recommendations, calling for a radical overhaul of social work practice. Like many other neo-liberals, he looks to the past for inspiration, arguing that social work should in future be based upon the individualist, self-help philosophy of the COS. What we require, he insists, *are the services of a friendly visitor trained in the COS approach, capable of assessing character, motivation and the relative significance of the behavioural and structural causes of welfare dependency in particular cases. Alas,* he laments, *no such cadre of helpers now exists.* The idea that social workers should seek to actively modify their service users' behaviour, teaching and coercing them to act as decent, law abiding citizens, has, he insists, *evaporated entirely*:

> *The reform of welfare will entail the reform of social work, and one option we might consider is taking it away from the state (certainly in so far as training is concerned) and returning it to the voluntary sector, where it began.* (Whelan, 2001, p96)

Conservative governments 1979–97

The election of Margaret Thatcher's Conservative government in 1979 is often seen as a defining political moment. It is frequently thought to have signalled an end to the social democratic consensus and the beginning of a radical new neo-liberal era. Conservative administrations governed Britain until 1997 and, during this period, neo-liberal values permeated all areas of welfare policy, including social work. That is not to say, of course, that what emerged was a mirror image of the ideal type neo-liberal welfare regime outlined above. As we stated in Chapter 3, politicians may be deeply influenced by their ideological convictions, but in formulating their policies they cannot always completely ignore electoral concerns or public opinion. Hence, Thatcher was reluctantly persuaded to curb her ideological instincts and to drop some of the more radical and politically unpopular proposals that she favoured, such as the outright privatisation of the National Health Service (NHS). In the particular case of the NHS, Thatcher's Health Secretary, Kenneth Clark, recalls having *ferocious rows* with her over the potential political implications of privatising the UK's health care system. Thatcher, he remembers, *wanted to go to the American system . . . She wanted compulsory insurance, with the state paying the premiums for the less well off. I thought that was a {political} disaster. The American system is hopeless . . . dreadful* (Rawnsley, 2014).

Nonetheless, the changes were significant. In the economic sphere, we saw the introduction of a range of measures designed to promote business interests, such as income tax cuts, financial deregulation, the privatisation of publicly owned industries, the erosion of workplace rights and the curtailment of trade union power. Government subsidies to 'ailing' manufacturing industries were also cut, leading to unprecedented, sustained levels of high unemployment, particularly in manufacturing areas. Meanwhile, the social policy sphere experienced radical reform, which included significant reductions in the value of social security. Child, unemployment, disability and lone-parent benefits were cut, as were housing subsidies and the value of the state pension. Unemployment benefits were worth the equivalent of 26.6 per cent of average earnings in 1979, but by 1997 their value had fallen to 13.7 per cent of average earnings. During the same period, the value of the basic state pension fell from 26 per cent to 16.7 per cent of average earnings. Child benefit also saw a real-terms reduction, from 4.46 per cent of average earnings for the first child, to just 2.97 per cent (Rutherford, 2013). In addition, eligibility for most forms of social security – in particular unemployment and disability benefits – was tightened, the assumption being that many fit and able people were simply 'choosing' not to work. In justifying such cuts, Conservative ministers utilised language similar to that used by the architects of the Poor Law Amendment Act, claiming that the 'pain' being suffered was a 'price worth paying' in the fight against 'welfare dependency'. Local authority social service budgets were also reduced, adding to the workload pressures of social workers, and restricting the support they could provide to service users (Jones, 2005).

At the same time, Conservative governments sought to encourage individuals to make provision for their own welfare, offering financial incentives for them to turn to the private sector for their education, housing, pension, health and social care needs. Indeed, the social care sector found itself at the centre of attempts to introduce competition, markets and private enterprise in the delivery of public services and was radically transformed. We saw the introduction of what has become known as the 'purchaser/provider split', whereby local authorities would become facilitators and enablers of services rather than direct providers of care. Social workers would become 'care managers', who would buy in services from a variety of different providers in the voluntary and private sector. The intention was to reduce the role of the state in the direct provision of care and increase the role of the private sector in particular. This 'purchaser/provider split' has now become well established in social work practice. Many practitioners believe that this has changed the nature of the profession for the worse, *as the task of social work intervention is now increasingly to assess clients' needs, not help them solve their problems* (Jones and Novak, 1999, p161). Jones (2005, p100) interviewed social workers who experienced these changes, and time and again found them referring to their frustration about how this had bureaucratised social work, diluting the welfare-focused ethos of the profession:

> *I was regaled by talk of budgets and not only their appalling paucity to meet the needs of clients, but also the manner in which budget management and control had become the key concerns of the agency, stripping out its welfare ideals in the process.*

Undoubtedly, there were many 'winners' during this period of Conservative governance, but all the contemporary analyses undertaken into economic and social conditions in 1979–97 point to widening inequality, poverty and social deprivation. The poorest and the most vulnerable benefited least from the Conservatives' economic and social policy reforms. Indeed, during 1979–94 the real incomes of the poorest 10 per cent of the population fell by 13 per cent. This was a period when average income rose by 40 per cent and the income of the richest increased by 60 per cent. In real monetary terms, by 1997 the poorest 10 per cent in the UK were £520 p.a. worse off after 18 years of Conservative government, whereas the richest 10 per cent were £12,220 p.a. better off (Ferguson and Woodward, 2009). At the same time, poverty soared. In 1979, 13 per cent of the population (7.1 m people) were living in poverty, but by 1996/7 this had increased to more than one-quarter of the population. During the same period, child poverty increased from 14 to 34 per cent (1.9 m–4.3 m). Such trends were unprecedented and inevitably led to accusations that the neo-liberal reforms pursued by the Conservatives were contributing to a divided, fractious Britain, where the well-off disproportionately benefited at the expense of the poor. The disregard Conservative ministers seemed to show for the casualties of their policies reinforced this perception. This was no more evident than in their refusal to accept that the growing levels of poverty identified by organisations such as the Child Poverty Action Group and the Joseph Rowntree Foundation were a problem. Indeed, as we have shown elsewhere, ministers denied the existence of any poverty in the UK. They claimed that everyone had access to the basic means of subsistence and hence nobody was 'poor' (Cunningham and Cunningham, 2014).

In summary, the welfare state inherited by New Labour in 1997 was radically different from that of 1979. Margaret Thatcher's first administration instigated a distinct ideological shift, one which was continued by successive Conservative administrations, including those led by John Major. As we will see later in the book, after 1979 many of the features of our ideal-type neo-liberal welfare model did shape future policy and practice, including, according to some commentators, that followed by Labour governments between 1997 and 2010.

Labour governments 1997–2010

During its 17 years in opposition, Labour had attacked the record of successive Conservative administrations, claiming that ideologically motivated neo-liberal policies had led to deep social divisions. When Labour was elected in 1997, many social democrats hoped to see Tony Blair's new government initiate a decisive break with neo-liberalism and a return to a traditional social democratic agenda. However, prior to the general election, the Labour leadership had made it clear that its election would not herald a restoration of 'old' social democratic values and that it would seek to develop a 'new' 'Third Way', a 'renewed' social democracy that would steer a more pragmatic course between the perceived extremes of 'left' and 'right'.

In practice, this approach led Labour governments to adopt a mixture of social democratic, structural interpretations for social problems and neo-liberal, behavioural ones. So, on the one hand, Labour acknowledged that it was the government's responsibility to help provide the environment and opportunities for individuals to develop and thrive, and to seek to promote social justice. On the other hand, as we will show in later chapters, Labour's social policies contained a strong moralistic undertone, at times embracing neo-liberal behavioural, pathological explanations for economic and social ills. The relative influence of structural versus behavioural explanations in shaping Labour's social policies is a matter of much debate. Some argue that Labour's policies did represent a 'renewed' social democracy that was more suited to the changed conditions of the late twentieth/early twenty-first century. They point, for instance, to Labour's introduction of the minimum wage, its commitment to the NHS and its pledge to eliminate child poverty as evidence of a social democratic influence. Others, however, argue that New Labour was little more than 'Thatcherism in trousers'. They accuse Labour of embracing the neo-liberal legacy that it inherited and argue that Labour's economic and social policies, like those of previous Conservative governments, were largely shaped by neo-liberal rather than social democratic principles (Hall, 1998). Much of the rest of this book is devoted to an analysis of the direction of social policy and social work since 1997, so we do not intend to discuss in any great depth the Labour government's record on social policy and social work in this chapter. Our brief comments here on Labour's period in office are simply intended to draw your attention to the ongoing debate over the ideological trajectory of its economic and social policies.

Coalition government and beyond

Prior to the 2010 General Election, David Cameron had sought to distance himself and his party from the widely held perception that Conservatives were ideologically wedded to a neo-liberal strategy that showed a casual disregard for the poor (Cunningham and Cunningham, 2014). He accepted that previous Conservative governments were wrong to deny the impact of their policies on levels of poverty and inequality, and in other areas he sought to distance the Conservatives from the 'extreme' policies they had traditionally been associated with. Hence, early on in his leadership of the party, Cameron criticised what he referred to as the 'Old Right' who, he stated, believed that the only way of promoting responsibility and social and economic well-being was to cut the supply of state services:

> *The fact is, we cannot arbitrarily withdraw welfare benefits for the most needy of our fellow citizens. Yes, if we did that, no doubt in 20 years' time people would have become more self-reliant – but think of the misery of those 20 years. Some people will always need help and support – and we should not imagine that government simply withdrawing from the social field will automatically and instantly cause new, independent bodies to spring up in their place.* (Cameron, 2006)

As we now know, no single party won an outright majority in the 2010 General Election, and between 2010 and 2015 the UK was governed by a Cameron-led, Conservative-dominated

Coalition government. Despite Cameron's pre-election criticisms of the 'Old Right', his Coalition government initiated a process of reducing and dismantling welfare rights at an unprecedented pace. In part, this process was justified by claims that the cuts were a necessary component of the government's deficit-reduction strategy. However, the Coalition's welfare reforms appeared to be accompanied by an ideological zeal that left many commentators questioning the extent to which the Conservative Party had, in reality, moved away from its unquestioning embrace of neo-liberal principles. In fact, it is not too difficult to detect a neo-liberal influence in the speeches Cameron made before the 2010 General Election. In these speeches, he frequently claimed that 'big government' had inhibited initiative, and that the welfare state had destroyed self-improvement and responsibility. In keeping with neo-liberal critiques of the welfare state, Cameron's proposed 'solution' to the problem of the 'broken society' was to move away from state welfare provided by 'big government' to what he referred to as the 'Big Society', where individuals and communities are responsible for securing their own economic and social well-being.

The 'Big Society'

David Cameron first floated his vision of the 'Big Society' in November 2009. Although many people remain unclear as to exactly what it entailed, it was a theme that Cameron returned to throughout his period as prime minister. At the heart of the 'Big Society' lay two key neo-liberal aims.

1. A determination to tackle 'dependency' by creating what Cameron referred to as a 'culture of responsibility', whereby individuals and communities would come together to solve their own problems.

2. A desire to radically reform public welfare services, expanding the role of the private and voluntary sectors.

The 'Big Society' and the 'responsibility' agenda

On the specific issue of responsibility, Cameron argued that individuals, families and communities should stop looking to the state for guidance or assistance and should search 'within' for the cures to their problems:

> We want to give citizens, communities and local government the power and information they need to come together, solve the problems they face and build the Britain they want. We want society – the families, networks, neighbourhoods and communities that form the fabric of so much of our everyday lives – to . . . take more responsibility. (Cabinet Office, 2010, p1)

Between 2010 and 2015, the Coalition did seek to encourage and indeed coerce individuals to take more responsibility for their own social and economic needs. On the 'coercion' side, the

Coalition's social security reforms, which continued apace under T
government, were designed to make life on welfare 'less attractive'
the incentives for people to support themselves rather than relying
followed a similar trajectory to the previous Labour government's r
significant acceleration of pre-existing policy trends, reducing the
tightening eligibility conditions still further.

These reforms have proven to be deeply controversial. Inevitably, social policy campaign groups, such as the Child Poverty Action Group and the Joseph Rowntree Foundation, have condemned the cuts to family support, arguing that they have exacerbated the hardship low-income families experience, punishing them for circumstances that are largely beyond their control. However, the reforms have also been criticised by the government's own Social Mobility and Child Poverty Commission and each of the UK's Children's Commissioners. The Social Mobility and Child Poverty Commission (2015, p131) concluded that the reforms mean that *many low-income working families with children will see big reductions in their income over the next few years, with lone parents, single-earner couples and large families seeing particularly large falls.* The UK Children's Commissioners (2015), who are tasked by Parliament with monitoring legislation for violations to children's rights, concurred with this negative assessment, drafting an unprecedented joint-memorandum calling upon the government *stop making cuts to benefits and welfare reforms in order to protect children from the impact of its austerity measures. The Children's Commissioners*, the memorandum stated, *are alarmed at the way the UK Government's austerity measures and changes to the welfare system have pushed more children into poverty.* More serious still, the welfare reforms faced censure from various United Nations organisations, who questioned their compliance with the UK's international human rights obligations. The Bedroom Tax, for example, which cut the housing benefit of social housing tenants deemed to be living in houses with more bedrooms than they required, attracted the condemnation of the UN's special rapporteur for housing. She argued that it *should be suspended immediately and be fully re-evaluated in light of the evidence of its negative impacts on the right to adequate housing and general well-being of many vulnerable individuals and households* (United Nations, 2013, p20). In addition, as we explained in Chapter 1, the UN Committee on the Rights of Persons with Disabilities (UNCRPD, 2016) has provided a damning indictment of the impact of Coalition and Conservative welfare reforms on disabled children. Moreover, as we discuss below, the UN Committee on the Rights of the Child has drawn attention to the negative impact of welfare reforms on children generally.

However, Coalition and Conservative ministers ignored these and other calls to mitigate or reverse their welfare reforms. Indeed, the austerity agenda continues to be driven apace, as evidenced by Theresa May's decision to press ahead with a new, reduced benefit cap. It is to an analysis of the benefit cap that we now turn. It is perhaps one of *the* most controversial aspects of the welfare changes introduced since 2010 and provides a useful gauge for assessing the extent to which the reform agenda has been driven by ideological considerations.

...efit cap

...13, the government introduced an overall benefit cap of £26,000 pa for families, or ...8,200 pa for a single person with no children. In part, ministers sought to justify this initiative with reference to the parlous state of the nation's finances and the need to make 'prudent' cuts. However, this was accompanied by a robust ideological justification, with ministers publicly claiming that individuals and families had a responsibility to look after themselves. Jeremy Hunt, then the Coalition's Conservative Culture Minister and at the time of writing the Health Minister, controversially argued that it was not the state's responsibility to fund the 'inappropriate' family-planning choices of 'shameless' individuals. *The number of children that you have, he insisted, is a choice and what we're saying is that if people are living on benefits, then they make choices but they also have to have responsibility for those choices . . . It's not going to be the role of the state to finance those choices* (cited in Gentleman, 2010, p14). The neo-liberal influences underpinning the benefit cap could also be detected in the justification advanced in support of the change by Iain Duncan Smith (2014), the Department for Work and Pensions Minister. The benefit cap was, he insisted, an attempt to initiate *striking cultural change . . . ending the something for nothing entitlement and returning fairness to the system.* The reform had *ended the perverse incentive to remain on welfare as a way of life and left the door open for a return to work.*

The measure received considerable support from the right-wing tabloid press, which portrayed it as a much needed attempt to restore responsibility and 'fairness' into the system. Perhaps not surprisingly, given the anti-welfare climate that had by then been fostered and cultivated by the media, Coalition politicians and Conservative commentators in the UK, ministers were also able to claim popular public support for the policy. One opinion poll commissioned by the government showed that 73 per cent of the public supported the benefit cap in principle (Department for Work and Pensions, 2013).

As we show below, concerns have been expressed about the impact that further reductions in support will have on the families affected by the new benefit cap. However, the government accused its critics of ignoring the positive impact the 'behavioural change' wrought by the cap would have on children's psychological, social and economic well-being. In language reminiscent of that used by the architects of the 1832 Poor Law Amendment Act, ministers claimed that the reduction in benefit income would 'help' recipient families and their children in the long term, by 'remoralising' them. In summary, the short-term financial 'pain' caused to families and children was a price worth paying in order to incentivise and encourage welfare-dependent households to support themselves and stand on their own two feet. The government's view was that the 'demoralising' effects of welfare dependency were far more corrosive to children's well-being than any discomfort that the depreciation in their family income might cause. *Children*, the government insisted, *can have their life chances and opportunities damaged as a result of living in households where no-one has worked for years*, and seeing their newly incentivised parents actively seeking work or in employment would improve the health, happiness and self-esteem of children, contributing to higher levels of well-being. Reducing the incomes of welfare recipients has thus been presented as a 'caring', 'morally invigorating' exercise; it constitutes part of a 'responsibilisation' process that will, ultimately, improve the quality of the lives of those who are temporarily and 'necessarily' plunged into hardship (DfWP, 2015a, p17).

Activity 5.2

- Do you share the government's view that the reductions in family income that result from the benefit cap are likely to contribute to improved levels of child well-being?
- What problems and difficulties has the benefit cap led to, and how might the reduced cap exacerbate these? In answering this question, you may find it worthwhile considering the views of the following organisations:

  - The Child Poverty Action Group
  - Shelter
  - The Children's Society
  - The UK Children's Commissioners
  - The UN Committee on the Rights of the Child.

Comment

Needless to say, the vast majority of organisations with an interest in the welfare of children and families opposed the introduction of the benefit cap. The Child Poverty Action Group condemned the policy immediately it was announced by the Coalition government in 2010:

> *Forcing children into destitution on the arbitrary basis of how many brothers and sisters they have is abhorrent. As families brace themselves to discover whether their jobs will survive the cuts it is awful that those with larger families should face this extra anxiety.* (Child Poverty Action Group, cited in Gentleman, 2010)

The homeless charity, Shelter, also expressed serious reservations about the potential of the cap to impact upon homelessness among larger families, whose benefit income would no longer be sufficient to meet their housing needs. It estimated that much of the south-east of England would become unaffordable to families on benefits who had more than two children, and many would simply lose their homes (Helm and Boffey, 2011). It soon became evident that Shelter's fears were not unfounded. Despite ministerial reassurances that the benefit cap

(Continued)

(Continued)

would not lead to destitution, it subsequently emerged that the Department for Communities and Local Government (DfCLG) estimated that it would make 40,000 families homeless. Moreover, the DfCLG had confidentially calculated that the costs of supporting these homeless families would be considerably more than the amount saved by the benefit cap itself (Sparrow, 2011). Such findings served to reinforce suspicions that ideology, rather than a pragmatic concern to reduce public spending, was driving the coalition's welfare reform programme. In fact, this was the conclusion of Sarah Teather, the Coalition's Children's Minister, who was at the heart of government when the benefit cap was first being considered. Looking back, she has no doubts that the policy was ideologically driven:

> *The policy was essentially conceived as a political device . . . I don't think it was even remotely conceived of as a financial cost cutting device . . . I think deliberately to stoke up envy and division between people in order to gain popularity at the expense of children's lives is immoral . . . Obviously not all of these children will be made homeless . . . but a substantial number will be required to move and that will have a destructive effect on their education . . . It will have a destructive impact on the support networks families have . . . My fear is that a lot of people will effectively just disappear from the area in which they were living. I think some very horrible things are going to happen.* (Helm, 2012)

Research summary

The benefit cap was fully rolled out in September 2013. At the time of writing, the full implications of the benefit reductions have yet to materialise, but the available evidence suggests that it is generating considerable hardship among affected families. As of November 2015, 69,900 households had faced reductions to their benefits, 45 per cent of whom were in London where housing costs are highest. The loss varied, but 22 per cent of capped households had experienced benefit reductions of more than £100 per week (House of Commons Work and Pensions Committee, 2014).

As the Department for Communities and Local Government predicted, this inevitably had a negative impact upon the housing tenure of affected families. The all-party House of Commons Work and Pensions Committee (2014) found that the mere fear that their tenants might be affected by the cap led many private sector landlords to begin prematurely evicting families before it had even come into operation. Where it had been applied, *tenants affected by the Benefits Cap were being made homeless as a result of accruing unmanageable levels of arrears* (p32). Another early evaluation of the impact of the benefit cap in Haringey served to confirm many of its critic's worst fears (Chartered Institute for Housing, 2013). London's local authorities, which, as already noted, are those most affected by the benefit cap, were being forced to remove families from communities that they had lived in for years and relocate them hundreds of miles away. Hence, in the first quarter of 2013, the number of families housed by London boroughs outside the capital almost doubled. In Haringey, *The feared mass evictions and relocation of benefit recipients . . . are visible on the horizon.* Children in Haringey had faced *instability in education, increasing tensions within the home, sudden relocation and loss of social and educational opportunities or networks.* There had also been *severe consequences for a small number of households which are likely to have longer term policy implications e.g. exacerbation of mental health problems, women left unable to flee abusive partners, children now in danger of being taken into care, and pre-emptive evictions of some private tenants* (Chartered Institute for Housing, 2013, p5–6).

Early evaluations of the benefit cap also suggest that the measure failed in its principle aims of either encouraging welfare recipients into work or significantly reducing welfare costs. Regarding its impact upon work activity, few of the families in the Haringey study had succeeded in finding employment. This was not due to 'laziness' on their part; it resulted from the fact that there were *still significant barriers to them gaining employment*, something that crude benefit reductions could do little to remedy (Chartered Institute for Housing, 2013, p5). Qualitative research undertaken by the London School of Economics, which involved interviews with those whose benefits had been cut, found similar barriers to work. All of its interviewees were actively seeking work, most had willingly and enthusiastically undertaken training to improve their employability and around half were engaged in volunteering with a view to enhancing their 'work-readiness'. In short, there was no evidence that its interviewees affected by the benefit cap lacked 'incentive' to work. *Tenants*, the evaluation concluded, *face many barriers to jobs* (Herden et al., 2015). A Work and Pensions Committee (2014, p36) inquiry into the benefit cap came to much the same conclusion, arguing that *for many people work was simply not an option, because of, for example, language barriers, skills barriers, or family commitments*.

In fact, research suggests that cuts to benefit entitlements can actually exacerbate the barriers to work faced by claimants, *decreasing* the likelihood of their finding employment. For example, an Oxford University/Oxford City Council evaluation of a government-backed employment support scheme in the city found that the stress, anxiety, debt, housing and financial difficulties caused by cuts to the support received by claimants *negatively* impacted upon their job search efforts:

(Continued)

(Continued)

> *For every pound increase in a customer's weekly loss, the odds of getting employed at the end of the project reduced by 2%. Again, conventional wisdom suggests that taking money off benefit claimants (e.g. by sanctions or cutting benefit rates) acts as a financial incentive to get a job. Our analysis says that the opposite is in fact true.* (Oxford City Council Welfare Reform Team, 2016, p51)

On the issue of 'savings', Haringey's housing benefit bill *was* reduced by £60,000 per week as a result of the benefit cap, but £960,000 worth of additional discretionary payments had been made in order to ensure families were not rendered destitute. The research also found evidence of 'cost-shunting', whereby services and support that were previously being paid for and provided by statutory agencies were increasingly being provided by the voluntary sector. Food insecurity was proving to be a particular problem and the study found that many Haringey families were now struggling to meet their nutritional needs and becoming increasingly reliant on food bank services (Chartered Institute for Housing, 2013).

The benefit cap has undoubtedly caused real hardship and in March 2015 the UK's Supreme Court ruled that the policy was not compatible with the UK's obligations under Article 3(1) of the United Nations Convention on the Rights of the Child (UNCRC), which states that *In all actions concerning children . . . the best interests of the child shall be a primary consideration*. In a damning judgement, the Deputy President of the Supreme Court, Lady Hale, said:

> *The prejudicial effect of the cap is obvious and stark. It breaks the link between benefit and need. Claimants affected by the cap will, by definition, not receive the sums of money which the State deems necessary for them adequately to house, feed, clothe and warm themselves and their children . . . It cannot possibly be in the best interests of the children affected by the cap to deprive them of the means to provide them with adequate food, clothing, warmth and housing, the basic necessities of life.* (Cited in Wilson, 2016)

Another critical judgement on the impact of the benefit cap on children's well-being has been provided by the United Nations Committee on the Rights of the Child (CRC). In its observations on the UK's compliance with its obligations as a signatory to the 1989 United Nations Convention on the Rights of the Child (UNCRC), the CRC concluded that the benefit cap undermined children's rights to an adequate standard of living because it arbitrarily restricted the amount of support a family could receive, irrespective of size or need, leaving many children susceptible to poverty, hardship and homelessness. The CRC stated that it was *seriously concerned at the effects that recent fiscal policies and allocation of resources have had in contributing to inequality in children's enjoyment of their rights, disproportionately affecting children in disadvantaged situations*. It demanded an immediate, comprehensive impact assessment of the government's welfare reforms, including the benefit cap, on children's rights and welfare. Moreover, *Where necessary*, the CRE insisted, the government should *revise the mentioned reforms in order to fully respect the right of the child to have his or her best interests taken as a primary consideration* (UNCRC, 2016, p18).

The new, reduced benefit cap

The Conservative Party's 2015 General Election Manifesto contained a commitment to reduce the benefit cap still further. Soon after its election, Cameron's government announced its intention to introduce a new family benefit cap of £23,000 in London (or £15,410 for single, childless adults) and £20,000 outside London (or £13,400 for single childless adults). The new cap became operative in November 2016, much to the dismay of children's rights campaigners. Again, it was interpreted as a triumph of ideology over social justice and children's well-being. The DfWP (2015) estimated that 120,000 additional households would be hit by the cap in 2017/18, losing on average £63 per week, but at least half would lose £50 or more per week. In all, these households contain 333,000 children, enough to fill more than 1,300 average size primary schools. According to one estimate, after rent and other essential housing-related bills, the cap will leave a family with four children living on the outskirts of London with a disposable income of just over one pound per day per household member (Chakrabortty, 2016). As the Chartered Institute for Housing (2016) point out, families and children across the UK will increasingly be affected by the cap and not just those in areas of expensive housing in the South East, with many simply not being able to afford their rent. Its evaluation concluded that the cap would have *a severe impact on these families, make housing in large sections of the country unaffordable and risk worsening what is already a growing homelessness problem*. Along with other children's charities and pressure groups, the Child Poverty Action Group condemned the new cap:

> *The government's own analysis shows the majority of households affected by the benefit cap are lone-parent households and the main victims are children – they're nearly seven times more likely to be hit by it than adults. Children are innocent. Why should they be deprived of the basic necessities of life because the government wants to send a message to adults? They haven't done anything wrong and cannot do anything about their circumstances. It's a cruel, costly and damaging policy.* (Butler and Arnett, 2015)

The Children's Commissioner for England (2015) also condemned the government's decision to reduce the benefit cap:

> *The new Government has the opportunity to truly commit to improving the lives of all children in England over the next five years. Some of the announcements made in today's Queen's Speech . . . are likely to do the opposite . . . I am . . . concerned that extending the benefits cap will push many thousands more children into poverty.*

At the time of writing (November 2016), the introduction of the lower benefits cap is imminent. As ever, the voices of those families who are to be affected by the cuts are largely absent from media commentaries. In the few instances that their views have been sought, they invariably express genuine anxiety and insecurity about their ability to cope. This is what Birkenhead resident, Steve, a lone parent with four children, told the *Guardian* about how he reacted when he was informed he would be affected by the cap:

> *When Steve opened the letter at the end of July he had a 'panic attack'. All that went round his mind was one question: 'How the hell am I going to pay this {the rent}?' Then came what he calls 'a depressive state' that lasted nearly two months. Now he bottles it up, for the sake of his boys. 'When they're not around, that's when I cry. When they're out at school, when they're asleep: that's when I break down.' It's the fear of losing the boys he fought so hard for custody of that haunts him most. So worried is he about a social worker taking them away that he requests a false name.* (Chakrabortty, 2016)

The 'Big Society' and the reform of welfare services since 2010

Significant though they were, the benefits cap and the host of other social security changes introduced since 2010 have comprised but one element of the post-2010 welfare reform agenda. More generally, Cameron's 'Big Society' plan for public services involved a dramatic rethink in the way welfare is delivered, with a much greater role for the voluntary and private sectors in education, health, social security and social work. In education, the 'free schools' initiative and the expansion of academies both sought to reduce the state's role in the delivery of schooling in the UK, and extend the influence of the private and voluntary sectors. The government's health care reforms also controversially significantly expanded the role of the private sector in the delivery of health care, despite public and professional concerns about the implications of this for patient care. For-profit private corporations have now become increasingly involved in health provision in the UK, delivering a range of general practice, community and mental health services, as well as many non-urgent hospital-based operations. In 2016, one-third of all NHS contracts were awarded to private companies, leading the Labour Party to accuse Coalition and Conservative governments of presiding over the *piecemeal break-up and privatisation of the NHS* (Abbott, 2016). The same trends can be found in social security provision, where the private and voluntary sectors are key providers of the welfare-to-work reforms introduced since 2010. Probation services in England and Wales have also been privatised and for-profit Community Rehabilitation Companies (CSCs) are now responsible for supervising around 80 per cent of all prisoners released. In each instance, the shift away from public sector provision has been justified by the claim that the private and voluntary sectors are both more 'efficient', and 'attuned' to the needs of users of services. The infusion of greater heterogeneity in the provision of welfare will, Coalition and Conservative ministers have argued, increase choice, but also drive up standards, as providers are forced to improve the quality of their services in order to attract 'consumers' and indeed government funding.

Research summary

Is, as neo-liberals claim, the private sector more efficient in delivering welfare than the state sector? Despite the apparent plausibility of claims concerning the 'superiority' of the private and voluntary sectors in delivering welfare, evidence from the UK and elsewhere points to a more nuanced picture. The US's private health care system, for instance, is desperately inefficient, consuming more than 17 per cent of GDP in 2014 (compared with the UK's 9.1 per cent), while at the same time leaving tens of millions, including children, without any health insurance at all (World Bank, 2016). Closer to home, research has shown that UK Jobcentres have a more effective record at delivering welfare-to-work schemes than either the voluntary or private sectors. It is simply not true, noted the Department for Work and Pensions (2009, p13) all-party Select Committee of MPs, *that either the private or the third sector has a consistently better record in the provision of employment services than in-house staff.* Concerns have also been expressed about the quality of provision under the newly privatised probation services in England and Wales. The National Audit Office (NAO, 2016a, p7) heard evidence that the new for-profit CRCs *had become too focused on their commercial interests as opposed to the best interests of offenders.* Financial considerations, it seemed, had begun to take priority over service provision, resulting in overworked, stressed staff, who were unable to perform their supervisory roles effectively. A similar picture emerges in relation to social care. Hence, in 2007–8, 79 per cent of council-run services were rated as 'good' or 'excellent', whereas only 66 per cent of private sector ones were (Commission for Social Care Inspection, 2009). When we were writing the previous edition of this text, we suggested that the collapse of the private Southern Cross social care corporation, which found itself simply unable to make a profit from social care without compromising service users' needs, suggested that the private sector is not necessarily the panacea for shortcomings in social care provision. The Care Quality Commission's (2016) recent report, *The State of Health Care and Adult Social Care in England* lends support to this view. It found that private sector providers were increasingly withdrawing from domiciliary care because they were unable to provide dignified, good quality care while also generating profits for shareholders.

The NAO (2015) has also drawn attention to the 'perverse incentives' generated by the 'payment by result' schemes that tend to be built into government contracts with for-profit providers of welfare services. In the case of probation and welfare to work services, for instance, financial considerations often lead providers

(Continued)

(Continued)

to 'park', or neglect harder to help groups who genuinely need the most support. This allows them to focus their attention on assisting those service users who are 'easier to help', because less effort and expense is required to achieve the desired outcomes and hence receive payment. In short, they tend to seek *to maximise their profit margin . . . focus on activities that trigger payments and rely on quick wins that have no lasting impact on users' longer term outcomes* (NAO 2015b, p29–30). In its inquiry into the government's Work Programme, the DfWP Select Committee (2015, p6) referred to this as a process of 'creaming and parking'. It is, the Committee noted, *a common phenomenon . . . in which providers often choose to invest more time and resources in those claimants with the greatest chance of gaining employment, and therefore attracting a payment to the provider (creaming), while side-lining more challenging cases (parking)*. Again, such findings have helped reinforce accusations that recent attempts to expand voluntary and private provision are motivated primarily by ideological considerations, rather than an understanding of what works best.

The privatisation of social work?

As we have already hinted, social services and social work are not exempt from this neo-liberal-inspired privatisation agenda. Private sector initiatives have also been advanced by both the previous Coalition government and the Conservative administration at the time of writing, as methods of improving the quality of what are considered to be 'bureaucratically driven', 'inflexible', 'inefficient' statutory social work services. Of course, the private sector has long been involved in many aspects of social care and social work provision. However, recent policy trends indicate a desire to accelerate and expand this process. For example, the coalition expanded the previous Labour government's *Social Work Practice* (SWP) initiative. This was a pilot scheme involving the contracting out of social work services to social worker 'cooperatives', or private sector 'practices'. A number of 'pilot' SWPs were created, with the clear intention that these would be rolled out in future. Also evident was the Coalition's clear desire for a much more significant level of private sector involvement in the SWP initiative than had originally been envisaged by the former Labour government. The BASW and the Social Care Institute for Excellence initially supported the initiative, but front-line social workers and unions expressed concern that this would lead to the wholesale privatisation of social work, adversely impacting upon the welfare ethos of the profession, as well as the quality of care:

> *The Tory-led Government is enthusiastic about private social work practices because they fit into its 'Big Society' agenda. But we know that it is using mutualisation and social enterprise as a way to dress up wholesale privatisation plans. Without waiting for the*

evaluation of the initial 'pilot', the Government is rolling out private social work practices
and investing considerable effort and money (including set-up grants) to persuade local
authorities to go down this road. (UNISON, 2011, p1)

An independent evaluation of five SWPs was eventually undertaken and published.
Interestingly, it found that SWPs performed no better than their local authority equivalents,
despite ministerial claims that voluntary and private sector social work would be more
effective than local authority provision. As one of the key authors of the evaluation put it,
there was *no clear evidence* of whether SWPs performed better or worse. *The vast majority of*
children and parents in all the SWPs and LA {local authority} comparison sites in our evaluation said
allocated workers listened, cared and did their best for them. In addition, it was found that a number
of the SWPs actually cost more to run than equivalent local authority provision, a finding
that should perhaps lead us to question the notion that the non-statutory and private sector
is necessarily more efficient and cost-effective than its local authority counterpart (College of
Social Work, 2015, pp11 and 13).

The absence of an evidence base pointing to advantages of privatisation has failed to weaken
the resolve of ministers to press ahead with the marketisation of social work services. Indeed,
it is envisaged that even sensitive child protection work will be opened up to private sector
providers. Hence, in 2013, the Coalition introduced powers allowing local authorities to
delegate responsibility surrounding the management of care plans for looked-after children
to voluntary and private providers. Soon after, the Coalition sought to move a controversial
late amendment to the Children and Families Bill, which would have allowed voluntary and
private sector organisations to initiate care or adoption proceedings. Thereto, such coercive
powers had been restricted to just local authorities and the NSPCC. The desired trajectory
of policy was clear; ministers were determined to remove all legal obstacles to private sector
involvement in even the most delicate and complex areas of child protection work. The
government's controversial advisor on children's services, Martin Narey (2014), defended the
proposal, arguing that there was *no reason why a properly managed private sector organisation . . .*
could not compete to play a role in child protection. In his former role as Director General of the
Prison Service, Narey had presided over the privatisation of prisons and his experiences had
left him with the view that there was *nothing intrinsically wrong about making a profit* out of
welfare services, including child protection. The Coalition's plans prompted 40 leading social
work academics to write to *The Guardian*, expressing their concerns at the potential risks of
privatisation and drawing attention to the failure of private sector involvement to deliver in
other areas of welfare provision, including prisons:

England has one of the most successful child protection systems in the world. This is
based on strong accountability, stability, continuity, good local partnership working
across professionals and agencies, and with experienced and committed professionals and
leadership. The intention that private sector organisations such as G4S, Serco, Atos

> *and others should be able to run child protection services causes considerable concern.*
> *Their track record elsewhere has hardly been unblemished in providing Olympics*
> *security, over-claiming payments for tagging offenders, misreporting on GP out-of-hours*
> *contracts, and delaying and denying disability benefits . . . Child protection is much*
> *too important to be exposed to their fickleness and failings.* (Malnick, 2014)

In the weeks that followed the publication of this letter, an online petition opposing the
Coalition's plans to allow private sector companies to bid for work involving care and adoption
proceedings attracted 10,000 signatures and it would eventually achieve more than 72,000
(Jones, 2014b). Meanwhile, an opinion poll commissioned by the trade union UNISON
(2014) found that only five per cent of the British public felt that private companies were
best placed to make decisions about child protection work, serving to illustrate widespread
public scepticism towards the involvement of the private sector in children's social work.
In all, 79 per cent of the public feared a potential conflict of interest if companies that
already made money out of children's homes provision were involved in making decisions
about taking children into care. The same conflict of interest concerns were also raised by
Children England, an umbrella group for the country's principal children and family charities,
including Action for Children, Barnardo's, the Care Leavers Foundation, Gingerbread,
the NSPCC and the Children's Society. It feared that private companies would have direct
financial incentives to refer vulnerable children to their own residential services rather than
considering more suitable alternatives to care proceedings. Its survey of members' uncovered
widespread opposition to the government's plans. *A large proportion of respondents*, it found,
had strong reactions to the idea that it could ever be ethically or morally acceptable for any company's
shareholders to be able to profit from involvement in the protection of maltreated and traumatised children
(Labour Research, 2014).

Heightened levels of concern over the Coalition's proposed privatisation of child protection
services led to a short, six-week consultation period on its proposals. Tellingly, only two per
cent of the 1,300 respondents to the consultation supported the government's plans (Children
England, 2016). The Association of Directors of Children's Services were unequivocal in their
opposition. *Decisions taken about a child's life*, it argued, *should only ever be based on what is in*
the best interests of the child as assessed by skilled and qualified social workers and the courts system.
These decisions cannot, and must not, be subordinate to the pursuit of financial profit (cited in Lords
Hansard, 6 July 2016, Vol. 773, c230).

Such concerns did little to dampen the Coalition's enthusiasm to push ahead, though ministers
did seek to assuage widespread public concern raised by the Children and Families Bill by
announcing that profit-making companies would be excluded from directly bidding for child
protection work involving care and adoption proceedings. However, critics pointed out that
such work would still be allowed to be outsourced to third-sector organisations, and that
companies would be permitted to set up 'shadow' not-for-profit subsidiaries, which they could

then potentially use to funnel children (and the revenue that flowed with them) to their parent profit-making residential care companies (Butler, 2014a). In fact, it subsequently emerged that the government fully intended to allow the formation of such 'shadow' subsidiaries and had been in private talks with outsourcing social care companies, such as Virgin Care, G4S, Serco and Amey with a view to them acquiring such a 'stake' in work involving care and adoption proceedings. One of the attendants described the meetings as *a sales pitch for privatising core children's social work activity. This is radically different to existing outsourcing,* they stated. *This is the crown jewels stuff* (Butler, 2014b).

The regulations were passed, though private sector enthusiasm to purchase the *crown jewels* of child protection failed to materialise in the short term. There can be little doubt that the potential for major child protection scandals to cause 'reputational damage' to their 'brands' deterred many corporations from bidding for this work. However, the ideologically driven quest for what in 2015 David Cameron described as 'market-insurgents' to spearhead a market in social work continued under Theresa May's Conservative government, in the form of the Children and Social Work Bill.

The Children and Social Work Bill contained a number of contentious clauses, which, if passed, would have removed 'barriers' that have discouraged private sector involvement care and adoption proceedings. One key clause, which was justified on the grounds that it would encourage 'innovation', envisaged giving ministers wide-ranging powers to exempt local authorities from providing local child protection and other children's services. This clearly opened up the possibility of local authorities outsourcing provision to private companies. Under the proposals, social service departments would also be exempted from ensuring a host of safeguards are in place to protect vulnerable children, including independent scrutiny of foster families, a duty to visit care leavers, the requirement for an independent review before children are moved, and a duty to assess the suitability of carers from a child's own family. Again, critics feared that this proposed 'bonfire' of legal protections was designed to enhance the 'appeal' of children's services to private corporations. Freed from the 'burden' and cost of guaranteeing these key safeguards would, it was envisaged, make child protection social work a more 'attractive' and profitable proposition for the private sector. Inevitably, Ministers denied their proposals constituted part of a process of 'back-door' privatisation. However, Children England, like opposition politicians, remain unconvinced, as were the 100,000 plus concerned citizens who signed a petition calling for the government to drop its unprecedented plans to excuse local authorities from their legal duties to protect vulnerable children and care leavers. In a Parliamentary briefing for MPs, Children England set out its case for the government to accept an amendment to the Bill which explicitly ruled out privatisation:

> *Our concerns about the influence of profit motives centre upon two key issues. Firstly, an*
> *organisation could seek to generate a profit from budgets delegated to them by reducing its*
> *expenditure through, for example, cutting back on staff hours, reducing staff terms and*

conditions, employing less experienced staff or choosing not to intervene in a family in need of support . . . Secondly, a company that had been delegated social care responsibilities could refer a child, and therefore also direct revenue, towards other services it provides – or indeed other services in which it has any other financial interest as an investor or 'parent company' for a subsidiary . . . However sincere current ministers may be in assuring everyone of their intentions to honour the profit ban they agreed to place in regulation two years ago, we do not believe this is an adequately robust or enduring basis for such an important safeguard. (Children England, 2016)

Ultimately, children's campaigners and charities succeeded in forcing the government to drop the most contentious elements of the Children and Social Work Bill. Nonetheless, this development should be seen within a wider context of government attacks on local authority social work, as well as a series of reforms to practice and training, all of which, some argue, point to a concerted attempt to reshape the profession along neo-liberal lines. These include the government's very public criticism of 'failing' local authority child protection services, the closure of the College of Social Work, the undermining of social work education and the funding of short, skills-focused qualifying programmes such as Frontline, which are said *to threaten the internationally recognised theory and social science knowledge base that is the bedrock of social work* (BASW et al., 2015). Ray Jones (2013), a long-time critic of the government's reforms to social work, claims to have identified a series of trends which point to an ideologically influenced, multi-stage plan to privatise social work:

- Firstly, the government has deliberately criticised local authority social workers for their incompetence and 'political correctness', reinforcing and inflating already existing negative media reporting of the profession.

- Secondly, when tragic, high-profile child protection cases have arisen, ministers have ensured that very little attention is devoted to the role or failings of other, non-social work professions, such as the police, doctors, schools and health workers. This way, support for the profession has been further undermined.

- Thirdly, the government has sought to discredit existing professional social work education and introduced/funded fast-track, skills-focused qualifying social work programmes for 'bright' graduates, which are largely devoid of social science content and have no roots in social work traditions/values. These programmes, Jones argues, will provide a 'cadre' of largely uncritical, ambitious managers whose role it will be to lead the newly privatised child protection system.

- Fourthly, government cuts to local authority funding have engineered a scenario whereby the child protection system is on the verge of breakdown, increasing workloads and undermining the capacity of local authority social workers to perform their roles effectively.

- Finally, ministers have simultaneously utilised other organisations and 'expert' appointees to fuel the privatisation agenda. OFSTED, in particular, has been used as a national 'hit-and-run inspectorate' to highlight the 'failings' of local authorities, without paying any reference to the deliberate, chronic underfunding of the profession.

Jones's claims may seem somewhat conspiratorial, but many of the developments that he identifies have occurred. Moreover, the concerns he raises about the trajectory of policy are shared by leading organisations within the profession. In what was described as a 'historic', unprecedented development, representatives of leading social work organisations, including the BASW, the Social Work Action Network, the Joint University Council Social Work Education Committee, the Association of Professors of Social Work and representative trade unions, released a joint statement expressing their concerns that the *raft of recent political initiatives is set to significantly undermine social work education and training and the profession more generally*. They appeared to be *part of the transformative project to privatise large swathes of the welfare state* (BASW et al., 2015).

Inevitably, ministers have denied that their reforms are ideologically driven and the rhetoric used to justify the government's plans to increase the private sector's role in social work has been uniformly progressive. The Children's Minister, Edward Timpson, claims that the government are merely seeking to create *an environment where excellent practice can flourish* and that practitioners should ignore *conspiracy theories* which claim that the government's agenda for social work is ideologically driven (McNicoll, 2016). However, concerns remain that the rhetoric represents little more than an ideological smokescreen, disguising what is a neo-liberal-influenced attack on the welfare state. It is, critics argue, a crude attempt to roll the country back to a mythical 'golden age' of individualism and self-improvement, where the state provided only a bare minimum of conditionality-based, judgemental social protection and where most individuals were left to provide for themselves in a 'welfare marketplace'.

Chapter summary

As we have shown in this chapter, neo-liberals oppose state intervention in the welfare sphere, believing it to be a morally corrupting, dependency-inducing influence. While neo-liberals do not doubt that the architects of the post-war welfare state, such as Sir William Beveridge, were well intentioned, they argue that the welfare services developed after 1945 have exacerbated the economic and social problems that they were designed to solve. Echoing the architects of the New Poor Law, they argue in favour of a restoration of the 'principles of 1834' and advocate a strong dose of 'self-help'. State welfare services should be cut and individuals should be

(Continued)

(Continued)

encouraged, and where necessary coerced, into supporting themselves through their own efforts and initiative. Governments can legitimately provide a very basic, means-tested safety net for the very vulnerable, but anything over and above this minimum should be provided by the voluntary and private sectors in a competitive 'welfare market'. As we have illustrated, in policy terms neo-liberalism has been at its most influential since 1979, and it is particularly associated with Conservative govern-ments between 1979 and 1997. However, as noted above, there are those who argue that Labour's economic and social policies were infused with neo-liberal principles. Moreover, a clear neo-liberal thread can be detected in the post–2010 welfare reform strategies of Coalition and Conservative administrations. Nowhere is this more evi-dent than in the welfare reforms, such as the benefit cap, as well as the attempts that have been made since 2010 to expand the role of the private sector in delivering welfare and social work.

As future welfare practitioners and social workers, you can hopefully now see why it is important for you to have a basic understanding of the key principles underpin-ning neo-liberalism. Firstly, neo-liberal ideas and values have led to a fundamental transformation of the welfare state, as well as social work practice. There is now a much greater emphasis upon marketisation, competition, consumerism and the voluntary and private provision of welfare, and this will inevitably impact upon your professional futures. Secondly, and just as crucially, it is important to bear in mind the impact of neo-liberal economic and social policies upon vulnerable service users. The 'legacy' of neo-liberalism in the 1980s and 1990s was a more divided, unequal, fractious society, which was characterised by unprecedented levels of poverty and associated social problems. This inevitably led to increased caseloads for social work-ers, at a time when funding for social work services was cut. Alongside this, we saw the restoration of behavioural interpretations for disadvantage, which apportioned blame for misfortune upon individuals and families themselves. These developments inevitably created a difficult environment for social workers to operate in. Social workers were portrayed as overly sentimental, politically motivated 'do-gooders', whose misguided 'help' was encouraging and reinforcing fecklessness and irrespon-sibility. Current policy trends seem to be pointing in the same direction. Just as social service departments are feeling the impact of austerity-driven public expenditure cuts, inequality, poverty and the range of ills associated with these problems are set to increase. At the same time, we have seen a resurgence of the seductive language of the 'undeserving' poor, which holds individuals morally culpable for the marginali-sation that they experience. What seems clear is that these developments look likely to create an extremely challenging environment for social workers to operate in.

Further reading

The following texts are written from a neo-liberal perspective and provide a classic neo-liberal interpretation of the welfare state:

Bartholomew, J (2014) *The Welfare State We're In*. London: Biteback Publishing.

Bartholomew, J (2015) *The Welfare of Nations*. London: Biteback Publishing.

Marsland, D (1996) *Welfare or Welfare State? Contradictions and Dilemmas in Policy*. New York: St. Martin's Press.

The following texts offer a radical critique of the impact of neo-liberalism on social policy and social work practice:

Ferguson, I (2008) *Reclaiming Social Work: Challenging Neo-liberalism and Promoting Social Justice*. London: Sage.

Ferguson, I and Woodward, R (2009) *Radical Social Work in Practice: Making a Difference*. Bristol: Policy Press.

6: Marxism, social policy and social work

- **Professional leadership** – take responsibility for the professional learning and development of others through supervision, mentoring, assessing, research, teaching, leadership and management.

The chapter will also introduce you to the following academic standards which are set out in the 2016 QAA social work benchmark statements:

4   Defining principles
5.2   Social work theory
5.3   Values and ethics
5.4   Service users and carers
5.6   The organisation and delivery of social work services
5.13   Analysis and synthesis
5.16   Skills in working with others
6.4   Learning methods
7.3   Knowledge and understanding

Introduction

As we noted in Chapter 4, the emergence of neo-liberalism was not the only important ideological trend emerging from the crisis of British social democracy in the late 1960s. A concurrent development was the resurgence of Marxism, an ideology based upon the work of the nineteenth-century political philosopher, Karl Marx. Although Marxism would have little or no influence in shaping the policy programmes of the established political parties in the UK, its influence within academic, activist and practitioner circles was and remains relatively significant.

Karl Marx

Karl Marx (1818–83) was a German nineteenth-century revolutionary political philosopher who lived in England at a time when the emergence of industrial capitalism was creating widespread economic and social division. He was deeply uncomfortable with what he witnessed; people whose lives were blighted by utter poverty and despair, coexisting with those whose lives were characterised by opulent riches and affluence. Marx's life work was devoted to exposing the economic and political arrangements that he felt led to such gross and unjust inequalities, and in doing so he identified two main groups in capitalist society: the bourgeoisie (rich manufacturers) who owned the means of production (factories), and the proletariat (or workers) who were forced to sell their labour to the bourgeoisie in return for a wage. In their insatiable search for profits, the bourgeoisie exploited the proletariat remorselessly, forcing them to work long hours, in appallingly unhealthy conditions, for wages that were barely enough to meet their subsistence needs.

Marx referred to this exploitative economic system as *capitalism*. It was, he argued, bolstered by the state elite (including governments, senior civil servants, judges and military officers), whose policies and interventions were always, ultimately, designed to promote the interests of the rich and economically powerful. As Marx and Engels argued in their *Manifesto of the Communist Party*, published in 1848, *The executive of the modern state is but a committee for managing the common affairs of the whole of the Bourgeoisie* (Marx and Engels, 1969, p44). Even nineteenth-century welfare measures, which ostensibly seemed to help the poor, were, from a Marxist perspective, actually influenced by economic rather than altruistic concerns. Thus legal restrictions on the employment of children were, from this viewpoint, motivated less by humanitarian sentiment or popular democratic pressure, and more by recognition that the brutalising inhuman conditions under which the nation's children were forced to toil threatened future profit levels. It was, as one Marxist has subsequently argued, a fear that children – the next generation of wage labourers – were being *literally worked to death,* which *underlay a series of attempts by the state to control the hours and conditions of {their} work* (Gough, 1979).

Marx believed that at some point in history, the proletariat would come to see the true nature of their exploitation, and combine in a state of true class consciousness to overthrow the system that had always oppressed them. In its place, there would be a fairer communist society. Private property would be abolished and no one social group would exploit another. *The proletarians*, he proclaimed, *have nothing to lose but their chains. They have a world to win.* He optimistically called for *Working men of all countries unite!* (Marx and Engels, 1969, p96).

Marxism

Clearly, the communist revolution that Marx hoped for and predicted had not arrived in Britain in the 1960s, and society had obviously changed since Marx's death in 1883. For some, though, this had done little to dent the importance or relevance of his ideas for interpreting contemporary events. As we saw in Chapter 4, the post-war welfare state may have reduced some of the excesses of social and economic inequality but, as in Marx's day, British society continued to be characterised by poverty amid plenty. The political climate of the 1960s was also conducive to a resurgence of Marx's ideas. It was a decade of civil rights protests and political turmoil, and Marx's revolutionary critique of capitalism appealed to a new generation of activists, academics, practitioners and students. These Marxists argued that capitalist societies continued to be characterised by exploitation, widespread poverty and gross inequalities in income and wealth. Welfare policies, they insisted, had never really been designed to eradicate these problems. On the contrary, the primary objectives of welfare, including social work, were to promote economic interests by increasing profit accumulation and controlling the labouring population. Marxists accused social democrats of being delusional for assuming that it was possible to reform a system that was based upon naked exploitation, and that depended upon the fear of poverty to drive people into low-paid, unrewarding exploitative labour. Like Marx before them, this new generation of Marxists argued that capitalism could not ultimately be reformed and that the proletariat's true interests lay in the overthrow of the system, and the creation of a more just, egalitarian society.

At the heart of this developing critique of welfare was a challenge to the notion that the state in capitalist societies was a neutral entity, open to bargain, persuasion and reform. In this sense, a new generation of Marxists sought to develop Marx's analysis of the state, and demolish what they saw as the myth that the state was merely a democratic servant of the people, with no inherent bias towards any one class or group. One of the most influential attempts to do this can be found in Ralph Miliband's (1973) *The State in Capitalist Society*, first published in 1969. Like Marx, he argued that the state was primarily and inevitably the guardian and protector of the interests of the bourgeoisie. In explaining why, Miliband highlighted a number of factors, including:

- the similar educational and social class backgrounds of the state elite and the bourgeoisie;

- the sheer economic power possessed by major, privately owned corporations;

- the structural constraints imposed upon all governments in capitalist societies.

We examine each of these factors in greater detail below.

The similar educational and social class backgrounds of the state elite and the bourgeoisie

Miliband sought to highlight the links between the state elite (for him, this consisted of senior politicians, senior civil servants, judges and military officers) and leading sections of capital (business). Many of the state elite were, he pointed out, from business backgrounds themselves, with a number (particularly politicians) maintaining close links to important sectors of the economy. He argued that this inevitably gave them a vested interest in the implementation of business-friendly policies. Even where the direct links between the state elite and business were less tangible, their similar educational, social and class backgrounds meant that they were conditioned to think, speak, behave and react in the same way as each other. In the context of the UK, for example, the state elite and leading business figures had invariably attended the same small selection of elitist fee-paying independent public schools and studied at either Oxford or Cambridge universities. They knew each other, shared the same personal ties, connections, value base and world view. In short, the state elite were a product of the same mould as the bourgeoisie, and this led them to share their political and ideological outlooks, and to support policies conducive to the interests of capital. To quote Miliband (1977, p69), *a common social background and origin, education, kinship and friendship, a similar way of life, result in a cluster of common ideological and political positions and attitudes, common values and perspectives.*

Activity 6.1

In this activity we want you to consider whether today's 'state elite' is any more representative than it was in Miliband's day. The UK's Social Mobility and Child Poverty Commission (2014) has recently assessed the social composition of elite institutions that, in its words, *have such a profound influence on what happens in our country*. Its findings are set out in Table 6.1. As you can see, only 7 per cent of the British population attended private, fee-paying independent schools in 2014, and as few as one per cent attended either Oxford or Cambridge University (Oxbridge). However, the table shows that much higher percentages of privately educated individuals and Oxbridge graduates are found in Britain's elite institutions.

Table 6.1   Elitist Britain (2014)?

	Percentage who have attended fee-paying independent schools	Percentage who have attended either Oxford or Cambridge University (Oxbridge)
Whole population	7%	1%
Senior judges	71%	75%
Senior armed forces officers	62%	Not available
Civil service permanent secretaries	55%	57%
Senior diplomats	53%	50%
Members of the House of Lords	50%	38%
Chairs of public bodies	45%	44%
Members of the Sunday Times Rich List	44%	12%
Newspaper columnists	43%	47%
Members of the Cabinet	36%	59%
Members of Parliament	33%	24%
BBC executives	26%	33%
Shadow Cabinet	22%	33%

- What does this tell us about the representative nature of these institutions and the social backgrounds of those who wield power and influence in Britain?
- Do you agree with Miliband's assertion that unrepresentative elite institutions are problematic and can have *immense policy implications* (p71)?

The first question that we have asked you to consider is relatively straightforward to answer. Britain's elite institutions *are* wholly unrepresentative of the population as a whole. As already noted, only 7 per cent of British children are privately educated, yet 33 per cent of MPs in 2014 had attended fee-paying independent schools, as had 36 per cent of David Cameron's Coalition Cabinet. Remarkably, as many as 59 per cent of Cameron's Cabinet had attended one of just two universities – Oxford or Cambridge – compared to only one per cent of the population as a whole (Social Mobility and Child Poverty Commission, 2014). Of course, Parliament is unrepresentative in many other respects too. In 2016, only 3 per cent of MPs (19 out of 650) were from working-class manual backgrounds, a much smaller percentage than in 1979, when 15.8 per cent were. The remaining 97 per cent of MPs are drawn overwhelmingly from business or professional backgrounds. Only 29 per cent of MPs (191 out of 650) are women and only 6.3 per cent are from black and minority ethnic (BME) group backgrounds, despite the fact that 12.9 per cent of the UK's population are BME (Audickas, 2016). The same lack of diversity can be found in each one of the influential elite institutions listed above, all of which recruit from an extremely narrow, unrepresentative range of society.

Is this necessarily a problem? *Daily Mail* columnist Tom Utley, a former pupil at the £36,000 per year Winchester College and Cambridge University graduate, has defended Oxbridge's grip on influence and power:

> *Well, I have to say I don't find it particularly disturbing that so many who land influential jobs went to Oxford or Cambridge. In most fields, these are the two best universities in the land and it cannot, surely, be a bad thing that our top judges had the best legal education available or that our politicians were taught by some of the country's best teachers.* (Utley, 2014).

Peter Hitchens (2015), another conservative-minded *Daily Mail* commentator, makes much the same point; because elite institutions *can choose from huge numbers of applicants for every job, it is no surprise that they pick men and women from the best universities, who are confident, fluent and literate.*

However, serious reservations have been expressed over the unrepresentative nature of Britain's elite institutions. Nor, by any means, are such concerns the sole preserve of the Marxist 'left'. For instance, despite having presided over an Oxbridge-dominated Cabinet, the former Conservative Prime Minister David Cameron (himself a former pupil at the £32,000 per year Eton College and an Oxford University graduate) has condemned the elitism that characterises so many of the institutions in which state and communicative power resides. As he acknowledged:

> *You only have to look at the make-up of the high levels of parliament, the judiciary, the army, the media. It's not as diverse; there's not as much social mobility as there needs to be . . . I want to see a Britain where no matter where you come from, what god you worship, the colour of your skin, what community you belong to, you can get to the top in television, the judiciary, armed services, politics, newspapers.* (Mason and Wintour, 2013, p1)

The government's Social Mobility and Child Poverty Commission concurs, arguing that the dominance of a narrow, unrepresentative economically privileged elite within key power-holding institutions creates a democratic deficit that we would be ill-advised to ignore:

> *Where institutions rely on too narrow a range of people from too narrow a range of backgrounds with too narrow a range of experiences they risk behaving in ways and focussing on issues that are of salience only to a minority but not the majority in society. Our research shows it is entirely possible for politicians to rely on advisors to advise, civil servants to devise policy solutions and journalists to report on their actions having all studied the same courses at the same universities, having read the same books, heard the same lectures and even being taught by the same tutors.* (Social Mobility and Child Poverty Commission, 2014, p2)

From this perspective, the unrepresentative nature of government, the senior civil service, leading sections of the media and other influential institutions *really does* matter. As Alan Milburn, the chair of the Social Mobility and Child Poverty Commission (2014, p2) argues, it means that those who determine policy, who shape public opinion and who have profound influence over our daily lives are *far less familiar with the day-to-day challenges facing ordinary people in the country.*

Less still, it could be argued, are they likely to be familiar with the difficulties experienced by vulnerable groups of social work service users, or with the challenges faced by often under-resourced, over-burdened social work practitioners whose role it is to support them. According to Jones (2014a), this ignorance among the 'establishment' of the 'real-world' issues faced by vulnerable, marginalised groups leaves those within elite institutions susceptible to the embrace of inaccurate, pathological interpretations of economic and social ills. Hence recipients of welfare and social work services are frequently accused by those in elite institutions – politicians, newspaper editors and correspondents – of being lazy, feckless and the architects of their own misfortune, despite widespread evidence to the contrary. Nowhere is this more evident than in commentaries around welfare fraud, an issue which is constantly at the forefront of media and political debates, and one that reinforces the perception that those reliant upon state support are 'irresponsible shirkers' undeserving of assistance.

Meanwhile, as Owen Jones (2011 and 2014a) argues, the transgressions and crimes of the affluent, as well as the dubious business practices of major corporations, are ignored: *While the law cracks down on the misdemeanours of the poor, it allows, even facilitates, the far more destructive behaviour of the rich* (2014a, p104). Thus, while welfare 'scroungers' are roundly castigated, the dubious (but technically legal) widespread tax evasion practices engaged in by major corporations are largely condoned. Starbucks, Apple, Facebook, Amazon and Google are just a few of many major corporations that have managed to use 'sharp' accounting techniques to avoid paying tax in the UK. Starbucks, for instance, paid absolutely no corporation tax between 2009 and 2012 (Ebrahimi and Wilson 2012; Wright, 2012), and it is not alone in this respect; in 2012/13 one-fifth of the largest businesses in the UK paid no corporation tax (National Audit Office, 2015a). Those within elite institutions therefore stand accused by Marxists of protecting members of 'their own' class, while demeaning 'others' with whom they have no affinity or connection.

Marxists accept that this 'bias' is not necessarily a conscious process, and that members of the elite within the establishment are often genuinely affronted when accused of attacking the vulnerable and of protecting the economically advantaged. They are, Miliband (1973) accepts, frequently genuinely blind to their class bias, and are the most ardent and eloquent exponents of the view that their sole aim is to serve the whole nation, without favouring any particular class interest. Thus many of those within elite institutions who engage in the demonisation of welfare recipients genuinely do not experience any 'guilt' or sense of contradiction when condemning users of welfare services and slashing expenditure on social policy programmes, while at the same supporting and implementing fiscal policies that favour the already advantaged.

Of course, Marxists accept that this apparent 'bias' towards business and the rich is not *solely* a product of the shared social and educational backgrounds of business leaders and those within elite institutions. As we show below, Marxists point to other ways that 'capital' is able to ensure that elite institutions serve its interests. They would, for instance, note that almost one-third of MPs elected to Parliament (and 44 per cent of all Conservative MPs in 2015) are themselves from business backgrounds (Audickas, 2016). In addition, of course, many MPs maintain their business links while in Parliament, continuing to work as directors for major corporations. As Jones (2014a) highlights, 46 of the UK's top 50 firms have a parliamentarian as either a director or as a shareholder, giving many MPs and peers a direct personal stake in policies that promote and enrich corporate interests (2014a, p71). *The borders between the political and business elite*, he argues, *are now so porous that it is increasingly difficult to treat them as separate worlds*.

However, Marxists maintain that *social background* matters too, and that the pro-business 'bias' is at least *partly* a consequence of the personal and ideological links between leading sectors of capital and those occupying the higher echelons of elite institutions. Conversely, the absence of any meaningful knowledge of or interaction with less privileged groups is seen as one of the reasons the elite fail to appreciate the debilitating impact of poverty, unemployment, homelessness and other forms of exclusion on individuals and families, or comprehend the structural causes of their marginalisation. In short, those within elite institutions have little or no affinity with 'the poor', yet they have a great deal in common – in terms of their educational backgrounds, ideological affinity and world view – with 'the rich'.

The sheer economic power possessed by major corporations and privately owned industries

As we have shown, the social origins of the state elite are seen by some Marxists as a crucial factor in shaping the class bias of the state, but it is not the only factor. The sheer economic power of the bourgeoisie – their ownership and control of economic, technological and media interests – means it possesses immense coercive power, which it can use to encourage or force states to adopt policies conducive to its interests. It can do this through bribes or political donations, or via the funding of negative media campaigns, or through threats to remove investment from the country. While this may sound far-fetched, it is important to bear in mind that some of the world's corporations have higher turnovers of income than many nation states. As the World Bank (2010) note, the oil companies Royal Dutch Shell and ExxonMobil each have higher annual turnovers than any of Egypt, Pakistan, Belgium, Sweden, Greece, Switzerland, Austria, Norway and a host of other countries that would be too long to list here. Wallmart's annual revenues alone are more than double the GDP turnovers of the Ukraine, Denmark, Finland or Ireland. Marxists argue that this economic clout gives corporations (and businesses generally) considerable political power and influence. In fact, there are occasions in relatively recent British political history when governments have been coerced into modifying their political agenda in order to accommodate the needs of business. For example, when the Labour Party won the General Election in 1964, the head of the civil service informed the new Prime Minister, Harold Wilson, that it would be 'unwise' from a business point of view to implement Labour's manifesto commitments. As Wilson recalled in his autobiography, *a newly elected Government with a mandate from the people {was} being told . . . by international speculators, that the policies on which we had fought the election could not be implemented* (Wilson, 1971, p65).

Structural constraints imposed on all governments in capitalist societies

Marxists also point to the in-built, structural constraints that force all governments in capitalist societies to introduce pro-business policies, irrespective of the social origins of the state elite or their political allegiances. To quote Miliband (1977, p72): *There are structural constraints which no government, whatever its complexion, wishes and promises, can ignore or evade. A capitalist economy has its own rationality to which any government and state must sooner or later submit, and usually sooner.* In a sense, Miliband is right. Governments in capitalist countries such as Britain – whether left or right wing – are presiding over economies that are closely integrated into the world capitalist system, and the success or failure of these economies depends upon their ability to attract investment and compete. In such a capitalist context any reform is bound to be limited to measures which enhance, or certainly do not threaten, the economic efficiency and profitability of businesses. Thus, to give one hypothetical (and perhaps extreme) example, a UK government may wish to introduce a minimum wage of £200 per hour, but to do so in the context of a world capitalist economic system would be economic suicide. Such a policy would increase the costs of UK businesses dramatically, affecting their ability to compete with lower-waged countries, potentially leading to job losses and crippling the economy. In this sense, the system itself constrains governments to act in a way that promotes business interests.

Marxism and welfare

If, as Marxists assert, the state always acts in the interests of capital, why does it fund and provide welfare services that ostensibly help the poor, the marginalised and the vulnerable? This was a question that Marxist-influenced social policy academics sought to answer in the 1960s, when we saw the development of an explicitly Marxist critique of the welfare state. This critique sought to demystify social policies, aiming to shatter the notion that the welfare state was motivated by humanitarian sentiment. In doing so, Marxists drew attention to the 'legitimation' and 'accumulation' functions of welfare.

Legitimation functions of welfare

By 'legitimation', Marxists meant that the welfare state served an ideological role, creating the image of a caring capitalism that is interested in the welfare of its citizens. Marxists noted that welfare had historically been presented as the compassionate, civilised face of capitalism, and was genuinely seen by many as an example of society's preparedness to care for and support some of the most vulnerable members of society. In this sense, welfare provided legitimacy to existing exploitative economic and political arrangements, acting as an ideological smokescreen. It detracted attention from the exploitative nature of capitalism, and the fact that workers' interests lay in its overthrow.

Accumulation functions of welfare

Welfare was also said to perform a crucial 'accumulation' function in that it served to enhance profits. For example, education and health care systems helped maintain a relatively healthy and educated workforce, key prerequisites for modern capitalist societies. Likewise, social security systems ensured that redundant workers were fed, maintained and disciplined at the public's expense, providing employers with an acquiescent 'reserve army of labour' when necessary. Those who did stray from the 'straight and narrow' would be subjected to targeted interventions from social workers and other welfare professionals, with a view to 'reintegrating' them into society. Put simply, by providing employers with an appropriately educated, healthy and disciplined workforce, welfare states in capitalist societies actively promoted business interests.

Activity 6.2

- How convincing do you find Marxist interpretations of welfare?
- Does the UK's benefit system serve a 'disciplinary' function?
- Are Marxists correct when they argue that the welfare state performs crucial legitimation and accumulation functions?

(Continued)

(Continued)

Comment

At first glance, this interpretation of welfare policies in capitalist societies may seem somewhat conspiratorial. It appears to imply that the sole purpose of social policy is to 'dupe' us into thinking that the rich and powerful care about us, whereas in reality their sole aim is our ruthless exploitation. Many of the claims made by Marxists are, however, not without foundation. For example, one need not be a Marxist to accept the notion that certain welfare initiatives, such as education and health care, do help to produce an educated, technically proficient and healthy workforce, thereby promoting economic efficiency and profitability. Thus, when the then British Prime Minister, Tony Blair, famously extolled the virtues of 'education, education, education', his justification for doing so was couched as much in economic terms as it was in social justice terms.

Nor can there be any doubt that the benefits system serves a disciplinary function, punishing those who are deemed 'lazy', thus reinforcing bourgeois work ethic norms and forcing workers to engage with an increasingly insecure, low-paid labour market. In fact, the disciplinary nature of the benefits system has been brought into sharp focus since 2010, as eligibility criteria have been tightened and the number of sanctions applied to the so-called 'workshy' has soared. In 2009/10, the year Labour left office, 10.8 per cent of Jobseeker's Allowance (JSA) claimants were sanctioned, but by 2013/14 this had increased to 18.4 per cent – almost one in five. In the 12 months prior to 30 June 2015, 284,436 claimants faced sanctions (Webster, 2016). As we note in Chapter 8, where we discuss this issue in greater detail, considerable concern has been raised about the inappropriate use of sanctions against vulnerable and disabled people who are simply not fit to work. According to one study, for example, the tightening of the disability benefit regime alone can be linked to 590 additional suicides, 279,000 cases of self-reported mental health problems and 725,000 additional anti-depressant prescriptions (Barr et al., 2015).

Regarding the 'accumulation' functions of welfare, a number of commentators have identified what they refer to as a 'corporate welfare state', which provides direct financial benefits to business. Tax credits are an obvious form of 'corporate welfare'. The fact that millions of people depend upon them to meet their subsistence needs should not detract from the fact that they are, as Jones (2014, p18) argues, in effect, *a subsidy to bosses for low pay*. These state-funded wage subsidies – which cost £176.64 billion between 2003–4 and 2010–11 – only exist because businesses, in order to boost profits, fail to pay workers an adequate living wage. Farnsworth (2015) has identified a host of other forms of 'corporate welfare' that serve to promote the accumulation of capital. He estimates that in 2012/13 businesses based in the UK benefited from £145 billion in direct corporate benefits (such as tax subsidies and capital grants) and indirect benefits (for instance, wage subsidies and spending on education and public health care). This annual subsidy to business is the equivalent of almost 40 years' worth of spending on unemployment benefits in the UK (£3.47 billion in 2014/15). As Farnsworth (2015, p2) argues: *Publicly-funded benefits and services that are aimed at meeting the needs and/or wants of private businesses is a key part of what governments do and have always done.* However, unlike the stigmatised, under-funded, shrinking welfare state used by social work service users, this 'corporate welfare state' is booming, expanding and remains largely free from political scrutiny or controversy.

Of course, business has also benefited enormously from the increasing tendency for the state to contract out public services, such as health provision, welfare to work and residential care, to the private sector. This process, which has gathered pace since the ascendency of neo-liberalism (see the previous chapter), also arguably constitutes a form of 'corporate welfare', providing businesses with a lucrative source of profit. In fact, around half of the £187 billion now spent on public services goes to private contractors. As Jones (2014, p18) argues: *Much of Britain's public sector has now become a funding stream for profiteering companies.* As we saw in the previous chapter, it appears that this also includes key, sensitive child protection services, which are currently being 'touted' to corporations like Virgin Care and Amey.

Perhaps the most spectacular recent example of 'corporate welfare' occurred in the aftermath of the 2008 financial crisis, when almost £1 trillion of public money was poured into the banking sector to prevent it collapsing. As Jones (2014a) notes, this bank bailout, which resulted from widespread malpractices within the sector, was the principal cause of the Coalition and Conservative governments' austerity measures that did so much damage to the public services that ordinary citizens rely upon.

In summary then, Marxists accuse bourgeois politicians of cutting welfare for the least well off while simultaneously bestowing huge sums of taxpayers' money upon already extremely profitable businesses in the form of government subsidies. For Marxists, therefore, Miliband's (1973, p72) assertions about the crucial role played by the state in guaranteeing the accumulation of capital remain as relevant today as they did in 1969 when he first made them:

> *Capitalist enterprise . . . depends to an ever greater extent on the bounties and direct support of the state, and can only preserve its 'private' character on the basis of such public help. State intervention in economic life in fact largely means intervention for the purpose of capitalist enterprise. In no field has the notion of the 'welfare state' had a more precise and apposite meaning than here: there are no more persistent and successful applicants for public assistance than the proud giants of the private enterprise system.*

(Continued)

(Continued)

Finally, it is fair to say that Marxists do point to other influences when interpreting welfare policies. For example, social policies are, to an extent, also said to have been introduced in response to direct pressure 'from below'. The labour movement and workers have always fought for improved standards of welfare, and at certain periods in history it has been politically impossible for the capitalist state to ignore these demands, a good example being the immediate aftermath of the Second World War. From this perspective, therefore, the welfare state should also partly be seen as a 'ransom' that the bourgeoisie have been prepared to pay in order to prevent more radical, revolutionary reform. Of course, Marxists accept that the hard fought for welfare services that have emerged as part of this 'ransom' have delivered real, tangible benefits for working-class families, and Marxist scholars and activists are at the forefront of campaigns to protect welfare services from cuts, and calls for their improvement and extension (Turbett, 2014). However, as the aftermath of the 2008 financial crisis seemed to illustrate, for Marxists progressive social policies are often merely temporary concessions which can be (and usually are) reversed when political and economic conditions change:

> *The welfare state that marked the lives of a generation in a number of advanced capitalist societies after the second world war {sic} now appears as a relatively brief interlude in the otherwise dismal role of state policy in its dealings with the poor . . . There is no longer much sense that the welfare state is there to help in periods of crisis . . . During the last quarter of a century, social policy has taken on a more authoritarian, less compassionate and more coercive tone . . . The gains in peoples {sic} welfare achieved over a century of struggle are being swept away, and the vile maxim of the masters has returned, without disguise or embarrassment to the centre stage.* (Jones and Novak, 1999, pp139, 201)

Radical social work

The emergence of radical social work theory in the 1970s was one example of the growing influence of Marxism within academic, activist and practitioner circles. While other theoretical traditions could be found within radical social work, most of those who embraced it were socialists, attracted to the movement because of its commitment to revolutionary change. The publication of Bailey and Brake's seminal text, *Radical Social Work* (1975), is seen as a formative moment in the development of the movement. It represented a devastating critique of British social work, and at the same time it sought to map out a radical approach for future social work practice. A key premise of the radical social work movement was the notion that social democratic welfare strategies in capitalist societies were always doomed to failure. The capitalist economic system itself was the cause of inequality and oppression, and until this was abolished social justice and equality could never be achieved. The ruling class and its representatives within the state apparatus might be prepared to grant concessions to workers in the form of piecemeal welfare policies, particularly in periods of economic boom and high employment. However, these reforms were inadequate, tentative and always at risk of reversal in less certain economic times. Moreover, they could never be sufficient to meet the need. *The idea of the state as a neutral arbiter between different sections of society was*, it was argued, *wholly inadequate*, and there was a need to appreciate the extent to which social reform, and indeed social work itself, was shaped with a view to safeguarding *the interests and development of British capitalism* (Case Con Manifesto, 1975, p146).

Those influenced by radical social work called for a critical reappraisal of the nature and role of social work in capitalist societies. There was, they argued, a need to eliminate oppressive pathological casework approaches from social work practice and acknowledge the fact that *for most of the working-class material deprivation lies behind many of their problems* (Bailey and Brake, 1975, p9). Hence, the traditional casework method was dismissed as *a pseudo science, that blames individual inadequacies for poverty and so mystifies and diverts attention from the real causes – slums, homelessness and economic exploitation* (Case Con Manifesto, 1975). In addition, the myth of the 'caring' welfare state needed to be challenged, and the social control element of social work – the extent that it sought to manipulate and control the unwitting casualties of capitalism – had to be confronted. It was also important to acknowledge the limitations of social work, that is the extent to which social workers themselves were *trapped in a social structure which severely delimits their power and hence their ability to initiate significant change* (Bailey and Brake, 1980, pp7–8).

Social work training was also targeted for specific criticism. According to Pearson (1975, pp34–6), social workers, were provided with a *pre-packed work problem*, because their training failed to provide them with an awareness of the limitations of reform under capitalism. He argued that social work training was *punctuated by bad promises*, because it misleadingly offered a *spirit of hopefulness and betterment* and the vacuous promise of *a germ of advancement in capitalist society*. It put forward *a professional vision of a promised land of social welfare before the eyes of its recruits which is shattered in the world of work*. Training courses encouraged students to *act on the ideals of social work in a less than ideal world,* neglecting to impress on them the constraints on their actions imposed by the economic system itself. There was therefore a need, according to Leonard (1975, p49), for social workers to be aware of *the pathology of wider economic and political structures*. As long as capitalism existed, social workers could be little more than *social bandits, noble robbers*, or Robin Hood-like characters, blindly groping against social injustice. They were, Pearson argued (1975, p40), taught to *oppose injustice not by struggling for the defeat of injustice, but by getting round the edges of it* and their practical function was *at best to impose certain limits to traditional oppression in traditional society.*

Finally, there was a more optimistic strand to radical social work, which emphasised the social worker's role both in mitigating individual suffering caused by capitalism and as a vanguard of revolutionary change. Regarding this latter point, social workers should, Leonard (1975, p57) argued, seek to play a crucial educational role, developing among themselves, other professionals and users of welfare services *a critical consciousness of their oppression, and of their potential.* Clearly, they needed to help alleviate immediate suffering, but their long-term objective should be to actively fight for revolutionary change. Here is an extract from the Case Con Manifesto (1975, p147), which constituted a statement of political aims that many supporters of radical social work adhered to:

> *Case Con believes that the problems of our clients are rooted in the society in which we live, not in individual inadequacies. Until this society, based on private ownership, profit and the needs of a minority ruling class, is replaced by a workers' state, based on the interests of the vast majority of the population, the fundamental causes of social problems will remain. It is therefore our aim to join the struggle for the workers' state.*

One of the main criticisms radical social work faced was its emphasis upon the need for revolutionary change and its alleged failure to appreciate the importance of tackling injustice in the 'here and now'. It was, some argued, all fine and well for radicals to place their efforts into generating revolutionary ferment, but what about the social and economic well-being of service users in the meantime? As Pearlman, a contemporary critic of the movement, stated, *Man runs his short life span in six or seven decades. He should not have to wait – suffering, struggling, withering, as the case may be – while the wheels of social justice grind out social change* (cited in Pearson, 1975, p35). Linked to this criticism was the allegation that radical social work rarely moved beyond a critical mode, and that with the exception of proposals for revolutionary change, it offered little in the way of a practical programme for a progressive alternative. Radical social work was also accused of being gender and race blind and of overly focusing on ruling-class oppression at the expense of racist and sexist practices.

Langan and Lee, in their reappraisal of the impact of radical social work, accept that there is an element of justification to some of these criticisms, but their overall assessment of the impact and legacy of radical social work is overwhelmingly positive. The socialist 'workers' state' may not have been achieved, but radical social work's powerful critique of pathological casework techniques, as well as the primacy it gave to user involvement and structural explanations for the difficulties facing service users, constituted an enormously positive contribution to the future shape of social work training and practice. According to Langan and Lee (1989, p2), the movement was a jolt to the complacency of a profession that was beginning to insulate itself from the essentially political nature of its tasks, and *many of the attitudes and values of the radical movement entered mainstream practice.* Nor should we think of Marxism or radical social work as being a distant phenomenon, a peculiar characteristic of the 1960s and 1970s. Recent years, for example, have seen the publication of a range of social policy and social work texts written from a radical, Marxist perspective, as well as the emergence of a practitioner movement – the Social Work Action Network (2009) (SWAN) – committed to pursuing many of the original radicals' aims.

Radical social work today

This 'new' variant of radical social work shares many of the concerns that motivated the 'original' radicals. Turbett (2014), for example, hints at the *pre-packaged work* problem first discussed by Pearson in the 1970s, pointing to the disappointment that many newly qualified social workers feel when their social work values come into conflict with the realities of capitalism. The need for practitioners to be aware of the limits to which social work, in isolation, can dramatically improve the lives of service users is, Turbett insists, even more important today than it was in the 1970s. Citing Mullaly's comments on the importance of critical analysis, he argues that radical social workers *at least have an analysis that explains why mainstream interventions and traditional approaches to social problems do not work* (Mullaly, cited in Turbett, 2014, p144). Rogowski (2016) also discusses the 'moral distress' practitioners feel when they are unable to 'do the right thing' and take ethically appropriate action which is in accordance with their value base. He too hints at the risks posed to practitioners if they enter the world of work without any appreciation of the barriers capitalism presents to those who wish to engage in progressive, emancipatory social work. Without a critical understanding of the wider political and economic context within which social work operates, even the most resilient practitioner's sense of purpose, integrity, self-worth and authenticity can, he argues, be severely compromised, leading to stress, burnout and even resignation.

Like their predecessors, the 'new' radicals also emphasise the need for social workers to avoid and challenge pathological, neo-liberal interpretations for disadvantage, and to acknowledge the structural causes of the oppression that service users face. As Turbett (2014, p32) argues, within today's 'radical' literature there is *broad agreement that service users are not the architects of their own misfortune but that other forces are responsible for the oppression and division in society*. The 'new' radicals also share a belief that, ultimately, true emancipation will involve the abolition of capitalism and a move towards a more equal, socialist society. *Radical approaches*, states Turbett, *assume that society requires fundamental socialist change*.

Where the 'new' radical social work literature does perhaps differ from its original variant is the greater emphasis that it places on the need to articulate 'here and now' strategies for defending service users from the corrosive impact of neo-liberalism, which, it argues, has exacerbated pre-existing tendencies towards greater marginalisation and inequality. It has, therefore, sought to respond to concerns that radical literature has hitherto been overly theoretical, pessimistic and utopian. As Turbett (2014, p25) insists: *Whatever one's vision might be of a future where the resources of the world are shared more equally . . . it is out of the struggles of the present that the future will be shaped*. Hence, a series of practical guides to radical social work 'in action' have been published, which seek to provide practitioners with the information, advice and tools they need to challenge oppression and promote social justice. Turbett's appropriately titled book, *Doing Radical Social Work*, is a good, influential example of this genre, as it seeks, through practical examples, to illustrate the *small and good deeds that show the way to a better world.* Together with other radical texts, Turbett's book sets out the opportunities that exist for social workers to engage in resistance at a local and national level, drawing attention to areas of discretion and collaboration that be can be exploited by the radical practitioner.

Other texts have sought to apply a radical, Marxist perspective to particular areas of social work provision. Garrett (2013) and Rogowski (2012 and 2016) focus on social work with children and families, arguing that practice in this field, as in other areas of social work, is not an entirely benign, emancipatory activity and should not be sentimentalised. They point to the neo-liberalisation of social work with children and families, a process which is increasingly divesting practice of its progressive, emancipatory potential. *Relationship-based work*, Rogowski (2012, p921) argues, *has been transformed into a bureaucratic focus on the assessment of risk and rationing of resources and services, together with a more controlling, moral policing role.* In his most recent book, where he reflects upon his forty year career as a social worker, he calls for radical practitioners to resist the pressure for them to embrace a form of *muscular authoritarianism*, whereby children and family social workers descend into little more than *community surveillance and rationing officers* (Rogowski, 2016):

> *Critical practice is needed because otherwise social workers will be increasingly locked into a system whereby they become hard-line state agents . . . rather than the 'soft cops' of the 1970s. In such a scenario the emphasis would be upon working to prop up and ensure the status quo rather than working towards a more just and equal world. My argument is that despite the reduced and limited discretion that practitioners now have, requiring critical thinking and practice remains possible.* (p9)

Other groups of service users have also been subjected to the radical 'gaze'. Elsewhere, Rogowski (2014) has applied a radical perspective to social work with young offenders, where he again criticises the authoritarian neo-liberal 'twist' that has shaped policy and practice. He calls for practitioners to avoid the tendency to *condemn more and understand less. Rather than notions of punishment and control being to the fore, attention should be paid to the social and economic conditions that shape young people's lives and behaviour* (p7). Ferguson and Lavalette (2014) adopt a similar approach in their radical analysis of recent developments in social work with adults. Mental health policy and practice (Weinstein, 2014) and personalisation (Beresford, 2014) have also been analysed utilising a radical perspective. While presenting a radical critique of mainstream practice, each of these contributions, to varying degrees, attempts to move beyond critique and, in the words of Turbett (2014, p159), promote *the practical application of the values of the political left within the work context of social work.*

Another noteworthy development is the growing interest shown internationally in the radical social work tradition. As Ferguson and Smith (2012) point out, this has been prompted primarily by growing global dissatisfaction over the impact of neo-liberalism on policy and practice. For example, the austerity programmes implemented in Southern European nations in the aftermath of the 2008 financial crisis prompted the emergence of a number of radical social work activist networks. Like the UK-based SWAN, these sought to re-emphasise the political nature of social work, calling upon practitioners to defend services and engage in radical street-level acts of civil disobedience in order to insulate service users from the impact of cuts. In Greece, Spain and Portugal social work activists have successfully frustrated the imposition of policies and practices that they consider contravene the human rights of service users. The respective social work associations in each of these countries have been driven in a more critical and politically informed direction by more activist practitioners influenced by the radical tradition (Ioakimidis et al., 2014). Similar 'radical turns' can be detected within the social work professions of other countries, as evidenced by the internationalist flavour of the contributions to the academic and practitioner journal that has been created to promote radical perspectives, *Critical and Radical Social Work*.

In summary then, this new domestic and international revival of Marxist-inspired radical social work literature calls upon practitioners to build alliances and coalitions with the other radical, progressive groups, professions and movements that are challenging the neo-liberal trajectory of policy. It implores social workers to 'reclaim' a political dimension to their practice and resist and oppose initiatives that undermine progressive work with service users. Indeed, Ferguson and Woodward (2009, p159), have encouraged social workers to perceive themselves as *outlaws* engaging in *guerrilla warfare* against neo-liberal pressures to stigmatise service users and ration provision. While acknowledging the practical, organisational constraints that may make such *guerrilla warfare* difficult, they argue that social workers *need to be much more vocal, both about the way social policies are impacting on the lives of their clients and also about the value (as well as the limits) of their own role* (Ferguson, 2008, p136). Most of all, they should aim to promote *a modern engaged social work based around such core 'anti-capitalist' values as democracy, solidarity, accountability, participation, justice, equality, liberty and diversity* (Jones et al., 2004). According to Ferguson (2008, p136), it is only then that *social work can finally stop being a 'quiet profession' and can begin to play its proper role in the struggle for a more equal, more just society.*

Activity 6.3

In this activity we want you to reflect on some of the themes and debates that we have covered in this chapter. Firstly, download the SWA Manifesto for a new engaged practice (http://www.socialworkfuture.org/articles-resources/uk-articles/103-social-work-and-social-justice-a-manifesto-for-a-new-engaged-practice). Once you have done this, try answering the following questions.

- Can you detect a Marxist/radical social work influence in the Manifesto?
- What do you think of the Manifesto and how might its principles be translated into practice?

Chapter summary

As we have seen in this and previous chapters, by the late 1960s, there was a general feeling across the political spectrum that the social democratic welfare state had failed to deliver the 'New Jerusalem' promised by its architects. The evolution of Marxist interpretations of social policy and social work can be traced back to this period. Although Marxists agreed with many of the aims of social democrats – in particular the creation of a more equal, socialist society built upon the principles of fairness and egalitarianism – they rejected social democratic strategies for achieving these objectives. As we saw in Chapter 4, social democrats believe that it is possible to reform capitalism from 'within' and for a benevolent, social democratic government to create a 'better world' through the enactment of progressive social reform. Marxists dismiss such claims, highlighting what they see as the powerful, entrenched bourgeois forces within the state apparatus which, they argue, will frustrate, check and dilute attempts to create a more equal society. At the same time, they argue that the structural constraints that capitalism imposes upon any government – the need to make profits and to compete with other capitalist countries – means that all governments, irrespective of their political orientation, are forced to introduce policies that are conducive to business interests. It is, Marxists insist, for these very reasons that ostensibly social democratic Labour governments have always failed to radically transform, or 'tame' capitalism. For Marxists, this also explains why welfare services, including social work, have ultimately always had at their heart the promotion of the status quo rather than progressive economic and social change.

Further reading

The following texts will be useful for those of you wishing to further explore Marxist interpretations of welfare:

Gough, I (1979) *The Political Economy of the Welfare State.* London: Macmillan.

Ferguson, I, Lavalette, M and Mooney, G (2002) *Rethinking Welfare: A Critical Perspective.* London: Sage.

The following two texts are seen as seminal in terms of the development of radical social work in the UK:

Bailey, R and Brake, M (1975) *Radical Social Work.* London: Edward Arnold.

Bailey, R and Brake, M (1980) *Radical Social Work and Practice.* London: Edward Arnold.

These texts will be useful for those of you wishing to further explore more recent analyses written within a radical social work perspective:

Ferguson, I (2008) *Reclaiming Social Work: Challenging Neo-liberalism and Promoting Social Justice*. London: Sage.

Ferguson, I and Woodward, R (2009) *Radical Social Work in Practice: Making a Difference*. Bristol: Policy Press.

Garrett, PM (2013) *Children and Families*. Bristol: Policy Press

Lavalette, M (ed.) (2011) *Radical Social Work Today: Social Work at the Crossroads*. Bristol: Policy Press.

Rogowski, S (2016) *Social Work with Children and Families: Reflections of a Critical Practitioner*. London: Routledge.

Turbett, C (2014) *Doing Radical Social Work*. Basingstoke: Palgrave Macmillan.

Part two

Social policy, social work and service users

7: Children, social policy and social work

Achieving a social work degree

This chapter will help you to meet the following capabilities from the Professional Capabilities Framework:

- **Professionalism** – identify and behave as a professional social worker, committed to professional development.
- **Values and ethics** – apply social work ethical principles and values to guide professional practice.
- **Diversity** – recognise diversity and apply anti-discriminatory and anti-oppressive principles in practice.
- **Rights, justice and economic well-being** – advance human rights and promote social justice and economic well-being.
- **Knowledge** – apply knowledge of social sciences, law and social work practice theory.
- **Critical reflection and analysis** – apply critical reflection and analysis to inform and provide a rationale for professional decision-making.
- **Intervention and skills** – use judgement and authority to intervene with individuals, families and communities to promote independence, provide support and prevent harm, neglect and abuse.
- **Contexts and organisations** – engage with, inform and adapt to changing contexts that shape practice. Operate effectively within own organisational frameworks and contribute to the development of services and organisations. Operate effectively within multi-agency and inter-professional settings.

(Continued)

(Continued)

The chapter will also introduce you to the following academic standards which are set out in the 2016 QAA social work benchmark statements:

4   **Defining principles**
5.1   **Subject knowledge and understanding**
5.2   **Social work theory**
5.3   **Values and ethics**
5.5   **The nature of social work practice**
5.11 **Manage problem solving activities**
5.13 **Analysis and synthesis**
6.2   **Teaching learning and assessment**
7.3   **Knowledge and understanding**

Introduction

Children have been at the forefront of social policy and social work practice developments over the past decade. Within social work, the Victoria Climbié inquiry and more recently the Baby Peter Connelly and Daniel Pelka cases have placed a very public spotlight on social workers' attempts to safeguard children. However, in this chapter we argue that overly concentrating on 'safeguarding' and 'protection' can serve to divert attention away from the pressing need to address other factors that impinge upon children's life chances, such as poverty, poor educational opportunity and health inequalities. As future practitioners who may be working with children, it is crucial that you possess an awareness of this wider societal context that shapes children's lives. This chapter examines the UK's record on children's welfare and looks at the wider social policy developments that shape the environments within which children live. We begin by discussing the emphasis that is placed upon issues relating to child protection in narratives on children's welfare. We then seek to introduce you to a broader conception of children's welfare, focusing upon wider structural determinants that impact upon their well-being.

Child protection or children's welfare?

Hardly a month goes by without some exposé of child abuse or neglect in the media. Clearly some cases achieve more prominence than others, but issues relating to the safeguarding and protection of children dominate media and political commentaries around children's welfare. Regarding the media, our own analysis of newspaper sources found that in the 12 months prior to 23 June 2016, UK national newspapers published more than 1,200 *substantive* articles on 'child abuse', 'child neglect' or 'child protection'. Their Internet-based formats published an additional 1,500. By contrast, during the same period, these same sources only published around 350 substantive articles on 'child poverty', despite its long-standing recognition as a problem that blights the life chances of millions of UK children. In addition, the vast majority of 'child poverty' articles were published in 'highbrow' broadsheet newspapers and their online equivalents, whose circulations are far lower than 'opinion-forming' tabloid newspapers. Thus the *Guardian* and the *Independent Online* featured 70 articles each on child poverty, whereas the influential *Daily Mail* and *Mail on Sunday* only published four (two of which were devoted to questioning the existence of child poverty!).

To an extent, the emphasis the media place upon 'child abuse' is understandable. As we have seen with the Victoria Climbié, Baby Peter Connelly and Daniel Pelka cases, the tragic circumstances surrounding many child protection cases are newsworthy. These three child deaths were the subject of detailed public inquiries, generating a huge amount of media, political and public interest. Indeed, the names of the children concerned are now recognisable to even those with the most fleeting knowledge of social policy and social work. As Franklin (2014, p29) notes, *The roll call of the children involved is unforgettably imprinted on society's collective memory.* When we wrote the previous edition of this text in 2012, the Baby Peter Connelly case alone had already been the focus of over 2,500 substantive national newspaper articles. The Daniel Pelka case has generated similar levels of press interest since his death in 2012. By June 2016, it had been the subject of around 750 national newspaper articles, and almost 300 articles on newspaper Internet formats. Naturally, the horrifying catalogue of neglect documented in the reporting of such child death cases has the propensity to shock, and it is easy to see why child abuse as an issue resonates with the general public and politicians.

Nor, of course, should we underestimate the extent of child abuse and neglect, or their seriousness as problems. As Lord Laming's (2009) report showed, on 31 March 2008, 29,000 out of 11 million children in England had child protection plans in place and 37,000 were the subject of care orders. Laming also estimated that in 2007/08, 55 children were killed by their parents or somebody known to the child. Since then, the numbers of children on child protection plans has increased – to 62,200 in 2015 (Department for Education, 2016). The number of children the subject of care orders has also grown, to 42,030 in 2015 (Zayed and Harker, 2015). Children also continue to die as a result of neglect and harm.

Clearly, it is a tragedy when any child is put at risk, seriously injured or dies unnecessarily as a result of neglect or intent to cause harm. However, the cumulative emphasis placed upon child protection by the media, social commentators and politicians helps to create and sustain the impression that extreme child abuse and neglect are *growing* problems, and indeed are *the* most important issues affecting children's welfare. There are two points to be made here.

Firstly, this impression is contradicted by evidence showing that significant improvements have been made in tackling the worst forms of child neglect. As Polly Toynbee pointed out in the wake of the Baby Peter Connelly case:

> *. . . the number of children killed has fallen steadily – down 50 per cent in England and Wales since the 1970s . . . Britain was fourth worst among Western nations in the 1970s. Now it is among the best: only four countries have fewer child murders per million. Compare America, where child murders have risen by 17 per cent since the 1970s.* (Toynbee, 2008, p35)

The number of child killings has continued to fall since Lord Laming's report was published. Between 1 April 2013 and 31 March 2014, thirty children died as a result of either neglect or a non-accidental injury perpetrated by a parent or carer in England, a 45 per cent decrease since 2007/08 (OFSTED, 2015). Again, when any child dies under such circumstances, it should not be considered anything less than an appalling, unacceptable tragedy. However, this should not be allowed to detract from the fact that the overall trajectory of such deaths is downwards. The UK's child homicide rate has also fallen significantly over the past decade. Taking a longer term view, since the 1980s there has been a 69 per cent decrease in the five-year average rate of child deaths caused by assault or undetermined intent (Bentley et al., 2016).

Secondly, the 'skewed' focus upon abuse and neglect means that other narratives, such as those which emphasise the damaging impact of poverty, poor educational opportunity and health inequalities on children's welfare are 'crowded out'. The promotion of children's welfare is reduced to a concentration on 'abuse' and 'neglect', with little space given to the possibility that poor outcomes for most children are a result of structural problems that are largely beyond parental control. We are left with a one-sided account that ignores a whole range of other crucial variables that impact upon children's well-being. The continued existence of these endemic social problems does, some argue, represent a form of 'abuse' that is actually far more harmful to children than the physical dangers they face from parents, relatives or strangers. Lavalette and Ferguson (2009), for example, argue that:

> *. . . children in Britain continue to face all manner of societal abuse. The evidence shows that Britain, in comparison to other economically advanced countries, is failing its children. It also shows that the lives of poor and working class children are worse, more restrictive and more dangerous than their middle class peers on every front.*

The media, the welfare state and child protection

In the section above, we hinted at the disproportionate emphasis the media place on child abuse, neglect and protection when they publish stories on children's welfare. However, it is not just the media's over-concentration on these issues that is potentially problematic. We also need to assess whether the nature and content of the material published impact upon how issues relating to children's welfare are perceived. Likewise, it is important to consider whether the way the media report child neglect cases may influence the way people think more generally about the legitimacy of the welfare state and its impact upon recipients of services.

In fact, the media's portrayal of child abuse and neglect is rarely balanced. As with the reporting of welfare news generally, there is a tendency to focus on the more lurid, scandalous elements of stories, in a way that undermines support for the principles underpinning welfare. The impression given is that of a welfare state that corrupts families, destroys personal responsibility and acts to the detriment rather than the benefit of children's interests. Analyses into the media's portrayal of welfare news have shown that this picture is not inadvertent or accidental; rather it is part of an orchestrated attempt to manage welfare news in a way that corresponds with the media's own material interests and ideological allegiances.

The media and 'welfare'

Studies conducted into the media and welfare emphasise the extent to which media organisations tend to look for certain 'triggers' when choosing what issues to cover, focusing on aspects of stories that are most likely to boost sales, and/or which reinforce their own ideological positions. Newspaper editors, for instance, are well aware that lurid headlines sell newspapers and they carefully filter their welfare-related news accordingly. A link to crime, fraud and/or sex and an ability to apportion blame will increase the likelihood of publication, as will the ability to identify 'villains' and link issues to wider social ills (Brindle, 1999). As one journalist who specialises in welfare-related news stories has put it:

> A good story – contrary to popular social work belief – is not about some worthy policy development, practice initiative or social services personality. It is about raw emotion, disagreement between professionals and, best of all, culpability. (Fry, cited in Brindle, 1999, p43)

The reporting of social policy issues is also shaped by the ideological predications of particular news corporations. As Franklin (2014, p32) argues, hostile reporting of social policy-related issues certainly offers the prospect of good copy, a circulation spike and enhanced profitability, but other political imperatives are at work here. UK newspapers, least of all the tabloid variety, are not renowned for their sympathy for either welfare recipients or welfare professionals. Those in receipt of state welfare are invariably portrayed as selfish scroungers, fraudsters and feckless deviants, while those who administer services (including social workers) tend to be depicted as self-serving, 'bungling', politically correct bureaucrats. This portrayal of welfare recipients has a long historical pedigree and despite it invariably being based upon inaccuracies, partial truths and wildly inflated generalisations, it continues to resonate with the wider public (Golding and Middleton, 1981).

The media and child protection

In this context, it is easy to see the appeal of child abuse, neglect and protection stories to news editors. They invariably hit all the 'triggers' that constitute a 'good' welfare story, providing lurid, compelling, sensational copy that appeals to the more voyeuristic instincts of their readers. There are, for example, no shortages of 'villains' to blame, whether these are the 'evil' perpetrators of abuse, or the 'neglectful' social workers who are said to have failed in their duty to protect children. On this latter point, Warner (2013, p217) has shown how in the aftermath of Peter Connelly's death, social workers were cast as *cold-hearted bureaucratic folk devils*, targeted by the press for their alleged lack of competence or 'common sense'. As we saw with our discussion of the 1945 Dennis O'Neill case in Chapter 4, hostile media coverage of child protection social work is not a new phenomenon, and the media furore that followed the death of Peter Connelly should not be seen as *particularly* novel. It followed a similar pattern to that which emerged in the wake of the deaths of Maria Colwell (1973) and Victoria Climbié (2000), and is representative of what Greenland (1986, p164) has described as the *peculiarly British sport of social worker baiting* within the media. As with these previous high-profile child protection incidents, the complexities and nuances of the Peter Connelly case were side-lined, as tabloid newspapers held social workers culpable for the tragic event, initiating *a campaign of vengeance and vilification directed at those who gave their professional lives to assisting and protecting children* (Jones, 2014a, p1). Indeed, Butler and Drakeford (2011, p199) argued that in this particular case the press engaged in *entirely new levels of irrationality*, where the *worst excesses of tabloid reporting woefully and reprehensibly wove a web of meaning around a child's death, largely for their own political purposes*. Likewise, Warner (2014) accused the media of *manufacturing dissent*, a process which served both its publishing interests and its ideologically motivated desire to undermine support for the welfare state and the social work profession.

Accompanied by powerful, inflammatory rhetoric, such narratives have gained resonance, and the social work profession is now frequently accused of embracing a 'liberal political correctness' which leaves practitioners too willing to excuse and sanction the irresponsible behaviour of feckless 'dangerous' parents. In her post-Baby Peter review of child protection undertaken on behalf of the Coalition government, Eileen Munro (2011, p124) commented on the difficulties such *one-dimensional* media interpretations of child protection work generate for practitioners. This negative, blame-seeking approach is, she argues, counterproductive, contributing to a besieged, *less safe* child protection system that lacks public confidence. She also points to the collapse in morale among practitioners engendered by the negative imagery that surrounds the profession. Certainly, as we observed in Chapter 1, survey evidence suggests that many children and families social workers are experiencing heightened levels of stress and 'burnout', a trend corroborated by official workforce data, which shows that only around half of England's children's social workers now remain in post beyond five years, and that 45 per cent of those leaving the sector are under the age of 40 (Department for Education, 2016b). Today, the average social work career is less than eight years, compared to 16 for a nurse and 25 for a doctor (Department for Education, 2016c).

Media reporters also often seek to link child abuse and neglect to wider social malaise, and the claim is often made that particular cases of abuse or neglect are representative of the much wider problem of declining morals or the 'broken society'. As Warner (2013) argues, newspaper coverage presented Peter Connelly's death as being symptomatic of the emergence of *an imagined dangerous, contaminating underclass*, whose welfare-induced fecklessness needed to be countered by closer surveillance and moral regulation by social workers. In this sense, as we have already hinted, the media's coverage of child protection cases can also often be structured in a way that links into the anti-welfare bias of particular newspapers, adding to their appeal to editors. The reporting of the high-profile Shannon Matthews case was fairly typical in this respect. Shannon's mother, Karen Matthews, had faked the kidnapping of her daughter, allegedly in order to profit from a reward when her daughter was found. The media reacted with predictable outrage when it discovered that Karen had numerous children while 'on welfare'. As has happened in previous cases, 'welfare' was seen to lie at the heart of Britain's 'child abuse problem'. Melanie Phillips (2008, p12), a columnist in the *Daily Mail*, claimed the case was *but the latest of a series of child abuse horrors which have left people aghast at Britain's culture of brutishness and its link with welfare dependency.* It was clear, according to Phillips, that *child benefit, and all the multifarious other welfare incentives to irresponsibility, are intrinsically linked to the emergence of households where, in truth, civilisation has given way to barbarism.* As the following extract on the Baby Peter Connelly case from *The Times* illustrates, such interpretations of child abuse are not uncommon in even the more 'serious-minded' sections of the media:

> *The unspeakable case of Baby P raises profound questions about the state of Britain today. The welfare state has created some communities with no morality . . . The story of Baby P is one that will haunt Britain for years to come. But for some, its message is already all too clear: that this has become a country where the State's largesse can be a lifelong livelihood; where parents can have as many children with as many partners as they please without feeling obliged to care for any of them.* (*The Times*, 2008, p37)

This portrayal of child protection cases has a significance that stretches well beyond social work practice. As we have suggested, the 'incompetence' and 'political correctness' of social workers themselves are often the target of such articles, but more often than not it is the welfare state itself that is in the 'eye of the storm'. In this sense, we can perhaps see the appeal of this interpretation of child abuse and neglect to neo-liberals, who are ideologically committed to the retrenchment of state welfare. It seems to provide corroboration to their claims that welfare is a morally corrupting influence, which seduces recipients into lives of deviancy and dysfunctionality. Indeed, what more shocking justification for retrenching welfare can there be than the claim that it contributes to child abuse and neglect? The policy-making implications of this kind of an approach are clear. Cuts in social security to families are thus portrayed as being necessary and in the interests of society, families and children themselves:

> *Rather than encouraging social cohesion, indiscriminate welfare weakens the bonds that should hold us together. In the climate of dependency, initiative is sapped and enfeeblement rewarded . . . Our addiction to welfarism . . . has restricted economic growth, fueled mass*

> *unemployment, trapped people in poverty and dependency, increased births outside marriage and fostered a culture of crime and corruption . . . Disturbingly, children from broken homes are over-represented in official reports of child abuse and are more likely to be drawn into crime . . . The present degraded approach is not helping anyone: not the poor, nor taxpayers, nor wider society.* (Bartholomew, 2015a)

In relation to social work practice, progressive, community development and family support-based initiatives are dismissed as counter-productive distractions from the 'real' role of social work – the policing of 'abuse' and 'neglect'. Clapton et al. (2013, pp803–4) thus point to the emergence of *a pervasive climate of panic relating to child and young person endangerment* which has negatively impacted upon social work practice with children and families. This has *had a detrimental effect on child protection, contributing to a coarsening of attitudes towards families in child protection work, a retreat from preventative practice and a deterioration in relationships between social workers, service users and members of the public more generally.* Rogowski (2015, p102) links this development to the demise of the collectivist, welfare-orientated social democratic consensus and the growing influence of individualist, neo-liberal values, with their focus upon pathological interpretations for economic and social difficulties. As neo-liberal reforms gripped the profession, *social workers became investigators, managers . . . designers of surveillance systems, rather than consultants and parents became objects of enquiry; the move was essentially one from therapy and welfare to surveillance and control.* At the same time, we have seen growing political support emerge for a radical overhaul of social work training, and for a renewed focus to be placed upon the need for social workers to be equipped to detect and address the immoral behaviour of 'feckless' families and their 'feral' children (see Cunningham and Cunningham, 2014)

As we discuss below, there is no empirical evidence linking welfare dependency with 'abuse'. Nonetheless, this interpretation is now rarely challenged in the mainstream media or by large sections of the public, whose critical faculties have become desensitised by the dramatised presentation and shocking images associated with particular tragic cases. We would, though, caution you to view this interpretation of child abuse and neglect through a more critical lens. The assumptions that seem to underpin it, that the best way to promote children's welfare is to reduce the financial support available to needy families and to adopt a more disciplinary, moralistic form of social work, are clearly problematic.

Child neglect and welfare

Claims that child neglect and abuse are a consequence of 'lavish', over-generous welfare are simply not borne out by the evidence. As the Child Poverty Action Group argued in response to media suggestions of a link between the Baby Peter Connelly case and welfare dependency, *there is no evidential basis for suggestions that the welfare state has made such appalling cases more common*:

No domestic correlation exists between the number of benefit claimants and infanticide.
Internationally, there is no evidence linking countries with the best welfare provision to
higher rates of child abuse and infanticide. The legacy of the welfare state is the protection
of millions of children from suffering caused by homelessness, hunger, sickness and disability.
Without the welfare state child protection would be far worse. (Green, 1999, p37)

In fact, contrary to popular perceptions, the UK's benefit system is one of the least generous among all developed capitalist countries. UK families are therefore afforded far less social and economic protection than their counterparts in other comparable nations and this is one of the key reasons that the UK has one of the worst child poverty records levels of all developed capitalist counties. Internationally, the link between child poverty and poor levels of child well-being is widely acknowledged, pointing to the conclusion that more welfare (not less) could provide the panacea to improving children's welfare in the UK (we expand on this theme in more detail below).

Finally, if there was a correlation between generous welfare support and child abuse, we would expect to find soaring rates of neglect in Scandinavian nations, where welfare really is set at relatively generous levels. This is not the case. Indeed, as we discuss later, research shows that Scandinavian countries are characterised by the world's highest levels of child well-being.

In the next section we want to broaden our analysis of child well-being, moving away from a focus on 'abuse' and 'neglect' towards a more rounded appreciation of the many different factors that can impact upon outcomes for children. As the United Nations Children's Fund (UNICEF) argues, any effective assessment of child well-being must involve a much broader analysis of factors other than 'safeguarding' and 'protection', and include other indicators such as poverty, educational opportunities, health status and risk behaviours (UNICEF, 2016).

Child well-being in the UK

You would be forgiven for thinking that the UK has a strong record in terms of the provision it makes for children's welfare, given the multitude of measures and procedures that exist to safeguard and protect children from physical harm. Indeed, some commentators argue that our children are 'too protected' and 'mollycoddled' and that their development is seriously hampered by a combination of risk-averse social policy and the 'paranoid parenting' of overbearing, anxiety-ridden parents. These two mutually reinforcing traits are said to have created an environment which has frustrated and stifled children's sense of adventure and independence (Furedi, 2002). Certainly, as we have already discussed, as a society we do place a disproportionate emphasis upon the need to protect children from harm, and this does have wider implications, not least for social policy and social work practice.

However, in this chapter we are seeking to move beyond a narrow conception of children's welfare which sees it as being primarily about 'safeguarding' and 'protection'. If we adopt a much wider definition of child well-being – such as that utilised by UNICEF – we find that the UK's record is far from adequate. Indeed, comparative welfare studies have consistently shown it to be one of the worst in the developed world. UNICEF has published a number of influential studies ranking countries according to their records on securing child well-being, most notably in 2007, 2013 and 2016. Each of these has positioned the UK below most comparable nations. Indeed, in its landmark 2007 study the UK occupied the bottom place in the organisation's league table of child well-being in 21 developed OECD nations. This and subsequent UNICEF studies have been based upon an analysis of a number of social and economic indicators in each country, including:

- lack of material well-being or child poverty;

- health and safety of children;

- children's educational well-being and opportunities;

- children's risk behaviours.

We examine the UK's record on each of these four indicators below.

Lack of material well-being or child poverty

According to UNICEF, poverty and material deprivation are key factors that detrimentally affect children's lives. Poverty, more than any other variable, presents *a decided and demonstrable disadvantage* to children because it is so closely linked to other social problems:

> *Poverty . . . affects many aspects of child well-being in many well-documented ways: particularly when prolonged, poverty has been shown to be likely to have an effect on children's health, cognitive development, achievement at school, aspirations, self-perceptions, relationships, risk behaviours and employment prospects.* (UNICEF, 2007, p39)

International surveys have consistently shown the UK to have one of the developed world's worst child-poverty records. UNICEF's (2000) *A League Table of Child Poverty in Rich Nations* placed the UK 20th out of 23 in its child-poverty rankings, with only Italy, Mexico and the United States having worse records. A follow-up UNICEF (2005) survey of poverty in 26 'rich' nations found that the UK had the 20th worst record. In all, 27 per cent of children were living in households with below 60 per cent of median income (the internationally accepted definition of poverty chosen), compared with 7.5 per cent in Norway, 8 per cent in Finland and 9.2 per cent in Sweden. The latest child poverty data indicates a worsening situation in the UK, with 29 per cent of children (3.9 million) living in poverty in 2014/15 (McGuiness, 2016), an increase of 200,000 on the previous year. Moreover, the UK's record remains one of the worst in the European Union (EU). For instance, under the EU's broader measure of child poverty and social exclusion, which combines income poverty data with data relating to childhood material deprivation and levels of work insecurity within families, 31.3 per cent of UK children were suffering from or at risk of poverty and social exclusion in 2014. This compares to 11.9 per cent in Norway, 14.5 per cent in Denmark, 15.6 per cent in Finland, 16.7 per cent in Sweden, 17.1 per cent in the Netherlands, 19.6 per cent in Germany and 21.6 per cent in France (Eurostat, 2016a).

Internationally, there is a broad consensus over the notion that poverty has a profoundly harmful effect on the immediate and future life chances of children. Hence, the importance of combating child poverty is enshrined in the Article 27 of the 1989 UN Convention on the Rights of the Child (UNCRC), which states that *children should have access to a standard of living adequate for their physical, mental, spiritual, moral and social development*. Article 11 goes on to stipulate that children should have a right to *the continuous improvement of living conditions*. The inclusion of these clauses in the UNCRC, both of which emphasise the need to maintain children's relative living standards, reflects a growing international recognition of the detrimental impact of poverty on children's lives. The UN argues that this poverty is morally unacceptable and that 'rich' nations such as the UK should develop poverty reduction strategies. As UNICEF argues, it is *fundamental to shared concepts of progress and civilisation that an accident of birth should not be allowed to circumscribe the quality of life* (UNICEF, 2000, p3).

All UK governments elected since 1997 have claimed to share these concerns and a series of child poverty strategies *have* been developed. For example, the previous Labour government's commitment to eradicating child poverty by 2020 was based upon an acknowledgement of its harmful impact on children's lives. Labour ministers described child poverty as one of the most corrosive issues facing the country, and before leaving office Gordon Brown's government passed a Child Poverty Act (2010) committing it and future governments to a target of reducing relative child poverty to less than 10 per cent by 2020. In Opposition the Conservative Party supported the passage of this Act (see our discussion of child poverty in Cunningham and Cunningham, 2014). Hence, senior neo-liberal Conservatives, such as the Conservative Prime Minister, Theresa May, claim to share Labour's concerns about the extent and nature of child poverty:

> *Eradicating child poverty is an ambitious but important aspiration for any Government of this country. Not only is it an economic imperative, as no advanced economy can afford to waste the potential of so many of its citizens; more importantly it is a moral imperative, as no decent society should allow children to grow up in poverty. Let us be clear that poverty exists in 21st century Britain, and for some communities it is the norm and not the exception. That situation is shameful and destructive.* (May, cited in Commons Hansard, 20 July 2009, Vol. 496, c611)

The Social Mobility and Child Poverty Commission (2015) (now the Social Mobility Commission), whose task it is to monitor levels of child poverty in the UK, has also sought to illuminate the hardship and distress that lie behind the UK's child poverty statistics:

These numbers hide the day-to-day tragedy of child poverty, from the effects of low-quality and insecure housing, through a lack of new, quality clothes that other children take for granted, to unhappy and anxious early years. Child poverty imposes a lasting burden. When doors to opportunity are closed off early in life, the chance to do well as an adult is much reduced.

These assertions are supported by the findings of a number of surveys, which serve to confirm the debilitating impact poverty has on children's educational, social, physical and emotional well-being in the UK. They are also reflected in the Coalition government's *Child Poverty Strategy 2014–17*, which at the time of writing still provides the framework for government thinking on child poverty. *Whilst some children thrive despite the poverty they grow up in*, the *Strategy* states, *for many children growing up in poverty can mean a childhood of insecurity, under-achievement at school, poor health and isolation from their peers* (HM Government, 2014, p11).

However, while there is something of an academic and political consensus over the negative consequences of child poverty, there is little agreement as to its causes, or the solutions that should be adopted to reduce its incidence and tackle its symptoms. We will examine these differences later.

Health and safety of children

The UK's record on securing the health and safety of its children – assessed by a comparison of indicators related to deaths from accidents and injuries (including murder and violence), infant mortality rates and low birth weights – is more mixed. Interestingly, its record on deaths from accidents and injuries is very good. Indeed, in its league table of child deaths from intentional and unintentional injuries, the European Child Safety Alliance (2012) ranks the UK third out of 27 European countries, with only Sweden and the Netherlands having better records. The UK is only one of four countries, the others being Sweden, Germany and the Netherlands, to have reduced the incidence of deaths from unintentional injuries to the remarkably low level of fewer than 5 per 100,000. These findings corroborate the point we made earlier about the UK's relatively good safeguarding record on reducing child deaths.

However, the UK performs poorly on a whole range of other child health indicators, such as low birth weights and infant mortality. In the UK, 7 per cent of babies weighed less than 2,500g at birth in 2013, whereas the equivalent rates for Iceland, Finland, Sweden and Norway were 3.7, 4.1, 4.3 and 4.6 per cent respectively (OECD, 2016). As UNICEF (2007) notes, low birth weight has been linked not only to increased risk to life and ill-health in the early stages of life, but also to longer-term cognitive and physical development.

The UK's infant mortality rate also lags behind that of many other developed nations. The infant mortality rate is one of the most commonly used and widely accepted indicators of child health. It reflects a basic provision of the Convention on the Rights of the Child, which calls on all countries *to ensure the child's enjoyment of the highest attainable standard of health, including by diminishing infant and child mortality* (UNICEF, 2007). The UK's relatively high levels of infant mortality are, therefore, deeply concerning. Its rate of 3.9 per 1,000 live births in 2014 was almost twice that of Iceland's (which was just over 2 per 1,000) and almost twice as high as other Scandinavian countries such as Sweden and Finland (both with rates of 2.2 per 1,000) (Eurostat, 2016b). According to the Royal College of Paediatrics and Child Health, if the UK's infant mortality rate was the same as Sweden's, 1,951 fewer UK children would die each year (Wolfe et al., 2014).

Research summary

The links between infant mortality and material well-being

In England and Wales alone, 2,517 children died before reaching their first birthdays in 2014 (Office for National Statistics, 2016). All the evidence suggests that these deaths do not occur 'randomly' and that there is a direct correlation between infant mortality and poverty. Infant mortality rates across the UK are not uniform – they vary geographically and by social class. For instance, in 2013 the infant mortality rate for babies with fathers in lower-paid 'routine' occupations (7.5 per 1,000 live births) was around five times that for those in higher paid managerial occupations (1.5 per 1,000 live births) (Office for National Statistics, 2015a).

Regarding geographical variations, infant mortality rates are significantly higher in deprived areas than in non-deprived areas. In Birmingham, where 56.2 per cent of the population reside in areas of high deprivation (i.e. they live in the 'most deprived' quintile), the infant mortality rate is 7.2 per 1,000 live births. By contrast, in nearby Shropshire, where only 2.7 per cent of the population live in areas of high deprivation, the infant mortality rate is just 3.3 per 1,000 live births. If Birmingham's infant mortality rate was the same as that of Shropshire's almost 200 infant lives would be saved each year (Public Health England, 2016). Just to put this into context, this is more than six times the numbers of children who died as a result of either neglect or a non-accidental injury perpetrated by a parent or carer in England in 2014. Of course, the patterns identified here are not unique to the West Midlands or England and similar trends can be found in almost every geographical area and town and city across the UK.

All the evidence, therefore, points to infant mortality and low income or poverty being strongly linked. Indeed, the strong association between poverty, inequality and poor infant and child health is now so well established it is beyond refute. In recent decades, the Black Report (1980), the Health Divide (1986), the Acheson Report (1998) and the Marmot Report (2010) have all pointed to the fact that poverty kills children prematurely. Moreover, each of these 'landmark' studies rejected pathological, behavioural explanations for high levels of infant mortality in deprived areas, highlighting the need for concerted action to be taken to tackle the structural causes of social class inequalities in health, such as low incomes, poor housing, unemployment and work insecurity. As the Marmot Report (2010, p9) argued:

> *In England, people living in the poorest neighbourhoods, will, on average, die seven years earlier than people living in the richest neighbourhoods . . . Health inequalities result from social inequalities. Action on health inequalities requires action across all the social determinants of health . . . These serious health inequalities do not arise by chance, and they cannot be attributed simply to genetic makeup, 'bad', unhealthy behaviour, or difficulties in access to medical care, important as those factors may be. Social and economic differences in health status reflect, and are caused by, social and economic inequalities in society.*

In this sense, as Wolfe et al. (2014, p18) argue, *Social and economic policy do matter to children's chances of survival . . . Social policy can save lives.* Indeed, the Department of Health (2007) has long acknowledged this. Its *Good Practice Guide* for reducing infant mortality emphasises the need to tackle child poverty and to *provide adequate financial support for families.* This approach is supported by virtually all the research that has been undertaken into infant mortality rates in particularly deprived areas, which suggests that tackling poverty – by improving incomes – is the most effective mechanism of cutting infant deaths.

Educational opportunity and well-being

Educational opportunity is another key indicator of child well-being. Once again the UK's record on this is poor. UNICEF's (2013) league table of educational well-being ranks the UK's performance as 24th out of 29 developed nations. A key contributory factor in this low ranking is the UK's relatively high level of educational inequality. In fact, research has consistently shown that the UK's education system is characterised by significant social class variations in attainment. Poor children tend to perform less well academically and gain fewer educational qualifications than their more affluent peers. Indeed, the evidence suggests that poverty impacts upon children's cognitive abilities well before school age, and clear differences between the poorest fifth of children and others are evident when children are as young as three (Goodman and Gregg, 2010). Inequalities in educational attainment in the UK become more pronounced once children attain school age, continuing to deteriorate as they progress through their school careers. At age 11, 25 per cent of children from the poorest fifth of families fail to achieve the government's expected levels at Key Stage 2, compared to only 3 per cent of children from the most affluent fifth (Goodman and Gregg, 2010).

Poverty continues to blight the opportunities of children at secondary schools. The receipt of free school meals is often seen as an indicator of disadvantage, since eligibility is based upon parents' entitlement to means-tested income support. How, then, do the educational attainment rates of children receiving free school meals compare with those who do not? In the UK, the data consistently show that children who receive free school meals are far less likely to achieve five A*–C grade GCSEs (including Maths and English) than those who do not receive free school meals. In 2015, only 33.1 per cent of children in receipt of free school meals in England did so, whereas the equivalent figure for non-free school meal children was 60.9 per cent. However, under-attainment at GCSE level is not just a phenomenon affecting children who are *currently* entitled to free school meals. The Department for Education has developed a wider 'disadvantage index', classifying children as 'disadvantaged' if they have claimed free school meals in the previous six years, or have been looked after for at least one day, or are recorded as being adopted. Here, a similar pattern of inequality prevails, with only 36.7 per cent of 'disadvantaged' pupils in England achieving five or more GSCEs (including Maths and English), compared to 64.7 per cent of their non-disadvantaged peers (Department for Education, 2016d). Research also shows a clear correlation between areas of income deprivation and poor levels of educational attainment. For example, only approximately 43.6 per cent of children living in England's most deprived areas receive five A*–C GCSEs (including English and Maths), compared with 74.5 per cent of those living in the least deprived areas, an alarming 30.9 percentage point difference (Department for Education, 2015).

The UK also performs poorly on many other indicators of educational well-being, including the percentage of 15–19s remaining in education. Only around 74 per cent of 15–19 year olds in the UK are involved in full- or part-time education, considerably fewer than their peers in most other OECD countries. In Belgium, 93 per cent of children are involved in full- or part-time education, and numbers approaching 90 per cent can be found in Germany, France, Sweden, Finland and Norway. The percentage of UK 15–19 year olds who were not in education, employment and training (NEET) is also worryingly high. UNICEF (2013) ranks the UK's NEET record as 24th out of 28 European nations. In all, almost 10 per cent are NEET, compared with less than three per cent in Norway and Denmark and less than five per cent in Germany and the Netherlands. As UNICEF (2013, p19) states, *Research in different countries has also shown associations between NEET status and mental health problems, drug abuse, involvement in crime, and long-term unemployment and welfare dependence.*

Children's risks and behaviours

UNICEF (2013, p23) describes children's 'risks and behaviours', such as diet, exercise levels, substance misuse, experience of violence outside the home and teenage pregnancy, as *critical to the present and future well-being of children*. Once again, the UK's record on such indicators lags behind that of many other developed countries. Regarding diet, almost 40 per cent of UK children fail to eat breakfast each day, compared to just 15 per cent of children from the Netherlands and around 25 per cent in Denmark, Sweden and Iceland. Recent UK-based research suggests that this may underestimate the scale of childhood food insecurity. The

All-Party Parliamentary Inquiry into Hunger in the UK (2014, p10) found that one-quarter of pupils *routinely* arrive at school hungry, negatively impacting upon their ability to fully benefit from their education. The key causes of this hunger are *delays and errors in the processing and payment of benefits, the sometimes heavy-handed issuing of benefit sanctions by Jobcentre Plus, a sudden loss of earnings through reduced hours or unemployment, the absence of free school meals, the accumulation of problem debt or, for some, even a lost purse,* and not neglect on the part of parents. The proliferation of the number of children reliant upon food charity also serves as testimony to the UK's worsening record on food security for families. According to the Trussell Trust (2016), one of the UK's networks of food banks, almost half a million children relied upon its charity for their sustenance at some point in between April 2015 and March 2016.

Teenage pregnancy is understandably seen by UNICEF as another key area of risk for children's well-being. *Giving birth at too young an age,* UNICEF (2013, p23) argues, *puts at risk the well-being of both mother and child. The mother is at greater risk of dropping out of school, of unemployment, of poverty, and welfare dependence – so helping to perpetuate disadvantage from one generation to the next. The child is also at greater risk – of poverty, of poor health, and of underachievement at school.* As with many of the other indicators of child well-being we have discussed, the UK's teenage conception rate is considerably worse than most other developed countries. Despite some improvement since the late 1990s, the UK's rate of around 30 per 1,000 live births is significantly higher than the Netherlands, Denmark, Sweden, Norway, Finland, Germany and France, all of which have rates of less than 10 per 1,000 live births. In fact, UNICEF's league table of teenage fertility in 29 developed nations places the UK third from bottom, with only Romania and the United States having worse records.

Research summary

Material disadvantage and teenage pregnancy

The links between material disadvantage and teenage pregnancy are now well established. As with infant mortality rates, there is a close link between the incidence of teenage pregnancy and area deprivation. The Labour government's Social Exclusion Unit (1998) estimated that teenage pregnancy rates in the poorest areas in England were more than six times those found in the most affluent areas. This pattern continues to hold true. Hence, between 2009 and 2011, the highest under-18 conception rates could be found in Blackpool (58.5 per 1,000 women aged 15–17) and Middlesbrough (58 per 1,000 women aged 15–17). Blackpool is ranked the 6th most deprived out of 324 English local authorities, whereas Middlesbrough is ranked the 8th most deprived. By contrast, the lowest levels of teenage pregnancy were found in Rutland (11.7 per 1,000 women aged 15–17) and Waverley (12.4 per 1,000 women aged 15–17), which are among England's least deprived local authorities (they are ranked 305th and 321st respectively)

(Office for National Statistics, 2014a). Data on the social backgrounds of teenagers who become pregnant seem to confirm the link between teenage pregnancy and income. One estimate suggests that the risk of becoming a teenage mother is almost ten times higher for a girl born into an unskilled manual family than a professional one (Cater and Coleman, 2006).

International comparative data on teenage pregnancy provide further corroboration of the links between poverty and teenage pregnancy. As Wilkinson and Pickett (2010) have shown, the highest teenage pregnancy rates are found in those nations with the highest levels of poverty. Hence, the UK and the US have particularly poor records. By contrast, countries with the lowest levels of teenage pregnancy, such as Sweden, Denmark, Norway and the Netherlands, are those that are characterised by much lower levels of inequality and poverty.

Activity 7.1

In this group activity, we want you to discuss among yourselves the following questions.

- How surprised are you at the UK's record on children's well-being?
- Do you think a consideration of such issues is of relevance to you as students wishing to work in a welfare or social work-related field?
- Linking back to our discussion of ideologies in Chapters 3 to 6, briefly try to sketch out how you might think a neo-liberal explanation for the UK's poor record on child well-being might look like. How might this differ from a social democratic interpretation?

Comment

Many of our students are often surprised when confronted with this child well-being data. To an extent, this is understandable. The UK is, after all, the world's fourth richest nation and hence it should be in a position to ensure that its children's social and economic needs are well catered for. However, children born in the UK are more likely than those in most other developed countries to die in infancy and to suffer from low birth rates, they engage in more risk behaviours and are also far more likely to be brought up in families that are materially poor.

An understanding of this broader context of child well-being is crucial to you as future social workers and welfare practitioners. On a practical level, on graduating many of you will be seeking to discourage vulnerable children from engaging

(Continued)

(*Continued*)

in risk behaviours that you know will detrimentally affect their life chances and opportunities. You may also be working with disaffected young people who are finding it difficult to engage with education, training or employment. In addition, many of you will undoubtedly encounter children who are living in materially disadvantaged families. As individuals who have chosen to pursue a social work or welfare-related career, you must be curious as to why it is that children in the UK are more likely to be affected by these problems than those in most other developed countries. In short, you should be interested in these issues because they are directly relevant to your chosen career path.

We would, however, go further and argue that as future practitioners you have a duty to consider the wider environment within which the children you may be working with live their lives. Welfare and social work with children are concerned, primarily, with improving outcomes for children, and hence it would be negligent to ignore the many different variables that can affect their life chances and opportunities. Embracing this broader conception of child well-being can, of course, have important implications for practice. It may, for instance, lead to a questioning of the overarching emphasis that seems to be placed upon abuse and protection in debates on children's welfare, to the exclusion of other equally important factors.

Competing explanations for children's poor outcomes: neo-liberalism versus social democracy

In the discussion below we examine two contrasting interpretations that have been advanced to account for the UK's relatively poor record on child well-being. The first is essentially a neo-liberal approach, which sees it as a consequence of welfare-induced dysfunctional patterns of behaviour within certain families. The second interpretation, which has more in common with social democratic approaches, seeks to draw attention to the impact of wider structural inequality on children's opportunities and life chances.

A neo-liberal approach to child well-being

The publication of reports drawing attention to the UK's relatively poor levels of child well-being have naturally generated considerable alarm among politicians. Following the publication of UNICEF's first league table of child well-being in 2007, David Cameron (2007), the former Conservative Prime Minister, then leader of the opposition Conservative Party, described the findings as *a clear call to action*. Cameron's analysis mirrored that of other conservative commentators, drawing strongly on traditional neo-liberal interpretations of social ills. The UK's poor record was, he argued, a consequence of an over-generous, bloated, administratively lax welfare system, which had sapped individual responsibility and encouraged the emergence of an inter-generational dependency culture, which had:

- encouraged the growth of welfare dependent 'dysfunctional' families;
- destroyed the traditional two-parent family.

Subsequent revelations of poor levels of child well-being across the UK have been interpreted in much the way by conservative, neo-liberal-minded politicians, commentators and think-tanks. The neo-liberal-leaning Centre for Social Justice (CSJ) typifies this approach. Created by Iain Duncan Smith, the former Minister for Work and Pensions and architect of some of the most controversial Coalition and Conservative welfare reforms, the CSJ sees 'profligate' welfare as lying at the heart of the UK's child-well-being 'problems', whether this be child poverty, health inequalities, educational failure or teenage pregnancy.

We examine these claims in greater detail below.

The erosion of individual responsibility and the growth of welfare dependency

For many families, Cameron (2007) argues, *welfare has become a way of life – a generational pattern of dependence and unemployment which is a complete denial of the responsibility of adulthood.* Families, he insists, are being seduced into a life 'on welfare' by a system that *has sent out some incredibly damaging signals* and *created a culture of entitlement*. Rather than supporting and nurturing themselves and their children independently through their own initiative, effort and hard work, parents are increasingly expecting the state to perform these functions, with devastating effects on children's well-being. *Quite simply*, he argues, *we have been encouraging working-age people to have children and not work, when we should be enabling working-age people to work and have children* (Cameron, 2012). Cameron's successor as Conservative Prime Minister, Theresa May, also believes that 'welfare' lies at the heart of the UK's poor record on child well-being. *Benefit dependency*, she argues, puts *children and young people at risk*, weakening incentives to work, leaving millions of children growing up in households with relatively low incomes, where access to a benefit income is seen as a 'way of life' (Commons Hansard, 20 July 2009, Vol. 496, c611). From this perspective, welfare is having a morally corrosive impact, encouraging parents to neglect their responsibilities for socialising children appropriately, meaning that they fail to discipline them, or instil in them a sense of right or wrong.

For neo-liberals such as Cameron and May, the psychological impact of this experience is just as damaging as its impact upon material living standards. Children in such families lack effective role models, and hence inherit their parents' dysfunctional, fatalistic outlooks on life. They disengage from education and emerge into adolescence without any sense of responsibility or work ethic, lacking aspiration or hope. This, more than anything, helps explain the UK's poor record on child well-being. Welfare has created a 'culture of dependency', which is passed down from one generation to the next, increasing the likelihood of children engaging in behaviour that is deleterious to their well-being.

This approach has much in common with Charles Murray's influential neo-liberal explanation for the emergence of a so-called 'underclass' in Britain. According to Murray (1999, p26), the welfare state has created a scenario whereby *Britain has a growing population of working-aged, healthy people who live in a different world from other Britons, who are raising their children to live in it, and whose values are now contaminating the life of entire neighbourhoods* (p26). Murray's work inevitably attracts a great degree of controversy, but it has been politically influential. In policy terms, it helped shape the welfare reform strategies of successive Conservative governments in the 1980s and 1990s, which were geared towards cutting welfare and tightening eligibility. Murray's ideas also have much in common with the approach adopted by the recent Coalition and Conservative governments to welfare reform.

Research summary

Frank Field, 'The foundation years' and the Coalition's child poverty strategies

On entering government David Cameron commissioned Frank Field, a Labour MP and long-standing commentator on poverty-related issues, to undertake an inquiry into child poverty. Field is a former director of the Child Poverty Action Group and was previously a vociferous opponent of neo-liberal interpretations for poverty. In particular, he had been a fierce critic of Murray's 'underclass thesis', which he accused of ignoring the structural determinants of social and economic problems (see Field, 1989). However, in recent years, his position has changed. Field is now a proponent of behavioural explanations for disadvantage and social exclusion. This sea change in Field's thinking is reflected in the report he produced for the Coalition, *The Foundation Years: Preventing Poor Children Becoming Poor Adults* (2010), in which he rejected redistributive solutions for tackling child poverty:

> *I no longer believed that the strategy of concentrating on income transfers could achieve the goal of abolishing child poverty . . . Something more fundamental than the scarcity of money is adversely dominating the lives of these children. Since 1969 I have witnessed a growing indifference from some parents to meeting the most basic needs of children, and particularly younger children, those who are least able to fend for themselves.* (p16)

Throughout the report, Field highlights the 'futility' of strategies for tackling child poverty that are geared towards boosting the incomes of the poor. *It is*, he argues, *family background, parental education, good parenting . . . that together matter more to children than money, in determining whether their potential is realised in adult life* (p5). He insists that any 'modern' approach to child poverty *must take into account those children whose parents remain disengaged from their responsibilities* (p15). The report chimed well with the Conservative-led Coalition's desire to shift the focus away from structural determinants of child poverty towards interpretations that concentrated on 'problematic', 'irresponsible behaviour', and the 'perverse incentives' generated by the welfare state. Commenting on the report, Maria Miller, a minister in the Department for Education (2010), stated that Labour's attempts to tackle child poverty by improving incomes had resulted in *5 million people trapped in welfare dependency, a benefits system which actually disincentivises work, and a complete failure to address the reasons behind so many children growing up in poverty.* The report, she insisted, provided ample justification for the Coalition's plans to engage in the most comprehensive and radical reform to the welfare system since its inception.

As well as shaping the welfare reforms that we discussed in Chapter 5, this behavioural interpretation has underpinned the approach to poverty enshrined in the two *Child Poverty Strategies* that have been published since 2010, both of which contain a distinct neo-liberal hue. The most recent strategy, published by the Coalition in 2014, locates the blame for what it describes as *the cycle of poor children going on to be poor adults* primarily with *the poor home environment of the child in poverty.* Poor parenting, substance misuse, welfare dependency, financial mismanagement and worklessness within families, it implies, leads to *under-developed character skills (e.g. social skills, self-esteem, self-reliance)*, and an inter-generational cycle of poverty. As a number of authoritative commentators pointed out, the strategy provides an ideologically biased, partial view of child poverty, because it gives very little attention to its wider structural causes – for instance, high child care costs, welfare retrenchment, involuntary unemployment, disability and discrimination. Most of all, it ignores the problem of low pay. In all, 66 per cent of children in poverty in 2015/16 were living in households where somebody was in work (Child Poverty Action Group (CPAG), 2016). The CPAG (2014, pp4–5) therefore have accused the Coalition of concentrating solely on *individual and family characteristics*, arguing *that a strategy that takes no account of structural factors is unlikely to have enduring impacts on child poverty.* Such an approach, CPAG argued, *is likely to place ever-increasing pressure on low-income parents to take steps at an individual level despite the structural conditions that conspire against them.* The Children's Commissioner for England (2014) also gave a damning assessment of the strategy's interpretation of child poverty.

The strategy focuses on individual and family characteristics which suggest that the cause of poverty is solely the result of individual or family characteristics. A more robust approach would include structural characteristics which make it harder for people to move out of poverty. For example the supply and quality of jobs and/or the levels, availability and accessibility of benefits have a profound impact on the levels of child poverty and longer term social mobility . . . the current draft child poverty strategy has significant gaps that, if left unaddressed, will do little to halt, or even slow, the worrying increase in the numbers of children and young people living in poverty across England.

The government's own Social Mobility and Child Poverty Commission (2015) concurred, accusing ministers of failing to acknowledge either the extent of 'in-work' poverty, or the negative impact of its own welfare cuts. Indeed, it described the failure of the child poverty strategy to acknowledge the impact of the government's welfare reform agenda, which cut working age benefits by billions of pounds, as the *elephant in the room.* Ministers needed to explain *how savings on this scale – equivalent to 13% of the 2014–15 non-pensioner benefit and tax credit budget – can be made while avoiding a sharp increase in absolute and relative child poverty.*

The growth of 'dysfunctional' family units and the 'destruction' of the two-parent family

The welfare state also stands accused by neo-liberals of destroying family life, once again to the detriment of children's interests. 'Profligate' welfare is said to have encouraged an explosion of family breakdown and lone parenthood, which in turn has led to greater levels of neglect and poorer outcomes for children. Underpinning this approach is the view that the traditional, heterosexual two-parent family is by far the most effective means of rearing and socialising children. In the words of David Cameron (2010), *children are more likely to do well when both parents are there for them, together providing the love and the discipline.* Indeed, he goes further, arguing that it is *the poverty of the parent–child experience* generated, in particular, by 'non-traditional' families *that leads to poor child outcomes rather than poverty of a material kind.* Again, Cameron's successor, Theresa May, agrees with these sentiments:

> *Britain has one of the highest rates of family breakdown in Europe. There is widespread evidence showing the impact that family breakdown can have on a child's outcomes in life. We know, for example, that children who experience family breakdown are 75 per cent more likely to suffer from failed education; 70 per cent more likely to experience problem drug use; and 35 per cent more likely to experience unemployment or welfare dependency.*

Those shocking figures, May argues, *surely provide all the evidence we need to accept that family breakdown is one of the most serious challenges we face* when it comes to improving child well-being (Commons Hansard, 20 July, 2009, Vol. 496, c611).

The notion that lone parenthood is necessarily linked to poor levels of child well-being is an often repeated claim among right-wing commentators and politicians. James Bartholomew (2014, p275), for example, argues that children of lone-parent families are more likely to be depressed, to be emotionally and educationally stunted, to have underage sex, to smoke, to consume drugs and alcohol, to engage in criminal or violent disruptive behaviour, and to be vulnerable to physical and sexual abuse:

*The epidemic of ruptured and never-formed families has . . . caused misery for the children . . .
The lives of such children have been ruined and they, in turn, have damaged the safety and
quality of life of others.* (p281)

As we saw in Chapter 2, this is not a novel argument. Similar claims about teenagers and
other young women 'working the system' and being 'enticed' into lone parenthood by the
prospect of lavish, morally corrupting welfare provision were made in the nineteenth century.
The solutions proposed then – to end public support for lone mothers and 'let nature take its
course' – are not too far removed to those advocated by many neo-liberals today. For example,
Charles Murray's (1999, p127) demand for the elimination of benefits for unmarried women
altogether, and for the state to *stop intervening and let economic penalties occur*, contains more than
a faint whiff of the Malthusian principles we discussed in Chapter 2.

From this perspective, increasing the attractiveness of welfare payments will exacerbate the
problems it is intended to solve and welfare-induced deviant patterns of behaviour will continue to
be passed down to succeeding generations. The solution lies in a radical reform of the welfare state,
involving cuts in support and a reinforcement of the notion of personal responsibility. Once again,
we see links here between past and present debates about the role, function and impact of welfare
provision. Indeed, the similarity between the statements made by neo-liberals today bear a striking
resemblance to those made by the architects of the Poor Law Amendment Act in the 1830s.

Implications for social work

The acceptance of this neo-liberal interpretation for low levels of child well-being in the UK
would clearly have implications for social work training and practice. The sociological and social
policy content of social work courses would be rejected in favour of a more moralistic syllabus
designed to teach student social workers the skills they need to imbue 'deviant' families with
a strong sense of personal responsibility (Whelan, 2001). Hence, in advocating a model for the
future, neo-liberals look backwards: to the late nineteenth and early twentieth-century work of
the Charity Organisation Society (COS). Welfare, and more specifically social work, should be
geared towards modifying behaviour, closely monitoring 'at risk' groups and 'educating' them
in the habits of self-reliance and effective parenting. Indeed, some neo-liberals, such as David
Marsland, have gone further, suggesting that social workers should be provided with powers
to recommend irreversible sterilisation for 'at risk' groups such as alcoholics, drug addicts and
people experiencing mental health problems, who he feels are unfit to raise children effectively.
He claims that this is the only effective way to prevent the abuse and neglect of children whose
parents are incapable of looking after them:

*We have to prevent such people from abusing or gravely neglecting children . . . Permanent
sterilisation . . . is the only way to reduce and control the killing, torture and neglect of our
children. Decisions would be taken by and within the child protection system, involving
social workers, the police and crucially and ultimately the courts.* (Marsland, 2010)

Activity 7.2

In April 2010, a US-based organisation, Project Prevention, was launched in the UK by Barbara Harris. It described itself as an *agency committed to raising public awareness to the problem of addicts/alcoholics exposing their unborn child to drugs during pregnancy.* Like Marsland, it was a vociferous advocate of the sterilisation of drug users. Its tactics involved outreach workers scouring inner cities for drug users and offering them £200 incentives to become 'voluntarily' sterilised. Its sister organisation in the US goes further, offering additional financial incentives to drug users who successfully 'refer a friend' for sterilisation. Project Prevention was eventually forced to cease paying for sterilisations in the UK, due to the controversy they generated and also the opposition of the British Medical Association. However, it continues to fund other long-term birth control techniques for those suffering from substance misuse problems. In addition, it still pays for sterilisations in the US and in a number of developing countries (Project Prevention, 2016). It does, therefore, provide useful case study for assessing the merits of the birth control measures favoured by some neo-liberals such as Marsland.

Like Marsland, Harris has encouraged social workers to embrace her organisation's approach, and to this end, when it first began operating in the UK, Project Prevention distributed leaflets to social service departments in an attempt to educate social workers about the 'benefits' of its work. Sterilisation will, it argued, *reduce the burden of this social problem on taxpayers, trim down social worker caseloads, and alleviate from our clients the burden of having children that will potentially be taken away* (Project Prevention, 2010).

Not surprisingly, the organisation's work generated a good degree of controversy. In one incident, the police were called after its volunteers were found randomly harassing mothers leaving a health centre in Glasgow who were thought to 'look like' people with substance misuse problems. Barbara Harris sought to defend her organisation's strategy:

> *We don't allow dogs to breed . . . We spay them. We neuter them. We try to keep them from having unwanted puppies, and yet these women are literally having litters of children . . . Women have told me about leaving their babies in a shoe-box in a crack den, selling their children to dealers for sex, even leaving babies in the trash – things so bad I can't even tell you . . . I didn't know who I was more angry with – the mothers for having these children or the system for allowing it to happen . . . If you pay a woman not to abuse a child, it's the best £200 you can spend . . . These women have so many children that even if they do get clean they have more children than they can care for.* (Appleyard, 2010, p36)

In this task, we want you to engage in a group discussion about the strategy and aims of schemes such as those organised by Project Prevention. In particular, we would like you to critically analyse its work, and think of a number of reasons why such strategies may be inappropriate and counter-productive. You might want to consider the following questions.

- As future social work practitioners and welfare workers, how comfortable do you feel with the strategies adopted by Project Prevention? How might its strategies conflict with the social work value base?
- Does the 'voluntary' nature of Project Prevention's strategies make them morally acceptable?
- Is there a danger that Project Prevention's work might lead for calls for sterilisation and birth control to be extended to other 'undesirable' groups of people?

Comment

Firstly, with regard to its initial sterilisation programme, although the scheme was 'voluntary', there is the obvious question of whether drug users are in a sound state of mind when asked to make such a radical and (for the most part) irreversible step in their lives. So even if one accepts the validity of the highly contestable principle of 'sterilisation by consent', there is still a serious ethical issue over whether consent in what are often desperate, fraught circumstances can ever be seen as 'voluntary'. As Julian Shearer, the British Medical Association's (BMA's) Ethical Manager asked at the time: *Would the addiction render consent invalid? Is the payment a coercive means of getting people to agree to a sterilisation they would otherwise not contemplate?* (Doward, 2010, p3). Critics feared that drug users coming into contact with Project Prevention ran the very real risk of making fundamental, life-changing decisions that they would subsequently regret, to the detriment of their long-term psychological and emotional well-being.

Secondly, an implicit assumption underpinning Project Prevention's policy of sterilisation seemed to be that drug users are 'incurable' and cannot be trusted to be responsible parents in the future. What this ignores is that many drug-using parents often reduce their misuse, or often completely cease misusing drugs. Many inevitably go on to have children, providing them with caring and stable environments. Indeed, according to Martin Barnes, Chief Executive of DrugScope, *for many parenthood has proved to be the catalyst for change, and been the powerful motivation to seek help with their addiction and other problems in their lives* (Doward, 2010, p3). Recent international research seems to corroborate the view that parenthood significantly improves the success rate of substance misuse treatment, particularly when parents are supported in a holistic, non-judgmental way (Jeong et al., 2015).

Thirdly, Project Prevention's strategies are based upon the flawed assumption that all drug users are not responsible parents. While parenting can undoubtedly

(Continued)

(Continued)

be affected by substance misuse, many children of drug-using parents do live happy, well-adjusted lives. One estimate suggests that around 200,000 to 300,000 children have parents with a serious drug problem in England and Wales and around 41,000 to 59,000 in Scotland (Advisory Council on the Misuse of Drugs, 2011). It is thought that around one half of these live with their parents, with the active support of social services (Forrester and Harwin, 2007). Hence, an approach based upon restricting or terminating the fertility options of drug users not only ignores the fact that addiction is not incompatible with adequate parenting; it also carries with it the danger that attention and resources will be diverted away from the very necessary programmes of support needed by parents with substance misuse problems, exacerbating the difficulties such families face. As the chief executive of the drugs and alcohol charity Addaction argues: *It doesn't deal with addicts who are already parents, it doesn't help people recover and it doesn't offer any positive solution* (Davies, 2010, p11).

Finally, if we accept the principle of long-term birth control or sterilisation in the case of drug users, what rationale have we got for opposing calls from those such as Marsland for it to be extended to other so-called 'undesirable' groups? As Martin Barnes argues: *Where should the line be drawn – women who drink? Women who smoke? Women with mental health problems? Women who themselves have been the victim of abuse?* (Doward, 2010, p3). Perhaps even women living in poverty should have their fertility rights restricted? Bizarre though it may sound, this is the intention of another Project Prevention initiative, which is aimed at sterilising women in Haiti, for no other reason than they are living in abject poverty. *The women in Haiti*, Harris states, *are having children they can't even feed, so why are they getting pregnant?* As an 'incentive' for them to sacrifice their fertility, her organisation intends to offer vulnerable, poverty-stricken women food vouchers (Kleeman, 2010, p14).

Despite Project Prevention's claim that it is altruistically motivated, the ethos underpinning its strategies has much in common with that of the eugenics movement, which was influential in many countries during the inter-war years. As we have shown elsewhere, eugenicists used pseudo-scientific claims to support their assertion that certain groups or races were 'genetically inferior' to those within the 'mainstream'. The dubious 'evidence' they accumulated was subsequently used to justify a range of injustices, from compulsory sterilisation programmes for 'undesirables' in some countries to Hitler's programmes of mass murder of millions in the 1930s and 1940s (Cunningham and Cunningham, 2008). As we have already mentioned, Project Prevention has, reluctantly, temporarily ceased paying for sterilisation procedures in the UK, due to the opposition of the BMA. However, its work in other countries continues unabated, and the organisation has made it clear that it is seeking to influence a shift in the BMA's stance here in the UK.

A social democratic approach to child well-being

We examined the key principles underpinning social democracy in Chapter 4. As we stated there, social democrats tend to embrace structural explanations for economic and social ills. Hence, in explaining the UK's poor record on child well-being, social democrats emphasise causal factors that they believe are largely beyond the family's control, such as unemployment, low family income, poor housing conditions and poverty. Like UNICEF, they believe that poverty, in particular, is one of the key factors detrimentally affecting children's well-being. This is the variable that needs to be most urgently addressed through, for instance, the provision of improved benefits and greater opportunities to families. In advocating a model for the future, social democrats, not surprisingly, look towards Scandinavian countries such as Sweden, Denmark, Norway and Finland. These nations have for many years accepted responsibility for securing their citizens' welfare and their records on child well-being are among the best in the world. In fact, the term 'social democratic' model is frequently utilised to describe the welfare regimes in these countries, out of recognition that their development has been shaped by social democratic principles (Esping Andersen, 1990). The summary below, which provides a brief comparison of various benefits available to citizens in the UK and Sweden, illustrates the generosity of levels of services and provision found in nations characterised by 'social democratic' welfare regimes.

Research summary

A comparison of welfare between Sweden and the UK

Table 7.1 Welfare comparisons

Sweden	UK
In 2016, there was a maximum monthly charge for child care of around £113 per month in Sweden, irrespective of the income of the family, the number of children utilising child care or the numbers of hours utilised. In reality, Swedish parents pay less than this for their child care, since child care costs are capped at between 1 and 3 per cent of income. Hence, a family with income equivalent to £1,000 per week would not be expected to pay more than £30 per week in child care costs. In all, 55 per cent of Swedish children under three and 96 per cent of those aged between three and six are enrolled in formal child care (European Union, 2016).	By contrast, there is no maximum monthly charge in Britain, and in 2015 the average cost of sending just one child under two to a nursery (for only 25 hours) was £115.45 per week. In London, the costs were as high as £152.06 per week (Rutter, 2015).
Swedish parents are entitled to 480 days' parental leave, per child, anytime between children being born and reaching eight years of age. While undertaking their leave, they receive 80 per cent of their previous income for the first 390 days (up to a limit of around £769 per week in 2016). This can be divided between fathers and mothers, and is intended to enable parents to bond with their children and enhance their social, physical and emotional well-being. Parents also receive an additional tax-free 'bonus' of around £1,200 if both utilise the same amount of parental leave, a policy designed to promote gender quality (European Union, 2016).	In contrast to this, UK parents are entitled to apply for 18 weeks unpaid parental leave, per child, anytime between the child being born and it reaching 18 years of age. Employers can turn requests down if they feel it is detrimental to their business interests (UK Government, 2016a).

(Continued)

(Continued)

Sweden	UK
Basic unemployment insurance benefits in Sweden are worth around £145 per week. In addition to this, most Swedish citizens are enrolled in earnings-related unemployment insurance schemes, which provide additional benefits worth between 70 and 80 per cent of previous earnings (up to a limit of around £306 per week in 2016). Hence, many unemployed Swedish citizens receive around £451 per week in support, as well as being eligible for other benefits, such as children's allowances and housing benefits. The intention is to ensure that family incomes are not drastically reduced as a result of unemployment, to the detriment of either adults or children (Nordic Social Insurance Portal, 2016).	In the UK, unemployment benefit is paid at a flat rate and in 2016 this was £73.10 for those over the age of 25. No attempts are made to ensure family living standards are maintained during periods of unemployment. Indeed, the opposite is the case and benefits are kept deliberately low in order to maintain work incentives (UK Government, 2016a).
Higher (university) education in Sweden is free. Students do not pay tuition fees, and there are a range of grants and loans available to support their maintenance costs.	In England, students are required to pay tuition fees. At the time of writing, tuition fees are capped at £9,000 per year, though Theresa May's Conservative government expressed an intention to remove this cap for certain 'high-performing' institutions (HE funding arrangements are different for Scottish and Welsh students). According to one estimate, students attending university in England will owe around £41,000 when they graduate under the existing arrangements in 2016 (Bennett, 2016). Perhaps not surprisingly, recent research suggests that one in three 18–35 year olds who went to university in England now regret doing so due to the debts that they have incurred (Shaw, 2016).
The pension system in Sweden is earnings-related and designed to provide a decent retirement income for pensioners. For those on average incomes, compulsory pensions provide Swedish citizens with more than half of their pre-retirement income when they retire (56 per cent) (OECD, 2015). Social care for elderly citizens is also largely free in Sweden and only 4 per cent of the cost of elderly social care is met by patient charges (Sweden.se, 2016). Again, the intention is to maintain the previous living standards of recipients, a key feature of the Swedish welfare state.	The UK's state pension is a flat-rate benefit, which provides single pensioners who retired after April 2016 with just £155.65. Those retiring before April 2016 receive a basic state pension of only £119.30 per week. The OECD (2015) estimate that those pensioners who have previously been on average incomes receive around one-fifth of pre-retirement income when they retire. Unlike Sweden, social care in England is means tested and anyone with savings or assets (including the value of their home) of more than £23,250 is expected to pay for the full costs of their care. Moreover, as we show in Chapter 10, those with lower levels of savings and assets can invariably only receive support if they have high needs.

Many of our students express surprise at the generosity of the level of welfare provision in Sweden. The high rates of taxation needed to fund such services should, they tell us, have a stifling effect on the Swedish economy. The standard rate of income tax in Sweden is just over 50 per cent, compared with the UK's 20 per cent, so surely this will impact adversely on entrepreneurial activity, putting the Swedish economy at a competitive disadvantage? In addition, the generous levels of support that are a characteristic feature of Sweden should theoretically encourage idleness and the other dysfunctional behavioural traits that in the UK are said to be linked to benefit 'dependency'. In relation to children specifically, if the neo-liberal interpretations of the UK's poor record on child well-being are correct – and it *is* a result of a lavish, morally corrupting welfare state – then we would expect Sweden to possess an even worse record.

In fact, none of these assumptions turns out to be true. Regarding Sweden's economic performance, the influential World Economic Forum (2015) ranks the Swedish economy ninth out of 133 nations in its Global Competitive Index. The UK's position was 10th. In addition, Sweden, like the other Scandinavian countries, emerged from the recent global recession much earlier than the UK, and in 2015 its economy grew by 4.2 per cent compared to the UK's 2.2 per cent (Eurostat, 2016a). Levels of unemployment are (and have historically been) broadly similar, serving to dispel the myth that generous welfare necessarily encourages 'voluntary' unemployment.

Nor have the generous levels of support provided to families – both couples and lone parents – contributed to 'poor parenting' or a 'culture of irresponsibility'. On the contrary, 'responsibility' is actively encouraged by mechanisms of support that enable citizens to balance their work and family responsibilities. For example, good-quality, cheap child care and flexible parental leave arrangements enable parents – including lone parents – to remain engaged with the labour market and to support themselves independently. This is reflected in comparative labour market data, which shows that in 2011 only 3.2 per cent of Swedish children in lone parent families were living in workless households compared to almost 50 per cent in the UK (OECD, 2014).

One feature that the UK does have in common with Sweden is a high level of family breakdown and lone parenthood. For example, the divorce rates for Sweden (2.5 per 1,000 population in 2012) are higher than those of the UK (2 per 1,000 population) (Eurostat, 2016c). Levels of lone parenthood are also higher in Sweden. In 2012, 54.5 per cent of births were outside marriage, compared to 47.6 per cent in the UK (Eurostat, 2016e). However, Sweden is not characterised by the poor levels of child well-being that senior UK Conservative politicians, such as David Cameron and Theresa May, claim are associated with 'family breakdown'. As we have already seen, Sweden's record on child well-being is among the best in the world. What this suggests is that neo-liberal claims that there is a direct and definite correlation between lone parenthood, family breakdown and poor outcomes for children are incorrect. The experiences of Sweden (and other Scandinavian countries) imply there is not necessarily a link between family structure and poor outcomes for children. When support mechanisms are put in place to enable all families to balance work and family life responsibilities (such as affordable child care, flexible parental leave schemes and income transfers), family structure becomes a far less relevant factor in determining children's material and social well-being.

Relevance to the UK?

Social democrats have long argued that we have much to learn from the way Scandinavian countries organise their welfare provision (Mishra, 1984). The welfare policies adopted by Scandinavian nations are seen to provide a viable, working 'alternative' to the failed, socially divisive neo-liberal policy prescriptions that have been implemented in the UK. In relation to children specifically, Scandinavian countries' excellent records on child well-being are seen to be a direct result of their distinctly social democratic approach to welfare. More than anything else, it is this that explains their high ranking in international league tables on child welfare.

By contrast, the UK's relatively poor record on problems such as infant mortality, teenage pregnancy and the high number of youngsters who are NEET can be traced to its equally poor record on material well-being. In short, the UK suffers from a high incidence of these problems because it also has relatively high adult and child poverty rates. These claims are supported by international evidence which shows that societies that are characterised by greater income equality, less poverty and well-funded, generous welfare states possess the world's best child welfare records (Wilkinson and Pickett, 2010). From this perspective solutions should focus upon improving the opportunities and incomes of families living in deprived areas. Rather than cutting already low levels of benefits, a strategy that will exacerbate the difficulties such families face, welfare policies should be targeted at providing them with the incomes, support and opportunities they need to lift them out of poverty. Neo-liberal claims that the welfare state is to blame for enticing individuals and families into a state of feckless dependency are therefore dismissed. Governments should follow the Scandinavian, social democratic model and provide citizens with greater opportunities to balance work and family life responsibilities. More, rather than less, state intervention is thus required.

Implications for social work

Social workers would also have an important role to play in any social democratic strategy designed to tackle the underlying causes of poverty-linked problems. The nature of social work practice with children would, though, have to change. In particular, more resources would be needed to ensure that children's social workers are liberated from the intensive 'protection' and 'safeguarding' work that currently dominates their caseloads. Because they are currently understaffed and overwhelmed with work, social workers naturally focus on what is, in reality, the most pressing and immediate issue – protecting the most vulnerable children from harm. However, this is a resource-led, crisis-response approach, which is shaped by a policy environment that has consistently denied the profession the resources necessary to undertake truly effective, preventative social work with children and families. Social democrats, therefore, would argue in favour of a greater injection of resources into children's social work in order to 'free up' practitioners to engage in crucial, preventative welfare-related work that their current workloads preclude them from undertaking.

Surveys suggest that significant numbers of practitioners would support such a programme. In fact, as we illustrated in Chapter 1, many social workers have expressed frustration at the way resource constraints make it extremely difficult for them to engage in community-based, preventative welfare work with children and families. They feel that they are forced to crisis-manage overstretched child protection cases, and are unable to engage in the progressive welfare work that they know will prevent less urgent cases from escalating into more serious ones. The following comments, made by one children's social worker in BASW's 2014/15 Social Work Survey, were representative of those made by many others who replied to the association's request for information:

> *The team is really struggling to do everything that is required. It means that less serious cases are not being dealt with properly and a lot of our interventions are when there is a crisis. Working in these conditions is difficult and heart-breaking for our team who want to have the time to help each child to the best of our abilities but unfortunately time does not allow.* (Children's Social Worker, South East) (Munro and Liquid Personnel, 2015, p18)

Similar issues were raised by other children's social workers who responded to BASW's survey. The ability of practitioners to engage in preventative work was, many stated, being challenged by the need to deploy nearly all their resources into child protection and high-level statutory work. Others commented upon how resource and time constraints left them with little time to reflect or consider the long-term interests of the children that they work with:

> *Sometimes, I feel like all I do is spend time on catch up, moving from one priority task to another with no rest and time for reflection. It's like I don't have time to even take a breath.* (Children's team manager, North East) (Munro and Liquid Personnel, 2015, p21)

For social democrats, such comments point to the need for a better resourced, more liberating, welfare-focused form of practice with children. Rather than concentrating almost all their efforts upon protection work and 'controlling' 'at risk' groups, the efforts of social workers should instead be geared towards, for instance, ensuring that families have sufficient income and opportunities to meet their needs and requirements. At a national level, they and their professional associations would be expected to campaign for improved, more comprehensive welfare provision for deprived families. At a practice level, one of their roles would be to ensure that families receive their full entitlement to benefits and support, and to direct them to agencies and organisations that can help provide for any needs not provided for by an inadequate welfare system. They might also become involved in encouraging community-led action, helping families in deprived areas to organise their own campaigns for improved welfare provision.

More generally, the welfare state should follow the model of Scandinavian countries and be infused with principles that place a primacy on citizens' welfare needs. This might lead social workers to become involved in a whole range of tasks that are currently performed by unqualified administrators in the UK, few of whom have been trained to consider the holistic, long-term needs of service users. In Sweden, for instance, social assistance benefits are administered by social workers, and this changes the whole ethos of the way they are delivered. Unlike the UK, where provision is highly stigmatised and recipients tend to be treated with suspicion, in Sweden a welfare-first principle predominates. As Jones et al. (2006, p430) argue, the more generous and crucially less stigmatising 'welfare'-orientated nature of Swedish social assistance means the poor are more 'resilient' in Sweden – they are *not made to feel so useless, or so guilty for their plight.* Other studies have shown how particular groups of service users, including children and young people, benefit from this broader conception of social work, which places the welfare service users and their families at the heart of any intervention.

Chapter summary

We began this chapter by drawing attention to the overwhelming emphasis placed upon issues relating to child abuse and neglect in media and political commentaries on children's welfare. As we pointed out, this has led to a scenario whereby children's social work has become all but synonymous with child protection, to the exclusion of other factors that impact upon children's well-being. We have sought to counter this perception and hope that our discussion has encouraged you to embrace a much broader conception of children's welfare than that which you commonly encounter. As we have shown, while it is clearly important for you as students to be aware of issues relating to child protection, your education and training should also encompass an analysis of other factors that affect children's welfare.

Finally, we also hope that our discussion prompts you to think critically about some of the 'common sense' assumptions that tend to govern thinking on welfare in the UK, many of which are based upon inaccuracies, mistruths and popular myths rather than established fact. In this respect, our discussion of welfare in Sweden has perhaps led you to challenge some of your own preconceptions about the welfare state, and introduced you to an alternative welfare model which contributes to very different outcomes to those generated by the UK's welfare system.

Further reading

For a useful introduction to issues relating to the media and welfare see:

Franklin, B (1999) *Social Policy, Media and Misrepresentation.* London: Routledge.

For an analysis that focuses more specifically on media and societal reaction to some of the UK's major child protection cases, in particular the Maria Colwell inquiry, see:

Butler, I and Drakeford, M (2011) *Social Work on Trial: The Colwell Inquiry and the State of Welfare.* Bristol: Policy Press.

The following analysis into the Baby Peter 'story' provides an excellent illustration of the way the media is able to shape societal perceptions of the nature of social work and indeed influence the trajectory of policy and practice:

Jones, R (2014) *The Story of Baby P: Setting the Record Straight*. Bristol: Policy Press

For a first-hand account of the media's attacks on social workers, see Sharon Shoesmith's harrowing account of the climate of fear and blame that saw her hounded from her job following the Baby Peter case:

Shoesmith, S (2016) *Learning from Baby P: The Politics of Blame, Fear and Denial*. London: Jessica Kingsley.

If you are interested in comparative data on children's welfare and well-being, the following influential UNICEF publications are informative, well written and accessible:

UNICEF (2005) *Child Poverty in Rich Countries*. Florence: UNICEF. www.unicef-irc.org/publications/pdf/repcard6e.pdf.

UNICEF (2007) *An Overview of Child Well-being in Rich Countries*. Florence: UNICEF. www.unicefirc.org/publications/pdf/rc7_eng.pdf.

UNICEF (2013) *Child Well-being in Rich Countries: A Comparative Overview*. Florence: UNICEF. http://www.unicef.org.uk/Images/Campaigns/FINAL_RC11-ENG-LORES-fnl2.pdf.

UNICEF (2016) *Fairness for Children: A League Table of Inequality in Child Well-being in Rich Nations*. Florence: UNICEF. https://www.unicef-irc.org/publications/pdf/RC13_eng.pdf.

For an influential introduction to different 'models' of welfare pursued by different countries see:

Esping Anderson, G (1990) *The Three Worlds of Welfare Capitalism*. London: Polity Press.

For a useful analysis of how social policy and social work is organised in other countries see:

Lawrence, S, Lyons, K, Simpson, G and Huegler, N (2009) *Introducing International Social Work*. Exeter: Learning Matters.

More generally, we would recommend you consult the websites of organisations such as the Child Poverty Action Group (www.cpag.org.uk) and the Joseph Rowntree Foundation (www.jrf.org.uk), both of which contain a wealth of information on children's well-being.

8: Youth, social policy, social work and the 'crisis of youth'

The chapter will also introduce you to the following academic standards which are set out in the 2016 QAA social work benchmark statements:

4   Defining principles
5.1   Subject knowledge and understanding
5.3   Values and ethics
5.2   Social work theory
5.5   The nature of social work practice
5.11 Manage problem-solving activities
5.13 Analysis and synthesis
6.1   Teaching learning and assessment
6.2   Teaching learning and assessment
7.3   Knowledge and understanding

Introduction

Young people have always been the subject of social policy and social work interventions. One of the reasons for this is that 'youth' is seen as a formative, but potentially troublesome, 'transitional' period between childhood and adulthood; it is perceived as a life stage which offers great opportunities, but one that is also fraught with potential risks. This view of young people was reflected in the Labour government's influential Green Paper, *Youth Matters*, which set out its strategy for ensuring that all young people achieved their potential. *Life for teenagers*, the Secretary of State indicated, *is full of opportunities, and most take full advantage of them* (DfES, 2005, p1). However, the Green Paper's concern was that, despite the opportunities that were then available, a sizeable minority were still experiencing marginalisation and exclusion. In this chapter we will look at competing explanations for youth exclusion and marginalisation, contrasting neo-liberal 'behavioural' interpretations with social democratic 'structural' ones. We also discuss the trajectory of recent youth-related social policy, in particular the response to the riots in England in 2011, assessing the relative influence of each of these ideological perspectives. We end the discussion by outlining an alternative, Marxist, interpretation for youth exclusion. The chapter begins, though, with an examination of societal perceptions of youth exclusion, and an activity that is designed to elicit your perceptions of 'young people'.

Perceptions of youth

Research suggests that there does seem to be a general agreement about the characteristics and behaviour patterns that are associated with 'youth' and 'young people'. Indeed, it is quite likely that you, yourself, will associate 'youth' and 'young people' with certain features and behavioural characteristics.

Activity 8.1

This activity is designed for use in groups. Here, we want to assess your perceptions of 'young people' in order to encourage you to think about how these might impact upon your future practice. This is important because many of you will be working with and providing services to young people, and it is crucial that you are aware of how your own preconceived perceptions might impact upon your practice.

We want each of you to write down on a piece of paper half a dozen words or phrases that come to mind when you hear the terms 'youth' or 'young people'. It is important that you try to be as honest as possible and, in order to facilitate this, we would suggest that you complete this exercise anonymously, without writing your name on the piece of paper.

Once you have completed this, gather all the separate pieces of paper, shuffle them together and nominate one person to read out the responses.

Comment

Over the years, we have tried this exercise with different cohorts of our own students. Their responses are invariably the same, which suggests to us that the concepts of 'youth' and 'young people' do conjure up certain images in most people's minds. The words and phrases that our students have associated with 'youth' and 'young people' tend to contain an interesting mix of what could loosely be categorised as 'positive' and 'negative' elements. On an ostensibly positive note, they seem to associate 'youth' with 'adventure', 'fun', 'energy', 'excitement', 'freedom' and 'partying'. Young people, our students tell us, are 'lively', 'fast-living' and 'fun-loving'; they are 'active', 'full of life', live 'carefree lifestyles' and have 'few ties'. We describe these words and phrases as having 'ostensibly positive' connotations, because on closer inspection it is also possible to detect a 'less positive' undertone of 'hedonism' and 'risk' within them. For example, for many people the 'freedom', 'energy', 'sense of adventure' and 'carefree' nature of 'youth' is deeply problematic, contributing to a series of risk-taking behaviours that are associated with far more negative undertones and outcomes. Hence, our students also tell us that young people are 'troublemakers', 'thugs', 'out of control', 'selfish', 'immature', 'wild', 'loud', 'temperamental', 'disrespectful', 'moody', 'risk taking', 'lazy', 'impulsive' and 'arrogant'. They also associate young people with 'alcohol', 'drugs', 'sex', 'rebellion' and 'anti-social behaviour'. There is also a tendency to characterise young people into loosely related pejorative groupings, and they are often referred to as 'hoodies', 'chavs', 'yobs' or 'hooligans'.

We suspect that some of your group's comments will not have been too dissimilar to those we describe above. This is hardly surprising, because young people do tend to be perceived in a negative light, and they are increasingly associated with anti-social behaviour, crime and community breakdown. As Muncie (2015, p2) notes, *While 'child' and 'adult' are largely neutral terms connoting what is generally viewed as a normative period in life, 'youth' and 'adolescence' usually conjure up a number of emotive and troubling images.* This is corroborated by opinion poll surveys which indicate a widespread feeling that youth crime and anti-social behaviour are escalating, and that young people are responsible for a large proportion of crimes that are committed. In one such 2006 survey, 62 per cent of respondents stated that they felt that the number of young offenders had increased in the previous two years, while only 4 per cent stated that the numbers had fallen. Respondents to the same survey said that they believed that young people were responsible for almost one-half of all crime committed in the UK (Ipsos MORI, 2006). A more recent survey of public opinion found that 36 per cent of the population felt that crime amongst 16–18 year olds had increased between 1995 and 2015 (YouGov, 2015). Other forms of 'recklessness' among youth were also thought to have become far more common. Half of those of those asked felt that young people's alcohol consumption had increased, and as Table 8.1 illustrates, significant percentages said the same about other forms of negative risk behaviours that tend to be associated with young people.

Table 8.1 Percentage of people thinking that certain risk behaviours associated with young people have increased, decreased or stayed the same between 1995 and 2015

	Increased	Decreased	Stayed the same
Alcohol consumption	50%	24%	15%
Sexually transmitted disease	44%	16%	20%
Pregnancy	35%	30%	22%
Drug taking	56%	9%	21%
Politeness	9%	57%	24%
Truancy	25%	15%	35%
Crime in general	36%	20%	30%

(YouGov, 2015)

To what extent, though, do people's 'feelings' about young people's declining morals accord with the evidence? In fact, such perceptions are contradicted by research. In 1998, for example, more than a quarter of participants in the British Crime Survey felt that young people were responsible for 'most' crime, yet fewer than one-quarter of offenders committing indictable offences in 1998 were aged between 10 and 17 (Halsey and White, 2008). Recent crime data also shows a clear and persistent decline in young people's offending. In fact, the number of proven offences committed by young people declined by 70 per cent between 2005 and 2015. This is reflected in youth justice data, which shows much lower levels of youth interaction with the criminal justice system. Hence, the number of cautions received by young people fell by 81 per cent between 2005 and 2015, from 106,403 to 20,080. In 2007 there were around 110,000 first-time offenders aged 10–17, yet by 2015 the number had fallen to around 10,000. The number of children and young people aged 18 or under held in custody has also fallen dramatically, from around 3,100 in 2005 to approximately 1,100 in 2015 (Youth Justice Board/Ministry of Justice, 2016).

Negative perceptions of young people are also contradicted by research which suggests that most young people are more rather than less positively 'engaged' in society than ever before. The evidence points to a high degree of conformity between young people's aspirations and societal norms, values and expectations. One inquiry into young people's aims and goals in life found that more than nine out of ten agreed that *working hard at school/aiming to do the best you can will help their future success in life*, and a similar proportion thought that having good qualifications/exam results would help their future success (Ipsos MORI, 2010, p4). Indeed, the educational attainment rates of young people – at GSCE, advanced and degree level – are now higher than ever. In the late 1980s less than 30 per cent of young people achieved five or more GCSEs, but by 2011/12 more than 80 per cent did, a development which suggests that predictions about growing levels of 'irresponsibility' among young people may be inaccurate (Bolton, 2012). Other indicators of youth 'engagement' also suggest positive rather than negative trends. For instance, levels of youth volunteering are at unprecedentedly high levels. The National Council for Voluntary Organisations (2016) estimates that 49 per cent of young people participate in volunteering each year. Around 32 per cent of these volunteer at least once a month, making important and positive contributions to the communities in which they live. As Smith (2008, p17) argues, such developments suggest that there is actually *much to celebrate* about the state of 'youth' today.

Why, then, do people's perceptions of young people continue to be shaped by the view that their outlooks and behaviour are increasingly problematic? As we have argued elsewhere, successive media-inspired moral panics around 'youth' have frequently served to reinforce inaccurate, negative stereotypical attitudes about young people (Cunningham and Cunningham, 2014). As Cohen (2006) argues, *Working-class yobs are the most enduring of suitable enemies* of the press. They are, to be blunt, an 'easy target' and when newspaper editors decide to publish sensational, salacious stories about 'feral', anti-social young miscreants they know that they are able to tap into long-standing fears and prejudices about youth. Widespread, sweeping generalisations are made on the basis of the most limited evidence, yet the persistence and regularity of the message means that it resonates. As one government report acknowledged, young people are rarely portrayed in a positive light by the media and this inevitably impacts upon the way they are perceived:

> *Young people are . . . faced with the challenge of growing up in a culture that has widespread negative perceptions of youth. Adults and the media commonly associate young people with problems such as anti-social behaviour – 71 per cent of media stories about young people are negative, a third of articles about young people are about crime . . . Sometimes,*

these views have been an unintended consequence of Government policies to tackle some serious problems affecting the lives of some teenagers. Rather than presenting a positive vision for youth development, national priorities and local services have been organised and targeted around avoiding and addressing problems, such as crime, substance misuse, or teenage pregnancy. While it is right to continue to focus on addressing these issues . . . it {is} also important to be aware of the influence this has on popular perceptions. (HM Treasury and Department for Children, Schools and Families, 2007)

The point made here about public perceptions of young people being influenced by the disproportionate emphasis placed upon the negative aspects of youth by both the media and government is important. Indeed, coming as it does from an official government document, it constitutes something of an admission that social policies have served to reinforce the inaccurate, negative imagery of young people propagated by large sections of the media. The quotation suggests that this has been an unintended consequence of government policy, though many academics would take issue with this. They argue that successive Home Office ministers have pandered to such sentiments, utilising concerns about the 'problematisation of youth' to divert attention away from the structural causes of (and costly solutions to) the problems many young people face. Rather than challenging inaccurate stereotypes, ministers stand accused of embracing them, utilising heightened anxieties about 'youth' as justification for implementing coercive social policies. Certainly, as the influential report published by the Independent Commission on Youth Crime and Anti-Social Behaviour (2010, pp17, 23) argued, senior politicians have not been averse to indulging in sensationalist rhetoric that can only serve to strengthen pathological conceptions of 'youth'. *For many years*, this Independent Commission concluded, *politicians appear to have been caught in a war of words on the basis that public opinion would favour whichever party sounded 'tougher'.* It accused politicians of engaging in an *exceptionally fierce, punitive arms race*, with each party seeking desperately to sound 'meaner' than its opponents on youth crime, *despite sound evidence that it has been falling for the past 16 years.*

A mythical 'golden age' of youth?

Hardly a day goes by without some commentator or politician discussing the decline in the public morals of today's youth, contrasting our current 'worrying' predicament with a previous 'golden age' of harmony and respect. According to Pearson (1983), this view of British history as one founded on stability and decency is deeply ingrained in the self-understanding of the British people and is based upon a number of key assumptions.

- Firstly, it is assumed that public and political concerns over the problematic behaviour of young people are relatively recent in origin. Civility, adherence to the law and an unquestioning respect for authority were, it is claimed, once characteristic features of the British way of life, but these have now given way to a 'deluge' of anti-social behaviour.

- Secondly, it is felt that the customs, laws and regulations that traditionally ensured that young people conformed to appropriate moral and legal boundaries have somehow been diluted or lost, and that this is the principal cause of the exclusion and marginalisation many young people face. There is, it is assumed, a deep malaise at the heart of Britain, one which has led to an erosion of the traditional 'checks' that regulated young people's behaviour.

- Thirdly, it is assumed that it is possible to create conditions that are conducive to the restoration of 'civility' and the rehabilitation of 'youth'.

Many of these assumptions have faced criticism for offering an overly simplified, 'romanticised' view of young people in both the past and the present. However, there can be little doubt that they are largely shared by the general public and policy-makers alike. As we have already seen, many people today agree with the claim that the behaviour of young people has progressively deteriorated. The question of whether young people in Britain are engaging in more anti-social behaviour is now rarely asked – the focus instead is on why this is so. The notion that young people are increasingly uncontrollable and badly behaved is invariably taken as given. All the evidence, we are told, seems to point to a lost 'golden age' of youth.

Activity 8.2

Although we tend to think of the problematisation of youth as being a relatively recent phenomenon, historical research shows this not to be the case. As Pearson (1983) illustrates, successive generations have always identified young people as a threatening 'social problem group' in need of close surveillance and control. In addition, individualised explanations for the difficulties young people face, which locate their causes within a breakdown in young people's respect for authority and in an absence of parental control, have been a regular feature of commentaries around 'youth' for centuries.

In this fairly straightforward task we want you to try to date the quotations below. In order to help you with the task, we have provided you with dates. All you have to do is match the quotation to the correct date! You can find the answers to this task located at the end of the chapter:

c.4000 BC	4th century BC	AD 1274
1900	1960	1977

1. We live in a decaying age. Young people no longer respect their parents. They are rude and impatient. They frequently inhabit taverns and have no self-control.
2. The young people of today think of nothing but themselves. They have no reverence for parents or old age. They are impatient of all restraint . . . As for the girls, they are forward, immodest and unladylike in speech, behaviour and dress.

3. What is happening to our young people? They disrespect their elders, they disobey their parents. They ignore the law. They riot in the streets, inflamed with wild notions. Their morals are decaying. What is to become of them?

4. What are we to do with the hooligan? . . . Every day in some police court are narrated acts of brutality of which the sufferers are unoffending men and women . . . There is no looking calmly, however, on the frequently recurring outbursts of ruffianism, the systematic lawlessness of groups of lads and young men who are the terror of the neighbourhoods in which they dwell . . . The most obvious and popular remedy for this organised lawlessness is that the guilty should be flogged freely.

5. On one point we must all agree. The spirit of bravado or whatever it is called, has led to a wave of senselessly destructive hooliganism that shows no signs whatever of dying down . . . kindly and inspiring efforts to reform the little thugs have, beyond question, been . . . ineffective . . . Unfortunately, there is no question but that, as matters stand, they laugh, often openly at attempts to control them.

6. No group in the community has a more rapidly rising crime rate than young people, especially those in their teens. Burglaries and crimes of violence in particular tend more and more to be committed by younger and younger people.

Comment

We are sure that, like our own students who have undertaken this task, many of you will have found it difficult to identify the correct dates for these quotations. If so, this tells us something about the accuracy of claims surrounding a supposed 'golden age' of youth. As Pearson (1983) has shown, British society has been shaped by a remarkable degree of continuity in terms of its anxieties and fears surrounding 'youth'. While the labels attached to young people may have changed – ranging from the nineteenth-century 'artful dodgers', 'street arabs' and 'hooligans', to their twentieth-century equivalents, the teddy boys, mods, rockers, skinheads and punks – the message has remained broadly the same. Each, in its own time, has been accused of varying degrees of insubordination, depravity and anti-social behaviour, just like their twenty-first-century forebears, the 'chavs' and the 'hoodies'. British history is littered with a liberal scattering of moral panics about youth, and hence it is important to put today's concerns about young people in context. In short, we would caution you against uncritically accepting the notion that we are facing an unprecedented 'crisis of youth', whereby young people are becoming increasingly unruly and disaffected.

Youth exclusion and the 'crisis of youth'

Despite evidence to the contrary, over the last 30 years or so, politicians, journalists and various social commentators have undoubtedly come to the conclusion that 'youth' *is* 'in crisis'. Such concerns cross the political spectrum and tend to centre on debates about 'youth exclusion'. Although explanations for and solutions to youth exclusion differ, it is possible to identify two broad strands of thought in mainstream debates, one which embraces a neo-liberal perspective, the other a social democratic perspective. We examine each of these in turn below, ending the discussion with an alternative Marxist interpretation of youth exclusion.

Neo-liberalism and youth exclusion

Neo-liberal interpretations of the 'crisis of youth' often have a strong moral undertone, with young people, or their families, increasingly being held personally responsible for the difficulties they face. The problems experienced by young people are seen to be largely a result of their own, or their parents', making, sometimes reinforced by an over-generous, perverse welfare system. Welfare, it is argued, has seduced parents and young people into a life of irresponsibility and dependence, and this, together with 'soft', liberal criminal justice policies, is said to have encouraged a host of dysfunctional, deviant patterns of behaviour. From this perspective, the solution to the 'crisis of youth' is quite straightforward. This is to introduce stringent criminal justice policies that will deter delinquent behaviour, while at the same time reinforcing parental responsibility and reducing the welfare available to young people.

Neo-liberal interpretations of youth exclusion are perhaps best epitomised in the work of the American sociologist Charles Murray (1999). In 1989, he claimed to have identified a burgeoning youth 'underclass' in the UK, which was characterised by growing levels of illegitimacy, labour market 'dropout' and criminal activity. 'Welfare' was said to lie at the heart of each of these social problems. Illegitimacy, for example, was said to have risen because misguided social policies had eroded the punishing, but necessary, social and economic penalties that used to be associated with it. Put simply, the provision of benefits meant that the *economic feasibility of raising a baby without the support of a father has changed fundamentally since the end of the Second World War* (p48). Youth unemployment was also said to result from the generosity of welfare provision. Murray insisted that labour market dropout, or 'idleness' among young people, had been encouraged by an irresponsible culture of welfare, which allowed *young men to grow up without being socialised into the world of work* (p41). Murray also maintained that 'liberal' welfare policies had contributed to a proliferation of youth offending and anti-social behaviour. Echoing the architects of the 1834 Poor Law Amendment Act, he argued that welfare-induced idleness provided greater opportunities for young people to engage in criminal activity. In addition, the criminal justice system had been 'captured' by well-meaning but fundamentally flawed rehabilitative values, which meant that crime *has become dramatically safer in Britain throughout the post-war period, and most blatantly safer since 1960* (p45).

Perhaps not surprisingly, Murray's ideas were embraced by ministers in Margaret Thatcher's Conservative government. His explanations for 'youth exclusion' were very much 'in tune' with this government's own ideological outlook, and his claims, which were actually based upon very little substantive evidence, provided justification for the government's plans to reduce welfare. The links between Murray's ideas and the social policies of successive Conservative administrations can be seen in the numerous social security and housing benefit cuts that have affected young people since the 1980s. The assumptions underpinning Murray's 'underclass thesis' have subsequently provided the inspiration for a number of UK-based neo-liberal social policy commentators, who have adopted an identical position (Marsland, 1996; Bartholemew, 2014 and 2015b). A number of conservative-leaning research institutes also embrace neo-liberal interpretations for youth exclusion, including the Institute of Economic Affairs, CIVITAS and the Centre for Social Justice. Like Murray, they argue that the solution to youth social exclusion lies in coercive, targeted interventions designed to deter and control the inappropriate, 'deviant' patterns of behaviour that lie at its heart. The focus of attention (and intervention) is on a relatively small group of 'recalcitrant' young people and their families, and little attempt is made to understand the underpinning economic and social structures that constrain their lives.

Media and political commentaries on the 'crisis of youth' have tended to be shaped by similar neo-liberal principles, which point to its allegedly pathological, behavioural causes. What is needed, from this perspective, is less 'welfare' and 'care' and more 'control'. Indeed, it is 'soft', 'caring' social-democratic-inspired social policies and social work interventions that are said to be responsible for the 'crisis of youth'.

Activity 8.3

The following comments, taken from an article in the Express newspaper, are fairly typical of the media's representation of young people. After reading the extract, try answering the questions we have posed.

Instead of protecting the public the state acts as the simpering ally of juvenile thugs and bullies. Hand-wringing social workers, enfeebled youth officers, nervous probation staff, dripping-wet judges and cowardly politicians all collude in a destructive culture that allows vicious young criminals to swagger through our streets with impunity . . . The justice system has become so soft because of a malign cocktail of sentimentality and Marxism. Since the Sixties, our civic institutions have been increasingly gripped by a politically correct ideology which holds that young offenders are really the victims of social disadvantage. Therefore, according to this dogma, what they need is constant support rather than punishment . . . It {is} true that a large proportion of delinquents come from broken homes, partly because the vast welfare state provides so many perverse incentives towards family breakdown and mass idleness. (McKinstry, 2011, p 12)

(Continued)

(Continued)

- Why are social workers and other welfare practitioners portrayed in this way?
- How can the above quote be criticised? You may wish to think about some of the young people whom you have come across on placement.

Comment

As we discussed in Chapter 7, the media's portrayal of welfare-related issues is rarely balanced. There is a tendency for it to focus on the more lurid, scandalous elements of stories, in a way that undermines support for the principles underpinning welfare (Brindle, 1999). This is particularly the case with youth-focused stories (Cohen, 2006; Muncie, 2015). The impression given is that of a welfare state that corrupts 'youth', destroys personal responsibility and acts to the detriment rather than the benefit of young people's interests. Hence, young people are frequently portrayed as violent, selfish scroungers, fraudsters and feckless deviants who have been seduced by a lax, over-generous welfare state into a life of irresponsibility and idleness. Welfare practitioners who provide services to young people hardly fare any better. As is the case with the above article, they are invariably depicted as 'left-wing', politically motivated, misguided do-gooders, whose interventions generate more harm than good. Clearly, this is an overly simplistic misrepresentation of young people and an inaccurate portrayal of welfare work with young people, but the regularity and pervasive nature of the media's message resonates with the public. As we have already seen, this interpretation of the 'crisis of youth' has gained a good deal of currency, and opinion poll surveys tell us that it is a view shared by large sections of the general public.

Neo-liberal influence on youth policy?

There can be little doubt that in recent years there has been a discernible shift in both policy and practice to an approach which focuses upon young people's irresponsibility or behaviour rather than their potential social and economic needs. A negative 'deficit' model has predominated, focused on what young people are said to 'lack', whether this be aspiration, motivation, appropriate values or moral decency. By contrast, analyses that point to the structural barriers that inhibit the effective participation of young people in society appear to have been missing from official policy documents. Some, such as Levitas (2005), argue that the social exclusion strategy pursued by Labour governments (1997–2010) was typified by this 'deficit model' approach. She suggests that the ostensibly progressive rhetoric underpinning Labour's approach to social exclusion was little more than a smokescreen, disguising its underlying neo-liberal influences. Structural interpretations for youth exclusion were, she insists, largely marginalised by an agenda that focused attention upon relatively small groups of young people who were deemed to pose a threat to the social order. Hence, Labour's Social Exclusion Unit (SEU) reports focused on issues such as truancy, youth homelessness, teenage pregnancy and young people who were NEET, prioritising concerns about behaviour rather than material hardship. Where references to structural inequality were made – as in its *Teenage Pregnancy* report – these were effectively obscured by the behavioural recommendations of the reports and the pathological rhetoric subsequently utilised by ministers (see Cunningham and Cunningham, 2008 and 2012, for discussions of Labour's social exclusion strategy).

Youth policy has followed a similar neo-liberal trajectory since 2010 under the Coalition and Conservative governments. Nowhere was this more evident than in the Coalition government's response to the series of riots that swept across Britain in 2011. The media and political responses to these riots warrant a detailed analysis because they illustrate the extent to which ideology, rather than research evidence or pragmatism, continues to shape key elements of youth policy.

Research summary

The riots in England in 2011

Between 6 and 10 August 2011, a series of riots and acts of civil disobedience broke out across England. The all-party House of Commons Home Affairs Select Committee (2012, p3) described the disorder that took place *as unprecedented in the modern era*. In the ensuing disturbances, five people were killed and billions of pounds worth of damage was caused, as the initial protests in Tottenham, North London, spread to approximately 66 locations in numerous towns and cities across England (Kelsey, 2015). As the Home Affairs Select Committee noted, a significant factor in igniting the initial spark for the riots was the Metropolitan Police's handling of its fatal shooting of Mark Duggan, a young black male from Tottenham. However, the precise cause of the rapid *spread* of the civil disobedience across England remains the subject of much debate. For some, including the then Coalition government and the mainstream press, the riots were opportunistic, random acts of mindless, criminal violence, committed by gangs of a-social, feckless youths. Echoing Charles Murray's language, Kenneth Clark (2011), the then Justice Secretary, described the riots as an *outburst of outrageous behaviour* by a young *feral underclass*. Kit Malthouse, deputy mayor of London with responsibility for the capital's policing, also pointed the finger at irresponsible, *feral* lawless youth who were *looking for the opportunity to steal and set fire to buildings and create a sense of mayhem* (cited in Sparrow, 2011a). The media's interpretation of the riots was broadly similar. The *Mail*'s response was representative of other tabloid newspapers:

(Continued)

(Continued)

> *What we witnessed was despicable . . . it was nothing more than a mixture of mindless criminality and opportunistic materialism. These young people wholly buy into a shallow culture of instant gratification. Oblivious to traditional ideas of hard work and social obligation, they seek to grab what they want, whether it be a new set of trainers from JD Sports or a flat-screen TV from Currys.* (Johns, 2011)

It subsequently became evident that children and young people under the age of 18 only constituted a minority of those arrested – just 26 per cent (Home Affairs Select Committee, 2012). However, this did little to dampen the media's enthusiasm to hold young people culpable for the disorder. Indeed, before long, *all* young people were in the dock, as the riots were portrayed as being symptomatic of a much wider moral malaise within the nation's youth. The riots were, we were told, a generational issue, the result of a 'crisis of youth' on an epidemic scale. *Years of liberal dogma*, railed the *Mail*'s Max Hastings (2011), had *spawned a generation of amoral, uneducated, unparented, welfare dependent, brutalised youngsters*. For the *Express*, this was a wide scale *anti-social uprising by the 'Me Generation'*, and not just a series of random acts committed by a small section of 'lawless youth':

> *It seems that young people from all walks of life have been swept along in the riots, which have tarnished Britain's reputation and left communities facing a clean-up bill running into millions of pounds . . . It is now emerging that many of the accused are not hopeless cases or feral teenagers but people who hold down good jobs, have a decent education and come from upstanding family backgrounds.* (Roycroft-Davies, 2011)

Little evidence was cited to support such claims, but the charge that *all* young people were potential rioters, or at risk of contagion, added to the sense that the nation's youth was in 'meltdown'. *The spectre of nihilistic and feral teenagers, seemingly devoid of any semblance of morality, ransacking shops and torching homes and businesses for their own vile personal gratification* had, the *Mail* stated, *shattered the image of Britain as an ordered and civilised society* (*Daily Mail*, 2011). *The Telegraph* struck an equally apocalyptic tone about the state of the nation's young people:

> *The Tottenham summer, featuring children as young as seven, is an assault not on a regime of tyranny but on the established order of a benign democracy . . . Watch the juvenile wrecking crews on the city streets and weep for all our futures. The 'lost generation' is mustering for war.* (Riddell, 2011)

As we illustrate below, some commentators offered a more nuanced analysis of the cause of the riots, pointing to young people's exasperation over, for instance, growing levels of youth unemployment, poverty and homelessness. However, in his initial response to the riots in the House of Commons on 11 August, the

Prime Minister, David Cameron, dismissed the notion that the young people participating in the disturbances were motivated by anything more than violent, acquisitive thuggery, and he rejected calls for a wider inquiry into the causes of the riots. *This was not*, he insisted, *political protest, or a riot about protest or politics – it was common or garden thieving, robbing and looting, and we do not need an inquiry to tell us that . . . Young people stealing flat-screen televisions and burning shops – that was not about politics or protest, it was about theft.* (Hansard, 11 August 2011, 1075). He elaborated upon this theme in subsequent comments on the riots. *I think there is a danger sometimes*, he stated, *of people seeking very, very complicated answers when there are quite simple explanations . . . These {young} people who were nicking televisions were not complaining about the reform of the Educational Maintenance Allowance or tuition fees. They were nicking televisions because they wanted a television and they weren't prepared to save up and get it like normal people* (D'Ancona, 2011).

This refusal to countenance more complex, structural explanations for the riots was reflected in the tone of media reporting. *Left-wing politicians*, argued the *Mail*, *have cynically sought to make political capital out of the riots, blaming government cuts for the orgy of violence. Labour MPs and activists lined up to make excuses for the thugs, spouting claims that disadvantaged youth had no option but to smash up high streets* (Shipman, 2011). The following comments, made by the *Mail*'s right-wing columnist Richard Littlejohn (2011), typified media responses to claims that the riots may have had wider structural determents:

> *There have been several times this week I've come close to putting my foot through the plasma screen. Frankly, I don't know what's worse: Harriet Harman {Labour's Deputy Leader} on Newsnight disgracefully trying to blame the Tory cuts for this weeks robfest, or the rolling news channels giving airtime to masked criminals . . . The BBC and Channel 4, in particular, have been anxious to portray these violent thugs and looters as victims. We've heard the usual garbage about social exclusion and police hostility to minorities. Every lame excuse has been trotted out, from lack of job opportunities to tuition fees . . . Do me a favour. We're talking about a wolfpack of feral inner-city waifs and strays who spend their time smoking dope, drinking lager and playing Grand Theft Auto on their stolen PlayStations.*

In the House of Commons, Cameron located the blame for the riots upon familiar neo-liberal 'demons' – feckless, irresponsible parents, the welfare state and an allegedly 'lax' criminal justice system:

> *Responsibility for crime always lies with the criminal. These people were all volunteers; they did not have to do what they did, and they must suffer the consequences. But crime has a context, and we must not shy away from it. I have said before that there is a major problem in our society with children growing up not knowing the difference between right and*

(Continued)

(Continued)

wrong. This is not about poverty; it is about culture – a culture that glorifies violence, shows disrespect to authority and says everything about rights but nothing about responsibilities.

In too many cases, the parents of these children – if they are still around – do not care where their children are or who they are with, let alone what they are doing. The potential consequences of neglect and immorality on this scale have been clear for too long, without enough action being taken. As I said yesterday, there is no one step that can be taken, but we need a benefit system that rewards work . . . We need more discipline in our schools; we need action to deal with the most disruptive families; and we need a criminal justice system that scores a clear, heavy line between right and wrong – in short, all the action that is necessary to help mend our broken society. (Hansard, 11 August 2011, c1054)

Over and above that, we must recognise that the responsibility for the fact that some of these children – I use the word 'children' advisedly – are out on the streets rests with their parents. We need parents to take more responsibility for their children, teach them the difference between right and wrong, and point out that this sort of behaviour is completely unacceptable. (c1063)

Of course, the 'broken society' that Cameron refers to in his speech had, for him and other prominent Coalition politicians, resulted from *moral* breakdown, rather than *social and economic* breakdown. As Kelsey (2015, p243) argues, Coalition ministers sought to portray the actions of the rioters as being *symbolic of a sick society that could be cured by Conservative social policy*. On the one hand, this would involve the imposition of harsh criminal sanctions against those arrested in the riots. On the other, it would entail intrusive, targeted family intervention, designed to 'turn around' the lives of what Cameron referred to as the *completely dysfunctional . . . deeply broken and troubled families*, whose children he deemed responsible for the disorder (Cameron, 2011).

The criminal justice response to the riots was rapid and punitive. Around 2,000 arrests had been made within a week of the riots. By 22 February 2012, 4,000 had been arrested, after hundreds of police officers were deployed to scour CCTV and media footage. Those arrested, around half of whom were under the age of 20, were frequently 'fast-tracked' through the courts, and in the febrile political climate surrounding the riots, there was little opportunity given to them or their representatives to plead mitigation. Political and media pressure for judges to 'throw away the rule book' and incarcerate those arrested meant that pre-sentencing reports provided by social workers and probation officers were largely ignored. The following comments were made by two probation officers who were frustrated at the refusal of judges to take into account their views before sentencing:

They did ask for pre-sentence reports but it felt like they were just going through the process but always intended to send them to prison.

There was a blanket approach. I wrote a report proposing a community order but there was no chance and a one size fits all approach was adopted without taking into account individual circumstances. Professional assessments were not listened to so what was the point of asking for a pre-sentence report proposal if you were going to send people to prison for two years. (Cited in Fitzgibbon et al., 2013, p454)

The majority of those found guilty were sentenced to immediate custodial sentences. Bridges (2012) has calculated that these riot-related offenders received 'immediate custody' sentences at approximately three times the rate of those normally found guilty of committing similar offences, and the duration of their sentences were almost four times longer than the 'norm'. As he argued, the courts had *clearly responded to political demands that riot offenders be seen to be severely punished.* Defence lawyers who contacted the *Guardian*'s Reading the Riots project, described the court proceedings as a 'tragic farce'; they were, they reported, *kangaroo courts, dispensing 'conveyor belt justice'* (Bawdon and Bowcott, 2012). The courts have since been accused of engaging in *prosecutorial zeal and judicial abandon*, as pre-riot sentencing guidelines were simply ignored, particularly in relation to young people. Court proceedings were, Lightowlers and Quirk (2015, pp78–9) argue, *akin to show trials, with the district judge addressing the press gallery as much as the defendants*, and no consideration was given to the long-term impact of sentencing on young people's well-being.

In the week following the riots, Cameron announced what would be the Coalition's key non-criminal justice-related social policy response to the riots – the troubled families programme. This coercive, sanction-based form of family intervention would 'turn around' the lives of 120,000 families who Cameron claimed were gripped by a *culture of disruption and irresponsibility that cascades through generations.* Children and young people from these families, he argued, were indeed responsible for the recent disorder, but their corrosive influence was said to stretch way beyond these one-off, spontaneous outbreaks of lawlessness. They, and their children in particular, were *the source of a large proportion of the problems in our society*, costing the taxpayer up to £9 billion per year. Predictably, perhaps, Cameron's interpretation for the 'dysfunctional' behavioural characteristics of these families focused upon the 'morally corrupting' influence of a 'broken' welfare system, which had for too long encouraged and rewarded family breakdown and illegitimacy. Troubled families, including the lawless young miscreants who they spawned, were the victims of *an excess of unthinking, impersonal welfare*; they had *been subjected to a sort of compassionate cruelty . . . smothered in welfare yet never able to escape* (Cameron, 2011).

Cameron's focus on welfare had the inevitable support of neo-liberal-leaning tabloid newspapers, who had already associated the riots with a 'corrupt, 'broken', 'lavish' welfare state. *If anything*, argued the *Telegraph*'s Phillip Johnston (2011), *the biggest problem has been the creation of a sense of entitlement sustained by an overly generous*

(Continued)

(Continued)

(and no longer affordable) welfare system, which expects nothing in return for the benefits dispensed. Meanwhile, the *Mail's* Melanie Phillips reinforced Cameron's claim that 'indiscriminate' welfare was responsible for the proliferation of 'dysfunctional' family units. The *breaking of the family* was *condoned, rewarded and encouraged by the Welfare State*, which *subsidises lone parenthood and the destructive behaviour that fatherlessness brings*. In the immediate aftermath of the riots, an e-petition, which demanded that all rioters be denied access to all welfare support, had received 250,000 signatures, serving to confirm the extent to which attempts to link the riots to 'welfare' had widely resonated (Reeves and de Vries, 2016).

In policy terms, the troubled families programme was influenced by little more than a belief that the roots of the August 2011 disorder (and, more generally, the economic and social problems facing the country) could be solved by 'gripping' 'troublesome' families and forcing them back onto the 'straight and narrow' through a combination of coercion and sanctions, running alongside a series of welfare reforms designed to clamp down on 'shirkers' and the 'feckless'. We have discussed the neo-liberal ideological inspiration underpinning the troubled families programme elsewhere (see Cunningham and Cunningham, 2014). As we pointed out there, the programme was beset by controversy from the outset and it continues to be so.

The programme was not without implications for social work practice either. For example, the introduction of the 'troubled families' initiative was accompanied by a rising tide of criticism of the profession for its supposedly 'liberal', 'hand-wringing' approach towards the difficulties experienced by 'problem families'. There can be little doubt that this criticism was deliberately orchestrated by Coalition ministers, who seemed to have viewed the riots and the 'troubled families' initiative as an opportunity to question the social work value base. For example, Eric Pickles, the Communities and Local Government Minister whose department was responsible for the 'troubled families' programme, sought to justify the scheme by accusing social workers of failing to challenge, and indeed promoting, an 'it's not my fault' culture of excuses among young people and their 'problematic' parents. Social workers, gripped by naive, liberal-minded political correctness had *run away from categorising, stigmatising, laying blame*, something his department's 'troubled families' initiative would, he stated, deliberately avoid (cited in Chorley, 2012). The implication here was clear. 'Traditional' social work values, which emphasised the importance of empathy, non-judgemental and anti-oppressive practice were part of the problem, contributing to the culture of 'irresponsibility' that fuelled the riots, and acting as an obstacle to turning these families around. Young people in troubled families, Pickles insisted, *have got the language, they are fluent in social work*, and the social work profession needs to 'wise up' to the fact that it is being 'taken for a ride' by cunning, manipulative individuals.

How successful has the troubled families programme been? The Coalition government sought to claim that the programme had been an enormous success, suggesting that 105,000 of the 120,000 families targeted had been 'turned around' (Department for Communities and Local Government, 2015b). The government subsequently claimed a success rate of 99 per cent for the programme, arguing that it had succeeded in *getting children back into school . . . and cutting youth crime and anti-social behaviour*, saving the taxpayer approximately £1.2 billion. These claims have been contested. As we argued when the programme was introduced, the criterion for 'turning around' families was so vague and flexible, it was always going to be possible for the government to claim an extremely high success rate, even if no tangible changes had occurred to the circumstances or life chances of families and young people involved (Cunningham and Cunningham, 2014). As Crossley (2015, p6) argues:

> *The 99 per cent success rate of the programme is, in social policy terms, unbelievable. Local authorities, which have been hit by cuts and lost large numbers of staff, have allegedly 'turned around' almost the exact number of 'troubled families' they were required to work with, at a time when those families will potentially have suffered as a result of austerity policies, cuts to local authority services and welfare reforms.*

The National Institute of Economic and Social Research's Jonathan Portes (2015), a former Chief Economist to the Cabinet Office, is equally sceptical, describing the government's claims as *disgraceful*. They were, he argued, simply *making claims that are not true*. This was corroborated in August 2016, when it was discovered that an unpublished government-commissioned audit found that the troubled families programme had, in reality, achieved very little. Indeed, the audit concluded that the £1.3 billion scheme *did not have any discernable impact* on educational engagement, youth offending or employment levels among the children and young people in the participant 'troubled' families (O'Carroll, 2016).

Activity 8.4

Can you think of any criticisms of the neo-liberal interpretation of the riots promoted by David Cameron and his Coalition government? You might want to think about:

- the explanations advanced to account for previous riots in the UK, such as those that occurred in the early 1980s;
- the social, economic and political context within which the 2011 riots occurred.

Was a strategy that focused almost entirely upon the so-called 'pathological' behaviour of rioters and their families likely to get to the heart of the origins of the civil disorder?

Claims that the rioters were motivated by nothing more than hedonistic, mindless hooliganism *were* contested in the aftermath of the 2011 disturbances. The *Guardian's* Gary Younge (2011) argued that *Insisting on the criminality of those involved, as though that alone explains their motivations and the context* was *irrelevant* and *fatuous* (Younge, 2011). Commentators such as Younge pointed to young people's disaffection associated with youth unemployment, poverty, lack of opportunity, problems, they alleged, that had been exacerbated by the Coalition's austerity agenda. To an extent, this approach did chime with the general public's perceptions of the causes of the riots. Although there was also support for the Coalition's claims that 'bad parenting', 'criminality' and 'moral decline' were key factors, 69 per cent of the public felt that poverty was an *important* or *very important* cause of the riots; 79 per cent cited unemployment, 68 per cent policing, 65 per cent government policy and 56 per cent racial tensions (*Guardian*/London School of Economics, 2012). In this respect, the general public showed a willingness to accommodate the kind of 'social democratic' interpretations that emerged to explain earlier serious outbreaks of civil disobedience in the early 1980s.

The riots of 1981

Certainly, the context surrounding the August 2011 riots resembled that which surrounded previous riots that occurred in Brixton and Toxteth in the early 1980s, which, unlike the 2011 disturbances, *were* widely linked to social and economic deprivation and social division. As Newburn (2015, p50) notes, *An economic downturn, relatively high levels of unemployment, a right of centre government embarking on fairly radical reform, and rising levels of general social inequality characterized both periods*. However, the interpretations of these two outbreaks of civil disorder could not have been more different. In 1981, serious efforts were made to uncover and understand the complex causes of the riots by Lord Scarman, who chaired a major, influential judicial inquiry into the Brixton riots. In addition, far more space was given to the dissemination and promotion of explanations that focused upon more nuanced, structural determinants of the disorder (Cooper, 1985, p61).

As Fitzgibbon et al. (2013, p446) observe, the starting point for Lord Scarman's inquiry into the Brixton riots was where did *we*, as a country, fail our younger generation, and what could *we*, as a nation, do to ameliorate the structural causes of the riots. There was little discussion of 'bad parenting', 'family dysfunction' or welfare-induced criminality in the inquiry. Indeed, its analysis provided a tacit acknowledgement that the rioters' actions were based upon a clear set of genuine grievances. Discussing the motivations of the predominantly black youths who took part in the Brixton riots, Lord Scarman highlighted the pervasive levels of racism, discrimination and social and economic deprivation that they had been subjected to:

> *Their lives are led largely in the poorer and more deprived areas of our great cities. Unemployment and poor housing bear on them very heavily, and the educational system has not adjusted itself satisfactorily to their needs. Their difficulties are intensified by the sense they have of a concealed discrimination against them, particularly in relation to job*

opportunities and housing. Some young blacks are driven by their despair into feeling that they are rejected by the society of which they rightly believe they are members and in which they would wish to enjoy the same opportunities and to accept the same risks as everyone else.

Taken together, he argued, these multiple forms of deprivation provided *a set of social conditions which create a predisposition to violent protest.* Indeed, he concluded that in communities where marginalisation and frustration existed on such a scale, *the probability of disorder must . . . be strong.* Lord Scarman was not excusing the actions of the rioters, rather he was seeking to locate them in the context within which they occurred. As he stated, *the disorders in Brixton cannot be fully understood unless they are seen in the context of the complex, political, social and economic factors* that surrounded them. *In analysing communal disturbances,* he went on, *to ignore the existence of these factors is to put the nation in peril* (Scarman, 1981, p15). This is in complete contrast to the Coalition's refusal to contemplate the possibility that the young people involved in the 2011 disturbances may have been motivated by wider, social, economic or political grievances.

Of course, the political context of 2011 was very different to that of 1981, and in part this helps explain the differential in the political and policy response. True, in 1981, Britain *was* governed by a radical, right-leaning reforming Conservative government led by Margaret Thatcher. However, the neo-liberal project spearheaded by Thatcher was still at an embryonic stage in 1981 and neo-liberal interpretations for social and economic ills, such as youth disaffection and exclusion, had not then achieved 'hegemonic status' either among ministers or the general public. 'Hearts and minds' had yet to be won and key neo-liberal assumptions had not yet developed into a new 'common sense' (Hall and Jacques, 1983). While the key pillars of social democracy had been challenged and shaken, they were still relatively intact, hence the space given in the press and political arena to 'social democratic' interpretations of young people's motives for taking part in the 1981 riots. The following comments on the causes of the Liverpool riots made by an Oxford don in *The Times* could not be more different from those published in the wake of the 2011 riots:

> *Riots, Martin Luther King once famously decreed, are the voice of the unheard. It is probable that the Chief Constable of Merseyside is correct to observe that some groups that participated in the disorders did so with criminal intent . . . But it seems equally indisputable that unelequent {sic} though they may have been, the rioters have something to say, and that is about the intolerable circumstances which they have been condemned to endure.* (Waller, 1981)

These sentiments were reflective of the views of many other media commentaries, including those published in tabloid newspapers. To an extent, this 'social democratic' interpretation also shaped both policy recommendations and practice responses to the disorder of 1981. In relation to policy, Lord Scarman called for more job creation, more social expenditure (not less!), and a more concerted effort to tackle social division and discrimination. He concluded his recommendations by quoting US President's Lyndon Johnson's address to the nation, following widespread civil disorder in the US in 1968:

> *The only genuine, long-range solution for what has happened lies in an attack – mounted at every level – upon the conditions that breed despair and violence. All of us know what those conditions are: ignorance, discrimination, slums, poverty, disease, not enough jobs. We should attack these conditions – not because we are frightened by conflict, but because we are fired by conscience.* (Scarman, 1981, p136)

Recently released Cabinet files show that many of Margaret Thatcher's senior ministers were prepared to embrace such 'social democratic' inspired explanations for the riots. Douglas Hurd, the Home Secretary, Kenneth Baker, the Environment Secretary, and Lord David Young, the Employment Minister, all recommended positive government action to improve social and economic conditions and employment opportunities in riot-affected areas. Lord Young, in particular, called for millions of pounds to be spent on overcoming the barriers young black men faced in accessing jobs and developing business start-ups (Travis, 2015).

As we now know, successive Thatcher governments did little to ameliorate the deeply entrenched economic and social problems faced by citizens living in areas such as Brixton and Toxteth in the 1980s. It is also fair to say that there were elements close to the Conservative leadership who interpreted the riots differently Indeed, in the aftermath of the Toxteth riots, Thatcher's Chancellor, Geoffrey Howe, secretly advised her to simply 'write off' Liverpool. *I cannot help feeling,* he stated, *that the option of managed decline is one which we should not forget altogether. We must not expend all our limited resources in trying to make water flow uphill* (BBC News, 2011). Likewise, soon after the Brixton riots, Oliver Letwin, then a young advisor in Thatcher's policy unit, and Hartley Booth, her inner cities advisor, wrote a memorandum infused with neo-liberal and indeed racist undertones. They encouraged the prime minister to reject structural interpretations for the civil disorder, arguing, controversially, that any money spent would do little more than *subsidise Rastafarian arts and crafts workshops*:

> *The root of social malaise is not poor housing, or youth 'alienation' or the lack of a middle class . . . Lower-class unemployed white people had lived for years in appalling slums without a breakdown of public order on anything like the present scale . . . Riots, criminality and social disintegration are caused solely by individual characters and attitudes. So long as bad moral attitudes remain, all efforts to improve the inner cities will founder. David Young's new entrepreneurs will set up in the disco and drug trade.* (Travis, 2015)

Letwin and Booth's 'prescriptions' for the Brixton riots focused upon the need for greater efforts to be undertaken through the law to deter family dysfunctionality, to reinforce personal responsibility, school discipline, appropriate moral behaviour, honesty, and respect for the police among young people.

However, in public at least, Thatcher's Conservative administration gave Lord Scarman's recommendations its emphatic support when it was published, as did the media. In short, there was a much greater willingness to accept suggestions that there was a link between deprivation and social disorder (Neal, 2003). The practice response to the riots was often 'social democratic' in inspiration too. As one probation officer at the time recalls, the riots contributed to the development of a *completely different approach* within the probation service. Probation officers began to take a greater interest in social inquiry reports and research relating to youth exclusion. In addition, concerted efforts were made to make the probation service more representative of the communities it served, and a language of social justice began to permeate the work of probation officers (Fitzgibbon et al., 2013, p448).

Fast forward thirty years to August 2011, and the *political context* could not have been more different. As we discussed in Chapter 5, three decades of neo-liberal consensus had contributed to the ascendency of pathological, behavioural interpretations of social and economic ills. A neo-liberal 'common sense' now prevailed, shaping the ethos of policy and practice, and this, we would argue, shaped political and social policy responses to the 2011 civil disorder. Letwin and Booth's neo-liberal prescriptions for the Brixton riots now had something of a contemporary resonance, in that (racist overtones aside) they were not too dissimilar from Cameron's response to the 2011 riots. It is, perhaps, no coincidence that by the time of the 2011 riots Oliver Letwin had risen to the rank of chief policy advisor to Cameron.

How different, though, was the *social and economic context* facing young people in August 2011 from that experienced by their peers in 1981? In fact, socio-economic data shows that young people across Britain had as much reason to feel disaffected in 2011 as had their counterparts in Brixton and Toxteth. The youth unemployment rate in August 2011 was the highest it had been since comparable records began in 1992. In all, 37.4 per cent of 16–18 year olds (205,000) were unemployed; 30,000 had been so for over 12 months. A further 21.3 per cent of 18–24 year olds (991,000) were unemployed and more of a quarter of these had been without work for more than a year (Office for National Statistics, 2011). At the same time, young people were bearing the brunt of the Coalition's austerity measures, facing cuts to welfare provision and funding reductions to youth services and housing support. In its annual survey of youth homelessness for 2011, the housing charity, Homeless Link (2012, p6) argued that this policy context had created *the perfect storm for an increase in homelessness amongst young people, especially the most vulnerable, and with severe consequences*. In fact, the official rate of youth homelessness by June 2011 had leapt by 15 per cent, the largest year-on-year increase since records began (Centrepoint, 2011). Young people had also witnessed the abolition of the Educational Maintenance Allowance and higher university tuition fees, both of which had prompted widespread demonstrations and civil disturbances in November/December 2010. The anger generated by these changes culminated in around 50,000 school, college and university students laying siege to the Conservative Party's headquarters on 10 November. In a separate incident on 9 December, around 500 young people protesting against increased university tuition fees surrounded Prince Charles' chauffeur-driven Rolls Royce in the West End of London, imploring him to speak out against tuition fees before daubing his car with paint (Cunningham and Lavalette, 2016).

Young people were also among those most affected by the Coalition's intensification of the benefit sanctioning regime, with many finding their welfare support terminated for the most minor of oversights. In 2010/11, a remarkable one in ten Jobseeker's Allowance (JSA) claimants under the age of 25 had sanctions applied to their benefits, often inappropriately, creating enormous hardship and resentment. As the Joseph Rowntree Foundation (2013) argued, there was widespread evidence of *direct or indirect discrimination within the welfare system . . . placing young people at particular risk of financial penalties*. This was corroborated in April 2011, when a *Guardian* investigation revealed that Jobcentre advisors were encouraged to arbitrarily target vulnerable people, including young people, with the imposition of sanctions. This is what one Jobcentre advisor told the newspaper about the ethos that now shaped their day-to-day work:

> *Suddenly you're not helping somebody into sustainable employment, which is what you're employed to do. You're looking for ways to trick your customers into 'not looking for work'. You come up with many ways. I've seen dyslexic customers given written job searches, and when they don't produce them – what a surprise – they're sanctioned. The only target that anyone seems to care about is stopping people's money . . . Saving the public purse is the catchphrase that is used in our office . . . It is drummed home all the time. Feel good about stopping someone's money, you've just saved your own pocket. It's a joke . . . We were told suddenly that {finding someone to sanction} once a week wasn't good enough, we were far behind other offices, and we went to a meeting where they compared us with other offices, and said we now have to do three a week to catch up. Most staff go into work and they're thinking about it from moment one – who am I going to stop this week?. . . The young often fall into it, because they haven't been there long enough, they are generally a major target. The uneducated are another major target. I've seen people with . . . seriously low educational standards and it's easy to exploit them.* (Domokos, 2011, p 1)

A YMCA England (2014, p21) analysis into the intensified use of sanctions on the vulnerable people that it worked with accused the Coalition government of *simply punishing young people*, removing their sole source of income, without any consideration of its impact upon their well-being. The following comments made by its service users help illustrate the human cost of sanctions:

- *I didn't cope, I had no one.*
- *It's how long they left me with no money knowing I was pregnant and had to buy my own food.*
- *I was unable to eat and it was lucky they {the YMCA} could help.*
- *You have a much more negative attitude to life as a whole.*

- *It lost me my home and food.*

- *I had to borrow money just to make ends meet.*

- *I went three months living on food parcels . . . which is really degrading because you lose all your dignity. It's not just physically hard, it's mentally hard.*

In summary, then, the term 'perfect storm' is perhaps an appropriate description of the social, economic and political landscape faced by many young people in August 2011. As Bowman (2014) notes, the promise of social and economic stability and improvement in return for conformity and commitment to being a 'good citizen' had begun to ring hollow for many young people, who saw their safety nets, support mechanisms and opportunities dissolving before their eyes. Indeed, by the end of the year there was a general consensus that young people's aspirations and opportunities had been severely curtailed by the Coalition's response to the recession. By then, 65 per cent of people surveyed felt that it was unlikely that young people would have better living standards and opportunities than their parents. In 2003, only 12 per cent of people had felt this way. This was a remarkable shift in opinion, and illustrative of a wider recognition of the extent to which the changed political climate had impacted negatively on young people's opportunities (Helm, 2011).

While not condoning the behaviour of young people who were involved in the riots, there were those who argued that their actions could not be isolated from this wider political context of austerity and welfare cuts, which had disproportionately impacted upon the nation's youth. The leader of the Labour opposition, Ed Miliband, leaned tentatively towards this interpretation in his response to the riots. He accepted that the disorder represented acts of individual criminality, but argued that the government should seek to understand *the background, the reasons, the causes* that *lead people to feel they have nothing to lose and everything to gain from wanton vandalism and looting.* There was a need to consider *questions of hope and aspiration . . . the provision of opportunities to get on in life that do not involve illegality and wrongdoing* (Hansard, 11 August 2011, c1057).

Within months of the riots, the Ministry of Justice (2012) was lending plausibility to the suggestion that there was a link between poverty, inequality, unemployment, lack of opportunity and participation in the disorder. *Young people appearing before the courts*, it acknowledged, *came disproportionately from areas with high levels of income deprivation.* It found that 64 per cent of young people arrested lived in England's 20 per cent *most deprived* communities. The Ministry's data also showed that the children and young people arrested tended to be characterised by poor levels of educational achievement, thereby hinting at a link between educational inequality, lack of opportunity, disaffection and involvement in the riots. In addition, 42 per cent had been eligible for free school meals, a clear indication that they came from income-deprived backgrounds. Among adults, 35 per cent of those arrested were unemployed, implying a possible link between a lack of work opportunities and participation in the disorder. Subsequent academic research, which has analysed the geography of the riots in considerable detail, also seems to confirm a link between the 'anarchy' of 2011 and economic deprivation, social disorganisation, pre-existing dissatisfaction with the police and political grievances (Kawalerowicz and Biggs, 2015).

Qualitative analysis, in the form of interview statements of those who participated in the riots, also confirms that marginalisation and a perceived lack of opportunity was a key motivation for many. While this is not to suggest that acquisitive opportunism and criminal impulses did not play an important part in the disorder and looting, what it points to is a more nuanced collection of influences. As the *Guardian* and London School of Economics (2012, p5) Reading the Riots research project found:

> *Rioters identified a number of other motivating grievances, from the increase in tuition fees, to the closure of youth services and the scrapping of the education maintenance allowance. Many complained about perceived social and economic injustices. Anger over the police shooting of Mark Duggan, which triggered the initial disturbances in Tottenham, was repeatedly mentioned – even outside London.*

In fact, many of the young people interviewed for the Reading the Riots project expressed a pervasive sense of injustice as being the primary motive that led them to become involved in the disorder. As one Tottenham participant put it:

> *All I can tell you is that me, myself and the group I was in, none of us have got jobs, yeah? I been out of work now coming up two years . . . and it's just like a depression, man, that you sink into . . . . I felt like I needed to be there as well to just say 'Look, this is what's gonna happen if there's no jobs offered to us out there'.* (p25)

Social democracy and youth exclusion

The social democratic perspective to youth inclusion has much in common with this interpretation of the 2011 riots, rejecting many of the assumptions that underpin neo-liberal interpretations of youth exclusion. It sees the 'crisis of youth' as a manifestation of the growing, chronic levels of marginalisation experienced by certain sections of young people. Here, far less emphasis is placed upon the problems caused by young people and more on the problems experienced by them, such as family poverty, poor educational opportunities, inadequate housing provision and an increasingly punitive criminal justice system. Each of these factors shapes the lives of young people, constraining their opportunities for 'inclusion' and inhibiting their ability to achieve their full potential. Social democrats, therefore, point to a need to acknowledge the disadvantaged structural environments that many young people come from and are currently living in, which detrimentally impact upon their ability to secure 'inclusion'. They caution against the adoption of simplistic explanations for youth exclusion which fail to take into account the real difficulties that many young people have faced which may have contributed to the problems they experience.

With this approach, therefore, explanations focus on the far-reaching economic and social trends that have occurred which have made 'youth' a particularly precarious life stage. As Furlong and Cartmel (2007, p8) argue, *changes occurring over the last three decades or so have led to a heightened sense of risk and individualization of experiences of young people.* These include an increasingly deregulated, casualised, insecure labour market which has made it more difficult for young people to obtain good, sustainable, well paid work. Hence, although jobless levels among young people have fallen since 2011, improvements in job creation have not been shared equally and young people are now three times more likely to be unemployed than the rest of the population, the largest gap for 20 years (Boffey, 2015b). In all, 13.7 per cent of economically active young people (626,000) aged 16–24 were unemployed in April–June 2016 (Taylor, 2016).

At the same time, cuts in social housing provision and the promotion of home ownership have led to a boom in the price of houses, forcing many young people into longer periods of difficult, involuntary semi-dependency upon their parents. The impact of these developments has, it is argued, been exacerbated by neo-liberal inspired welfare reforms – in housing and social security – that marginalise or exclude young people from accessing social rights that most other citizens take for granted. For example, most 16–18 year olds are now prohibited from claiming social security and housing benefits and the welfare rights of 18–24 year olds are increasingly being curtailed. As our earlier discussion of the regime which imposes sanctions on benefits illustrated, there has been a more general marked 'coercive' turn in social policy directed at young people. From this perspective, solutions to youth exclusion should focus upon the urgent need for governments to address or reverse these changes, tackling the structural problems that blight the lives of many young people. They should *recognise the cumulative nature of some of the difficulties they encounter, whether these are the multiplier effects of different aspects of social exclusion . . . or the impact of unequal and discriminatory treatment* (Smith, 2008, p3).

While social democrats acknowledge that young people as a whole are disproportionately susceptible to exclusion, certain groups of young people who are thought to be especially vulnerable are singled out as being in particular need. Young people, they point out, are not a homogeneous entity, and some face a series of disadvantages and obstacles which increase the likelihood of their being exposed to a range of social problems and difficulties as they make the transition to adulthood. For example, disabled young people are more likely to experience exclusion than their non-disabled peers. Thus, 28 per cent of disabled 19-year-olds are classified as not being in education, employment or training (NEET), compared to 13 per cent of non-disabled 19 year olds. Disabled young people are also far more likely to have been NEET for longer periods than their non-disabled peers (Delebarre, 2016a).

Young people from minority ethnic backgrounds are also more likely to suffer from marginalisation in comparison with other young people. Hence, in the year to December 2015, the unemployment rate among black and black British 16–24 year olds was 27.5 per cent, compared to 13.1 per cent for their white counterparts. The rate for Asian 16–24 years olds was similarly high – 24.3 per cent (Delebarre, 2016b). Young minority ethnic people are also more likely to be caught up in the criminal justice system than their white peers. A *Guardian* analysis of youth detention found that 40 per cent of children and young people held in the criminal justice system were from black, Asian, mixed race or 'other' minority ethnic backgrounds (Sloan and Allison, 2015). In each of these areas – employment and criminal justice – racial discrimination rather than moral culpability is likely to have been a significant factor in contributing to exclusion. Studies have continually shown that people from minority ethnic backgrounds face discrimination in the labour market and criminal justice system. Indeed, the UK's poor record in these areas was recently highlighted and criticised by the UN Committee on the Elimination of Racial Discrimination (2016), the body tasked with assessing whether or not countries are abiding by their obligations as signatories to the UN Convention on the Elimination of All Forms of Discrimination. In relation to employment, the Committee expressed its deep concerns over the higher rate of unemployment among young (and older) people of African and Asian descent, as well as *the concentration of persons relating to ethnic minorities in insecure and low-paid work* as well as the *discriminatory recruitment practices of employers*. It also condemned the fact that young (and older) African and Asian people *continue to be disproportionately targeted throughout the criminal justice system*.

Care leavers are another group who are susceptible to higher levels of exclusion than other young people, including educational disadvantage and unemployment. In 2013/14, 41 per cent of 19-year-old care leavers were NEET compared to 15 per cent of all 19-year-olds. Care leavers are also more likely to be homeless and experience other housing problems. According to one study, 33 per cent of care leavers experienced homelessness between six and 12 months after leaving care. It is also estimated that 25 per cent of all homeless people have been in care at some point in their lives (National Audit Office, 2015c). Care leavers are also more likely to be criminalised. Indeed, according to the National Audit Office almost half of all young men under the age of 21 who have been in contact with the criminal justice system have had been looked-after children at some point in their lives. Given the difficulties that these young care leavers have faced, and indeed continue to experience, social democrats argue that it would be absurd to hold them responsible for the situations in which they find themselves. Their exclusion cannot be seen in isolation to the other aspects of their lives over which they have very little control. Frequent and abrupt changes in living arrangements, regular interruptions to education, variable standards of care, cuts in funding for care leavers as well as potential histories of neglect and abuse are bound to have an impact on their life chances and opportunities.

Herein, social democrats argue, lies one of the fundamental flaws of the neo-liberal approach to youth exclusion. The real world is far more complicated than neo-liberals imagine, and far more nuanced explanations need to be embraced in order to understand the dynamics that contribute to young people's marginalisation and indeed their frustrations. Many require high-quality, well-resourced, tailored support that recognises the particular difficulties they face in, for example, accessing education and employment opportunities and decent-quality housing provision. Instead, they tend to be treated as a 'problematic' homogeneous 'mass', by a poorly resourced, inflexible, increasingly coercive welfare system that is simply incapable of meeting their complex needs. Solutions, from a social democratic perspective, should not be based around negative, pathological assumptions, which locate the blame for exclusion with vulnerable young people themselves and their families, such as the troubled families programme. On the contrary, there should be an open acknowledgement of the obstacles and barriers that many groups of young people face in securing inclusion. Interventions at an individual level may be necessary in order to enhance, for instance, skills and improve the low levels of confidence of young people. Just as importantly, though, societal change will be necessary and genuine, life-enhancing opportunities should be provided. Good-quality welfare support would also be considered fundamental to any social democratic approach to tackling youth exclusion.

Social workers would also have a crucial role to play in any 'social democratic' solution to the problems faced by young people. In their practice, social workers come across young people who are experiencing difficulty and marginalisation and are consequently ideally placed to help mitigate the difficulties they face. They do, though, need to ensure that their interventions are informed by an understanding of the structural constraints that shape young people's lives and not influenced by negative, value-laden perceptions of their 'culpability'. This is not an easy task. Like other members of society, social workers and welfare professionals are constantly bombarded with narratives and images which locate the blame for young people's marginalisation on the shoulders of young people themselves. As we have discussed in relation to the government's troubled families programme, since 2010 social workers and other welfare practitioners have increasingly been exhorted to embrace more pathological interpretations of social and economic ills. In addition, as Smith (2008) argues, in many scenarios (though by no means all) it is young people's perceived problematic behaviour that prompts social work intervention in the first place, reinforcing the notion that young people themselves are to 'blame' for their situation. This makes it all the more important that welfare professionals are able to challenge common-sense assumptions and acknowledge the fact that the difficulties faced by many young people frequently stem from the disadvantage, discrimination and marginalisation that they have faced or are experiencing. As Smith (2008, p12) states, *The fact that wider society harbours a considerable degree of apprehension and uncertainty about its younger members should not, of itself, lead us to believe that this is based upon a fair or accurate portrayal of the underlying reality of their lives.*

Marxism and youth exclusion

We end this chapter with a discussion of Marxist interpretations of youth exclusion. As we pointed out in Chapter 6, Marxism has enjoyed something of a renaissance recently, and it is worth considering how Marxist approaches to youth exclusion might differ from the two we have already outlined. In fact, Marxists tend to share some of the concerns expressed by social democrats. They too accuse neo-liberals of ignoring the structural constraints that detrimentally impact upon young people's opportunities. However, Marxists see youth exclusion, and the state's punitive response to it, as an inevitable feature of the capitalist economic system itself. Moreover, they accuse social democrats of being naive for assuming that it is possible to reform capitalism into a more humane, progressive system. Capitalism, they argue, is a system which is based upon naked exploitation. It depends upon the fear of poverty to drive people into low-paid, unrewarding exploitative labour, and until capitalism is abolished the marginalisation and exclusion young people experience cannot be fully addressed.

Marxist interpretations of youth start from the premise that the state views young people solely in terms of their future potential as workers, or 'proletarians in the making', who needed to be moulded into acquiescent, mature adult workers. Wyn and White (1997) point out that 'youth' is the *threshold to adulthood* and as such the capitalist state takes a close interest in those experiencing this life stage, seeking to monitor young people's behaviour and shape it in a way which is conducive to the future interests of capital. The state's interventions are therefore designed to socialise young people into becoming future loyal, law-abiding, compliant citizen-workers, and it is in this context that punitive coercive interventions in youth policy must be interpreted. Behaviours that are deemed to contravene bourgeois values, or which are seen as being deemed 'inappropriate' to the effective functioning of capitalism – such as economic inactivity, teenage pregnancy, youth protests or 'misbehaviour' – are accordingly subjected to swift, targeted interventions from the state. However, it is not fear of young people themselves that prompts intervention; indeed, for Marxists, *the popular image of young people presenting a 'threat' to law and order represents young people as more powerful than they actually are* (Wyn and White, 1997, p12). Rather, it is the prospect of a future disaffected, potentially rebellious adult population that compels the state to pay extremely close attention to this particular life stage.

Marxists argue that this desire to instil conformity and an acceptance of the status quo into young people has been a constant influence on youth-related social policy since capitalism's inception. They point to historical research which shows that 'youthful rebellion', whether this be protests over corporal punishment and discipline in schools or demonstrations over youth unemployment and the cost of university tuition, has always been met by a swift, coercive response by the state. For example, in 1972, the Conservative Prime Minister, Edward Heath, reacted to school student protests over corporal punishment and school discipline by instructing MI5, the British secret service, to spy on the pupil agitators and 'disrupt' their political activities. Likewise, in 1985, the Conservative Prime Minister, Margaret Thatcher, condemned a half-day nationwide school pupil strike against the government's Youth Training Scheme, claiming that the pupils' demonstrations *were a clear political act of a totally negative nature*. In these and other instances when school pupils have sought to highlight their genuine grievances – for instance over the Iraq war in 2003 and the abolition of the Educational Maintenance Allowance in 2010 – the state, in the form of the police and education authorities, have moved to rapidly suppress their protests (Cunningham and Lavalette, 2016, p196).

For Marxists, attempts to discipline children and young people are said to have intensified in recent years. According to Jones and Novak (1999), the emergence of youth unemployment as an endemic feature of capitalist societies has led to an intensification of efforts to ensure labour discipline. The potential of youth unemployment to undermine traditional work ethic norms and lead young adults to question the validity of capitalism is too great to be ignored. Punitive social security reforms (such as the regime which imposes sanctions on benefits discussed earlier) and dubious 'training' schemes, such as the Labour's New Deal for Young People and the Conservative's Work Programme, have been the principal means the state has used to force young people into accepting their fate and resigning themselves to the prospect of insecure, unrewarding, low-waged work. At the same time, harsh criminal-justice policies and sentences, such as those applied to those convicted during the 2011 riots, ensure that young people are 'kept in check' and actively discouraged from engaging in active resistance and protest against their marginalisation. In recent years, the trajectory of such policy in the UK has, Jones and Novak (1999, pp64–6) argue, been *unrelenting and peculiarly vicious*, having a marked negative effect on the living standards, opportunities and civil rights of young people:

> *The assault on young people has involved the imposition of new work disciplines, lower expectations in terms of both social security benefits and job security, pay and conditions, and a sexual, social and moral agenda that the neo-liberal project has pursued in the face of both uncertain evidence and immense hardship to some of the most vulnerable of the young.*

This attack on young people's eligibility to support is seen as an attempt to reduce future welfare expectations of citizens in capitalist societies. As, Jones and Novak argue, *The depression of young people's expectations – and especially the expectations of young working-class people – has been a hallmark, even a target, of government policy since 1979* (1999, p64). Marxists argue that instilling in young people a sense of acceptance of their fate will lead them to be more resigned to their future roles:

> *As future generations of adults, parents and workers their experience is crucial in determining what in the future will or will not be considered as acceptable, or at least unchallengeable.* (p66)

The point, for Marxists, is that this coercive direction of youth-related policy is an inevitable and indeed necessary requirement in capitalist societies, whose labour markets are increasingly reliant upon the supply of cheap, amenable, disciplined workforces. From this perspective, a more humane, progressive approach cannot ultimately be implemented and sustained.

The structural constraints of the capitalist system – that is, its need to generate a compliant workforce that is willing, or unable to be unwilling, to engage in exploitative, low-waged work – means that all governments, whatever their political complexion, are compelled to introduce policies that guarantee the requirements of business are met. This is the context within which Marxists interpret policies such as the government's Work Programme and its youth justice agenda, and indeed its response to the riots in 2011. They reject the rhetoric that accompanied the introduction of such policies and initiatives, claiming that they represented little more than an attempt to force young people to conform with bourgeois values and to engage with an increasingly insecure, low-paid, exploitative labour market.

What role then is there for social workers in youth-related policy? A Marxist approach to social work with young people would begin with an acknowledgement that social work practice cannot in itself solve the endemic exclusion they experience. Social workers working with young people can have as their aim the creation of a more fair, just society, but they cannot themselves achieve the fundamental changes that are needed to significantly improve the lives of marginalised young people. As Bailey and Brake (1980, pp7–8) argue, the potential to do this is constrained by the fact that social workers, like their young service users, are *trapped in a social structure which severely delimits their power and hence their ability to initiate significant change.*

This is, however, not to say that there is no role for social workers. Indeed, the early pioneers of Marxist approaches to social work made it clear that their intention was not to underestimate the potential of social work in the 'here and now'. *Our purpose*, Bailey and Brake insisted, *is not to discourage radical students from taking up social work, nor to depress those workers already struggling in contradictions which have not been created by them* (p9). As 'social bandits', or 'noble robbers', social workers have a crucial ideological and practical role to play in mitigating the injustices capitalism imposes upon young people's welfare, while at the same time fighting against the system itself. On the one hand then, they can operate as a 'buffer', alleviating some of the more destructive elements of capitalism by doing their best to ensure that young people's services are delivered in a non-judgemental way that acknowledges the structural constraints that have caused or contributed to their difficulties. They need to move away from a form of practice that has hitherto tended to focus upon the social pathologies of 'defective' youth and embrace a more emancipatory form of youth work that acknowledges the exclusionary barriers that constrain the lives of many young people, restricting their opportunities and contributing to their disaffection (Cooper, 2012). On the other hand, they can seek to undermine capitalism from 'within', operating as 'grit' in the capitalist machine, wherever possible offering recalcitrance, resistance, obstruction (Ferguson and Woodward, 2009, p78), and seeking to encourage an awareness among young people and others of the need to transcend capitalism. This latter ideological/political role is one that is emphasised by Marxists such as Skott-Myhre (2005, p142), who point to *the potential of revolutionary collaboration between youth and adults.* Skott-Myhre argues that 'youth' has always historically been at the vanguard of protest and revolution, and suggests that social workers have a role to play in cultivating this revolutionary potential. Likewise Cooper (2012, p62) argues that youth workers and other practitioners have an obligation to create an environment which encourages young people not only to *express views on the planning and delivery of services that are responsive to their needs but also to reveal aspects of their oppression and to engage in 'acts of resistance'*. Rogowski (2014, p14) recommends a similar strategy when working with young offenders. He calls for practitioners to embrace *politicisation and consciousness-raising strategies*, which inform young offenders about *the societal, structural issues that lie at the root of crime*:

> *For instance, it could be pointed out that issues of boredom and material gain could be resolved by ensuring that adequate, publicly funded, recreational, educational and employment/training opportunities were available to all young people. Discussions could turn to the need for social justice and equality in terms of both opportunities and outcomes.*

Such consciousness-raising strategies, it is hoped, can help channel the frustration and anger of disaffected young people against the capitalist system that lies at the heart of the difficulties they face.

Clearly, there are many professional and organisational constraints which make it difficult for social workers to develop such a liberatory form of practice with young people. As Ferguson and Woodward (2009, p79 and 132) accept, *In the current controlled and controlling climate, such practice can be seen as radical, even subversive*. It can, they acknowledge, *be difficult, and, from an employment point of view, potentially hazardous to practise radical social work in isolation* (p132). Wherever possible, though, practitioners should seek to rise above these constraints, and build alliances with colleagues and like-minded welfare workers in related professions, in order to create a truly emancipatory form of practice with young people.

Chapter summary

This chapter began by challenging some of the more 'common-sense' perceptions surrounding 'youth' and 'young people'. As we saw, the notion that we are witnessing an unprecedented 'deluge' of youth irresponsibility and misbehaviour is not borne out by either historical or contemporary evidence. Indeed, as we stated, there is much to celebrate about the conduct and achievements of young people today. However, 'youth' is a life stage that is characterised by a higher likelihood of exclusion and marginalisation and certain groups of young people do experience particular difficulties. As we showed, different theoretical explanations have been advanced to account for this exclusion, but neo-liberal, pathological interpretations do appear to have been most influential in shaping UK youth exclusion policy.

Further reading

The following, now classic text by Geoffrey Pearson provides an excellent analysis of the history of concerns about 'hooligan' behaviour among young people:

Pearson, G (1983) *Hooligan: A History of Respectable Fears.* London: Macmillan.

For those of you interested in moral panics around youth, Stanley Cohen's original classic text would be an excellent starting point:

Cohen, S (2006) *Folk Devils and Moral Panics*, 3rd edn. London: Routledge.

The following text provides an excellent, thorough introduction to issues relating to social work with young people:

Smith, R (2008) *Social Work with Young People*. London: Wiley.

Answers to Activity 8.2

Quote 1 = *c*4000 BC. This quote was found in an Egyptian tomb (cited in Byron, 2009).

Quote 2 = 1274, Peter the Hermit (cited in Byron, 2009).

Quote 3 = 4th century BC, Plato (cited in Byron, 2009).

Quote 4 = 1900, *The Times* (30 October).

Quote 5 = 1960, *The Times* (13 June).

Quote 6 = 1977, *The Times* (20 April).

9: Adults, social policy and social work: the personalisation agenda

---

Achieving a social work degree

This chapter will help you to meet the following capabilities from the Professional Capabilities Framework:

- **Values and ethics** – apply social work ethical principles and values to guide professional practice.
- **Diversity** – recognise diversity and apply anti-discriminatory and anti-oppressive principles in practice.
- **Rights, justice and economic well-being** – advance human rights and promote social justice and economic well-being.
- **Knowledge** – apply knowledge of social sciences, law and social work practice theory.
- **Critical reflection and analysis** – apply critical reflection and analysis to inform and provide a rationale for professional decision-making.
- **Intervention and skills** – use judgement and authority to intervene with individuals, families and communities to promote independence, provide support and prevent harm, neglect and abuse.
- **Contexts and organisations** – engage with, inform and adapt to changing contexts that shape practice. Operate effectively within own organisational frameworks and contribute to the development of services and organisations. Operate effectively within multi-agency and inter-professional settings.

(Continued)

205

(Continued)

The chapter will also introduce you to the following academic standards which are set out in the 2016 QAA social work benchmark statements:

4   Defining principles
5.1   Subject knowledge and understanding
5.2   Social work theory
5.3   Values and ethics
5.5   The nature of social work practice
5.11 Manage problem-solving activities
5.13 Analysis and synthesis
6.1   Teaching learning and assessment
6.2   Teaching learning and assessment
7.3   Knowledge and understanding

Introduction

In their practice, social workers engage with a number of different groups of adult service users. By 'adults' we are referring to service users who are over the age of 18 and under the age of 65 (we examine policy in relation to older adults in Chapter 10). As with other service user groups, the work carried out by social workers with adults is shaped and constrained by wider ideological and policy trends. Recent policy developments, in many cases influenced by the views of user movements themselves, have focused upon the need to empower certain groups of adult service users by giving them more control over their services. The emphasis that is placed upon the need for the development of more personalised systems of support is perhaps the most consistent theme to be found in recent policy documents relating to adult social care. Indeed, personalisation is universally portrayed as the new panacea or the 'holy grail' of adult social care and its arrival on the social policy agenda has been welcomed by academics and politicians of all political shades. However, we will also show how this ostensibly progressive development should not be interpreted entirely uncritically.

Personalisation

Personalisation formed a key part of the previous Labour government's strategy for adult social care (Glasby and Littlechild, 2009) and by 2007/08 some 86,110 adult service users and 30,425 carers were in receipt of personalised services in the form of direct payments (Commons Hansard, 17 November 2010, c973–8). The Labour government's enthusiasm for extending personalised services was shared by the Conservative-dominated Coalition government. The Coalition's strategy document, *A Vision for Adult Social Care*, reiterated the positive messages contained in Labour's earlier policy documents:

> *People not service providers or systems should hold the choice and control about their care. The time is now right to make personal budgets the norm for everyone who receives ongoing care and support – ideally as a direct cash payment, to give maximum flexibility and choice.* (Department of Health, 2010, p15)

As was the case with previous Labour governments, Coalition ministers claimed that their motivations were entirely altruistic and geared towards delivering *greater choice, control and independence, and ultimately better quality of life.* Personalisation, in short, is seen to provide the long sought-after radical solution to the problems that have previously beset adult social care, and will progressively transform the way it is delivered. As a result of the 2014 Health and Social Care Act local authorities are now required to give all eligible service users a personal budget by April 2015, and consequently the number of people receiving them has increased. In 2014/15, 500,000 service users had been allocated personal budgets (House of Commons Public Accounts Committee, 2016).

Later in the chapter, we place some of the assumptions that underpin the 'personalisation agenda' under a more critical lens. One of the issues we examine is the extent to which political support for 'personalisation' is genuinely based upon benevolent, progressive principles. This is an important question because, as Spandler (2004) argues, the policy implications associated with personalisation can hold an appeal to those of both progressive and reactionary tendencies. For example, direct payments (a key mechanism of delivering personalisation) may, on the one hand, be interpreted as a progressive attempt to provide service users with a greater level of self-determination, improving and strengthening collectively funded provision. In this sense, one can see the attraction of personalisation to social democrats. On the other hand, direct payments could be seen as part of a less altruistic strategy to abrogate responsibility for 'difficult' service users and to transfer responsibility for securing welfare from the state to the individual. Herein lies the appeal of personalisation to neo-liberals who are committed to the retrenchment of state welfare. We will assess the complex confluence of ideological interests that shape current personalisation strategies in greater detail later. First, though, we examine some of the concerns that have provided impetus to the current shift towards personalisation.

Has statutory provision been unresponsive to the needs of adult service users?

As we explained in Chapter 4, the development of the social democratic welfare state after 1945 led to an unparalleled improvement in levels of economic and social well-being.

In 1948 a universal National Health Service was established, which for the first time provided free health care to all on the basis of need. In addition, better social security and housing provision helped alleviate some of the chronic levels of poverty and destitution that were a feature of life before the welfare state. However, as we also saw in Chapter 4, the post-war welfare state was far from perfect and there have always been calls from within the social policy community for improvements to be made to the level and quality of provision. This has been particularly so in relation to adult social care provision. Research evidence has consistently highlighted significant levels of marginalisation and exclusion among adult service users. In addition, inquiries have pointed to a systematic failure of welfare services to meet the needs of certain groups of adult service users. Indeed, some investigations have shown services to be oppressive, demeaning and entirely unresponsive to the preferences of those whose needs they are designed to meet.

Adults with mental health and learning disabilities

The poor standard of care offered to adults with mental health and learning disabilities in the relatively recent past has long been acknowledged. The post-war years, for example, were littered with scandals, where professionals who were entrusted with caring responsibilities for vulnerable adults were found guilty of committing appalling levels of neglect. In the late 1960s and early 1970s consecutive inquiries in Ely, Farleigh and Whittingham hospitals uncovered a dreadful catalogue of abuse. There was, in short, an utter breakdown in care in these institutions, and it was clear from the major inquiries that were undertaken at the time that some welfare professionals placed their own selfish interests above the needs and wishes of their patients.

These scandals were illustrative of one of the darker periods in the history of British post-war welfare and, partly as a consequence, we saw a shift towards community care and the acknowledgement of the need for welfare to be more responsive to the needs and preferences of adult service users. There was, therefore, a general recognition that welfare should not simply be 'imposed' by professionals upon vulnerable service users. There can be little doubt that as a result of this, standards of care for adults with mental health and learning difficulties have now improved. For instance, many of the old Victorian long-stay hospitals have closed and those who would have previously been resident in these institutions now receive social care and support in the community. Indeed, only approximately 3,000 people with learning disabilities continue to live as NHS inpatients (Health and Social Care Information Centre, 2015).

However, various inquiries and investigations have drawn attention to the continued failure to provide for the needs of many mental health and learning-disabled adult service users. In 2006, for instance, a joint inquiry undertaken by the Healthcare Commission and Commission for Social Care Inspection (CSCI) (2006, p5) into the supported living arrangements for learning-disabled adults in Cornwall's NHS Trust found evidence of abusive practices that were reminiscent of those uncovered in the 1960 and 1970s.

Cornwall's NHS Trust's service users were being provided with support in the 'community', but the quality of that support was in many ways no better than that provided in the old Victorian 'asylums'. Adult service users in the Trust's 'supported housing', for example, were found to have no choice over where they resided, over who provided their care or over the nature or quality of that care. 'Residents' were overly sedated, locked in their rooms and denied access to basic facilities like food and running water. There was, the inquiry found, evidence of *physical restraint being used illegally and of excessive use of . . . medication to control unacceptable behaviour in the Trust's assessment, treatment and supported living services.* Incidents uncovered by the CSCJ/Healthcare Commission included:

> *. . . hitting, pushing, shoving, dragging, kicking, secluding, belittling, mocking and goading people who used the trust's services, withholding food, giving cold showers, overzealous or premature use of restraint, poor attitude towards people who used services, poor atmosphere, roughness, care not being provided, a lack of dignity and respect, and no privacy.* (p31)

Much of the abuse stemmed from the poor treatment meted out by certain members of staff. However, the inquiry also pointed to culpability of the hospital trust itself, in particular its failure to ensure its staff treated service users with dignity, respect and compassion. The following extract is taken from the Healthcare Commission's report:

> *The trust's own investigations . . . have shown that some people using its services have had to endure years of abusive practices and some have suffered real injury as a result . . . Our investigation found that institutional abuse was widespread, preventing people from exercising their rights to independence, choice and inclusion. One person spent 16 hours a day tied to their bed or wheelchair, for what staff wrongly believed was for that person's own protection. One man told investigators that he had never chosen any of the places he had lived as an adult.*

Learning-disabled people who utilised the trust's services were *'looked after', instead of being supported to develop their skills. This*, the report concluded, *limited their ability to make informed choices and communicate their needs*, rendering them *largely powerless to control their environments or their lives* (pp7–8). There was, therefore, a fundamental failure to understand or acknowledge the wishes of individual service users. Managers and staff at the Trust simply assumed that 'they knew best'; they determined the shape and quality of provision and no attempts had been made to empower service users or enable their voices to be heard. *The Trust's services*, the report concluded, *did not reflect the principles of rights, independence, choice and inclusion, set out in the Valuing People strategy* (p6).

In the light of such findings, one can understand the growing demands that have emerged for user empowerment to be at the heart of adult social care provision. Clearly, the abuses found at Cornwall's NHS Trust are not representative of provision generally, but as a 2012 BBC *Panorama* investigation into abuse at the Winterbourne View assessment and treatment unit illustrated, such scandals continue to occur.

Activity 9.1

The BBC's Winterbourne View documentary can be found on a variety of video-sharing platforms, including *YouTube*. Take time to watch the documentary and then read through the report produced by the serious case review, which was undertaken by Margaret Flynn. You can access this, as well as a shorter summary of the findings and recommendations, here: http://sites.southglos.gov.uk/ safeguarding/adults/i-am-a-carerrelative/winterbourne-view/.

- What does the documentary tell us about the veracity of the claims that Winterbourne View's owners had made about the 'person-centred approach' pursued by its staff, which, they alleged, was built around providing service users with *a range of therapeutic, educational and recreational activities that address individual need and choices*?
- In Chapter 5 we discussed neo-liberal claims that private sector organisations are better able and more likely than statutory providers to provide efficient and personalised care to service users. What do the findings of the Winterbourne View serious case review tell us about the potential conflict between the requirement for private sector providers to make a profit and the ability to deliver effective, dignified care to service users?

Comment

Winterbourne View was a relatively small £3,500 per week, privately run unit for adults with learning disabilities, near Bristol. It was owned by a company called Castleback Ltd, which ran more than 50 other care homes and had an annual turnover of around £90 million. Unlike many cash-strapped local authority services whose incomes had been affected by the Coalition's austerity programme, the 24-bed hospital's annual turnover of £3.7 million was more than sufficient to enable it to meet the care needs of its service users in an effective, humane and dignified manner. Certainly, in its brochures, Winterbourne View's owners boasted of its *recruitment, development and retention of dedicated, well trained and appropriately registered staff*, who were committed to promoting *the development of each individual through the application of the key principles of Valuing People: rights, independence, choice and inclusion. All interventions*, the publicity material stated, were *based on current best practice that embraces the ethics and principles of non-aversion, non-punitive, multi-elemental approaches* (Flynn, 2012, p7).

If you have watched the BBC documentary, which was filmed by an undercover reporter posing as a support worker, you will already be aware of the groundless nature of these claims. The film documented an appalling litany of abuse, showing poorly trained, often sadistic staff harassing, punching and kicking learning-disabled patients in their care. In one scene, a member of staff was seen goading a service user to jump out of a second floor window. In another, a support worker was seen impersonating a Nazi camp commander, screaming 'Nein, nein, nein' at a service user, before slapping her across the face with leather gloves. He then added to her humiliation by throwing the water from a vase of flowers, which had been a gift from her parents, into her face (Flynn, 2012).

The film's broadcast on 31 May 2011 was greeted with a palpable sense of shock. *The Telegraph* accused Winterbourne View of subjecting service users to *Victorian levels of abuse and cruelty* (Swinford, 2011), while *The Guardian* was *appalled at the depiction of a regime of casual, vicious physical and verbal abuse of some of society's most vulnerable members*. Winterbourne View was little more than *a warehouse for people with 'challenging behaviour'* (Brindle, 2011). Savage images of the cruelty were emblazoned across news bulletins and newspapers, and the scandal gripped the nation's news agenda. Stung into action, the Coalition set up a serious case review to look into the appalling treatment of service users at Winterbourne View. The serious case review's report described the cruelty exposed in the BBC film as *a bleak collage of the phenomenon of institutional abuse* (Flynn, 2012, p143). Here is how it commented upon the 'treatment' received by one of the service users, Simon.

Alli {one of the female support workers} bounced forcefully on the lap of a male patient, Simon, in the lounge and yelped as she did so. Later, she shouted at him, 'Don't push it or I'll put your head down the toilet' . . . Alli and her colleagues knew that Simon was fearful of toilets. She took Simon's favourite drinking bottle and told him, 'It's going out the window' . . . Jason, a support worker, engaged in another unequal game – this time, of boxing with Simon. As Simon cowered in a chair, Jason towered over him, boxing his head . . . Wayne {another support worker} exploited Simon's fear of toilets by crushing him against the wall of a toilet. Simon cried out in distress . . . Later in the lounge, and without provocation, the back of his knees were kicked by Wayne. Simon fell backwards to the floor where he was heard to cry out as he was pinned down by Wayne. A woman patient was heard to ask, 'Why are you fighting at us all?' {Later} Wayne pulled down his {Simon's} shorts and slapped his exposed buttocks hard. He adopted a fighting posture over Simon claiming, 'I'm warmed up – let's go. Why don't you want it? I'm gonna bite your face off then'.

(Continued)

(Continued)

Sadly, the abuse experienced by Simon was the norm rather than the exception. Here is the serious case review's description of the treatment of another service user, Simone:

> *Simone, a patient at Winterbourne View Hospital for four months, was pinned on her back under a chair by Wayne. She managed to turn onto her front and Wayne jerked back her head by her hair while simultaneously pulling her arm up . . . Thirty minutes later, he had Simone in a head lock as another member of staff distributed sweets. Wayne was heard slapping Simone . . . Four days later, Simone was again pinned under a chair, this time on her side, with her right wrist pinned under Wayne's foot as he watched TV. She was crying out with pain. He slapped her hard . . . On another occasion, when Simone was once again being pinned down on her back by Wayne, Michael {another support worker} dropped his knees heavily onto Simone's legs. Wayne slapped her hard and told her to 'shut up' . . . In another scene Wayne taunted Simone with the questions, 'Do you want me to get a cheese grater and grate your face off? Do you want me to turn you into a giant pepperoni? Get a razor and cut you up?' In other scenes Graham {another support worker} instructed Simone to 'suffocate in your own fat' and he called her a 'gimp'.*

Simone was physically assaulted by her support workers five times in a single day. On the final occasion, she was doused in cold water, thrown outside and left to lie, alone, shaking in sub-zero temperatures in the hospital grounds.

The serious case review found that Winterbourne View's service users had been chronically unprotected almost since the institution opened for business, and that the owners of the hospital – Castlebeck Ltd – had failed to act upon countless allegations of abuse and malpractice (Flynn, 2012). A Care Quality Commission (2011, pp5 and 7) Report, published in the immediate aftermath of the revelations, concurred: *The registered provider did not take reasonable steps to identify the possibility of abuse and prevent it before it occurred; and did not respond appropriately to allegations of abuse . . . Therefore the people, accommodated at Winterbourne View, were not fully protected from abuse, or the risk of abuse.*

Clearly, no attempts either were made at Winterbourne View to involve service users in decisions about their care, contrary to the grandiose claims contained in the unit's publicity material. The patients were *without voice or representation*, as were their relatives, who were not permitted to be fully involved in their lives, or even to visit the bedrooms of their loved ones (Flynn, 2012, p126). *Their silencing*, the serious case review concluded, *was scandalous*, making a mockery of the hospital's claims to provide person-centred care. *They did not receive customised support from skilled professionals* and their relatives *were rendered impotent or invisible* (Flynn, 2012, p143).

Clearly, the perpetrators of the abuse were themselves motivated by a twisted form of sadistic pleasure, and 11 of those responsible were identified, prosecuted and convicted as a result of their actions. However, attention soon turned to the failure on the part of Winterbourne View's owners to take action to protect patients. One of the most serious allegations was that Castlebeck Ltd prioritised its own financial gain above the care needs of service users in its charge. In fact, Castlebeck made strenuous efforts to conceal financial information from Margaret Flynn, the chair of the serious case review, citing 'commercial sensitivity'. Hence, it refused to disclose how much of the £3,500 per week it charged for each service user was spent upon their care. As a private sector organisation it was within its rights to do this, despite the gravity of the allegations and the fact that the information had been requested by the chair of a serious case review. However, documents that were obtained by Margaret Flynn showed that *from a financial perspective, Winterbourne View Hospital was one of the best performers in the group*. It seems that it was this financial success, as much as anything else, that led its owners to turn a blind eye to the countless complaints, high turnover of staff, poor levels of staffing and training, and allegations of emotional, physical and financial abuse of service users (p24). In short, Winterbourne View was perceived by Castlebeck Ltd solely in terms of its status as a financially buoyant, profitable enterprise. As the serious case review noted, Castlebeck Ltd *made decisions about profitability, including shareholder returns, over and above decisions about the effective and humane delivery of assessment, treatment and rehabilitation* (p144). It *took the financial rewards without any accountability* and *benefited financially to a substantial degree* from this arrangement (ppvii and 27). The judge who sentenced the 11 key perpetrators of the abuse alleged that Castlebeck's thirst for profit contributed to the actions of those in the dock:

> It is common ground in this Case that the hospital was run with a view to profit and with a scandalous lack of regard to the interests of its residents and staff . . . A culture of ill-treatment developed and as is often the case, cruelty bred cruelty. This culture corrupted and debased, to varying degrees, these defendants, all of whom are of previous good character. (*The Telegraph*, 2012a)

Castlebeck, the judge argued, saw Winterbourne View's residents primarily as a source of profit, stating: *The hospital's purported aim of assisting the residents so that they might return to homes in the community was cynically disregarded* (Lakhani, 2012).

Despite this conclusion, weak corporate governance regulations meant that Winterbourne View's owners, unlike those found guilty in the criminal trial, could not be prosecuted for their part in the scandal. The former Care Minister, Paul Burstow, expressed his frustration at his inability to hold Castlebeck to account

(Continued)

(Continued)

for its negligence: *When you look at Winterbourne View, the people who committed the abuse and the assaults were convicted, but what about the people making the money from that company?* (*The Telegraph*, 2012b).

The serious care review argued that the whole affair had exposed *a huge failure at the heart of our system of care.* It was *the worst kind of institutional care* and *recalled the endemic abuses which are known to have existed in long-stay, NHS hospitals in the past* (Flynn, 2012, p14). *We have been here before,* the serious case review concluded. *There is nothing new about the institutional abuse of adults with learning disabilities and autism,* but there was a need to ensure that abuse on this scale was prevented from ever happening again (p121). In its recommendations, the serious case review emphasised the need, wherever it was appropriate to do so, to phase out inpatient services for learning disabled adults, and for far greater levels of resources to be provided to fund more personalised, community-based forms of support and treatment. The Coalition government accepted this recommendation; in the light of the gravity of the scandal, it could hardly do otherwise. It also committed the government, wherever appropriate, to a policy of discharging inpatients with learning difficulties back to their homes and communities (with the required support) by 1 June 2014. Unfortunately, this target has not been met. As an all-party House of Commons Public Accounts Select Committee noted in 2015, the number of service users remaining as inpatients in hospitals and secure units remains roughly the same as it was in 2011 – around 3,230 in September 2014. One-third of these were in hospitals that were more than 50 km from their homes and one-fifth had been inpatients for more than five years. The government, the committee argued, needed to redouble its efforts for improving *community services provision and building the capacity in the community to support people, as well as preventing the need for admission in the first place* (p6). MENCAP and the Challenging Behaviour Foundation jointly condemned the *appalling failure of the government, the NHS and local authorities to meet their own deadline*:

> *Local areas have just not developed the right support and services . . . This means people remain in places where we know they are frequently overmedicated, restrained and are at significant risk of abuse.* (Spinks, 2015, p7)

The mere fact that pockets of neglect such as those found at Winterbourne View have continued to be exposed has, understandably, led to demands that the needs and views of service users must be far more central to future policy and practice. It is, critics argue, a failure to acknowledge the voices or wishes of service users that leads to neglect and poor quality provision. Consequently universal assumptions about what is 'good' for adult service users need to be rejected in favour of a more empowering, user-led model of policy and practice. Such concerns have been reflected in recent policy documents, which suggest that 'impersonal', inflexible welfare provision can, in some instances, serve to reinforce the disadvantages service users already face. As Labour's key strategy document *Putting People First* argued, *While acknowledging the Community Care legislation of the 1990s was well intentioned, it has led to a system which can be over complex and too often fails to respond to people's needs and expectations* (HM Government, 2007, p1). Labour's Green Paper, *Independence, Well-being and Choice*, continued this theme, this time identifying 'traditional' social work practices as a potential cause of marginalisation:

> *For too long social work has been perceived as a gatekeeper or rationer of services and has been accused . . . of fostering dependence rather than independence. We want to* create *a different environment, which reinforces the core social work values of supporting individuals to take control of their own lives, and to make the choices which matter to them.* (Department of Health, 2005, p10)

The Conservative minister, Earl Howe, made much the same point when introducing the 2014 Care Bill, which mandated local authorities to provide service users with access to personalised services. The social work and social care system, he argued, often *fails to live up to the expectations of those that rely on it*. Far too frequently, he stated, *the system can be confusing, disempowering and not flexible enough to fit around individuals' lives* (Lords Hansard, 21 May 2013, c745).

Universalism versus particularism? The challenge to universalism

As we have already explained, allegations that the welfare state is unresponsive and unsympathetic to the needs and wishes of those that use its services are not, in fact, particularly novel. This critique of welfare helped draw attention to the flaws associated with impersonal, 'institutionalised' care in the 1960s and 1970s and influenced the policy trend towards community care and services. However, concerns about 'top-down', professionally led rather than service user-led welfare services became increasingly influential in the 1980s and 1990s. The 'universal' nature of the UK's welfare services, it was argued, had led to the development of a 'one-size-fits-all' model, which meant that the particular needs of different groups of service users, particularly adults with disabilities, mental health issues and learning difficulties, had been largely ignored. While the worst excesses of 'institutionalised' services may, to an extent, have been tackled, service users were still often the unwilling recipients of services that were imposed upon them. This critique of the post-war welfare state sought to expose the extent to which the main institutions of collectivist welfare – health, social care, social work, social security, housing and education – had all failed to provide adequately for the diverse, conflicting and varied needs of different individuals and social groups. Fiona Williams (1992) was among those who were critical of the 'false universalism' of the post-war welfare state. It was, she argued, *built on a white, male, able bodied, heterosexual {nuclear family} norm*, and consequently those who failed to correspond to this 'norm' received inferior services, if any at all. The underpinning assumption, that uniform, standardised services were the most effective means of meeting the needs of all users of welfare services was, it was suggested, fundamentally flawed. This model of welfare provision may have been introduced with the best of intentions but, according to those such as Williams, it ignored the fact that users of welfare services often had differing and varied needs that 'mass', 'standardised', state-organised provision was failing to meet (Williams, 1989).

At the same time, the power and control wielded by 'expert' welfare professionals was subjected to critical examination. The post-war welfare state had, critics argued, always been characterised by a 'top-down' patronising mode of delivery, whereby users of welfare services had been expected to unquestioningly accept the prescriptions and services provided by welfare 'experts', such as nurses, doctors and social workers. Welfare professionals, including social workers, had *assessed and acted upon* service users, rather than engaging with them and giving them the control or power to tailor the services they received to their own individual needs. In short, it was argued that insufficient attention had been paid to the views and needs of certain service user groups, many of whom had been treated as 'passive' recipients of universal services rather than people with their own individual particular needs. Service users had, in many cases, been reduced to a *benign form of* state *clienthood* (Harris, 2004).

Case study

Arthur

Arthur is a 45-year-old service user with moderate learning disabilities, who lives in a local authority-funded sheltered housing project. In common with accepted practice at the time, Arthur attended a 'special' school as a child. His parents would have preferred him to be educated in a mainstream school, alongside non-disabled children, but in accordance with national policy Arthur's local authority felt it was better to educate disabled children separately. It was generally felt that disabled children would find it difficult to cope in a mainstream school environment, and that the 'demands' of catering for disabled children in mainstream schools would be too onerous.

Arthur was liked by his teachers at his 'special' school and was seen as one of the more academically able children in his cohort, but like the vast majority of his peers he left school with no formal academic qualifications. As was the case with many of the children in Arthur's class, it was assumed that on leaving school he would find employment in a government-funded 'sheltered workshop' for disabled adults, and would have no need for formal educational qualifications. Arthur worked in a sheltered workshop for a number of years after leaving school, but this closed two years ago as result of cuts in government funding. Since then, Arthur has applied for numerous paid jobs elsewhere, without any success. His social worker has sought to arrange

→

voluntary work experience for him and, along with a couple of other learning disabled adults, he currently helps out occasionally at a local charity shop.

- How might Arthur's life chances have been impeded by the 'universal' assumptions made by welfare professionals about the 'best' way to provide welfare services to people with disabilities?

Comment

Arthur's experiences of the welfare system serve to illustrate some of the problems associated with 'universal', 'professional-driven' forms of welfare. Such forms of provision can be based upon wide, often inaccurate generalisations about what is 'good' for service users. Individuals become categorised according to their collective, service-user-defined identities and they are subjected to universal, one-size-fits-all interventions, which take little account of their own particular needs, abilities and capabilities. In the case of children such as Arthur, the decision to segregate them into special schools will often have been taken without any assessment of their intellectual abilities, or without any appreciation of the consequences of denying them the opportunity of a 'mainstream' education. Likewise, the assumption that Arthur would be employed in a 'sheltered workshop' on leaving school will have been shaped by the belief that 'mainstream' employment was not right for Arthur. Welfare professionals who made decisions 'on behalf' of Arthur and his family may well have been motivated by the best of intentions, but the assumptions upon which they made those decisions have, over time, proven to be fundamentally flawed. The premise upon which they were based – that is, that it was unrealistic to think that disabled people should realistically expect to fully participate in society – is now widely acknowledged to be false and indeed oppressive. It is partly for this reason that welfare interventions that have been based upon wide, universal, generalised assumptions about what is 'appropriate' for service users were increasingly questioned in the 1980s and 1990s, and demands made for the implementation of a more empowering, user-led model of welfare.

Postmodernism and welfare

It is important to note that such critiques of the 'universal' post-war welfare state were articulated mainly by those on the social democratic left of the academic and political community who in no way wished to undermine support for the principles underpinning publicly funded state welfare. Many of these were attracted by 'postmodernism', an increasingly influential strand of sociological thought that seemed to provide a platform for the development of a more critical, emancipatory social policy and social work practice (Hillyard and Watson, 1996; Carter, 1998). They argued that while 'mass', 'universal' services may have been appropriate mechanisms for satisfying very basic, 'absolute' needs in the austerity-driven post-war decades of what they refer to as the 'modernist' era, there was now a need for a more nuanced approach. 'Mass', 'universal' welfare policy stood accused of failing to acknowledge the voices, desires and needs of many groups of service users. This, it was argued, could only be overcome though the injection of greater heterogeneity, diversity, flexibility and specialisation in the way welfare was delivered. Thus, a new political strategy, based upon a celebration of fragmentation and particularism was said to offer the basis for the development of a more progressive welfare model more befitting the new 'postmodern' world. Voices that had hitherto been ignored should, as a matter of principle, be acknowledged, commitments to 'old-style' universalism should be abandoned, and more specialised, targeted services should be developed to take into account the different and diverse needs of 'newly enfranchised' groups of service users.

As already stated, the intention of most of those who were attracted to 'postmodernism' was to strengthen the foundations of collectivist, statutory provision by making welfare and social care more responsive to the needs of service users. This, it was felt, would be of benefit to service users, ensuring an end to soulless, 'professionals-know-best' provision, but it would also help reinforce the legitimacy of the welfare state, making it more difficult for those on the political 'right' to pursue their ideologically motivated strategies of retrenchment and cuts. As we will see, it also reflected growing demands from adult service users themselves for more control of the welfare they received.

However, the growing influence of postmodernism within social policy was not without its critics. Peter Taylor Gooby (1994, p403), for example, accused its advocates of being blinded by the rhetoric of welfare pluralism, consumerism, decentralisation and choice, ignoring the fact that this same rhetoric was concurrently being used by neo-liberal Conservative governments to disguise policies which had actually reinforced inequalities and made the position of many vulnerable social groups much worse. The retrenchment of state welfare in the 1980s and 1990s and the movement from universalism to more targeted, means-tested forms of welfare provision had been justified by Conservative ministers through the rhetoric of 'choice' and 'flexibility', but the changes had heralded a shift towards a harsher, selective and stigmatising form of welfare delivery. Hence, while accepting that the welfare state was 'imperfect', those such as Taylor Gooby (1994, p403) cautioned against 'crude', generalised attacks on the principle of universalism. Such assaults, alongside an uncritical acceptance of the concept of 'choice', could, he argued, serve to *cloak developments of considerable importance:*

> *Trends towards increased inequality in living standards, the privatisation of state welfare services and the stricter regulation of the lives of some of the poorest groups may fail to attract the appropriate attention if the key themes of policy are seen as difference, diversity and choice.*

In summary, 'postmodern' approaches to welfare were accused by their critics of failing to have an adequate grasp of the power relations that often underpinned the rhetoric of 'choice' and 'flexibility'. The use of such language, it was argued, constituted little more than an 'ideological smokescreen', obscuring the regressive political interests that were driving the policies of successive Conservative administrations. 'Postmodernism' was, critics insisted, in danger of providing the 'right' with ammunition and support to amount an ideologically motivated assault on the very principles of the welfare state.

Service users' demands for greater autonomy

The articulation of this 'postmodern' critique within the social policy academic community coincided with growing dissatisfaction from within service user groups themselves with the services they received, many of whom consistently campaigned for the right to control their own welfare resources. Disabled people were one such group. Disabled activists had, for a number of years, been at the forefront of campaigns challenging the right of professionals to determine the shape of welfare provision, demanding that they be seen not as passive recipients, but as active participants in the design and delivery of the services they received (Morris, 1993). The expertise of these professionals and their ability to determine 'what was best' for disabled people was therefore increasingly questioned, and as part of this process disability activists championed the concept of independent living. They claimed that the money spent by the NHS and local authorities 'on behalf' of disabled people had previously had the effect of segregating and marginalising them. Welfare professionals, Morris (1997, p59) argued, *chose to spend large sums of money on segregated provision – which meant that disabled people had to live restricted and impoverished lives that the professionals concerned would* never *have chosen for themselves:*

> *For example, instead of spending money to help someone attend college, go to the cinema or pursue other leisure activities, visit friends and family and so on, money was spent on building Day Centres where people are still bused every day to do the kind of things that other people think are good for them.*

It would, disabled activists argued, be far better if disabled people themselves were given control over their own resources, allowing them to stay in their own homes and purchase the services they wanted. Organisations such as the Union of Physically Impaired Against Segregation, the British Council of Disabled People and the Disability Alliance were at the forefront of demands for greater choice and control (Leece and Bornat, 2006). Claims that disabled people were being 'duped' into inadvertently supporting a right-wing, ideologically motivated attack on collectivist welfare were rejected:

> *To support a system in which the individual who needs the help has the power to determine how that help is delivered is not to support an individualist right-wing agenda. Rather, it is about promoting collective responsibility for protecting individual rights.* (Morris, 1997, p59)

Partly as a result of the pressure applied by disabled people, in the late 1980s the Conservative government established the Independent Living Fund (ILF), which provided some disabled service users with small cash payments they could use to pay for their own care. What was initially intended to be a small-scale scheme designed to compensate only a few hundred disabled individuals who had lost income due to wider social security changes was quickly forced to expand to meet demand for more 'personalised' care. The scope of the ILF was still limited and circumscribed, and its funding was nowhere near adequate to meet need, but as Glasby and Littlechild (2002) point out, it did set an important precedent in the way it gave service users control over a portion of their care budget. They describe it as a 'Pandora's box' . . . which, once opened would be very difficult to close again (p17).

The 1996 Community Care (Direct Payments) Act

The 1996 Community Care (Direct Payments) Act, passed by John Major's Conservative government, came into force in April 1997 and placed the personalisation agenda firmly at the heart of government policy. The Act gave local authorities discretionary powers, enabling them to provide direct payments to adult disabled services users under the age of 65. John Bowis, the minister who steered the Bill though the parliamentary process, described it as representing a *significant step down the road of responding to people's wishes and enabling them to lead as normal a life as possible.* Henceforth, adult disabled people under the age of 65 would be given the opportunity to control social care resources that had previously been spent on their behalf by social service departments. They would be given the power to manage directly the services they received, deciding, for instance, from whom to buy services and who to employ to assist them. The crux of the government's case was that inflexible statutory social services had failed to respond to the varied and particular needs of adult disabled service users.

> *Time and again, I have heard from people who have a disability, but also hold down a job or voluntary work and whose working lives are obstructed by the rigidity of a council service rota; or people who do not like to complain, but would really like a different range of menus from the meal service; or people who have responsible jobs, but are treated by the care workers as if they were rather tiresome and untidy children. They have no real independence, no real choice and no real dignity. The Bill will change that.* (Bowis, cited in Lords Hansard, 6 March 1996, c372)

The Act would, the government argued, help revolutionise the organisation of adult social care, transforming the way in which services were delivered to and experienced by adult service users. Old 'top-down' approaches, whereby service users were the passive, sometimes unwilling recipients of second-class, bureaucratically driven services, would be consigned to the past. Welfare bureaucrats and professionals would no longer be in sole charge of the resources that determine the services that people are able to access. Resources, control, choice and power would be transferred to the 'service-user consumer', who was better placed to determine their own welfare needs and preferences. Although initially restricted to disabled adults under the age of 65, the government made it clear that it would consider extending the principle of direct payments to other categories of adult service users. The ultimate aim was for all adult service users to be given the power to purchase their own services and to tailor them to their fit around their own particular needs. Put simply, they, rather than welfare professionals, would have the power to decide what suits them best.

Altruism or ideology?

The rhetoric used by ministers to justify this strategy for adult social care drew heavily from the empowering principles that have shaped the campaigns of service user groups for greater autonomy. As we have seen, ministers claimed that they were simply delivering what service users had long demanded, and the process was the result of a bottom-up struggle to force the state to relinquish control of welfare resources and to develop a more progressive model of organising welfare. Benevolence, altruism and social justice were said to lie at the heart of the strategy. Personalisation, it was argued, held out the promise of a more democratised, self-determined model of welfare, one which would put the individual service user at the heart of provision. The message was clear. The move towards personalisation was motivated by progressive principles, and the outcome could not be anything but positive in terms of its impact upon the standard of services and quality of life afforded to adult service users.

Others remained less convinced of the government's claim that it was motivated by benevolent intentions. Conservative ministers had, for instance, previously been distinctly lukewarm towards the principle of direct payments, fearing that they would undermine accountability for public spending and, more importantly, lead to increased expenditure. Stung by the unexpected high demand for Independent Living Fund payments, ministers had previously feared that the costs of direct payments would become uncontrollable. Indeed, as late as 1993 John Major's Conservative government had reduced the scope for direct payments by closing the Independent Living Fund to newcomers and by establishing a new fund, the eligibility criterion for which was markedly more restrictive than the original scheme. The government's eventual 'conversion' to the principle of direct payments less than a year later was, some argue, motivated less by social justice concerns and more by a gradual realisation that 'personalisation' could actually be cheaper and more cost-effective than locally authority-provided services. As Pearson (2000) points out, the government's announcement that it was to legislate in favour of direct payments came less than a week after the publication of research suggesting they were between 30 and 40 per cent cheaper than service-based provision.

Direct payments also fitted in with John Major's Conservative government's wider neo-liberal ideological framework, which was focused upon privatising state provision, reducing the power of state welfare workers and promoting a marketised model of welfare. Some, such as Clare Ungerson (1997) (like Taylor Gooby earlier), feared that progressive social democratic language was being used to justify what was essentially a neo-liberal, cuts-led agenda. In embracing the powerful, persuasive, empowering rhetoric of service-user movements, neo-liberals were said by sceptics to have performed something of a *coup d'état*, 'co-opting' unsuspecting user movements into supporting their ideologically motivated strategy of welfare retrenchment. At the same time, the utilisation of the language of personalisation by Conservative ministers was said to have performed a powerful ideological function, allowing them to portray any criticisms of their policies for marketising social care as an extreme defence of 'old', 'oppressive' professionally driven services. Sceptics of the trajectory of policy, such as Ungerson, expressed their frustration at being cast as defenders of the 'unacceptable' status quo:

> *To query the empowerment of consumers of care is to appear to be against the interests of the vulnerable and the oppressed, and against the routes which might develop their currently very limited rights to full participation in society. The evidence is overwhelming that disabled people in the past have been demeaned, discriminated against, abused and ignored by those people funded by the state who were and are supposed to respond to their needs.*
> (Ungerson, 1997, p46)

Perhaps not surprisingly, disabled adult service users were less concerned about the ideological origins of the 1996 Community Care (Direct Payments) Act and more interested in the fact that it enshrined the principle of direct payments in law. They widely welcomed the legislation, seeing it as the beginning of an acknowledgement of their historical struggle for self-determination and control of welfare resources. Some were critical of its limited scope, particularly the fact that only disabled people under 65 were initially eligible to benefit from its provisions, but overall the reaction was positive. *The new system of direct payments – with all its imperfections*, Morris (1997, p60) argued, was *an important stage in the achievements of a civil rights movement.* The Act was also welcomed by the Labour opposition, though it too was critical of the government's decision to restrict eligibility to disabled adults under the age of 65. This restriction was removed by Tony Blair's Labour government in 2000, and in 2003 local authorities were mandated to offer direct payments to all eligible people living in their areas. As already indicated, the Coalition government's 2014 Care Act goes much further in extending the right of service users to determine the shape of their own care packages. There now appears to be little political disagreement over the principles of personalisation and all major political parties in the UK are committed to progressing this agenda, as are key service user organisations. As Beresford (2014, p1) notes, *it has become an article of faith for the English Department of Health and numerous consultancies and pressure groups work to advance its implementation.*

The benefits of personalisation

Analyses of the personalisation agenda have highlighted a number of beneficial outcomes and service users themselves have commented positively upon the greater autonomy afforded by direct payments. Surveys suggest that direct payments have contributed to higher levels of self-esteem among adult service users, increased control over their lives, as well as improved vocational and recreational opportunities. Research also suggests that significant cost-efficiency gains are associated with direct payments when compared with conventional services, with individual service users better able to micro-manage the care they receive (Stainton et al., 2009). The 'benefits' that are said to have been generated by personalisation are summarised below.

Better-quality services

Because the service user is the architect of provision, personalisation can lead to the development of more responsive, tailor-made services that are more finely tuned to match the particular needs of service users. Service users themselves are able to determine the type and shape of care they receive. They are also able to choose the staff/carers they feel are best qualified to deliver the support they require for their needs. In this sense, personalisation is said to provide much greater opportunities to develop closer, more continuous, trustworthy relationships with support workers, further enhancing the quality of provision (Spandler and Vick, 2005). In one recent survey of service users' experiences of personalisation, 68.5 per cent of participants stated that control over their budgets had a positive impact upon their relationships with the people paid to support them, and more than 80 per cent stated that it had improved their quality of life, independence and support (Hatton and Waters, 2015).

Case study

Arthur

In this case study, we want to return to Arthur, the learning-disabled service user we introduced you to earlier. When he is not volunteering at the charity shop, Arthur regularly attends a day care centre along with a number of other learning disabled adults. This is funded by the local authority as part of Arthur's package of care. The centre lays on some leisure activities and Arthur quite enjoys the company of other service users at the centre, though he is often bored and rarely stimulated by the activities it offers. Staff at the centre have noticed he is becoming increasingly withdrawn, but they are too busy to pursue the reasons why this is the case. Unbeknown to them, Arthur's two real passions are watching football and gardening. Arthur's interest in football was stimulated by a visit of his local football team, Preston North End, to the day care centre a couple of years before, and he would dearly love to be able to afford to go and watch them every week. Arthur's interest in gardening was developed while at school, where he and other pupils were encouraged to tend the school's grounds and vegetable plots. However, none of the supported housing he has lived in since leaving school has had gardens. Arthur recently saw an advert for allotments in his local newspaper, but knows he could not afford the annual fees, let alone the tools that he would need to tend the allotment. His growing frustration stems from his inability to afford to pursue these hobbies.

• How might personalised care offer up new opportunities and possibilities for Arthur?

→

Comment

Some of the money currently spent on Arthur's behalf by the local authority could, if given to him directly, be used in a more personalised way, tailored to fit around his particular interests and needs. Arthur could still attend the day care centre occasionally, but a portion of his social care budget could, for instance, be utilised to pay for rent and the tools he needs to tend his own allotment and to purchase tickets to see his local football team. He, rather than social services, would be in charge of his budget, and he (perhaps with advocacy support) could tailor a flexible package of provision that would fit around his particular interests and needs at particular times. He might, for example, wish to enrol on a short gardening course to improve his horticultural skills. Alternatively, he might decide that he wishes to travel to watch his favourite football team play away from home occasionally. He could even choose to employ personal assistants who share his passions for gardening and football. The point is, Arthur would not be 'tied' to an inflexible package of care that was planned months or even years in advance, which bore little or no relation to his current interests. In this sense, Arthur will benefit from the flexibility open to him to alter and adapt his programme of care as his interests and circumstances change. One can imagine the psychological benefits that could be derived from such empowerment and control, as well as its potential for enhancing Arthur's social and economic well-being.

Improved mental and psychological well-being

In fact, adult service users who utilise personalised services frequently report improvements to their psychological well-being. The *In Control* survey in 2015 of personal budget holders and family carers found that 70 per cent of respondents felt that holding their own personal budget impacted positively on their self-esteem. A further 71 per cent felt that it had improved their family relationships, 76 per cent felt safer and 78 per cent said that personalisation had improved their sense of dignity (Hatton and Waters, 2015). In part, this may be a result of improved service delivery. For example, in controlling how their own resources are spent, service users (like Arthur above) may be able to benefit from a whole range of health, education, training and leisure opportunities that would previously have been unavailable to them, and this will clearly contribute to enhanced levels of morale and mental health. This was the case with the following mental health service user, who was clearly appreciative of the opportunities his personalised budget provided to him:

> *Before this, I could not afford structured guitar lessons. It has given me a purpose in life because hopefully I might become a guitar teacher.* (Norrie et al., 2014, p182)

However, such improvements are also thought to result from the greater feelings of empowerment and control engendered by personalisation (Hamilton et al., 2016). As is the case with this mental health service user, recipients of direct payments often comment positively on the growing levels of self-respect and dignity derived from managing their own care packages and being in control of their lives:

Personalised budgets generally work better and give me more choice . . . It's improved my confidence, my ability to cope on my own . . . Yes it's made a big difference (Norrie et al., 2014, p181)

More economically efficient services

As already noted, one of the attractions of personalised services to politicians lies with the claim that they are more cost-efficient than 'traditional' local authority-organised services (Stainton et al., 2009). Service users, for instance, are said to have a direct vested interest in ensuring that 'their' resources are spent efficiently and that the money allocated to them is utilised as effectively as possible. On a practical level, for example, they are able to employ neighbours, friends and in some cases relatives. Unlike local authorities or private-sector service providers, which often charge by the hour irrespective of the time spent providing support, such individuals are more likely to be prepared to be and capable of being flexible with their working arrangements, leading to a reduction in overall costs as well as more effective care. Certainly local authorities do view personalised services as a 'cheaper' option than 'traditional' council-funded services. One recent survey found that 84 per cent of directors of adult social services felt that extending personalisation would lead to either medium or high levels of savings in 2016/17 (National Audit Office, 2016b).

In the light of these positive findings, it is hardly surprising that the personalisation agenda can count upon such widespread support among service users, commentators and politicians. It seems to offer the potential of revolutionising state-funded social care provision, putting the individual in the driving seat, while at the same time driving up standards and reducing the costs of provision. As Peter Beresford (2008a, p11) acknowledges, it could lead to *a new era of social care where the consumer becomes king, able to pull down a much broader and more imaginative menu of support, either directly for themselves or for those* close *to them – all with state aid.* Beresford is a prominent advocate of user empowerment and he clearly sees the potential of personalisation to transform adult social care for the better. However, like many others who have long advocated in favour of a much greater level of user involvement, he has cautioned against an uncritical celebration of the personalisation agenda.

A critical analysis of the personalisation agenda

Concerns about the direction of the personalisation agenda can be divided into two categories – 'practical' and 'ideological'. Practical criticisms focus upon issues such as the adequacy of resources devoted to personalisation, or the perceived inability of some service users to benefit from it. Such criticisms seek to highlight potential limitations of the agenda as it is currently being applied, but they do not necessarily represent a challenge to the general trajectory of policy. On the other hand, ideologically based criticisms seek to highlight what some believe are more fundamental flaws in the personalisation agenda.

Echoing those such as Taylor Gooby and Ungerson, they argue that politicians have utilised the progressive language of personalisation to justify neo-liberal-inspired strategies to reduce state welfare provision and transfer responsibility for securing welfare to individual service users. We discuss both these critiques in greater depth below.

Practical concerns

The (in)ability of some service users to benefit from personalised services

Clearly, for the reasons we outlined above, many adult service users will enthusiastically embrace the opportunities personalisation provides for them to control their own social care resources. However, some academics, as well as service user groups, have expressed concerns about the willingness or ability of many adult service users to exercise the 'choice' offered by personalisation. Not all adult service users, they argue, conform to the 'ideal' personalisation 'profile' presented by advocates of personalisation, and many may not wish to manage their own budgets, or they may simply be unable to do so. Rather than seeing personalisation as a 'liberating' experience, these service users may view the stresses associated with managing their own care with anxiety and trepidation. Hence, current plans to roll out personalised services are, some argue, in danger of marginalising the needs of those service users who value and rely upon 'traditional' services. The views of articulate, active and 'able' services users are, it is suggested, in danger of drowning out the voices of those, for example, with complex needs who are reluctant or unable to embrace the 'new opportunities' on offer. As Burton and Kagan (2006) state, *The complex health needs of many . . . and the need for knowledgeable and skilled specialists is not emphasised* in current policy discourses:

> *A kind of inadvertent trick takes place where the least impaired people are used in the imagery to stand for all the others (which reflects the higher profile of self-advocates), yet the life circumstances of many . . . are ignored.*

Activity 9.2

- Why might some adult service users be reluctant to embrace the 'opportunities' afforded by personalisation?
- What kind of support might those adults with complex social care needs require in order to benefit from personalisation?
- Does the requirement that personalisation be 'cost-neutral' restrict its potential to benefit such service users?

Comment

The questions raised in Activity 9.2 above are important, yet they are sometimes ignored in national debates which tend to focus upon the potentially progressive outcomes associated with personalisation. In fact, studies have shown that some service users are uneasy with the new 'opportunities' afforded by personalisation, viewing them with foreboding rather than enthusiasm. A major government-funded review of the impact of personalisation on service users provided some evidence to support this conclusion. It found that the introduction of individual budgets for adults with learning disabilities had led to significantly lower levels of self-reported health and increased levels of anxiety and stress (Individual Budgets Evaluation Network, 2008, p10):

> *They experienced the administration as stressful. 'What if I overspend?' 'I don't want to owe people money.' 'What if I don't fill the form in right?' 'What if there is no money left?' 'What if they cut my budget?' 'I can't recruit anyone!' Several interviewees . . . feared that relationships with directly employed carers could break down, leaving users and/or carers to dismiss the paid carer, face threats of legal action, and possibly be left for a period without a paid carer. This was contrasted with situations in which a relationship with an agency carer broke down, where the agency could send a replacement carer straight away. Direct employment of carers . . . was anticipated to carry more responsibility and risk for the user.* (pp72–3)

Subsequent research has confirmed that many service users continue to express concerns about their capacity to organise their own personalised services. A number of the mental health service users interviewed by Hamilton et al. (2016, p727) were worried about their *ability to manage the budget themselves, felt unable to cope with the monitoring requirements or perceived themselves to be too out of control in themselves to be able to act consistently and responsibly*. A recent all-party House of Commons Select Committee report also cautioned against assuming that personalisation is an appropriate 'fit' for all service users. As it argued, while personal budgets may work very well for some, *more vulnerable users, and those who lack mental capacity, will find it more difficult to take control of their care. They are*, the report concluded, *less likely to be able to make the good decisions on their own about how best to meet their care needs*. The Select Committee heard evidence from Citizens Advice, which warned that some service users were ill-equipped to take on responsibilities as employers, leaving them vulnerable to exploitation and debt (House of Commons Public Accounts Committee, 2016, p10).

In part, these fears may be unwarranted, and the reluctance to embrace personalisation may, understandably, stem from years of dependency-inducing reliance upon the direction of welfare professionals. Arguably, with encouragement and good-quality support, this reluctance could be overcome and even the most anxious and hesitant of service users may, in time, come to realise the potential of personalisation. Certainly, as we have already stated, research has drawn attention

(Continued)

(Continued)

to the positive impact personalised services have wrought on the self-confidence and well-being of many adult learning-disabled people. However, such anxieties are, for the moment, very real, particularly among adult service users with complex needs (Lawton, 2009; Abbott and Marriott, 2013). While good-quality advocacy and support might well eventually enable even those with the most severe disabilities to benefit from personalised care, such support is not itself cheap, and the government's insistence that personalisation be 'cost neutral' creates obvious difficulties for those service users with complex needs that require a high level of support to enable them to take advantages of personalised care. The question of a lack of adequate resources has, in fact, been highlighted by social workers as one of the most serious impediments to the success of personalisation. In 2013, 84 per cent of social workers questioned said that a lack of resources and government cuts to social care funding pose a threat to personalisation (Community Care, 2013).

The funding of personalisation

We have already explained how one of the attractions of 'personalisation' for politicians lies in the claims that were made regarding its potential to reduce the costs of social care provision. As Beresford (2014, p15) argues, *The promise of financial savings always appeals to politicians, and in relation to a service like social care, which has long been underfunded and strapped for cash, this appeal was visible and powerful.* Indeed, there is a general consensus that it was this, more than any altruistic concern to 'empower' service users, which convinced John Major's Conservative government to press ahead with direct payments in the mid-1990s. However, the notion that personalisation inevitably leads to reduced costs has been challenged:

> *Fawlty Towers got us used to saying: 'Don't mention the war'. But when it comes to personalisation, the difficulty is we aren't really meant to mention the money. Individual budgets were sold on being cheaper . . . they aren't. It is impossible to see how true self-directed support, accessible to all, within a broader customised system of personalised social care will ever become a reality without some fundamental rethinking about who pays and how much money will be needed.* (Beresford, 2008b)

Beresford, along with many other advocates of user empowerment, are concerned at the emphasis that has been placed upon cost containment and efficiency savings in debates on personalisation. Governments may have conceded to the principle of user-empowerment for adult social care but, critics argue, funding is still subjected to the same local authority needs-based, means-tested, resource-driven constraints that have always determined the financing of services. In short, no real additional funding is available and personalisation has, in practice, involved a process of service users choosing to spend their existing resources differently. However, if personalisation is to be a truly progressive, 'transformation agenda', then current funding restrictions may need to be removed, otherwise, its empowering ideals may never be fully realised.

For example, as we have already hinted, the success of personalisation may ultimately depend upon the availability of good-quality, independent advocacy support. As Beresford (2008b) argues, *Direct payments don't work as a simple consumerist transaction; they need a proper developed infrastructure of information, advice, advocacy and ongoing support to be accessible and empowering to all.* It is not only service users with complex needs that require such advocacy support, which can provide training in managing care and employees (for instance dealing with the sick and holiday pay and pensions rights of care workers), as well as assistance with budgeting, accounting and payroll services. However, there is a general consensus that support services providing help and guidance for service users to develop the organisational and management skills needed to manage their own care is woefully inadequate, mainly because of the significant costs involved in delivering it. In 2014, 55 per cent of service users in receipt of direct payments found it 'not easy' or 'difficult' to access information, advice and support to help them organise their care. The percentage was even higher where the direct payment was paid to a family member or friend (61 per cent), where the direct payment was paid to a broker (63 per cent) and where service providers were responsible for managing personal budgets (66 per cent) (House of Commons Public Accounts Committee, 2016). There is, as Beresford (2014, p23) notes, *a lack of capacity building through ensuring accessible information, advice, guidance and advocacy*. Resource constraints have also had an impact upon the ability of social workers to offer service users effective advice and guidance. Hence, in 2013, one-third of social workers responding to *Community Care*'s (2013) annual personalisation survey stated that training and support for professionals in delivering personalisation was 'very poor' or 'poor'. Forty-two per cent stated that they needed *substantially more* training if they were to provide adequate tailored support to service users and a further 35 per cent identified a need for a *little more* training. As Beresford (2014) argues, delivering and supporting properly organised, empowering personalised services is not cheap and requires additional necessary but 'hidden' costs that in the absence of sufficient funding threaten the emancipatory potential of personalisation. As Glasby and Littlechild (2009, p147) note, *there is a growing consensus that financial concerns may be a major obstacle to the success and progress of direct payments, preventing some local authorities from promoting their schemes and potentially leaving recipients without sufficient funds to purchase adequate care.*

Finally, the huge public expenditure cuts introduced by Coalition and the Conservative administrations since 2010 have exacerbated fears over government commitments to fully resource the personalisation agenda. The Association of Directors of Social Services estimates that adult social care budgets have been slashed by 31 per cent between 2010/11 and 2015/16, and it is clear that the funding and quality of personalised services, like those for social care generally, has been affected by this (House of Commons Public Accounts Committee, 2016).

The Department for Health admits that £72 million was shaved off personalisation budgets between 2012/13 and 2014/15, though in all likelihood budgets will have faced considerably higher cuts than this. More 'savings' are forecast for 2015/16. The influential, all-party House of Commons Public Accounts Committee (2016, p3) has expressed its concerns at the potential impact of these cuts on the ability of local authorities to meet their obligations under the 2014 Care Act:

> *We are not assured that local authorities can fully personalise care while seeking to save money and are concerned that users' outcomes will be adversely affected. Local authorities face a substantial challenge supporting sustainable local care markets which offer the diverse range of provision needed for users to personalise their care, while care providers are struggling to recruit and retain appropriately qualified staff as financial pressures increase.*

In fact, social workers across the country are reporting huge cuts in the resources they are able to devote to personalisation, as well as the imposition of tight constraints over what service users can spend their budgets on. In 2013, more than eight out of ten social workers felt that cuts to adult social care budgets had reduced service users' choice and control over their budgets (Community Care, 2013). As Glasby has acknowledged, *many of the social workers I meet seem to feel very isolated and alienated – as if personalisation is giving them empowering language but that they are being set up to fail by a financial context that makes it impossible to deliver* (cited in Association of Directors of Adult Social Services, 2011, p9). Service user groups have also expressed their alarm at the scale of cuts, and have sought to mobilise their constituents in opposition to them.

> *Independent living, that is being able to meet our support needs in the way we choose so that we can be equal citizens in society, is in crisis! Everything we have gained as a movement over the last 30 years is now being put in jeopardy. If we cannot get our support needs met then we will become institutionalised in our own homes living in intolerable conditions and unable to take part in community life. We will be forced to be dependent on family, friends and volunteers who we have no control over. Just like the old days. We cannot allow this to happen! NCIL is actively campaigning against these draconian public expenditure cuts joining with other sections of our society who are also opposed.*
> (National Centre for Independent Living, 2011)

The impact of personalisation on 'traditional' forms of provision

Others have expressed concerns that as individual budgets are rolled out, the ability of local authorities to fund and organise good-quality collectivist services will be undermined, a process which will effectively confine many vulnerable adult service users to second-class, 'Cinderella' services. In a bizarre twist of fate then, service users reliant upon 'traditional' provision may find the quality of their social care needs are detrimentally affected by a process that purports to be about empowerment and social justice. As Beresford (2008a, p12) states:

> *There is an anxiety that the traditional menu of collective social care services – such as day centres and respite care – will wither away, leaving people adrift in a complex and inadequately regulated market: existing collective services may be closed without adequate alternative support provision being offered in replacement.*

Many social workers share these concerns. In one survey, more than half of those questioned agreed with the statement that *Services such as day centres are being closed down in my area on the grounds that personal budgets will mean reduced use* (Dunning, 2010, p15). Service user groups have also noted that 'traditional' services are being cut without any alternatives being made available for those who previously wished to continue to use them. This was the case in Glasgow in 2015, when the closure of three day-care centres left 320 adults with learning disabilities without much needed and valued provision. Council officials claimed that the choice exercised by personal budget users to source their care from elsewhere meant that the centres no longer represented *best value for taxpayers* (Wollard, 2015). A local campaign, spearheaded by a group of actors, poets and social work academics, accused the council of utilising the personalisation agenda as an excuse for implementing swingeing cuts to social care services:

> *No-one can dispute the view . . . that adults with learning disabilities should have much greater choice and control over the services they receive, or that these services should be community-based. Yet there is growing concern that in Glasgow, a progressive self-directed support agenda is being used as a cover for cuts which will result in a withdrawal of much-needed services, increased social isolation for service users and added pressure on carers who are often already at breaking point.* (Ferguson et al., 2012)

A spokesperson for *In Control*, an organisation that itself has acted as a powerful advocate in favour of personalised services, has also expressed concerns about such developments:

> *The worst thing for personalisation is that it's used as an excuse to cut services. Personalisation is {supposed to be} about choice. We know a lot of people are still choosing day centres and, if day centres aren't there, people won't have a choice.* (Dunning, 2010, p14)

Reluctance among social workers to embrace personalisation

The attitudes and knowledge of social workers have also been identified as potential barriers to the successful implementation of the personalisation agenda. There is, in fact, evidence to suggest that some social workers have been distinctly reluctant to embrace personalisation. In one 2013 survey, only 15 per cent of social workers said that they felt that service users and their families were best placed to lead support planning for their care (Community Care, 2013).

In part, the lack of enthusiasm is said to stem from legitimate anxieties surrounding some of the issues we have discussed above. Social workers have expressed concerns over the risks associated with allowing vulnerable people to manage their own budgets. The absence of sufficient funding and the potential threat personalisation poses to collectivist services have also contributed to scepticism within the profession about the transformatory potential of personalisation. In addition, the practical pressures associated with working in busy, poorly resourced social work teams can operate as an additional disincentive for front-line workers to embrace an agenda that (initially at least) is resource-heavy and time-consuming. This was one of the findings of the Individual Budgets Evaluation Network (IBEN, 2008, p22), which conducted a detailed analysis into the provision of personalised services. As one adult services care coordinator told the IBEN researchers, *Care managers really do see the benefits but don't feel able to put in much time when they have such high caseloads.* On a more practical level, as we have already hinted, many social workers are said to lack knowledge about direct payments, which limits their ability to advise service users about the benefits of personalisation.

However, as Glasby and Littlechild (2009, p137) argue, *it may not just be a lack of knowledge that hinders implementation, but political and/or professional opposition.* There can, in fact, be little doubt that many social workers, like social work academics, have misgivings about the impact of personalisation on the professional autonomy of practitioners. It does involve *a radical rethink of the nature of modern social work,* and while many social workers have welcomed the challenge, others have interpreted it as a process which undermines their professional status and skills. The following comments, made by a care coordinator for adult services, illustrates the genuine concerns shared by many other social workers over the extent to which personalisation may lead to a dilution of the profession's skill-base:

> *I just feel like I'm doing an office job most of the time now. You know, when you train to be a social worker, you get trained in counselling techniques and different therapeutic approaches. What I do is go out with a tick box form and read it out to somebody and then get somebody to come back to tell me how much money they are allowed and that's not a social worker. It's getting worse and worse.* (IBEN, 2008, p189)

In fact, there is evidence that personalisation may contribute to a process of de-skilling in local authority social service departments as well as the social care sector generally. For example, many social work teams have reported a decline in qualified, experienced staff. Indeed, one survey found that one in eight social workers felt that personalisation had contributed to a reduction of social workers in their teams, while 16 per cent felt it had contributed to an increase in non-qualified staff (Samuel, 2010b). Regarding the social care workforce generally, early 'sceptics' of the trajectory of the personalisation agenda, such as Ungerson (1997), had argued that personalised care could lead to the development of an unregulated, low-paid, unskilled, potentially exploitative social care labour market. She was concerned that recipients of direct payments and individual budgets may be tempted to employ personal assistants informally, on an illegal, cash-in-hand basis, with no provision being made for employment rights of any kind. While Ungerson (2006, p217) accepted that her worst fears had not materialised, she continued to argue that the working conditions experienced by many personal assistants were *not wholly satisfactory* and at times were *deeply unsatisfactory*. Others feared that the rapid expansion of personalisation would lead to the development of a 'two-tier' social care workforce, *with trained and regulated workers employed by agencies, possibly under better terms and conditions; and a less qualified and unregulated workforce employed directly by individual service users* (Baxter et al., 2011). More recent research suggests the emergence of an even less optimistic scenario. For example, many workers providing support to those receiving personalised care are now employed by social care agencies, who have responded to the challenge of personalisation by developing 'brokerage' services that offer care packages to service users with personal budgets. As Cunningham (2016, p661) notes, these agencies – even those working on a not-for-profit basis – have increasingly responded to cuts in the funding they receive from local authorities by recruiting carers on low paid, exploitative casual, flexible, fragmented contracts. This is how one not-for-profit agency human resources manager described the impact of personalisation on his agency's working practices:

> *With personalization we'll have to change dramatically. So we've been increasing our relief workers, and also zero hour contracts and different variations of that . . . What I'm getting from some of the services as well is that we might start looking at split shifts. It's all going to be for the person we're working for, which might not be quite so good for employees.*

Other HR managers admit that personalisation has led to a power shift within agencies, from care workers to employers. HR managers themselves privately acknowledge that they are now able to justify exploitative working practices with reference to the personalised needs of service users, thereby disguising their own exploitative practices, whether this be the imposition of zero hours contracts or pressure to be available to work when needed, even when ill. One senior operational HR manager acknowledged the concerns that this had led to among staff:

> *The workforce has found it very difficult because they think personalization is just about job cuts. It's about the council saving money and putting it in a fancy way. They have really struggled because some of them are the only wage earner.* (Cited in Cunningham, 2016, p662)

Naturally, social work professionals and social care workers are concerned about such developments and this, partially, helps explain some of the professional resistance to personalisation that exists. Service user groups themselves have strenuously denied claims that they are culpable in the exploitation of workers (Morris, 1997), while others have highlighted the compensatory factors that, in practice, can mitigate what ostensibly appear to be poorer employment rights, such as more worthwhile, meaningful relationships with service users (Glasby and Littlechild, 2009).

Finally, it is also important to bear in mind that opposition to personalisation within the social work profession can also stem from genuine concerns about the ideological underpinnings of the agenda. Put simply, many social workers fear that 'personalisation' is, to an extent, 'a wolf in sheep's clothing', part of a skilful, ideologically motivated strategy to fundamentally retrench welfare and to transfer the burden of funding and administering care onto adult service users themselves. We examine some of the main elements of ideologically focused critiques of personalisation below.

Ideological concerns

As we have already outlined above, a number of academics and social workers have questioned the ideological motives of politicians who have embraced 'personalisation'. Politicians have, some argued, utilised the progressive language of personalisation to justify neo-liberal-inspired strategies to reduce state welfare provision. This critique shares much in common with the critique of postmodernism that we outlined earlier. While the personalisation agenda shares some of the appealing 'rhetoric of empowerment' of service user movements, ideologically, critics argue, it has very little else in common with it. It is, they insist, lacking any commitment to dramatically improve the state's funding of welfare services, as evidenced by the government's insistence that personalised services do not cost any more than 'traditional' services. It is, they argue, a market-led, consumerist approach, with the focus placed upon utilising the choices and preferences of service users to help drive up standards and secure efficiency gains. At best, this might lead to a greater element of participation and user input, but it will do little to address the issues related to discrimination and the underfunding of provision that acts to the detriment of adult service users (Beresford, 2014).

This variant of personalisation, critics argue, in reality constitutes little more than a diversionary tactic – an 'ideological smokescreen' – designed to draw attention away from the more fundamental, costly reforms that are necessary to secure the economic and social well-being of adult service users. At the same time, social workers and service users are in danger of becoming unwitting, *compliant collaborators* in the residualisation of welfare, as governments seek to transfer responsibility for the delivery and oversight of welfare from the state (and social workers) to individuals themselves (Scourfield, 2007, p112). Again, there are links here to Taylor Gooby's critique of postmodernism outlined earlier. As Scourfield (2007, p108) argues:

> *The danger of using independence and choice as central organising principles is to forget how and why the public sector emerged in the first place – to ensure that those who are necessarily dependent are treated with respect and dignity, to ensure a collectivised approach to risk, and to ensure that secure and reliable forms of support outside of the market or the family are available.*

As we showed in Chapter 5, neo-liberals are ideologically opposed to state welfare and suspicious of the motives of state welfare workers, who are often dismissed as a self-serving cadre of bureaucrats. In this context, it is not hard to see the attraction of certain aspects of 'personalisation' to those wanting to reduce the state's role in the provision of social care and to encourage a greater role for the private sector.

In addition, on a practical level, personalisation could potentially make it less difficult, or less politically problematic, for ideologically motivated governments to reduce expenditure on welfare in the future. As we have seen on numerous occasions in the past, the threatened closure of large-scale, collectively provided services has frequently prompted large-scale, collectivist opposition on the part of service users and communities. Communities and service users have come together, in many cases successfully, to defend provision that they feel common ownership with. The organised, collective nature of such protests is hard for elected politicians to ignore, making it politically difficult for them to press ahead with widespread retrenchment. By contrast, individualising provision may reduce the potential for such opposition. Resistance to cuts may become more individualised, making it considerably more difficult to develop organised opposition to ideologically influenced reductions in social care funding and services. In the current cuts-driven political and economic climate, one can certainly see the political attraction of a strategy that inhibits the potential of collective resistance to reductions in funding for social care.

In summary, ideologically based critiques of personalisation do not reject the principles of user empowerment, or the idea that the views of service users themselves should be central in shaping the provision they receive. Indeed, many of those who are suspicious of the ideological influences underpinning personalisation are themselves passionate advocates of the concepts of user empowerment and 'independent living'. Their criticisms are based upon their belief that what we are seeing implemented is a very much diluted version of the kind of personalisation that has been demanded by user movements. They fear that the personalisation agenda has been driven primarily by neo-liberal principles and that the appealing rhetoric of empowerment is helping to disguise an ideologically influenced strategy that, in reality, is rapidly becoming synonymous with public expenditure cuts, reduced choice and increased privatisation. Many of those opposed to the current trajectory of policy would prefer to see a much greater level of prominence given to the promotion of social democratic principles within the personalisation agenda.

Activity 9.3

As we have argued, personalisation has been embraced by commentators, academics and politicians of all political complexions. Certainly, the 'language' of personalisation has been utilised by both social democrats and neo-liberals to criticise existing provision and to justify different policy prescriptions. In this

(Continued)

> *(Continued)*
>
> activity, we want you once again to don your 'ideological spectacles' and to think critically how the concept can be used to justify different policy ends.
>
> - What aspects of the 'personalisation' agenda might be appealing to social democrats?
> - What might a social democratic approach to 'personalisation' look like, and how might it differ from one that is based upon neo-liberal principles?

A social democratic vision of personalisation

One can certainly see the appeal of the rhetoric of personalisation to social democrats who, as we saw in Chapter 4, place considerable emphasis upon the need to secure social justice, equality and the promotion of human welfare. To the extent that personalisation is, to cite *Putting People First*, said to be *driven by a shared commitment to social justice* (HM Government, 2007, p5), it does seem very much in tune with key social democratic principles. So too does the promise personalisation holds out to empower service users, *enabling them to participate as active and equal citizens, both economically and socially* (p2).

However, while welcoming the principle of greater participation, a social democratic-influenced personalisation agenda would also insist upon the need to address wider structural problems that shape the living conditions and standards of care experienced by adult service users. Hence, alongside an assurance to ensure greater user involvement, social democrats would insist upon an accompanying commitment to, for example, guaranteeing financial security and to ensuring that adequate funds are available to meet the health and social care needs of adult service users. Current funding for adult social care and social security, they argue, is woefully inadequate and governments – whatever their political complexion – should not be allowed to divest themselves of responsibility for this by seeking to locate the blame for inadequate provision solely upon the way services are organised and delivered.

Supporters of such a strategy argue that it would, in fact, have much in common with philosophies and programmes of various user movements, which for many years have been demanding greater participation in the formulation and delivery of services and more equitable and adequate mechanisms of funding. Participation is obviously a key demand for such movements, but they have also been driven by a commitment to social justice and radical social change (Beresford, 2014), sharing much in common with social democratic thought and indeed Marxism. Thus, while the question of procedural rights to participate in the design and delivery of services are seen as extremely important aims, the need to ensure adequate resources and to tackle structural inequality is perceived to be equally crucial. This is the approach adopted, for example, by many disability activists. They welcome the recent emphasis placed by government on the need for welfare practitioners to listen to and engage with people with disabilities, but insist that this in itself is insufficient. As Barnes (2004) has argued, *to achieve a lifestyle comparable to non-disabled peers disabled people need far more than simply user-controlled services*:

> *To attain 'independent living' disabled people need equal access to mainstream schools, jobs, transport, houses, public buildings, leisure etc. or 'all the things that non-disabled people take for granted'* . . . *It is a goal that is far from being achieved despite the introduction of the 1995 Disability Discrimination Act and subsequent amendments.* (Barnes, 2004, p13)

Beresford (2014) makes much the same point, drawing attention to the potential contradictions between the kind of user empowerment demanded by service-user movements and the personalisation model that he feels is currently being promoted by government. The former, he argues, grew out of positive, democratising, user-led collective campaigns which fought for the right for service-user control over welfare resources. These user-movement campaigns were designed to strengthen and improve the legitimacy and quality of collective state welfare provision. By contrast, the ideological origins of the government's personalisation model, he suggests, can be found in individualised, market/efficiency-driven neo-liberal agendas, the aims of which have ultimately been to weaken support for collective provision. Scourfield (2005, p473) agrees: politicians seeking to transfer responsibility for securing welfare from the state to individual citizens have, he argues, skilfully 'sat' their market-driven justifications for personalisation on top of service users' 'social rights' discourse, *producing a powerful hybridisation but one riddled with tensions*. Arguably, in what was until 2010 a fairly benign economic environment, the personalisation agenda had managed to reconcile these apparently contradictory ideological influences, with varying degrees of success. However, the election of the Conservative-dominated Coalition in 2010 and Conservative government in 2015 led to a seismic 'neo-liberal turn' in economic and social policy, one which many commentators felt had brought to the fore the ideological tensions underpinning personalisation and undermined the limited gains that had so far been achieved:

> *Sadly, current positive moves to personal budgets, self directed support and personalisation seem to be being undermined as they are being challenged by broader and bigger cuts leading to increased restrictions on eligibility criteria, cash ceilings and, of course, serious attacks on disability benefits. They are increasingly being seen as a cover for cuts rather than a real improvement.* (Beresford, cited in Association of Directors of Adult Social Services, 2011, p11)

Chapter summary

We began this chapter by drawing attention to some of the factors that have contributed to the emergence of personalisation on the social policy agenda. As we saw, the 'universal' post-war welfare state's perceived failure to meet the particular needs of different groups of adult service users led to calls for the injection of greater heterogeneity and user empowerment in the organisation and delivery of welfare. Service users' needs, it was argued, had been stifled by a professionally led, 'one-size-fits-all' model of welfare that took little account of their own wishes and preferences. This had contributed to the development of unresponsive, inappropriate, even oppressive welfare interventions which, in practice, served to reinforce rather than alleviate the difficulties faced by many adult service users. Giving service users control over the collectively funded welfare resources they consumed was promoted by service-user groups themselves as being the most effective means of developing a more responsive, emancipatory model of delivering adult social care. As we have shown, an initial reluctance on the part of governments to embrace 'personalisation' has now given way to an unbridled enthusiasm for the concept, and its arrival on the social policy agenda has been welcomed by academics and politicians of all political shades. However, agreement over the basic principles underpinning personalisation – greater user empowerment and choice – should not be allowed to disguise the real differences in opinion that exist over the general trajectory of policy, or the growing questions that are being raised about the ideological and political imperatives that are driving the personalisation agenda. As Scourfield (2005, p470) argues, *the hegemonic character of the transformative discourse that has emerged around direct payments has largely led to the silencing of critiques, usually by the construction of such critiques as being reactionary.* However, the sheer volume of such concerns, together with the fact that they are emanating from some of the most passionate advocates of user empowerment and independent living, means that they warrant our close attention. As future welfare practitioners and social workers, it is, of course, crucial that you are aware of the emancipatory potential of personalisation. However, it is equally important that you are able to identify the potential contradictions underpinning the personalisation agenda, as well as some of the concerns that have been expressed by some of its most passionate advocates.

Further reading

There are a number of sources that cover many of the issues examined in this chapter in greater detail. The following textbook provides an excellent summary of the history and nature of direct payments at what was a key stage in their development:

Glasby, J and Littlechild, R (2002) *Social Work and Direct Payments*. Bristol: Policy Press.

This text examines more recent developments in policy and practice:

Glasby, J and Littlechild, R (2009) *Direct Payments and Personal Budgets: Putting Personalisation into Practice*. Bristol: Policy Press.

The following edited collection contains useful chapters on policy and practice, as well as service user perspectives on personalisation:

Leece, J and Bornat, J (eds) (2006) *Developments in Direct Payments*. Bristol: Policy Press.

This Learning Matters text also provides a good critical overview of the personalisation agenda and reflects on the legislation, history, theories, values and collective voices that have influenced it:

Gardner, A (2014) *Personalisation in Social Work*, 2nd edn. London: Learning Matters.

The following short collection of essays was published as part of a critical collection of books on radical debates in social work. It provides an excellent, concise critique of the direction of personalisation under Conservative-led governments:

Beresford, P (2014) *Personalisation*. Bristol: Policy Press.

10: Ageing, social policy and social work

The chapter will also introduce you to the following academic standards which are set out in the 2016 QAA social work benchmark statements:

4   Defining principles
5.1   Subject knowledge and understanding
5.2   Social work theory
5.3   Values and ethics
5.5   The nature of social work practice
5.6   The organisation and delivery of social work services
5.11   Manage problem solving activities
5.13   Analysis and synthesis
6.1   Teaching learning and assessment
7.3   Knowledge and understanding

Introduction

In this chapter we examine a number of broad, policy-based issues that are of relevance to you as students of social work. Our intention here, as with other chapters in this book, is not to list and describe policies and strategies affecting older people. Nor is it our intention to provide a detailed description of day-to-day 'hands-on' work with older service users. There are other titles in the Learning Matters series that fulfil such functions (see, for example, Crawford and Walker, 2008). Rather, our aim is to examine a number of broad, interacting themes and debates, the outcome of which have a direct impact upon policy and practice affecting older service users. In particular, we seek to present a challenge to the dominant conception of older people as a burden, drawing attention to the extent to which ageist stereotypes impact negatively upon the life chances of older people, as well as the quality of services provided to them. We will show how a pervasive culture of ageism structures the lives of older people, leading them to experience inequality and discrimination across a whole range of areas of economic and social life.

The policy background

Most of us are now living much longer than before. In 1901 males in the UK could only expect to reach the age of 45 and females 49. By contrast, life expectancy rates for males and females born in the UK between 2012 and 2014 were 79.5 and 83.2 respectively. It is predicted that these rates will continue to rise in the coming years (Office for National Statistics, 2015a). The number of people reaching their 100th birthday has quadrupled in the last 30 years, from 3,250 to 14,450 (Office for National Statistics, 2015b) and it is estimated that one in three babies born in 2013 will live to reach 100 – 30 per cent of all males and 39 per cent of all females (Office for National Statistics, 2013a, 2013b). Contrast this to 1952, when the newly crowned Queen Elizabeth sent only 270 telegrams to people on their hundredth birthday (it has long been practice in the UK for personal 'royal' greetings to be sent to new centenarians) (Cayton, 1998). Of course, demands on future monarchs apart, population ageing should surely be seen as a cause for celebration, as a reflection of improved standards of living and the achievements of welfare institutions such as the National Health Service and other branches of the welfare state.

However, despite the positive sentiments expressed in some official policy documents, population ageing is invariably seen as a problem for society rather than something to be celebrated. Experts, academics, politicians, business leaders and media commentators all tell us that increased life expectancies and ageing populations will, in the near future, place an intolerable strain on the welfare states of nations such as the UK. We are said to be facing a 'demographic time bomb' of unprecedented proportions, and immediate action must be taken if we are to avoid a 'meltdown' in our social care, health and pension systems. To a certain extent, such claims are based upon factual statistical data, which does point to that fact that the UK's population (like that of other developed countries) is getting older. This is an issue which we examine later in this chapter, where we critically examine the 'demographic time bomb' thesis in greater detail. The claims are, though, also based upon a particular perception of ageing and older people, one which is shaped by age-based stereotypes which see older adults as 'helpless' and as a 'burden'. Put simply, older people are seen as unproductive and a drain on resources, and hence data suggesting there are likely to be more of them are deemed to point to a deeply problematic future.

Activity 10.1

This activity is designed for use in larger groups, and is similar to the activity we included in Chapter 8, where we sought to gauge your views of younger people. This time, we want to elicit your perceptions of older people and to encourage you to think about how these might impact upon your future practice. This is important, because working with and providing services to older people can constitute a significant part of a social worker's role, and you need to be aware of how your own perceptions of the ageing process might impact upon your practice. It is a fairly simple activity, and one that is based upon methodology that has been used to assess societal perceptions of older people.

- Firstly, we want each of you to write down on a piece of paper half a dozen words or phrases that come to mind when you hear the terms 'older people' or 'pensioner'. It is important that you try to be as honest as possible, and in order to facilitate this we would suggest that you complete this exercise anonymously, without writing your name on the piece of paper.
- Once you have completed this, gather all the separate pieces of paper, shuffle them together and nominate one person to read out the responses.

Comment

We have tried this exercise with cohorts of our own students and have, at times, been surprised at the generalised, stereotypical attitudes that some have about older people. They tend to associate 'older people' and 'pensioners' with negative words and phrases such as 'dependent', 'ill', 'burden', 'past it', 'sad' and 'inactive', all of which tell us a lot about how some of our students, many of whom will in future be responsible for providing services to older adults, view older people.

We suspect that some of your group's comments will not have been too dissimilar to those we describe above. As the research round-up below illustrates, this is hardly surprising – most members of the public seem to perceive older people in a negative light.

As we have already stated, the above task is based upon a commonly used methodology that has been utilised to gauge the public's views on older people. In 2006, for example, Age Concern published a survey entitled, *Ageism: A Benchmark of Public Attitudes in Britain* (Ray et al., 2006). The survey questioned a representative sample of the population about their views of older people, seeking to assess the public's perceptions of their relative levels of capability. The results are summarised below.

- One in three people viewed those over 70 as 'incompetent' and 'incapable'.

- One in ten people felt that people over the age of 70 were 'unfriendly'.

- Twenty-seven per cent of people viewed 'older people' with 'pity'.

- One-half of respondents agreed with the statement that, 'employers don't like having older people on their workforce as it spoils their image'.

- Seventeen per cent felt that older people took more out of the economy more than they put in.

- One-third of people felt that population ageing will make life 'worse' for all.

In summary, the Age Concern study found compelling evidence of *patronising or benevolent prejudice, ranging from the more hostile image of a 'cantankerous old codger' to less overtly negative images . . . whereby older people are perceived as . . . 'doddery but dear'* (p53).

A recent government-commissioned literature review of research which examined attitudes towards ageing in the UK confirmed the continued prevalence of ageist sentiment. It found that people tend to believe that *older people lack creativity, they are unable to learn new skills, are unproductive, a burden on family and society, and they are ill, frail, dependent, asexual, lonely and socially isolated.* Even when older people work, they are still perceived in a negative way, associated *with inflexibility, poor adaptability, resistance to change, cautiousness, low trainability and poor computing skills* (Abrams et al., 2015, pp9–10). Another government-funded literature review drew attention to the interplay between ageist stereotypes and overwhelmingly negative media representations of older people. It found that most newspapers tended to portray older people as *a burden on society* or as *frail non-contributors* (Kishita et al., 2015). The same is true of feature films, TV dramas, comedies and even advertising, all of which frequently depict older people in a stereotypical way – as 'grumpy' and 'cantankerous' or as isolated, inactive, unproductive and burdensome. As Age UK (2005) has argued, such negative representations would not be deemed acceptable if they were used to portray other social groups:

> *A recent advertisement for the betting shop 'PaddyPower' shows two women crossing the road. Odds are placed near their heads as to the likelihood of the approaching car running them over. The two women are older and walking slowly across the road to the frustration of the impatient driver. Can you imagine the same advertisement however if it was laying odds on running over the women because they were black, or gay, or Muslim, or severely disabled? Society has fought hard over the past three decades to ensure equality for all and to make clear that discrimination on grounds of race, gender, sexuality, religion or disability is unacceptable. Isn't it time that ageism was taken just as seriously?*

Of course, this kind of portrayal of ageing has a long historical pedigree, but it has contributed to the prevalence of inaccurate, yet deeply ingrained negative conceptions of older people. In the light of such representations it is perhaps understandable why many view population ageing as a problem and are susceptible to the claim that future demographic trends pose 'difficulties' for society.

Activity 10.2

Just how much of a burden do older people present to society? Clearly, large sections of the population seem to think that the burden is considerable, and that it is likely to become even more so as population ageing gathers pace. Once again, though, it is important for us to think critically about some of the assumptions that underpin this perception of older people, for they are often based on wildly inaccurate estimates as to the numbers in need of intensive residential and social care. They also underestimate the positive contribution millions of older citizens make to the economy and the communities within which they live.

- How many people over 65 do you think receive social care?
- How many people over 65 live in residential care?
- Is it right to describe older, retired people as 'unproductive' and a burden? What contributions do older people make to the effective functioning of society?

Comment

Many people tend to assume that old age is synonymous with dependency and decline. Consequently, when asked about the percentage of older people who need and receive social care, the answers given are often wildly inaccurate. In fact, only a small minority of those over 65 in England and Wales receive social care – around 15 per cent – and only 3 per cent live in residential care. Among the over-85s, the percentage living in residential care is still a relatively low 16.2 per cent, considerably less than popular stereotypes would have us believe (Office for National Statistics, 2014b). Hence, the pervasive image of older people as helpless, dependent 'geriatrics' is a myth, albeit a very powerful and persuasive one. As Alan Walker argues, the reality is that *People are living significantly longer and the majority are healthier and are active well into their 70s, so the perception that someone who is older is likely to require care and a big input of health resources is just out of tune with the demographic reality* (cited in Murray, 2014, p36).

Nor is it inevitable that people become 'unproductive' after they have reached retirement age. Contrary to popular perceptions, 1,113,000 people over the age of 65 continued to work in 2015, thus making important economic contributions to society. In fact, the employment rate of those over the age of 65 has doubled over the past 30 years, from 4.9 per cent to 10.2 per cent. All older age groups have seen an increase in economic activity, including those in the 70–74 age category, whose employment rate almost doubled between 2005 and 2015, from 5.5 to 9.9 per cent. In all, 258,000 citizens in this age group are in employment (Department for Work and Pensions, 2015b). Older people also provide a whole range of crucial, unpaid caring and voluntary activities. It is estimated that 58 per cent of grandparents (seven million in all) provide regular childcare, saving the economy billions of pounds per year. As Francis O'Grady, the General Secretary of the Trade Union Congress (TUC) argues:

> *The informal childcare that millions of grandparents regularly provide is one of the most important and unheralded forms of care in Britain today. The childcare provided by grandparents allows mums and dads to work, saves them money on nursery and childminder fees, and creates a special bond across different generations in a family.* (TUC, 2013)

Many other older citizens care for their partners or other aged relatives, receiving very little recognition or remuneration for their considerable efforts. Indeed, according to one estimate, around 1.2 million people over the age of 65 were carers in 2011, an increase of 35 per cent since 2001. The fastest growing group of carers is the 85 or over category, among whom 87,000 undertook caring

(Continued)

(Continued)

responsibilities in 2011. Among those carers in the 65–76 age group, 32 per cent provided 50 or more hours of unpaid care per week (Age UK, 2014).

Nor should we underestimate the positive, meaningful contributions older people make to their communities through their volunteering activities. Almost one in three (28 per cent) of those aged between 65 and 74 participate in formal volunteering, while well over one in three (38 per cent) engage in some form of informal volunteering. For those aged 75 or over, the formal and informal volunteering rates are 21 per cent and 31 per cent respectively (Communities and Local Government, 2009, p8). Such activity is obviously beneficial for older people themselves, in that they remain engaged and embedded in their communities, while at the same time obtaining a sense of status and worth. However, the knowledge and expertise of older volunteers is also indispensable to many third-sector organisations, whose operations are dependent upon the efforts of reliable, conscientious volunteer workers. One survey suggests that those over 60 contribute around 18 million hours a week in unpaid work, which if paid at the minimum wage level, would cost £4.3 billion per year (Binyon, 2009).

Older people are also more likely to contribute to the political and democratic culture of the country. They are more inclined than their younger counterparts to vote in national and local elections. In the 2015 General Election, for instance, 78 per cent of those aged over 65 exercised their right to vote, whereas only 43 per cent of those in the 18–24 category did (Ipsos MORI, 2015). Older people are also often more likely to be actively involved in shaping decisions and policy at a community level. Indeed, those in the 65–74 age category are more likely to take part in direct decision-making about a local service or issue (through, for instance, taking on a role such as a councillor, school governor or magistrate) than any other age cohort (Communities and Local Government, 2009, p8).

All these trends serve to contradict popular conceptions of the ageing process, which see it as an inevitable period of decline, deterioration and 'disengagement' from useful economic and social functions. Indeed, they point to a highly engaged, politicised older citizenry who are as involved, or perhaps even more involved, in shaping their communities than younger age groups. As one longitudinal survey of the ageing process concluded, the *myth of older age as uniformly characterised by decline and dependency is contradicted by the evidence of vigorous and active nonagenarians* (Banks et al., 2008). As future practitioners, it is crucial that you bear this in mind when considering the support needs of older people. As Qureshi and Walker argue, older people *do not give up their independence easily: with few exceptions they are reluctant subjects in caring and dependency . . . elderly people desire, often more than anything else, the preservation of their independence* (cited in Thane, 2000, p431). However, as we saw earlier, people's perceptions of older people remain fixated on the notion that they are a 'problem' to be managed rather than an asset to be valued and respected. As a society we tend to view older generations through an explicitly ageist lens which draws from inaccurate though pervasive negative images of older people. This has a direct and adverse impact upon older people's standards of living, as well as the quality of services that are provided to them.

Research summary

A Marxist interpretation of ageing and ageism

Some commentators have sought to provide a Marxist interpretation of ageing in capitalist societies. For Marxists, the origins of inaccurate, negative portrayals of older people lie with the capitalist system itself. In a system that is based upon production, efficiency and profit accumulation, 'unproductive' older, retired people are seen as an unnecessary drain on otherwise productive resources. They are, to put it bluntly, less essential to the needs of capital (Phillipson, 1982, p156). This is the reason why the state in capitalist societies has consistently failed to devote adequate funding to the health and well-being of older citizens. As Phillipson (1982, p102) puts it:

The need for the {capitalist} state to have a healthy workforce is one matter, whether it needs to have a healthy population of elders is quite another. The necessity for the former has been a major impulse in the creation of social policy. By comparison, the desirability of the latter has had only a marginal influence.

Consequently, Marxists argue that it is in the interests of the bourgeoisie for the majority of the population to perceive older people as a growing, expensive burden. This provides capitalist governments with the justification they need to retrench public spending on welfare provision for 'unproductive' older people (Phillipson, 1982). Once convinced of the 'myth' that older people present a rapidly increasing and intolerable burden, citizens are far less likely to protest against miserly retirement incomes and inadequate caring services, or actively resist cuts in social care and pensions budgets. In short, fewer demands will be made by older people, and their advocates, on the public purse. From this perspective, therefore, the 'problem' of ageing has been consciously 'manufactured' by the state in capitalist societies. It provides a powerful rationale for failing to address the poverty and exclusion experienced by many older people.

(Continued)

(Continued)

Capitalism benefits in other ways from the 'structured dependency' of older people. Mandatory retirement ages found in most capitalist societies are not, Marxists argue, 'natural', nor do they reflect the capabilities of many older workers. They are artificially imposed age categories, deliberately designed to fulfil the requirements of the capitalist economy. On the one hand, the removal of older people from the workplace provides employers with access to a younger, cheaper, more efficient, disciplined and conservative workforce. The old are thus *sacrificed in the corporation's drive for order and efficiency: speed-ups on the line, work-measurement techniques, etc., sealing the fate of the ageing worker* (Phillipson, 1982, p156). On the other hand, as we have seen above, retirement 'frees' older people up to provide crucial, unpaid caring functions, which capitalist societies cannot do without. In this way, the forced 'retirement' of older workers allows working-age parents to utilise the free domestic labour of older relatives, and to enter the labour market at no, or minimal, cost to business. Older people also provide extensive levels of care to older relatives which would otherwise cost billions of pounds. The manipulation of retirement ages also allows capital to use older people, like women, as a 'reserve army of labour', which can be drawn into or rejected from the labour market when economic conditions deem it necessary.

In summary, therefore, Marxists dismiss *over-deterministic assumptions about the universality and inevitability of poor health and low status in old age* (Vincent, 1995, p15). Not only are they misleading, they serve to mask the extent to which capitalism benefits from the myth that older people are an unproductive burden upon societal resources. In reality, *there is no good reason to assume a priori that a chronologically old person is necessarily or significantly different in hopes, abilities and potential capacity from a chronologically middle-aged individual* (p22).

Need and expenditure

So far, we have provided evidence to question the commonplace assumption that older people are necessarily a burden, who inevitably 'disengage' from society as they get older. However, it is clear that many older people in the UK are vulnerable to, for example, poverty, ill-health and disablement. According to one estimate, around 10 per cent of those aged over 65 are considered to be 'frail', while approximately one in five of those aged over 85 are thought to experience difficulties in undertaking five or more 'daily living' activities, such as eating, toileting and washing (Mortimer and Green, 2015). Meanwhile, around 1.6 million pensioners (14 per cent) were thought to be living in poverty in 2014/15 (McGuinness, 2016). It is, of course, the role of social policy and welfare practitioners, such as social workers, to provide various forms of welfare support to help address these issues.

The principle of cradle-to-grave security, whereby the state accepted responsibility for the welfare of citizens from birth and through old age, was perhaps the defining, underpinning theme of the welfare state that emerged after 1945. However, doubts have been raised about the extent to which older people's welfare needs are adequately met. For although older people do consume a higher proportion of welfare resources than other age cohorts, many of the services they receive remain underfunded and inadequate to meet need. As we show below, the resources that we as a society devote to the welfare needs of older people are far from sufficient, and the economic and social problems they face are tolerated to a far greater extent than they would be if they affected other groups.

Poverty, age discrimination and disadvantage

Older people's incomes in the UK

Older people are not a homogenous group and many older people have incomes which are more than sufficient to meet their needs. Numerous surveys, however, have drawn attention to the extent to which many older people are likely to be living in poverty. As we have argued elsewhere, as future social workers you need to be aware of the extent to which poverty structures the lives of the service users that you will be working with, impacting upon their social, economic and psychological well-being (Cunningham and Cunningham, 2014). With regard to older people specifically, poverty provides the context that can increase the likelihood of their coming into contact with social services. It can, as we will show, lead older people to cut back on food, heating, clothing and other essentials, which in turn can adversely affect their ability to live healthy, independent lives. It is therefore important that you, as future practitioners, are aware of the extent of poverty in old age, as well as its consequences.

Regarding the extent of poverty, as we have already indicated, in 2014/15 14 per cent of pensioners were living on incomes below the government's official poverty line (this was £134 per week for single pensioners and £232 for pensioner couples, after housing costs). A further 1.2 million pensioners had incomes which are just above the poverty line (Independent Age, 2016). The incomes of many pensioners actually fall well below these levels due to their failure to claim much needed means-tested financial support (see below). Consequently, many older people are unable to afford the basic goods and services they require. The inability to afford essentials, such as food, clothing, transport and fuel, means that many older people simply 'do without', detrimentally impacting upon both their physical and mental health and well-being. As one recent government-commissioned survey into pensioner poverty found, *respondents experienced varying limitations around being able to meet their basic and most immediate needs, including being able to have enough to eat and/or afford adequate quality of food, being able to afford clothes and care.* Those interviewed also *struggled to meet regular utility bills* and *were unable to keep their house as warm as they would like it* (Kotecha et al., 2013, pp14–15). In fact, as the following study showed, pensioners in the UK are far more likely than their counterparts in other countries to dread the onset of winter and to reduce spending on heating:

> *UK respondents are more likely than those in Germany and Sweden to have rationed their heating last winter. Indeed, they are four times more likely than those in Sweden to have avoided heating rooms in their home and to have turned off their heating even when they were cold because they were worried about the cost . . . UK respondents are also more likely to . . . worry about getting out and about in winter, and about being vulnerable to hypothermia, heart attacks and strokes.* (MORI, 2006, pp3, 8)

These fears are well founded, for in 2014/15 there were 36,300 excess winter deaths among those aged over 75 in England and Wales alone, a far higher level than that found in countries such as Sweden which have colder winters than the UK (ONS, 2015c). This shocking statistic serves to illustrate the very real impact poverty can have on the lives of older people. When compounded with the other crises that are often encountered in later life, such as bereavement, isolation, illness and the onset of disability, poverty can literally mean the difference between life and death for many older people.

One of the main causes of poverty in old age is the inadequate level of financial support provided by the UK's state pension system. As the all-party House of Commons Work and Pensions Committee (2009, p12) notes, it fails to provide an income sufficient to meet the minimal costs for healthy living in respect of requirements including *nutrition, physical activity, housing, psychological relations, mobility and medical care.* Certainly, there can be little doubt that UK pensioner incomes from state provision have fallen well behind those of their international counterparts. Low earners in the UK can only expect to receive 43.3 per cent of their pre-retirement income when they retire, compared to the 107.4 per cent received by their Danish equivalents. Not all countries offer as generous levels of pension support to low earners as Denmark, but very few offer as meagre levels of assistance as the UK. The Netherlands delivers a 'replacement rate' of 94 per cent for low earners and the equivalent rates for Iceland, Spain and Austria are 82.6, 82.1 and 78.1 per cent respectively. For those on average earnings in the UK (£26,500 in 2016) the UK pensions system provides an even less generous replacement rate of just 21.6 per cent. By contrast, those on average earnings in the Netherlands receive 90.5 per cent of their former salary when they retire, whereas those in Italy, Denmark and France receive 69.5, 67.8 and 55.4 per cent respectively. In fact, the UK's pension system provides the least generous levels of security for average earners out of the 34 major OECD world economies (OECD, 2016b).

Indeed, the real value of the basic state pension in the UK has fallen considerably and consistently since 1980, when a decision was taken by Margaret Thatcher's Conservative government to increase it annually in relation to prices rather than earnings. Claiming to be concerned about the 'burden' of providing for increasing numbers of 'dependent' older people, successive Conservative governments introduced this, and a range of other policies, designed to reduce the state's obligations to provide financial security in old age and to transfer responsibility on to individuals and families themselves. As we will see, although population ageing was cited as justification for this shift, a number of commentators argue that Conservative ministers were influenced primarily by neo-liberal, ideological concerns. In short, they were ideologically committed to rolling back the state and reducing welfare provision across the board, and 'apocalyptic demography' was used to justify ideologically influenced reductions in provision for older people (Cunningham, 2006). As a result of these changes, the real value of the basic state pension fell from 26 per cent of average earnings in 1979 to just 17 per cent in 2011 (Rutherford, 2013), and, in monetary terms a single pensioner was £3,075 worse off (National Pensioners Convention, 2011). By the time the Conservatives lost the General Election in 1997 almost one in three pensioners (29 per cent) had incomes below the official poverty line (House of Commons Work and Pensions Committee, 2009, p12). In addition, as the value of the basic state pension has continued to fall, many more pensioners have become reliant upon means-tested support to top up their incomes to what is deemed an 'acceptable' level.

Pensioner poverty has fallen somewhat since 1997 due mainly to Labour's improvement in the value of means-tested support (the Pension Credit) but, as outlined above, poverty among older people still remains at unacceptable levels. One of the main issues has been the continued reliance upon means-tested strategies to distribute financial support to vulnerable older people. As is often the case with means-tested benefits, there has been a significant problem of non-take-up.

Activity 10.3

As social workers, one of your roles will be to ensure that older people receive the financial support that they are entitled to. As we have just seen, even when in receipt of their full entitlements, in many cases pensioners will still be lacking an income that is sufficient to meet their needs. However, many older people in the UK are failing to receive even these minimal levels of support. After reading through the data presented below, try answering the questions that follow.

- In 2014/15, 38 per cent of older people eligible for the means-tested income support via the Pensions Credit failed to claim their entitlement, saving the government £3 billion per year (DfWP, 2016). Just to put this in perspective, this was considerably more than the £1.3 billion that was estimated to have been lost through benefit fraud for the same period (DfWP, 2015c).
- In 2014/15, 10 per cent of pensioners eligible for Housing Benefit did not claim their entitlement. The total saved amounted to £620–900 million (DfWP, 2016b).

(Continued)

(Continued)

- The government ceased publishing data relating to Council Tax Benefit take up in 2012, but we know that considerable numbers of pensioners fail to claim this entitlement too, In 2009/10, for example (the last period for which data is available), between 39 and 46 per cent of pensioners eligible for means-tested Council Tax Benefit failed to claim their entitlement, saving the government billions of pounds (DfWP, 2012).

In Chapter 2 we looked briefly at the issue of non-take-up of means-tested benefits and provided some hints there as to why people may fail to claim support they are entitled to. Why do you think there is a particular problem of non-take-up among pensioners?

Comment

Research suggests that there are a number of crucial factors that contribute to high levels of non-take-up among older people. Firstly, many are simply not aware that they are eligible for means-tested support, assuming (incorrectly) that they would be informed about any benefits to which they are entitled. As Moffatt and Higgs (2007, p455) note, *a significant proportion of older people have only a vague idea about the welfare benefits system and very little idea about what they are entitled to.* Other research points to a perception among pensioners that means-tested support is only available to the 'very poor'; a 'they don't mean me' attitude often prevails:

> *A commonly held view was that having modest savings (a few hundred pounds) meant an individual had too much money to be eligible for Pension Credit . . . A view of 'not being poor enough' was strongly held . . . essentially if you could afford to eat and live, you were unlikely to be successful in making a claim.*

> *'I thought* [Pension Credit] *was for people that were really rock bottom.'* (Male, North West)

> *'. . . well, I thought, I didn't know if we would be able to get any . . . well, because I didn't think we would . . . Well, I think you have to be really poor.'* (Female, North East).

> (Bhattachary and Slade, 2012, p16)

Secondly, among those who are aware of their eligibility, a sizeable proportion are deterred from claiming because of the complexity of the process. The 2016 version of the Pension Credit form, for instance, is a voluminous 23 pages, and there are an additional 19 pages of guidance to 'help' applicants fill in the form. The form itself asks complex, detailed questions about finances that many potential claimants find confusing, and it requires applicants to send in original copies of proof of evidence for any sources of income. The shift to the use of online forms by the DfWP has also failed to improve take-up – indeed it has generated anxiety and confusion among pensioners. Many lack computer literacy and the skills and resources to make online claims, while others express serious reservations about inputting their personal data online (Bhattachary and Slade, 2012). Faced with such obstacles and requirements, many older people view the claiming process as too onerous and simply fail to submit claims.

Finally, many associate claiming with the intrusive, stigmatising means tests of the inter-war years, and they resent having to reveal detailed financial information in order to claim benefits that they feel they should be entitled to as a right. Hence research shows that significant numbers of non-claimants are actually aware of their entitlements, but decline to claim because of the stigma associated with the process. One Department for Work and Pensions (DfWP) survey found that up to 5 per cent of non-claimants would still refuse to claim even if they received an extra £40 per week (cited in DfWP, 2005, p22). These were the findings of another DfWP-funded study:

> The key barrier preventing {a sizeable number of pensioners} from making a claim was their attitude towards Pension Credit – being too proud to accept any financial assistance. Often partners, particularly men, were reluctant to ask for help – holding the view that they should be able to provide for their families. This not only hindered the potential to gain financial support for themselves but also for their partner.
>
> 'I mean it's a bit embarrassing because you're on the take aren't you I think.' (Male, West Midlands)
>
> 'I heard about it, and a long, long time ago, someone said, well a relation, I can't remember which one it was, said, why don't you apply for Pension Credit, I said I won't get anything like that, and my hubby, said no we are not having that, you know, we'll manage as we are . . . Oh cos he's very proud, he was a very proud man, he said no.' (Female, South West)
>
> (Bhattachary and Slade, 2012, p20)

As Bhattachary and Slade (2012) note, the pensioners who fall in to this category are often the most vulnerable, tending to be older (in their seventies and eighties) and characterised by a variety of health and mobility problems. In short, they are precisely the kind of pensioners who need the greatest levels of financial support.

These surveys draw into question the current chosen method for distributing financial support for older people – means-tested assistance. As Goodman et al. (2003)

(Continued)

(Continued)

argue, if means-tested benefits are not taken up, then increases in entitlements, no matter how large, will not make a significant contribution to ending pensioner poverty. The evidence suggests that many of those failing to claim are the poorest pensioners and that hundreds of thousands are falling below this means-tested safety net and remaining in poverty due to missing out on their benefits. The 1.4 million pensioner households which failed to claim just their Pension Credit entitlement in 2014/15 lost on average £2,000 per year, which, in the context of the UK's already meagre system of pensions benefits, is a considerable sum of money (DfWP, 2016a). Just to reiterate, the issue is not simply one of complexity or lack of awareness. Research shows that significant numbers of non-claimants are actually aware of their entitlements, but decline to claim because of the stigma associated with the process. Hence, organisations representing older people, such as the National Pensioners Convention and Age UK, argue that the only effective way of getting additional resources to those pensioners who need them most is to introduce a truly universal citizens' basic state pension, which guarantees all older people an income above the official poverty line.

Age discrimination

In the light of our earlier discussions about societal perceptions of older people, it should come as no surprise to learn that older people face discrimination across a whole range of different walks of life. The prejudice older people face can take a number of forms. As consumers, older people face difficulty in accessing various financial products, such as loans, mortgages, and health, travel and car insurance, all of which can impact upon their ability to participate fully in society. In the labour market, we find that employers often discriminate against older candidates for jobs, assuming (incorrectly) they will be less motivated and more unreliable than younger applicants. Perhaps of more relevance to you as future social workers is the discrimination that older people often face in accessing welfare services.

Ageism and health care

The National Health Service (NHS) (2016) Constitution states that it should provide *a comprehensive service, available to all . . . irrespective of gender, race, disability, age, sexual orientation, religion, belief, gender reassignment, pregnancy and maternity or marital or civil partnership status.* The NHS, the Constitution goes on, has an obligation to ensure that *nobody is excluded, discriminated against or left behind.* However, difficulties that older people often experience in accessing health care services are now well documented. The following examples of discrimination in health services were outlined in a 1999 Age Concern report entitled *Turning Your Back on Us.*

- A 75-year-old women suffering from a build-up of cholesterol was told by her GP that the cut-off age for cholesterol treatment was 70. She was declined treatment on the NHS.

- A 71-year-old man with gallstones was told by a doctor *we wouldn't consider surgery at your age*.

- An elderly man with dementia had been placed on the floor with no bedclothes because he was being *demanding*. A sign had been placed next to him saying *good luck for tonight*, warning staff he was *troublesome*.

Turning Your Back on Us illustrated the extent to which the prejudicial, stereotypical attitudes we outlined earlier were influencing the views of health professionals, leading to inferior standards of care for older patients. Often this discrimination was inadvertent, based upon subtle, covert, often unconscious, ageist assumptions and attitudes. Practitioners had unwittingly internalised societal age stereotypes, and it was this rather than any conscious malicious intent which led them to assign older people a lower priority status than younger people.

However, Age Concern found evidence of more direct discrimination, whereby discriminatory practices were formally enshrined in policy. Thus, women aged over 70 were, as a matter of policy, not offered breast-screening opportunities, despite a clear risk, and in many areas there was an arbitrary cut-off of 60 in place for heart transplants and some other forms of care, including accident and emergency treatment, kidney dialysis and knee replacements (Lourie, 2001, p13). As we have already noted, an ageing population was one of the NHS's crowning achievements of the twentieth century, yet by the end of the century the NHS was being criticised for failing to meet older people's needs. As Harry Cayton (1998), head of the Alzheimer's Society, argued, the health service seemed to have responded to demographic change *not by redirecting resources to the old but by trying to ration care for them*.

The publication of the *National Service Framework for Older People* (NSFfOP) in 2001 was prompted by the then Labour government's acknowledgement that older users of health (and social care and social work services) were not being offered the same standards of care as other citizens. As the Health Minister, Alan Milburn, frankly admitted, services often *fail to meet older people's needs – sometimes by discriminating against them, by failing to treat them with dignity and respect* (Department of Health 2001, pii). There was, the NSFfOP stated, *evidence of poor, unresponsive, insensitive and, in the worst cases, discriminatory, services*, and the first of its eight framework standards pointed explicitly to the need for health and social care services to be geared towards *rooting out age discrimination*:

> *NHS services will be provided, regardless of age, on the basis of clinical need alone. Social care services will not use age in their eligibility criteria or policies, to restrict access to available services.* (Department of Health, 2001, p12)

Some eight years after the publication of the NSFfOP, the Department of Health commissioned the Centre for Policy on Ageing (CPA) to undertake a review of discrimination in the health and social care sectors. One of the resulting reports, *Achieving Age Equality in Health and Social Care*, provided a summary of the progress made in tackling ageism since 2001 (Carruthers and Ormondroyd, 2009). Some improvements had occurred, particularly in relation to overt age discrimination, and the report noted that a number of useful strategies had been introduced. Some of these are intended to tackle problems across the adult social care sector, but many were explicitly targeted at ensuring older people are able to access the same opportunities as other citizens. These initiatives included:

- the National Service Framework for Older People (2001);

- the Opportunity Age Strategy (2005);

- the Dignity in Care campaign (2006);

- Putting People First (2007);

- the End of Life Care strategy (2008);

- PSA Delivery Agreement 17: Tackle Poverty and Promote Greater Independence and Well-being in Later Life (2009)

- the Building a Society for All Ages initiative (2009).

- the National Dementia Strategy (2009).

However, despite these potentially positive policy campaigns and developments, the CPA found *clear evidence that discrimination remains* (p6). Once again, subtle, unconscious ageist attitudes of welfare organisations and professionals were highlighted as the major issue. Most examples of age discrimination, the report points out, *appear to be matters of thoughtlessness and misplaced assumptions, often reflecting those in wider society and are not the product of avowed prejudice* (p40). In one sense, this is a relief, since it suggests that the problem is not one of deeply held prejudice against older people. On the other hand, it is worrying in that it implies that many individual practitioners and welfare institutions are largely oblivious to their own discriminatory behaviour. The CPA called for professional bodies such as the General Social Care Council and the Nursing and Midwifery Council to redouble their efforts to ensure that all health and social care workers, through their training, are made aware of the need to identify and challenge ageism, and to base their practice *upon people's actual needs, preferences and aspirations, not assumptions about them derived from age* (p41).

Despite the introduction of initiatives such as those listed above, age discrimination was not *formally* prohibited within the NHS until 2012, serving to illustrate the lack of priority that had hitherto been attached to meeting the health care needs of the UK's older citizens. However, research suggests that this formal prohibition has failed to prevent discrimination and that the UK's health care system continues to deny older citizens the treatment that they urgently need. For instance, despite the incidence of breast cancer, cholecystectomy, inguinal hernia repair and knee replacement peaking at around the age of 80, a number of regional clinical commissioning groups (CCGs) across the country report that they undertake *no* surgical treatments for these conditions among the over-75s. Many other CCGs reported much lower levels of surgery among the over-65 and over-75 age groups. Age UK and the Royal College of Surgeons (2014, p7) describe these findings as a national scandal, pointing out that such surgery has the potential to be life enhancing for older people, reducing the debilitating impact of chronic, long-term conditions, enabling them to live more independent, fulfilling and longer lives. *We can no longer rely on outdated perceptions of fitness and old age*, they insist. Older citizens *have the right to expect that those making decisions about their care and treatment will base their decisions on an objective assessment of their health needs*.

Ageism and social care

Health care is not the only area of welfare that is characterised by differential levels of treatment. Age-related inequalities in standards of provision are also a characteristic feature of the social work and social care sectors and practices that would be deemed as wholly unacceptable for other groups, such as children, young people and disabled adults, are routinely tolerated when it comes to older service users.

Funding and social care

Firstly, there is the question of funding for social care services. Unlike the National Health Service, which provides free health care on a universal basis to all people irrespective of their incomes, the provision of social care (residential and home care) in England is subjected to stringent eligibility criteria and means tests. Regarding the means test, in 2015/16 individuals in England with assets of over £23,250 (including their homes) received no public support for social care, irrespective of the level of need identified. Those with assets of between £14,250 and £23,250 were also expected to make significant contributions to the costs of their care. These charges have been the subject of growing controversy and after much deliberation the Coalition government's Care Act 2014 included provisions which would have increased the means-test threshold to £118,000 for home owners needing residential care. It also included powers to introduce an overall cap on personal payments of £72,000, after which local authorities would become responsible for meeting the costs of social care. However, the implementation of these changes was delayed until at least April 2020, due to concerns about its impact upon public finances (Jarrett, 2015). The Alzheimer's Society (2015) argued that the decision to postpone the cap's introduction would *cause unacceptable costs to continue to be borne by people with dementia and their families into the next decade*.

Worryingly, one survey found that 31 per cent of the population are unaware of the obligation they are under to fund their own social care in old age, assuming that free social care will be available to them when they need it. This is a concern, and it epitomises the ignorance that surrounds social care funding, which in reality is heavily dependent upon private contributions. In 2015, for instance, it was estimated that total private expenditure on social care by older people, including user charges, top-up payments and privately purchased care, amounted to around £6.8 billion, which was roughly the same amount spent by local authorities. Of those in residential care, around 47 per cent (157,100) are forced to pay their care fees privately, without any assistance from the state or the local authority (Wittenburg and Hu, 2015).

However, being in receipt of a low income is in itself no guarantee that support will be provided. This will ultimately be determined by a complex assessment of needs, which is governed by the *Fair Access to Care Services* (FACS) guidance. Introduced by the Department for Health in 2002, FACS categorises individuals into four bands of 'risk':

- critical;
- substantial;
- moderate;
- low.

(For a more detailed description of these risk categories see Crawford and Walker (2008).)

FACS was intended to ensure that services were needs led and would be driven by a non-discriminatory, human-rights approach, though investigations by the Commission for Social Care Inspection and its successor, the Care Quality Commission (CQC), have revealed widespread variations in practice.

One of the main problems identified by the CQC is the artificial rationing of services by local authorities. As it notes, local authority funding for services has been drastically cut since 2010 and this has had an impact on social care resources:

> *According to the National Audit Office, local authority budgets have been reduced by 37% in real terms and on a like for like basis over the last five years. Local authorities have worked hard to protect social care budgets from these reductions . . . {but} . . . the result is that statutory funding for social care has decreased by £4.6 billion in this period, which is a 31% real-term reduction in net budgets.* (CQC, 2015, p11)

Concerned about their own dwindling resources for meeting their social care responsibilities, and in the absence of any political will to increase funding, many local authorities have increased eligibility thresholds. They have, the CQC (2015, p11), notes *had to prioritise care for those with the most severe need. They have tightened their eligibility criteria, cut back on what is provided in care packages and reduced spending on preventative care.*

So whereas previously service users with low or moderate needs may have been entitled to care, frequently only those with substantial or critical levels of need are now eligible. This may seem harsh, but it is perfectly legal. Although the four categories of need are set nationally, individual local authorities are able to choose themselves which categories should be used as a gateway to support. Also, under FACS guidance local authorities are allowed to take into account their own financial resources when making decisions about entitlement, which in itself makes something of a mockery of the claim that social care is distributed on a service user needs-led basis (CSCI, 2009, p20). Put simply, as demands on local authorities have increased, many of them have responded by 'changing the goalposts', increasing the level of need required to access care in order to ration provision and save resources. Thus, in 2006, 53 per cent of English councils funded the social care of service users with 'moderate needs', but by 2013/14 this had reduced to only 15 per cent, the remainder providing support only to those with 'substantial' or 'critical' needs (UNISON, 2015). The CQC estimates that there were 400,000 fewer people receiving publicly funded care services in 2014/15 compared to 2009/10, despite growing levels of need.

The CQC has identified a 'postcode lottery', whereby services may be available to people with particular needs in one area, but those with the same levels of need in neighbouring local authorities are ineligible for support. Inevitably, this *generates confusion and dissatisfaction among service users and carers, who do not understand how a system called 'fair' can result in the same level of need being met by provision of social care in one local authority and not another* (CSCI, 2009, p34). The resentment is, of course, compounded by the fact that those who do not meet these (often somewhat arbitrary) thresholds are expected to organise and pay for their own care.

Of course, it is front-line social workers who are tasked with the responsibility of managing the increasingly stringent eligibility criteria adopted by local authorities, a role that many naturally feel uncomfortable with. Many social workers are motivated to join the profession out of a profound sense of social justice and a desire to effect positive change in the lives of marginalised, vulnerable people. However, many feel that much of their time and energy is devoted to doing precisely the opposite, preventing vulnerable people from accessing services that will be of benefit to them. Assessments are, to cite one CSCI report (2008a, p23), *more concerned with using standardised procedures to screen people out of support rather than to assess their needs*. The King's Fund recently evaluated the impact of cuts to local funding on provision for older service users. This was the response it received from one local authority spokesperson:

> We ask individuals first of all what they can do for themselves, and then we turn to the family and say 'What can they do', then to the local community and say 'What can you do', then only after that do we think about what the council should do. (Humphries et al., 2016, p20)

As the following comments made by one local authority social care provider illustrate, the frustration felt by front-line practitioners is shared by many of their senior management colleagues:

> *It's horrible . . . {A} lot of the directors started off as social workers, they didn't go in there to cut services or make a service work . . . but they've been put in this very difficult position.* (Humphries et al., 2016, p18)

Funding cuts and the consequent need to severely ration and deny access to services inevitably affects morale among practitioners, many of whom believe such 'screening' contravenes the social work value base that they signed up to and passionately support. More concerning, however, is its impact upon those denied services who, according to a CSCI (2008b, p47) review into eligibility for social care, are simply *lost to the system*:

> *Without support people still had needs (and often, it appeared, significant needs that were simply overlooked) and they managed as best they could, but often at great cost in financial, emotional, personal and physical terms.*

Nor should we underestimate the broader climate of fatalism and resignation that such a system engenders among potential beneficiaries of services, many of whom are deterred from applying for assistance that they desperately need. As the Parkinson's Disease Society has argued:

> *The system is overly budget-driven with eligibility criteria being used to save money. People report that they feel social services are looking for excuses to exclude them, not to meet their needs . . . The word of mouth impact of this is that other potential users are put off even trying to get help.*(Cited in CSCI, 2008a, p37)

Clearly, all service user groups are affected by these shortcomings, but as the CPA (2009) argues, the failings we have identified often work to the particular detriment of older service users. For example, the fact that most local authorities restrict access to support to the two highest categories of need means that 'low' or 'moderate' levels of support, which can be crucial in enabling older people to live independently in the community, are not provided, leaving residential care as the only option for many. In fact, the CQC (2015) has confirmed that older service users have been disproportionately hit by local authority rationing of services. There has, it notes, *been a greater reduction in the percentage of older people receiving local authority funded or commissioned care, compared with 18–64 year olds* (p106):

> *Older people (those aged 65 and over) have been hit harder by reductions in local authority eligibility criteria, compared with other adults. More than 42,300 fewer older people in England received local authority-funded adult social care in 2013/14 compared with the previous year, a 4.7% reduction. The equivalent figure for those aged 18–64 was 12,500, a 2.9% reduction.* (p21)

What type of care for older people?

Despite the rhetorical emphasis placed upon 'choice', 'empowerment' and the psychological benefits of providing services in users' own homes, the underlying assumption that shapes practice still seems to be that 'residential care' is the most appropriate option for older people. This conclusion is supported by data which show a 30 per cent reduction in older people receiving local authority funded community-based council services since 2009 (Humphries et al., 2016). Worryingly, the evidence suggests that this trend has been driven less by the service users' needs or wishes, but more by the limited resources available to fund older people's care. As the CPA (2009) argues, *In practice, cost ceilings for packages of care can trigger reviews which might lead older people being pressured to accept residential care that is considered more cost-effective for local authorities at an earlier point than younger adults.* The following comments were made by professionals responsible for providing care services for older people and they serve to illustrate the inferior treatment received by older service users compared to their younger counterparts:

> *The limit for younger disabled is much higher . . . The market for older people is more 'pile 'em high, sell 'em cheap'. But also . . . there's a notion of 'it's more important to keep a young person at home'.*

> *There have been people who have been forced into care because we've refused to fund them any further {with domiciliary care packages}. They are told 'So you take your risk and stay at home or you go into care'.*

> *Generally . . . there's less per head for older people . . . {Older people are} placed in residential care homes so we don't overspend. It's discrimination because it's not how we would treat . . . children, then it's 'hang the cost'.*

> *So you could have an older person in the early stages of dementia or whatever it might be, who really wants to stay in their own home, but their package is going to be absolutely massive and you have got a spend ceiling for older people, so they can't have it. They have to go into residential care unless somebody tops them up, you know, their family. You could have a person with learning disability with dementia in their later stages of life being supported, and massively, to stay at home. Now that's the tension.*

> *We expect to pay significantly higher amounts for residential care for younger adults. It's historical, based on lower expectations . . . Some of that will be realistic and some is 'that's the way we've always done it'.*

> (CPA, 2009, pp19 and 34–5)

The quality of care for older people

There is also the question of the variable quality of care provided to older people. As the above quotations imply, inferior levels of spending inevitably equate to inferior standards of care.

Thus, in some residential care homes, often little is done to ensure that residents benefit from social, recreational and community activities. Inadequate funding is clearly a contributory factor here, though ageist stereotypes about what is an appropriate package of care for older people also play their part. As one inquiry into the conditions found in care homes concluded, the *prevalent model in care emphasises the debilitating effects of old age where staff take on the role of custodians who 'do things to' residents* (Owen, 2006, p68). CQC inspections confirm that the quality of care in adult residential care institutions is often not up to the required standard. Indeed, in 2014/15, around 40 per cent of the care settings that it inspected either required improvement (33 per cent) or were rated as inadequate (7 per cent). The quality of care in nursing homes, where many older service users with more complex health needs are placed, was even worse: 10 per cent were rated as inadequate and 45 per cent as requiring improvement (CQC, 2015).

Of course, this is not to suggest that residential care is an inappropriate choice for many service users, or that many residential care homes do not provide an excellent standard of care to their older service users. Nor is it to belittle the hard work and professionalism of social care workers working in many residential homes, the overwhelming majority of whom are dedicated to providing their service users with dignified, person-centred appropriate care. However, residential care for older people is often under-resourced and based upon a qualitatively different set of assumptions about the type of support that is needed. As Scourfield (2006, p1136) argues, *In both popular and professional discourses, people living in residential care are often homogenized, being defined in terms of 'complex needs' and 'dependency'*, and too little attention is paid to the possibility that they may wish to remain 'active' and 'engaged' citizens.

Even where home care packages are provided for older people, they tend to be focused upon personal care needs rather than seeking to support them in participating in useful, engaging, empowering activities, such as education or voluntary work. Different assumptions therefore seem to be made about what is an 'appropriate' quality of life for older people, and this is reflected in both the levels of financial resources devoted to their care as well as the standard of care provided. As we discussed earlier, the assumption that old age is a time of decline, mental and physical deterioration and dependency is widely held, and this, as the CPA (2009, p40) states, *can lead to assumptions about how older people should lead their lives . . . with an emphasis on managing dependency and decline.*

In summary, there is widespread evidence pointing to age discrimination in both health and social care provision in the UK, a problem that is in many cases compounded by the income poverty that many older people face. Utilising this evidence, groups representing older people argue that there is a clear, compelling case, based upon moral and social justice grounds, for enhancing the funding and quality of welfare provision for older people. However, the voices of those advocating such a policy shift are increasingly drowned out by the protestations of what we shall refer to here as 'demographic pessimists'.

Demographic 'pessimists'

Demographic pessimists accuse those calling for improved levels of provision for older people of naive sentimentalism and of ignoring demographic and economic realities. The position of the pessimists is fairly unequivocal. They argue that ageing populations in developed countries such as the UK are going to impose steep, unsustainable, health, social care and pensions costs, and immediate action is needed if we are to avoid a looming 'demographic timebomb'. The 'solutions' advocated by the pessimists vary. On the extreme end, we have those such as the author Martin Amis, who advocate voluntary euthanasia. He predicts a 'silver tsunami':

> *There'll be a population of demented very old people, like an invasion of terrible*
> *immigrants, stinking out the restaurants and cafes and shops. I can imagine a*
> *sort of civil war between the old and the young in 10 or 15 years' time.* (Cited in
> Chittenden, 2010, p7)

This 'silver tsunami', he suggests, can be avoided by the setting up of voluntary euthanasia booths on street corners, and those choosing to do the 'decent thing' can be offered a Martini and a medal for their trouble! Of course, not all pessimists agree with Amis's crude, unsophisticated musings on the implications of population ageing. Most focus upon what they see as the need to reduce public funding for older people's services. From this perspective, rather than improving public provision, governments should slash their obligations. They should increase retirement ages, cut the value of publicly funded health, social care and pensions, and state unambiguously that they cannot and will not meet the welfare requirements of future older people. Governments should also make it clear that today's workers must take more responsibility for their own future financial needs. The post-war 'cradle to grave' settlements, whereby states accepted responsibility for the welfare of citizens from birth and through old age, must therefore be 'reformed'. The alternative – intergenerational conflict and economic stagnation – is, we are told, too frightening to consider. The implications of this kind of agenda for social work practice are serious. Eligibility criteria for accessing publicly funded support will be tightened still further, and the social worker's role may become concerned with little more than rationing resources that are woefully inadequate to meet older people's needs.

As we saw at the start of this chapter, some of the statistical evidence presented to support this 'pessimistic' position is compelling. The perception of an imminent crisis is also reinforced on an almost daily basis in the media. Predictions of a looming demographic time bomb and intergenerational conflict provide newspaper editors with 'catchy' headlines, and for this reason they are more than happy to uncritically promote the view that there is an imminent crisis at hand. This has given the claims made by pessimists an aura of respectability and an unquestionable appearance of 'fact'. The uncritical manner in which certain politicians and official government publications utilise demographic data also serves to reinforce the 'pessimist case'. The Labour government's White Paper, *Building the National Care Service,* is a good example of this. While acknowledging that there was widespread popular support for a much improved, taxpayer-funded, comprehensive public system of social care in the UK, it explicitly rejected such an approach, citing concerns about ageing population trends. Significantly improving funding for social care would, it argued, be *unfair between generations.* It would *place a large burden on the working-age population – and this burden would increase significantly over time as the proportion of working-age people decreases, and the number of older people grows* (HM Government, 2010, p127). Likewise, Steve Webb (2010), the Coalition government's pensions minister, cited population ageing as justification for his government's decision to accelerate increases in the pension age. *People are now living longer and have healthier lives,* he argued. *Most 65-year-olds can now expect to live until their late-80s. State pensions need to reflect this and we need to make sure that the system is sustainable in the face of increasing longevity.*

Criticism of the 'pessimists'

However convincing the pessimistic case seems, as students of social policy we need to be aware that the questions raised by the 'sceptics' are not simply economic or, for that matter, demographic. As Vincent (1999) argues, debates over the most appropriate means of funding retirement incomes, like other aspects of social policy, are profoundly influenced and shaped by ideological principles. In this sense, it is important to acknowledge that the research bodies, academics, politicians and commentators warning us of the dangers posed by a 'demographic time bomb', are not ideologically or politically neutral. However, the ideological bias of these 'voices' is rarely, if at all, mentioned in the reporting of their claims. Their statements regarding the funding of the health, social care and income needs of older people are invariably portrayed as objective, authoritative and 'factual'. A largely uncritical media reports their 'findings' and recommendations, and little or no consideration is given to whether there is actually a 'crisis' that needs addressing. The question invariably posed is not, 'is there a problem', but rather, 'how can we cope with the imminent, looming catastrophe?' The voices of 'optimists', who argue that society is more than capable of meeting the financial, health and social care needs of future retired workers, are swept aside by an overwhelmingly sceptical discourse.

'Optimists' point out that ageing populations are not a particularly new phenomenon. They note that Britain's population has been ageing since the end of the nineteenth century, and although 'crises' relating to dependency ratios have been predicted throughout this period, they have never materialised. Mullan (2000, p74) argues that Britain *coped with a tripling in the proportion of over-64s between 1911 and 1991* and *in comparison a further 50 per cent rise over the next 50 years does not seem that onerous.* From this perspective, there is no demographic time bomb, nor will Britain's ageing population cause any insurmountable problems. The key to this argument is the acknowledgement that economic growth and growing tax revenues have historically been more than sufficient to ensure the increasing levels of resources needed to fund more costly public services for older people. This point was supported by the influential Wanless Review into the future of social care services for older people. It concluded that future projected levels of economic growth were more than sufficient to pay not just for current levels of care, but for a *much improved* social care system for older people. A movement towards a system which delivered *the highest levels of personal care* and which guaranteed older people were *socially included, able to participate socially, achieve a sense of well-being* was, it argued, eminently affordable, involving only a slight increase in the percentage of resources devoted to social care spending, from 1.4 per cent to 2 per cent of GDP by 2026 (Wanless, 2006, p180).

In the light of such projections, it is important to consider why, as a nation, we continue to be transfixed by the notion that decent, publicly funded social care for older people is becoming an increasingly unaffordable aim. As hinted at earlier, 'optimists' have linked the propagation of what they sometimes refer to as 'apocalyptic demography' in the UK to the rise of the neo-liberal right and its attempts to undermine state welfare. Thus, for Vincent (2003, p86), the notion that population ageing will create a demographic time bomb is a myth constructed by neo-liberals, who share a particular agenda and specific way of seeing the world. Put simply, they are seeking to heighten and exaggerate fears about population ageing in order to undermine support for otherwise popular publicly funded social care and pensions. Macnicol (2015, p66) agrees: *What has happened in the last forty years is that neo-liberalism has profoundly affected – indeed, contaminated – the demographic debate, reinterpreting population trends in such a way as to engender pessimism and justify the raising of state pension ages and cutbacks in social policies for older people.* Walker (2012, p818) has also commented upon the political imperatives that underpin recent tendencies to portray older people as a threat to the UK's economic future. The 'baby boomers', he argues, *have been mistakenly cast as the 'welfare generation' mainly because of the neoliberal antagonism towards the welfare state.* Optimists therefore accuse sceptics of being actually ideologically motivated, and of deliberately seeking to create a (false) sense of inevitability and certainty that public funding for older people's services is unaffordable.

In fact, numerous government-sponsored commissions of inquiry have confirmed that the UK is not facing a looming demographically induced financial meltdown. For example, the Royal Commission on Long-Term Care for the Elderly (1998) concluded that *there is no demographic 'timebomb'*. The UK, it argued, *has already lived through its 'time bomb' earlier this century. The future is much more manageable.* Confirming Mullan's (2000) analysis, the Commission noted that the UK's elderly population has always grown, and society has proven to be more than capable of finding the additional necessary resources to fund retirement incomes. On this specific point, a House of Lords (2003) inquiry offered further encouragement. It pointed out that projected productivity gains mean that per capita income will more than double over the next half century, delivering more than enough revenue to cope with the UK's ageing population. *We conclude*, the inquiry's report stated, *that population ageing does not pose a threat to the continued prosperity and growth of the United Kingdom economy; in this sense, therefore, there is no looming 'crisis' of population ageing in the United Kingdom* (House of Lords Select Committee on Economic Affairs, 2003, p15). A more recent House of Lords report adopted a somewhat more sceptical tone, mainly out of acknowledgement of the woeful levels of resources the UK devotes to funding the health, social care and pension needs of older citizens, but it too accepted that *Longer lives represent progress, and the changes do not mean a great economic or fiscal crisis*. As it argued, *the contribution to our society made by older people, which is already impressive, will be even greater as a result* (House of Lords Select Committee on Public Service and Democratic Change, 2013, p7).

However, the UK policy debate about funding the welfare needs of older people continues to be dominated more by predictions about the 'unsustainable' nature of current levels of public expenditure than it does by concern over the economic and social well-being of older people themselves. As 'optimists' such as Alan Walker argue, it is filled *by a demography of despair, which portrays population ageing not as a triumph for civilisation, but something of an apocalypse* (cited in Dean, 2004). Lodge et al. (2016) have argued that such 'apocalyptic demography' serves a number of important functions:

- For the print and broadcast media, who regularly propagate 'gerontophobia', it provides eye-catching headlines, boosting sales and viewing figures. At the same time, of course, privately owned media corporations are ideologically opposed to the state provision of welfare, including that delivered to older citizens, and news features that undermine support for publicly funded pensions and social care reflect their own ideological predispositions and political stances.

- For politicians (of all political shades), apocalyptic demography diverts attention away from their own failure to adequately fund pensions and social care, disguising the *political* causes of the financial hardship and poor standards of services experienced by millions of older citizens in the UK. A cursory glance at the levels of funding for pensions and social care found in other European countries seems to confirm that the UK's failure to adequately provide for its older citizens' needs is a result of *political choice* rather than demographic trends. As we noted earlier, the pensions systems of many other European nations are far more generous than the UK's, despite these countries facing precisely the same demographic trends as the UK.

- The 'demographic time bomb' thesis inappropriately locates the blame for underfunded, inadequate levels of welfare and services for the working age population on the shoulders of older citizens, who stand accused of hoarding resources to the detriment of younger generations. As Lodge et al. (2016, p56) argue, *We have lost count of headlines that begin 'Boomers to blame for . . .', including increased rudeness in society, shortage of hospital beds, difficulties in getting decent jobs or promotion, and student loans. You can add any social problems to this list.*

Most of all though, as we have already stated, apocalyptic demography is said to provide justification for ideologically motivated cuts to welfare and services to older people. Thus, according to Lodge et al. (2016, p61), the *myths of intergenerational conflict and the time bomb are promoted for political purposes.* These 'myths', they insist, have been remorselessly propagated by those on the political 'right' in an attempt to *drown out the reporting of the beneficial economic effects for our country of the increased number and proportion of older people* and to weaken resistance to neo-liberal-inspired reforms.

The personalisation agenda

Rather than spending more on social care for older people, governments seem to have chosen the route of changing the way services are delivered, with the personalisation agenda now at the forefront of social care reform. We examined the advantages and disadvantages of the current policy shift towards personalisation in Chapter 9, where we discussed it in relation to the provision for adult services. Certainly, one can see the possible advantages of such an agenda for older service users. As the Labour government's document *Putting People First* argued, personalised services, which allow older people themselves to determine the shape of the provision they receive, has the potential to liberate them from the ageist 'straitjacket' that has shaped many of the services they have received in the past. As we have seen, too often the assumption has been that residential care is the best option for older people, when other, more empowering and personalised packages of support would have been more appropriate. Hence, few would disagree with *Putting People First*'s aim to *replace paternalistic, reactive care of variable quality with a mainstream system focussed on prevention, early intervention, enablement, and high quality personally tailored services* (HM Government, 2007, p2). Likewise, the principle that older people should be seen and empowered to be *active and equal citizens, both economically and socially* – another key objective of *Putting People First* – should command widespread, universal support, particularly in the light of existing levels of exclusion. The promises personalisation holds out to older users of social care services, therefore, seem inherently progressive. They will no longer be treated as second-class citizens, and like those who privately fund their own provision, they will increasingly have *maximum choice, control and power over the support services they receive.*

As Lymbery (2010, p13) argues, it is difficult to marshal criticisms against an approach which seems so *warmly persuasive.* Those that do question the trajectory of policy can easily be portrayed as representing the *forces of paternalism, conservatism or reaction.* Who, after all, could possibly be opposed to the principles of empowerment and choice for older service users? However, some have questioned both the motives underpinning the personalisation agenda for older people, as well as the practical impact it may have upon the quality of services received (Ferguson, 2007). As was the case with 'community care' in the 1980s and 1990s, they argue that the benevolent rhetoric surrounding personalisation has the potential to mask a number of less than progressive developments (Cunningham and Cunningham, 2014).

On a practical level, questions have been raised about the willingness and ability of some older service users to exercise significant elements of choice over the care they receive.

Clearly, a large number of older service users will want to embrace some of the initiatives encompassed by personalisation, but at the same time many *may not wish to undertake the activities upon which self-directed support depends – nor indeed be capable of undertaking them* (Lymbery, 2010, p17). As Ferguson (2007, p396) puts it, many older service users do not conform to the 'typical' personalisation profile of the *choosing, deciding, shaping human being who aspires to be the author of their life*. A Department of Health-sponsored analysis of the trajectory of policy concurred with this view, pointing out that *the personal capacities of some very old people are inadequate to the challenge of orchestrating their own care* (Askham, 2008). Another government-funded review of the impact of personalisation on service users came to much the same conclusions. Indeed, it found that the introduction of individual budgets – a key part of personalisation strategies – led to *lower levels of well-being* and increased levels of anxiety and stress for older people:

> *The evaluation indicates that a potentially substantial proportion of older people may experience taking responsibility for their own support as a burden rather than as leading to improved control. Older people satisfied with their current care arrangements – particularly when this involved an established relationship with a current care worker – were reported to be reluctant to change.* (Individual Budgets Evaluation Network, 2008, p238)

The National Pensioners Convention (NPC), a user-led movement that seeks to promote the welfare and interests of older citizens, agrees. Expecting *some of our most vulnerable older people to take on the responsibility of micro-employers – recruiting, dealing with payroll matters, contracts, discipline, employment rights, paying tax and national insurance – is*, it argues, *simply unrealistic* (2009, p12). It also states that policies that promote independence and choice have implications for the protection of vulnerable adults, particularly physical and financial abuse, which advocates of personalisation have failed to address.

Of course, the NPC and others who are cautious about the impact of personalisation on older people are not suggesting that personalised services should not be available, but just that such an approach may sometimes be unwelcome or inappropriate, representing a hindrance rather than a benefit. There is, Lymbery (2014, p374) argues, *growing evidence . . . which casts doubt on the effectiveness of some elements of personalisation – particularly personal budgets – as far as older people are concerned*. As one recent qualitative study of older service users' experiences of personalised services concluded: *Older people in receipt of personal budgets were often very frail. It was difficult to imagine how such individuals would manage their personal budgets in the form of a Direct Payment without considerable support* (Norrie et al., 2014, p182). Critics are also concerned that in the current climate, where personalisation is seen to represent the magical panacea to the shortcomings in social care, the social care needs of those who do remain 'dependent' will be marginalised and overlooked, and that those who make a considered choice not to opt for personalised services may be pathologised.

Others have questioned the assumptions underpinning the personalisation agenda for older people, as well as the motives that have driven it. One of the key criticisms centres on the fact that the difficulties that older people face in accessing decent quality social care are seen to result from failings in the *style of delivery* of care, rather than one of *a lack of adequate funding* for care. They are seen to be a consequence of the 'old' paternalistic approach to organising provision rather than a failure to guarantee the resources needed to meet older people's needs. *Putting People First*, for instance, made it clear that any reformed system *must be constrained by the realities of finite resources,* and emphasis was placed upon the need to *spend existing resources differently* (HM Government, 2007, p5). Clearly, spending existing resources differently may well lead to improved outcomes from some or indeed many older people and, to the extent that it does, it is to be welcomed. The problem is, it is unlikely to address the significant relative underfunding of welfare and care services that works to the detriment of millions of older people, who are forced to live in hardship and to depend upon chronically underfunded social care provision. This has led some to question whether the promotion of the 'personalisation' agenda in relation to older citizens is motivated by less altruistic intentions than is commonly thought. Certainly, there are those who believe that one of the real objectives is to divert attention away from the costly, genuinely progressive, fundamental social care reforms that are desperately needed (Ferguson, 2007; Lymbery, 2010). From this perspective, changes in the style of delivery alone will be unable to bring about the significant improvements that are needed in social care for older people, unless they are matched by huge improvements in funding.

This is the approach adopted, for example, by the NPC. It welcomes the emphasis placed by government on the need to listen to and engage with older service users, but insists that this in itself is insufficient. If older people are to be treated with dignity and respect, the state needs to do much more than simply change the way existing resources are delivered. It must reaffirm the state's commitment to ensuring cradle-to-grave security, and significantly improve funding with a view to establishing a free, universal, taxpayer-funded National Care Service. This model of delivery of social care can be found in Sweden, where approximately 97 per cent of services are publicly funded from taxation and national insurance (CSCI, 2008b).

Chapter summary

The overarching theme to emerge from the discussion in this chapter is our failure as a society to meet the welfare needs of older citizens. Despite the introduction of a number of ostensibly progressive initiatives and developments, all the evidence seems to suggest that older people continue to suffer from a high incidence of hardship, and that the welfare services they receive are inadequate to meet their needs. As we have argued, these trends are undoubtedly reinforced by inaccurate but pervasive negative

(Continued)

(Continued)

societal perceptions of older people, which portray them as an 'unproductive burden'. This pejorative conception of older people, coupled with demographic arguments depicting Britain's ageing population as a threat to the nation's long-term economic and social well-being, provides justification for unequal, discriminatory treatment which, for other social groups, would be seen as unacceptable.

Our main aim in this chapter has been to challenge this negative conception of older people. We hope that our discussion will encourage you to exercise caution when considering issues relating to ageing and social care, and to treat some of the more alarmist claims made about population ageing with a degree of healthy scepticism. As we have intimated, predictions of a looming demographic time bomb can be, and often have been, prompted by ideological concerns rather than any genuine fears about the sustainability of supporting older people. The utilisation of 'apocalyptic demography' to justify ideologically influenced cuts in expenditure on older people is not a particularly novel phenomenon, but its apparent basis in 'statistical fact' gives it continued appeal to those wishing to implement policies that transfer the burden of responsibility for supporting older people from the state to the individual.

For the same reasons, we should perhaps exercise caution when analysing the trajectory of the current personalisation agenda for older people. Of course, few would disagree with the notion that the services older people receive should be based around their needs and preferences. However, as we pointed out in the previous chapter, the rhetoric of personalisation can also potentially be used to justify ideologically motivated strategies that, ultimately, will do little to advance the economic and social well-being of older service users. Improving user input and providing personalised packages of care are clearly important aims. However, the overarching focus on personalisation should not be allowed to obscure what for many is the pressing issue facing the provision of welfare services to older people – chronic, systematic underfunding. Unless this issue is addressed, then the rhetorical, progressive aims of personalisation may never be realised.

Further reading

Those of you wanting to read a good history of ageing and social policy that makes links between past and present debates will find the following book useful:

Thane, P (2000) *Old Age in English History: Past Experiences and Present Issues.* Oxford: Oxford University Press.

The following text, written by Chris Phillipson, provides a critical, Marxist analysis of ageing and social policy:

Phillipson, C (1982) *Capitalism and the Construction of Old Age.* London: Macmillan.

For an often cited, accessible critique of what the author refers to as the 'myth' of population ageing, see:

Mullan, P (2000) *The Imaginary Time Bomb: Why an Ageing Population Is Not a Social Problem.* London: IB Tauris.

The following text offers a more recent critique of the notion that population ageing is necessarily 'problematic':

Macnicol, J (2015) *Neoliberalising Old Age.* Cambridge: Cambridge University Press.

If you are interested in a practice-focused account of social work with older people we would recommend:

Crawford, K and Walker, J (2008) *Social Work with Older People.* Exeter: Learning Matters.

In relation to personalisation, we would recommend the texts listed in the 'Further reading' section of the previous chapter.

Conclusion

Throughout this book we have emphasised the important contribution social policy can make to your social work education. As we have shown, governmental responses to social and economic problems – their social policies – impact directly upon the life chances and opportunities of service users, and they can hinder as well as enhance the welfare of vulnerable, marginalised individuals and groups. Having read the book, we hope that you are now able to appreciate how the social and economic well-being of citizens is intrinsically linked to the social policy decisions that politicians make.

We have also seen how social work practice itself is shaped and circumscribed by legislation, policy and guidance that determine and constrain the levels, nature and quality of support that social workers are able to provide. As Ray Jones has recently argued, *Our work is shaped by the powerbrokers in Westminster and what we do is dictated by what they say* (cited in European Union News, 2016). Hence it is absolutely critical that you and other social work graduates moving into the profession have an understanding of politics and social policy.

As academics who have taught social work students for many years, we are well aware of the motivations that have led many of you to decide to become social workers. Some of you will have been driven by your own personal experiences of the social welfare system (good or bad) and a desire to support others who are experiencing similar circumstances to those that you faced. Others of you will have been motivated by a more general sense of social justice: you want to combat discrimination, 'help people' or ensure that vulnerable groups receive adequate support and are able to reach their full potential. However, as we have pointed out throughout this text, on occasions it is likely that you will not be able to provide service users with the support that you know they need. This will not be due to any professional incompetence on your part, but to the wider political and policy environments that restrict the decisions you are able to make. We hope, therefore, that we have succeeded in helping you to understand the limitations of social work and the barriers you will face in providing service users with the support they need. Of course, in drawing attention to the limits of social work practice, it has certainly not been our intention to disillusion or demotivate you before you embark upon your social work careers. On the contrary, we hope that a knowledge of such constraints might encourage you to become more critical, active and engaged practitioners, who are prepared to advocate and campaign on behalf of your service users.

We have also sought to draw attention to the way in which the ideological predispositions of politicians often influence the welfare policies they introduce when they are in government. Chapters 4 to 6 of the book provided a 'timeline' of influence of the three main ideological perspectives, social democracy, neo-liberalism and Marxism, assessing the respective influence of each. These, and subsequent chapters, point to a strong neo-liberal undercurrent in recent social policy developments. Conservative-led governments have tended to be more enthusiastic adherents to neo-liberalism than their Labour counterparts, but the social policies of all governments since 1979 have, to varying degrees, been influenced by neo-liberal ideals. In this very real sense then, political ideas and values do matter, and it is for this very reason that we have devoted a considerable amount of attention to analysing different ideological approaches to social problems and issues. In doing so, we have tried to provide you with an adequate understanding of not only the values that have been most influential in shaping the policy process, but also those of competing ideological perspectives. Our intention here has been to encourage you to think critically about alternative potential interpretations for (and solutions to) the economic and social problems experienced by the people with whom you will be working.

Finally, we would like to end the book by briefly reiterating once more the importance of embracing a social policy dimension to your studies. As academics who have taught social policy for many years, we are passionate in our belief that it is crucial for social workers to develop an appreciation of the wider social policy environment within which social work takes place. As future social workers, it is vital that you are encouraged at this early stage to develop your critical faculties and to be able to assess the underlying influences that shape welfare policy. The QAA (2008, p7) Benchmarks for Social Work state that you should be able to *think critically about the complex social, legal, economic, political and cultural contexts in which social work practice is located*. Hopefully, this text will have provided you with an appreciation of the causes of the problems and difficulties experienced by service users, and equipped you with some of the intellectual tools you require to critically analyse social policies.

Appendix 1

Professional capabilities framework for social workers

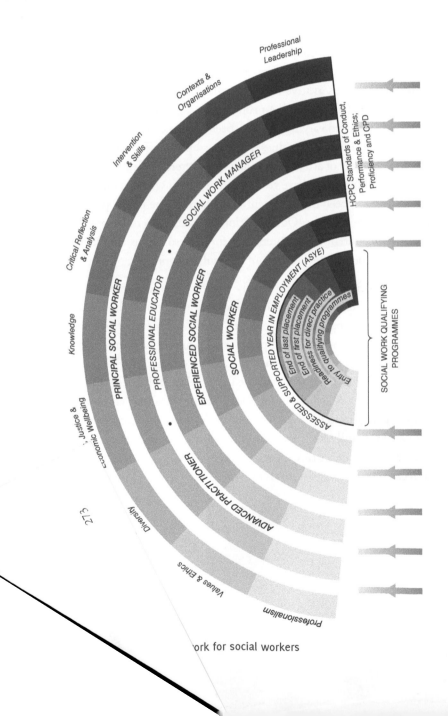

...ork for social workers

Appendix 2

Subject benchmark for social work (extracts)

4 Defining concepts and principles

4.1 The study and practice of Social Work in the UK reflects the key principles of the Global Definition of the Social Work Profession.[1] As an academic subject applied through professional practice, Social Work is characterised by a distinctive focus on practice in complex social situations to promote and protect individual and collective well-being. This underscores the importance of partnerships between higher education providers and service providers to ensure the full involvement of practitioners, employers, managers, academics and researchers, service users and carers with students in both academic and practice learning settings and in assessment processes.

4.2 Qualifying degrees in Social Work aim to develop the student as a social scientist, a professional, and a qualified practitioner.[2] At qualifying level, the study of Social Work involves the integrated study of subject-specific knowledge, skills and values and the critical application of research knowledge from the social and human sciences, and from Social Work (and closely related domains) to inform understanding and to underpin action, reflection and evaluation. Qualifying degree programmes are designed to help foster this integration of contextual, analytic, critical, theoretical, explanatory and practical understanding in a wide range of contexts.

---

[1]'Social work is a practice-based profession and an academic discipline that promotes social change and development, social cohesion, and the empowerment and liberation of people. Principles of social justice, human rights, collective responsibility and respect for diversities are central to social work. Underpinned by theories of social work, social sciences, humanities and indigenous knowledge, social work engages people and structures to address life challenges and enhance wellbeing.' See http://ifsw. org/policies/definition-of-social-work/.

[2]Croisdale-Appleby, D., *Re-visioning social work education: an independent review* (February 2014), available at: www.gov.uk/government/uploads/system/uploads/attachment_data/file/285788/DCA_Accessible.pdf.

Narey, M., *Making the education of social workers consistently effective* (January 2014), available from www. gov.uk/government/uploads/system/uploads/attachment_data/file/287756/Making_the_education_of_ social_workers_consistently_effective.pdf.

Scottish Executive, *Changing Lives: Report of the 21st Century Social Work Review* (2006), available at: www.gov.scot/resource/doc/91931/0021949.pdf.

4.3 Contemporary definitions of Social Work as a degree subject reflect its heritage in a range of different academic subjects and practice traditions. The precise nature and scope of the subject is itself a matter for legitimate study and critical debate. Four main issues are relevant to this.

- Social Work is located within different and changing social welfare contexts. Within the UK there are different traditions of social welfare (influenced by legislation, historical development, devolution and social attitudes) and these have shaped both Social Work education and social work practice in a diverse range of settings. In an international context, distinctive national approaches to social welfare policy, provision and practice have greatly influenced the focus and content of Social Work degree programmes and continue to do so.

- There are competing views in society at large on the nature of Social Work and on its place and purpose. Social Work practice and education inevitably reflect these differing perspectives on the role of Social Work in relation to social justice, social care and social order. These different dimensions are vital considerations in working closely with vulnerable people, families and communities.

- Social Work, both as an occupational practice and as an academic subject, evolves, adapts and changes in response to the social, political and economic challenges and demands of contemporary social welfare policy, practice and legislation.

- Social Work is responsive to change in supporting vulnerable people and families. While Social Work is undertaken in a wide range of settings, the relationship between society, state and Social Work remains central to the role of Social Work in protecting vulnerable people.

4.4 Qualified social workers therefore need to be equipped both to understand, and to work within, this context of contested debate about the nature, scope and purpose of Social Work, and be enabled to analyse, adapt to, manage and eventually lead the processes of change.

4.5 The nature of Social Work as an academic subject applied through professional practice means that practice is an essential and core element of learning. The following points clarify the use of the term 'practice' in this Statement.

- The term 'practice' in this Statement is used to encompass learning that not only takes place in professional practice placements, but also in a variety of other experiential learning situations. All learning opportunities that bear academic credit or which students are required to successfully complete are subject to methods of assessment appropriate to their academic level and are assessed by competent assessors. Where they form part of the curriculum leading to integrated academic and professional awards, practice learning opportunities are also subject to the requirements of the relevant regulatory body that further define learning outcomes, standards and modes of assessment.

- In programmes covered by this Statement, practice as an activity refers to experiential, action-based learning. In this sense, practice provides opportunities for students to improve and demonstrate their understanding and competence through the application and testing of knowledge and skills. Learning therefore transfers between practice settings and the 'classroom' and vice versa.

- Learning in practice can include activities such as observation of other professionals and of service users, skill development and analysis, shadowing, supervision, reflection analysis and research, as well as intervention within Social Work and related organisations. Practice-learning involves active engagement with service users and others in practice settings, and may involve, for example, virtual or simulated practice opportunities, observational and research activities.

4.6 Social Work is an ethical activity that requires practitioners to recognise the dignity of the individual, but also to make and implement difficult decisions (including the restriction of liberty) in human situations that involve the potential for benefit or harm. Programmes in Social Work therefore involve the study, application of and critical reflection upon, ethical principles and dilemmas as a core requirement. As reflected by the four care councils' codes of practice, this involves showing respect for persons; honouring the diverse and distinctive organisations and communities that make up society; promoting social justice and combating processes that lead to discrimination, marginalisation, inequality and social exclusion; all of which impact upon the individual, family or society. This means that Social Work students learn to:

- recognise and work with the powerful links between individual factors and the wider social, legal, economic, political and cultural context of people's lives;

- understand the impact of injustice, social inequalities and oppressive social relations;

- provide reasoned, informed arguments to address individual, institutional and structural discrimination;

- help people to gain, regain or maintain control of their own lives, choices and decisions, insofar as this is compatible with their own or others' safety, well-being and rights, and practise in ways that maximise safety work in partnership with service users and carers and other professionals to foster dignity, choice and independence, and effect change.

4.7 The expectation that social workers are able to act effectively in such complex circumstances requires that qualifying degree programmes in Social Work are designed to help students learn to become accountable, reflective, critical and evaluative. This involves learning to:

- think critically about the complex social, legal, economic, political, cultural, theoretical and research contexts in which Social Work practice is located;

- work in a transparent and responsible way, balancing autonomy with complex, multiple and sometimes contradictory accountabilities (for example, to different service users, employing agencies, professional bodies and the wider society);

- exercise authority constructively within complex frameworks of accountability and ethical and legal boundaries;

- understand the complexity of Social Work practice recognising the need for identified knowledge, skills and values which reflect the life course of individuals, families and communities;

- acquire and apply the skills of critical reflection, self-evaluation and consultation and use opportunities for professional supervision;

- make appropriate use of research in decision making and professional judgement about practice and in the evaluation of outcomes.

5 Knowledge, understanding and skills

Subject knowledge and understanding

5.1 During their qualifying degree studies in Social Work, students acquire, critically evaluate, apply and integrate knowledge and understanding in the following five core areas of study.

5.2 Social Work theory, which includes:

 i. critical explanations from Social Work theory and other subjects which contribute to the knowledge base of Social Work;

 ii. an understanding of Social Work's rich and contested history from both a UK and comparative perspective;

 iii. the relevance of sociological and applied psychological perspectives to understanding societal and structural influences on human behaviour at individual, group and community levels, and the relevance of sociological theorisation to a deeper understanding of adaptation and change;

 iv. the relevance of psychological, physical and physiological perspectives to understanding human, personal and social development, well-being and risk;

 v. social science theories explaining and exploring group and organisational behaviour;

 vi. the range of theories and research informed evidence that informs understanding of the child, adult, family or community and of the range of assessment and interventions which can be used;

 vii. the theory, models and methods of assessment, factors underpinning the selection and testing of relevant information, knowledge and critical appraisal of relevant social science and other research and evaluation methodologies, and the evidence base for Social Work;

 viii. the nature of analysis and professional judgement and the processes of risk assessment and decision making, including the theory of risk informed decisions and the balance of choice and control, rights and protection in decision making;

ix. approaches, methods and theories of intervention in working with a diverse population within a wide range of settings, including factors guiding the choice and critical evaluation of these, and user-led perspectives.

5.3 Values and ethics, which include:

i. the nature, historical evolution, political context and application of professional Social Work values, informed by national and international definitions and ethical statements, and their relation to personal values, identities, influences and ideologies;

ii. the ethical concepts of rights, responsibility, freedom, authority and power inherent in the practice of social workers as agents with statutory powers in different situations;

iii. aspects of philosophical ethics relevant to the understanding and resolution of value dilemmas and conflicts in both interpersonal and professional contexts;

iv. understanding of, and adherence to, the ethical foundations of empirical and conceptual research, as both consumers and producers of social science research;

v. the relationship between human rights enshrined in law and the moral and ethical rights determined theoretically, philosophically and by contemporary society;

vi. the complex relationships between justice, care and control in social welfare and the practical and ethical implications of these, including their expression in roles as statutory agents in diverse practice settings and in upholding the law in respect of challenging discrimination and inequalities;

vii. the conceptual links between codes defining ethical practice and the regulation of professional conduct;

viii. the professional and ethical management of potential conflicts generated by codes of practice held by different professional groups;

ix. the ethical management of professional dilemmas and conflicts in balancing the perspectives of individuals who need care and support and professional decision making at points of risk, care and protection;

x. the constructive challenging of individuals and organisations where there may be conflicts with Social Work values, ethics and codes of practice;

xi. the professional responsibility to be open and honest if things go wrong (the duty of candour about own practice) and to act on concerns about poor or unlawful practice by any person or organisation;

xii. continuous professional development as a reflective, informed and skilled practitioner, including the constructive use of professional supervision.

5.4 Service users and carers, which include:

i. the factors which contribute to the health and well-being of individuals, families and communities, including promoting dignity, choice and independence for people who need care and support;

ii. the underpinning perspectives that determine explanations of the characteristics and circumstances of people who need care and support, with critical evaluation drawing on research, practice experience and the experience and expertise of people who use services;

iii. the social and psychological processes associated with, for example, poverty, migration, unemployment, trauma, poor health, disability, lack of education and other sources of disadvantage and how they affect well-being, how they interact and may lead to marginalisation, isolation and exclusion, and demand for Social Work services;

iv. explanations of the links between the factors contributing to social differences and identities (for example, social class, gender, ethnic differences, age, sexuality and religious belief) and the structural consequences of inequality and differential need faced by service users;

v. the nature and function of Social Work in a diverse and increasingly global society (with particular reference to prejudice, interpersonal relations, discrimination, empowerment and anti-discriminatory practices).

5.5 The nature of Social Work practice, in the UK and more widely, which includes:

i. the place of theoretical perspectives and evidence from European and international research in assessment and decision-making processes;

ii. the integration of theoretical perspectives and evidence from European and international research into the design and implementation of effective Social Work intervention with a wide range of service users, carers and communities;

iii. the knowledge and skills which underpin effective practice, with a range of service-users and in a variety of settings;

iv. the processes that facilitate and support service user and citizen rights, choice, co-production, self-governance, well-being and independence;

v. the importance of interventions that promote social justice, human rights, social cohesion, collective responsibility and respect for diversity and tackle inequalities;

vi. its delivery in a range of community-based and organisational settings spanning the statutory, voluntary and private sectors, and the changing nature of these service contexts;

vii. the factors and processes that facilitate effective interdisciplinary, interprofessional and interagency collaboration and partnership across a plurality of settings and disciplines;

viii. the importance of Social Work's contribution to intervention across service user groups, settings and levels in terms of the profession's focus on social justice, human rights, social cohesion, collective responsibility and respect for diversities;

ix. the processes of reflection and reflexivity as well as approaches for evaluating service and welfare outcomes for vulnerable people, and their significance for the development of practice and the practitioner.

5.6 The leadership, organisation and delivery of Social Work services, which includes:

i. the location of contemporary Social Work within historical, comparative and global perspectives, including in the devolved nations of the UK and wider European and international contexts;

ii. how the service delivery context is portrayed to service users, carers, families and communities;

iii. the changing demography and cultures of communities, including European and international contexts, in which social workers practise;

iv. the complex relationships between public, private, social and political philosophies, policies and priorities and the organisation and practice of social work, including the contested nature of these;

v. the issues and trends in modern public and social policy and their relationship to contemporary practice, service delivery and leadership in Social Work;

vi. the significance of legislative and legal frameworks and service delivery standards, including on core Social Work values and ethics in the delivery of services which support, enable and empower;

vii. the current range and appropriateness of statutory, voluntary and private agencies providing services and the organisational systems inherent within these;

viii. development of new ways of working and delivery, for example the development of social enterprises, integrated multi-professional teams and independent Social Work provision;

ix. the significance of professional and organisational relationships with other related services, including housing, health, education, police, employment, fire, income maintenance and criminal justice;

x. the importance and complexities of the way agencies work together to provide care, the relationships between agency policies, legal requirements and professional boundaries in shaping the nature of services provided in integrated and interdisciplinary contexts;

xi. the contribution of different approaches to management and leadership within different settings, and the impact on professional practice and on quality of care management and leadership in public and human services;

xii. the development of person-centred services, personalised care, individual budgets and direct payments all focusing upon the human and legal rights of the service user for control, power and self determination;

xiii. the implications of modern information and communications technology for both the provision and receipt of services, use of technologically enabled support and the use of social media as a process and forum for vulnerable people, families and communities, and communities of professional practice.

Subject-specific skills and other skills

5.7 The range of skills required by a qualified social worker reflect the complex and demanding context in which they work. Many of these skills may be of value in many situations, for example, analytical thinking, building relationships, working as a member of an organisation, intervention, evaluation, and reflection. What defines the specific nature of these skills as developed by Social Work students is:

i. the context in which they are applied and assessed (for example communication skills in practice with people with sensory impairments or assessment skills in an interprofessional setting);

ii. the relative weighting given to such skills within Social Work practice (for example the central importance of problem-solving skills within complex human situations);

iii. the specific purpose of skill development (for example the acquisition of research skills in order to build a repertoire of research-based practice);

iv. a requirement to integrate a range of skills (that is, not simply to demonstrate these in an isolated and incremental manner).

5.8 All Social Work graduates demonstrate the ability to reflect on and learn from the exercise of their skills, in order to build their professional identity. They understand the significance of the concepts of continuing professional development and lifelong learning, and accept responsibility for their own continuing development.

5.9 Social Work students acquire and integrate skills in the following five core areas:

Problem-solving skills

5.10 These are subdivided into four areas.

5.11 Managing problem-solving activities: graduates in Social Work are able to:

i. think logically, systematically, creatively, critically and reflectively, in order to carry out a holistic assessment;

ii. apply ethical principles and practices critically in planning problem-solving activities;

iii. plan a sequence of actions to achieve specified objectives, making use of research, theory and other forms of evidence;

iv. manage processes of change, drawing on research, theory and other forms of evidence.

5.12 Gathering information: graduates in Social Work are able to:

i. demonstrate persistence in gathering information from a wide range of sources and using a variety of methods, for a range of purposes. These methods include electronic searches, reviews of relevant literature, policy and procedures, face-to-face interviews, and written and telephone contact with individuals and groups;

ii. take into account differences of viewpoint in gathering information and critically assess the reliability and relevance of the information gathered;

iii. assimilate and disseminate relevant information in reports and case records.

5.13 Analysis and synthesis: graduates in Social Work are able to analyse and synthesise knowledge gathered for problem-solving purposes, in order to:

i. assess human situations, taking into account a variety of factors (including the views of participants, theoretical concepts, research evidence, legislation and organisational policies and procedures);

ii. analyse and synthesise information gathered, weighing competing evidence and modifying their viewpoint in the light of new information, then relate this information to a particular task, situation or problem;

iii. balance specific factors relevant to Social Work practice (such as risk, rights, cultural differences and language needs and preferences, responsibilities to protect vulnerable individuals and legal obligations);

iv. assess the merits of contrasting theories, explanations, research, policies and procedures and use the information to develop and sustain reasoned arguments;

v. employ a critical understanding of factors that support or inhibit problem solving including societal, organisational and community issues as well as individual relationships;

vi. critically analyse and take account of the impact of inequality and discrimination in working with people who use Social Work services.

5.14 Intervention and evaluation: graduates in Social Work are able to use their knowledge of a range of interventions and evaluation processes creatively and selectively to:

i. build and sustain purposeful relationships with people and organisations in communities and interprofessional contexts;

ii. make decisions based on evidence, set goals and construct specific plans to achieve outcomes, taking into account relevant information including ethical guidelines;

iii. negotiate goals and plans with others, analysing and addressing in a creative and flexible manner individual, cultural and structural impediments to change;

iv. implement plans through a variety of systematic processes that include working in partnership;

v. practise in a manner that promotes well-being, protects safety and resolves conflict;

vi. act as a navigator, advocate and support to assist people who need care and support to take decisions and access services;

vii. manage the complex dynamics of dependency and, in some settings, provide direct care and personal support to assist people in their everyday lives;

viii. meet deadlines and comply with external requirements of a task;

ix. plan, implement and critically monitor and review processes and outcomes;

x. bring work to an effective conclusion, taking into account the implications for all involved;

xi. use and evaluate methods of intervention critically and reflectively.

Communication skills

5.15 Graduates in Social Work are able to communicate clearly, sensitively and effectively (using appropriate methods which may include working with interpreters) with individuals and groups of different ages and abilities in a range of formal and informal situations, in order to:

i. engage individuals and organisations, who may be unwilling, by verbal, paper-based and electronic means to achieve a range of objectives, including changing behaviour;

ii. use verbal and non-verbal cues to guide and inform conversations and interpretation of information;

iii. negotiate and where necessary redefine the purpose of interactions with individuals and organisations and the boundaries of their involvement;

iv. listen actively and empathetically to others, taking into account their specific needs and life experiences;

v. engage appropriately with the life experiences of service users, to understand accurately their viewpoint, overcome personal prejudices and respond appropriately to a range of complex personal and interpersonal situations;

vi. make evidence informed arguments drawing from theory, research and practice wisdom including the viewpoints of service users and/or others;

vii. write accurately and clearly in styles adapted to the audience, purpose and context of the communication;

viii. use advocacy skills to promote others' rights, interests and needs;

ix. present conclusions verbally and on paper, in a structured form, appropriate to the audience for which these have been prepared;

x. make effective preparation for, and lead, meetings in a productive way.

Skills in working with others

5.16 Graduates in Social Work are able to build relationships and work effectively with others, in order to:

i. involve users of Social Work services in ways that increase their resources, capacity and power to influence factors affecting their lives;

ii. engage service users and carers and wider community networks in active consultation;

iii. respect and manage differences such as organisational and professional boundaries and differences of identity and/or language;

iv. develop effective helping relationships and partnerships that facilitate change for individuals, groups and organisations while maintaining appropriate personal and professional boundaries;

v. demonstrate interpersonal skills and emotional intelligence that creates and develops relationships based on openness, transparency and empathy;

vi. increase social justice by identifying and responding to prejudice, institutional discrimination and structural inequality;

vii. operate within a framework of multiple accountability (for example, to agencies, the public, service users, carers and others);

viii. observe the limits of professional and organisational responsibility, using supervision appropriately and referring to others when required;

ix. provide reasoned, informed arguments to challenge others as necessary, in ways that are most likely to produce positive outcomes.

Skills in personal and professional development

5.17 Graduates in Social Work are able to:

i. work at all times in accordance with codes of professional conduct and ethics;

ii. advance their own learning and understanding with a degree of independence and use supervision as a tool to aid professional development;

iii. develop their professional identity, recognise their own professional limitations and accountability, and know how and when to seek advice from a range of sources including professional supervision;

iv. use support networks and professional supervision to manage uncertainty, change and stress in work situations while maintaining resilience in self and others;

v. handle conflict between others and internally when personal views may conflict with a course of action necessitated by the Social Work role;

vi. provide reasoned, informed arguments to challenge unacceptable practices in a responsible manner and raise concerns about wrongdoing in the workplace;

vii. be open and honest with people if things go wrong;

viii. understand the difference between theory, research, evidence and expertise and the role of professional judgement.

Use of technology and numerical skills

5.18 Graduates in Social Work are able to use information and communication technology effectively and appropriately for:

i. professional communication, data storage and retrieval and information searching;

ii. accessing and assimilating information to inform working with people who use services;

iii. data analysis to enable effective use of research in practice;

iv. enhancing skills in problem solving;

v. applying numerical skills to financial and budgetary responsibilities;

vi. understanding the social impact of technology, including the constraints of confidentiality and an awareness of the impact of the 'digital divide'.

6 Teaching, learning and assessment

6.1 Social Work programmes explicitly recognise and maximise the use of students' prior learning and experience. Acquisition and development of the required knowledge and skills, capable of transfer to new situations and of further enhancement, mark important staging posts in the process of lifelong learning. Social Work models of learning are characteristically developmental and incremental (so students are expected to assume increasing responsibility for identifying their own learning needs and making use of available resources for learning). The overall aims and expected final outcomes of individual degree programmes, together with the specific requirements of particular topics, modules or practice experiences, inform the choice of both learning and teaching strategies and aligned formative and summative assessment methods.

6.2 The learning processes in Social Work in qualifying degree programmes can be expressed in terms of four interrelated themes.

- Awareness raising skills and knowledge acquisition – a process in which the student becomes more aware of aspects of knowledge and expertise, learns how to systematically engage with and acquire new areas of knowledge, recognises their potential and professional accountability and becomes motivated to engage in new ways of thinking and acting.

- Conceptual understanding – a process in which a student acquires, examines critically and deepens understanding (measured and tested against existing knowledge and adjustments made in attitudes and goals).

- Practice skills and experience – processes in which a student learns practice skills in the contexts identified in Section 4 and applies theoretical models and research evidence together with new understanding to relevant activities, and receives feedback from various sources on performance, enhancing openness to critical self-evaluation.

- Reflection on performance – a process in which a student reflects critically and evaluatively on past experience, recent performance, and feedback, and applies this information to the process of integrating awareness (including awareness of the impact of self on others) and new understanding, leading to improved performance.

6.3 Programmes in Social Work acknowledge that students learn at different rates and in diverse ways, and learn best when there is consistent and timely guidance and a variety of learning approaches and opportunities. Programmes provide accessible learning approaches that enable students to engage with diverse learning and teaching methods in learning settings across academic and practice environments.

6.4 Learning methods may include:

- learner-focused approaches that encourage active participation and staged, progressive learning throughout the degree;

- the establishment of initial and developing learning needs and the formulation and review of learning plans;

- the development of learning networks, enabling students to learn from each other;

- the involvement of practitioners and service user and carer educators.

6.5 Students engage in a broad range of activities, including with other professionals and with service users and carers, to facilitate critical reflection. These include reading, self-directed study, research, a variety of forms of writing, lectures, discussion, seminars/tutorials, individual and group work, role-plays, presentations, projects, simulations and practice experience. Learning and teaching approaches include the use of technology to access data, literature and resources, as well as engagement with established and emerging technologies to support communication and reflection and sharing of learning across academic and practice learning settings.

6.6 Assessment strategies align programme content (theory and practice), learning outcomes and learning methods with assessment tasks. The purpose of assessment is to:

- provide a means whereby students receive feedback regularly on their achievement and development needs;
- provide tasks that promote learning, and develop and test relevant knowledge and skills, drawing on a range of sources including the contexts of practice;
- promote self-evaluation, and appraisal of their progress and learning strategies;
- enable judgements to be made in relation to progress and a final award, and to ensure fitness for practice, in line with professional standards.

6.7 Assessment strategies are chosen to enhance students' abilities to conceptualise, compare and analyse issues, in order to be able to apply this in making professional judgements.

6.8 In order to achieve the purpose of assessment across the diverse range of knowledge and skills which Social Work students develop, a variety of assessment methods are used. These may include case-based assessments, presentations and analyses, practice-focused assignments, essays, project reports, role-plays/simulations, e-assessment and examinations. The requirements of qualifying degree programmes in Social Work frequently include an extended piece of written work, which may be practice-based, and is generally undertaken towards the end of the period of study. This may involve independent study for either a dissertation or a project, based upon systematic enquiry and investigation. However, the requirements of research governance may restrict opportunities available to students to carry out research involving primary data collection.

6.9 Where practice competences are assessed, as identified through national occupational and capability standards or equivalent, opportunities are provided for demonstration of these, together with systematic means of development, support and assessment. Assessment methods may include those listed above, in addition to observed practice, reflective logs and interview records. Qualifying degree programmes in Social Work assess practice not as a series of discrete practical tasks, but as an integration of skills and knowledge with relevant conceptual understanding and demonstration of competencies. This assessment, therefore, contains elements that test students' critical and analytical reflective analysis. As a qualifying degree is an integrated academic and professional award, students must pass all core elements of the programme, including assessed practice components, to gain the final award.

7 Benchmark standards

7.1 Given the nature of Social Work as an academic subject applied through professional practice, and the co-terminosity of the degree and the professional award, students must demonstrate that they have met the requirements specified in relation to both academic and practice capabilities. These standards relate to subject-specific knowledge, understanding and skills (including key skills inherent in the concept of 'graduateness'). Qualifying students are expected to meet each of these benchmark academic standards in accordance with the specific standards set by the relevant country (see Section 3).

7.2 Levels of attainment vary on a continuum from the threshold to excellence. The benchmark standards set out below represent the threshold standard which all students graduating with a bachelor's degree with honours in Social Work must achieve.

Knowledge and understanding

7.3 On graduating with an honours degree in Social Work, students must be able to demonstrate:

  i. a sound understanding of the five core areas of knowledge and understanding relevant to social work, as detailed in Section 5, including their application to practice and service delivery;

 ii. an ability to use this knowledge and understanding in an integrated way, in specific practice contexts;

iii. an ability to use this knowledge and understanding to engage in effective relationships with service users and carers and relationships with other professionals and through supervision;

 iv. appraisal of previous learning and experience and ability to incorporate this into their future learning and practice, including engagement with supervision;

  v. acknowledgement and understanding of the potential and limitations of Social Work as a practice-based discipline to effect individual and social change;

 vi. an ability to use research and enquiry techniques with reflective awareness, to collect, analyse and interpret relevant information;

vii. a developed capacity for the critical evaluation of knowledge and evidence from a range of sources.

Subject-specific and other skills

7.4 On graduating with an honours degree in Social Work, students must be able to demonstrate a developed capacity to:

  i. apply creatively a repertoire of core skills as detailed in Section 5;

 ii. communicate effectively with service users and carers, and with other professionals;

iii. integrate clear understanding of ethical issues and relevant codes or standards of ethics, conduct and practice with their interventions in specific situations;

iv. consistently exercise an appropriate level of autonomy and initiative in individual decision-making within the context of supervisory, collaborative, ethical and organisational requirements;

v. embed skills of critical reflection on their performance and take responsibility for modifying action and learning in light of this, drawing on appropriate support mechanisms where necessary.

References

Abbott, D (2016) Jeremy Corbyn's vision for the NHS will rescue it from Tory dismantling. *Guardian*, 24 August.

Abbott, D and Marriott, A (2013) Money, finance and the personalisation agenda for people with learning disabilities in the UK: some emerging issues. *British Journal of Learning Disabilities*, 41(2), 106–13.

Abbott, E and Bompas, K (1943) *The Woman Citizen and Social Security*. London: Women's Freedom League.

Abel Smith, B and Townsend, P (1965) *The Poor and the Poorest*. London: G Bell & Sons.

Abrams, D, Swift, HJ, Lamont, RA and Drury, L (2015) *The Barriers to and Enablers of Positive Attitudes to Ageing and Older People, at the Societal and Individual Level*. London: Government Office for Science. https://www.gov.uk/government/uploads/system/uploads/attachment_data/file/454735/gs-15-15-future-ageing-attitudes-barriers-enablers-er06.pdf.

Abrams, F (2012) The age of innocence. *New Statesman*, 23–29 November, pp30–3.

Addison, P (1994) *The Road to 1945*. London: Pimlico.

Advisory Council on the Misuse of Drugs (2011) *Hidden Harm: Responding to the Needs of Children of Problem Drug Users*. https://www.gov.uk/government/uploads/system/uploads/attachment_data/file/120620/hidden-harm-full.pdf.

Age UK (2005) *How Ageist Is Britain?* https://kar.kent.ac.uk/24312/1/HOWAGE~1.PDF.

Age UK (2014) *Caring into Later Life*. http://www.ageuk.org.uk/Documents/EN-GB/For-professionals/Policy/care-and-support/caring_into_later_life.pdf?dtrk=true.

Age UK and Royal College of Surgeons (2014) *Access All Ages: Exploring Variations in Access to Surgery Amongst Older People*. http://www.guysandstthomas.nhs.uk/resources/our-services/acute-medicine-gi-surgery/elderly-care/access-all-ages-2.pdf.

All-Party Parliamentary Inquiry into Hunger in the UK (2014) *Feeding Britain: A Strategy for Zero Hunger in England, Wales, Scotland and Northern Ireland*. London: House of Commons.

Alzheimer's Society (2015) *Response to the Delay in the Implementation of the Cap on Care Costs*. https://www.alzheimers.org.uk/site/scripts/news_article.php?newsID=2417.

Appleyard, M (2010) The steriliser. *The Sun*, 6 March.

Askham, J (2008) *Health and Care Services for Older People: Overview Report on Research to Support the National Service Framework for Older People*. London: Department of Health.

Association of Directors of Adult Social Services (2011) *Policy: 2011 and Beyond.* https://www. adass.org.uk/media/4873/policy-2011-and-beyond-composite.pdf.

Attlee, CR (1920) *The Social Worker.* London: G Bell & Sons.

Audickas, L (2016) *Social Background of MPs, 1979–2015.* http://researchbriefings.files. parliament.uk/documents/CBP-7483/CBP-7483.pdf.

Bailey, R and Brake, M (1975) *Radical Social Work.* London: Edward Arnold.

Bailey, R and Brake, M (1980) *Radical Social Work and Practice.* London: Edward Arnold.

Banks, J, Breeze, E, Lessof, C and Nazroo, J (2008) *Living in the 21st Century: Older People in England.* London: Institute for Fiscal Studies.

Barnes, C (2004) *Independent Living, Politics and Implications.* Leeds: Centre for Disability Studies.

Barr, B, Taylor-Robinson, D, Stuckler, D, Loopstra, R, Reeves, A and Whitehead, M (2015) 'First, do no harm': are disability assessments associated with adverse trends in mental health? A longitudinal ecological study. *Journal of Epidemiology and Community Health.* http://jech.bmj. com/content/early/2015/10/26/jech-2015-206209.full.pdf+html.

Bartholomew, J (2014) *The Welfare State We're In.* London: Biteback Publishing.

Bartholomew, J (2015a) How welfare harms the poor. *Mail Online,* 28 March. http://www. dailymail.co.uk/news/article-3015429/How-welfare-HARMS-poor-Labour-attacks-Tories-cutting-benefits-damning-new-book-argues-handouts-destroy-communities-families.html.

Bartholomew, J (2015b) *The Welfare of Nations.* London: Backbite Publishing.

Bawdon, F and Bowcott, O (2012) Chaos in the courts as justice system rushed to restore order. *Guardian,* 3 July.

Baxter, K, Wilberforce, M and Glendenning, C (2011) Personal budgets and the workforce implications for social care providers: expectations and early experiences. *Social Policy and Society,* 10(1), 55–65.

BBC (1998) *Welfare for All: Social Policy: Welfare, Power and Diversity.* Course D218.

BBC News (2011) *Toxteth Riots: Howe Proposed 'Managed Decline' for the City.* 30 December. http://www.bbc.co.uk/news/uk-england-merseyside-16355281.

Bennett, R (2016) Student debt is third the size of mortgage. *The Times,* 9 August.

Bentley, H, O'Hagan, O, Raff, A and Bhatti, I (2016) *How Safe Are Our Children?* London: NSPCC. https://www.nspcc.org.uk/globalassets/documents/research-reports/how-safe-children-2016-report.pdf.

Beresford, P (2008a) Whose personalisation? *Soundings,* 40, 8–17. www.lwbooks.co.uk/ journals/soundings/articles/02percent20S40percent20beresford.pdf.

Beresford, P (2008b) Personalisation of social care can't be done on the cheap. *Guardian Online,* 22 October 2008. www.guardian.co.uk/society/joepublic/2008/oct/22/social-care-personalisationindividual-budgets.

Beresford, P (2014) *Personalisation*. Bristol: Policy Press.

Beveridge, Sir W (1944) *Full Employment in a Free Society*. London: George Allen & Unwin.

Beveridge, W (1942) *Social Insurance and Allied Services*. London: HMSO.

Bhattachary, D and Slade, Z (2012) *Investigating the Triggers into Claiming Pension Credit*. London: DfWP. https://www.gov.uk/government/uploads/system/uploads/attachment_data/file/214571/rrep785.pdf.

Bingham, J and Dominiczak, P (2014) Benefit cuts give people hope. *Daily Telegraph*, 19 February.

Binyon, M (2009) Hunt for the inspirational Britons age cannot wither. *The Times*, 1 October.

Boffey, D (2015a) Half of all services now failing as UK care sector crisis deepens, *Guardian*, 26 December.

Boffey, D (2015b) Youth unemployment rate the worst for 20 years, compared with overall figure. *Guardian*, 22 February.

Bolton, P (2012) *Education: Historical Statistics*. House of Commons Library. SN/SG/3452. http://researchbriefings.files.parliament.uk/documents/SN04252/SN04252.pdf.

Bowman, B (2014) 2011: Young rioters and imagined revolution in the British utopia of calm. *Postcolonial Studies*, 17(1), 90–103.

Boyson, R (1978) *Centre Forward: A Radical Conservative Programme*. London: Temple Smith.

Bridges, L (2012) Four days in August: the riots. *Capital and Class*, 51(1), 1–12.

Brindle, D (1999) Media coverage of social policy: a journalist's perspective. In Franklin, B (ed.) *Social Policy, Media and Misrepresentation*. Florence, KY: Routledge.

Brindle, D (2011) Private care homes have quietly taken over. *Guardian*, 1 June.

British Academy of Childhood Disability (2015) *Impact of Austerity Measures on Families with Disabled Children*. http://www.bacdis.org.uk/policy/documents/ImpactofAusterityMeasuresonfamilieswithDisabledChildren16Jan2015.pdf.

British Association of Social Workers (2011) *Social Workers Express Fears that Cuts Will 'Put Lives at Risk'*. https://www.basw.co.uk/news/article/?id=22.

British Association of Social Workers, Social Work Action Network, the Joint University Council Social Work Education Committee, the Association of Professors of Social Work, UNISON, University and College Union, Social Workers Union (2015) *Agreed Statement on the Safeguarding and Promotion of the Social Work Profession*. https://www.basw.co.uk/news/article/?id=1000.

Brown, M (1969) *Introduction to Social Administration in Britain*. London: Hutchinson University Library.

Brown, M (1983) The development of social administration. In Loney, M, Boswell, D and Clarke, J (eds) *Social Policy and Social Welfare: A Reader*. Milton Keynes: Open University Press.

Burton, M and Kagan, C (2006) Decoding valuing people. *Disability and Society*, 21(4), 299–313.

Butler, I and Drakeford, M (2005) *Scandal, Social Policy and Social Welfare*. London: Policy Press.

Butler, I and Drakeford, M (2011) *Social Work on Trial: The Colwell Inquiry and the State of Welfare*. Bristol: Policy Press.

Butler, P (2014a) Labour backing as MPs give the go-ahead to child protection outsourcing plans. *Guardian*, 10 September.

Butler, P (2014b) Outsourcing: government advisors finesse child protection 'sales pitch'. *Guardian*, 29 October.

Butler, P (2015) UN inquiry considers alleged UK disability rights violations. *Guardian*, 20 October.

Butler, P and Arnett, G (2015) Benefit cuts to hit huge number of children, government figures show. *Guardian*, 23 July.

Butterworth, E and Holman, B (1975) *Social Welfare in Modern Britain.* Glasgow: Fontana/Collins.

Byron, T (2009) We see children as 'pestilent'. *Guardian*, 17 March.

Cabinet Office (2010) *Building the Big Society*. http://www.cabinetoffice.gov.uk/sites/default/files/resources/building-big-society_O.pdf.

Cameron, D (2006) *Chamberlain Lecture on Communities*. Balsall Heath, Birmingham, 14 July. www.cforum.org.uk/blog/wp-content/uploads/2006/07/DavidCameronChamberlainlecture.doc.

Cameron, D (2007) *Civility and Social Progress:* Speech to the Royal Society of Arts, 23 April.

Cameron, D (2010) *Speech on Supporting Parents*, 11 January. www.conservatives.com/News/Speeches/2010/01/David_Cameron_Supporting_parents.aspx.

Cameron, D (2011) *Troubled families speech*. 15 December 2011. https://www.gov.uk/government/speeches/troubled-families-speech.

Cameron, D (2012) *Welfare Reform Speech*. 25 June. http://www.telegraph.co.uk/news/politics/david-cameron/9354163/David-Camerons-welfare-speech-in-full.html.

Care Quality Commission (2011) *Review of Compliance: Castlebeck Care (Teesdale Ltd)*. www.cqc.org.uk/sites/default/files/documents/1-116865865_castlebeck_care_teesdale_ltd_1-138702193_winterbourne_view_roc_20110517_201107183026.pdf.

Care Quality Commission (2015) *The State of Health Care and Adult Social Care in England, 2014/15*, HC 483. London: HMSO.

Care Quality Commission (2016) *The State of Health Care and Adult Social Care in England, 2015/16*. www.cqc.org.uk/sites/default/files/20161019_stateofcare1516_web.pdf.

Carruthers, I and Ormondroyd, J (2009) *Achieving Age Equality in Health and Social Care*. London: Central Office for Information.

Carter, J (1998) Postmodernity and welfare: when worlds collide. *Social Policy and Administration*, 32(2), 101–15.

Case Con Manifesto (1975). In Bailey, R and Brake, M (1975) *Radical Social Work*. London: Edward Arnold.

Cater, S and Coleman, L (2006) *Planned Teenage Pregnancy: Perspectives of Young Parents from Disadvantaged Backgrounds*. York: JRF.

Cayton, H (1998) Over 65? The NHS couldn't care less now. *The Independent*, 5 July.

Centerpoint (2011) *Youth homelessness jumps by 15%*. Press release, 9 June. http://www. centrepoint.org.uk/archive/about-us/news/2011/june/youth-homeless-increase-15.

Centre for Policy on Ageing (2009) *Ageism and Age Discrimination in Social Care in the United Kingdom: A Department of Health-Commissioned Review from the Literature*. London: CPA.

Chakrabortty, A (2016) Creating child poverty for a whole new generation. Take a bow, Theresa May. *Guardian*, 31 October.

Charted Institute for Housing (2013) *Experiences and Effects of the Benefit Cap in Haringey*. London: Charted Institute for Housing.

Chartered Institute for Housing (2016) *New Benefit Cap Will Have 'Widespread and Severe Impact'*. Press release, 1 November. http://www.cih.org/news-article/display/vpathDCR/ templatedata/cih/news-article/data/New_benefit_cap_will_have_widespread_and_severe_ impact_-_new_research.

Checkland, SG and Checkland, O (1974) *The Poor Law Report of 1834.* Harmondsworth: Penguin.

Child Poverty Action Group (2014) *Consultation on the Child Poverty Strategy, 2014–17*. www. cpag.org.uk/sites/default/files/CPAG%20child%20poverty%20strategy%20consultation%20 response%20May%202014.pdf.

Child Poverty Action Group (2016) *Child Poverty: Facts and Figures*. www.cpag.org.uk/child- poverty-facts-and-figures#footnote5_wz4pl8b.

Children England (2016) *Briefing on the Children and Social Work Bill*. https://www. childrenengland.org.uk/Handlers/Download.ashx?IDMF=c28fb782-b12c-440d-ad0c- 8d015c7a3b7.

Children's Commissioner for England (2014) *Response from the Office of the Children's Commissioner to the Government's Child Poverty Strategy, 2014–17*. www.childrenscommissioner. gov.uk/sites/default/files/publications/Child_poverty_strategy_response.pdf

Children's Commissioner for England (2015) *The Queen's Speech: Press Release*, 27 May. www. childrenscommissioner.gov.uk/news/queen%E2%80%99s-speech.

Chittenden, M (2010) Amis calls for euthanasia booths on street corners. *The Sunday Times*, 24 January.

Chorley, M (2012) Eric Pickles: the man who wants to bring back blame. *The Independent*, 10 June.

Clapton, G, Cree, VE and Smith, M (2013) Moral panics and social work: towards a skeptical view of UK child protection. *Critical Social Policy*, 33(2), 197–217.

Clark, K (2011) Punish the feral rioters, but address our social deficit too. *Guardian*, 5 September.

Cohen, S (2006) *Folk Devils and Moral Panics*, 3rd ed. London: Routledge.

College of Social Work (2015) *Children's Social Work Practices: Key Lessons for Children's Social Work*. http://cdn.basw.co.uk/upload/basw_101637-2.pdf

Colwill, J (1994) Beveridge, women and the welfare state. *Critical Social Policy*, 14(41), 53–78.

Commission for Social Care Inspection (2008a) *Analysis of Evidence Submitted to the CSCI Review of Eligibility Criteria*. London: CSCI.

Commission for Social Care Inspection (2008b) *Cutting the Cake Fairly: CSCI Review of Eligibility Criteria for Social Care*. Newcastle: CSCI.

Commission for Social Care Inspection (2009) *The State Of Social Care in England, 2007/08*. London: CSCI.

Commons Hansard: Various dates.

Communities and Local Government (2009) *Citizenship Survey: April–September 2008, England*. www.communities.gov.uk/documents/statistics/pdf/1133115.pdf.

Community Care (2013) *The State of Personalisation, 2013*. www.communitycare.co.uk/state-of-personalisation-2013/.

Contact a Family (2014) *Counting the Costs, 2014*. www.cafamily.org.uk/media/805120/counting_the_costs_2014_uk_report.pdf.

Cook, D (1989) *Rich Law, Poor Law: Differential Responses to Tax and Supplementary Benefit Fraud*. Milton Keynes: Open University Press.

Cooper, C (2012) Imagining 'radical' youth work possibilities – challenging the 'symbolic violence' within the mainstream tradition in contemporary state-led youth work practice in England. *Journal of Youth Studies*, 15(9), 53–71.

Cooper, J (2011) News. *Community Care*, 5 May.

Cooper, P (1985) Competing explanations for the Merseyside riots of 1981. *British Journal of Criminology*, 25(1), 60–9.

Crawford, K and Walker, J (2008) *Social work with Older People*. Exeter: Learning Matters.

Cree, VE and Myers, S (2008) *Social Work: Making a Difference*. Bristol: Policy Press.

Crosland, CAR (2006) *The Future of Socialism: 50th anniversary edition*. London: Constable & Robinson.

Crossley, S (2015) *Troubled Families Programme: The Perfect Social Policy?* London: Centre for Crime and Social Studies. www.crimeandjustice.org.uk/sites/crimeandjustice.org.uk/files/The%20Troubled%20Families%20Programme,%20Nov%202015.pdf.

Cunningham, I (2016) Non-profits and the 'hollowed out' state: the transformation of working conditions through personalizing social care services during an era of austerity. *Work, Employment and Society*, 30(4), 649–68.

Cunningham, J and Cunningham, S (2008) *Sociology and Social Work*. London: Learning Matters.

Cunningham, J and Cunningham, S (2012) *Social Policy and Social Work: An Introduction*. London: Learning Matters.

Cunningham, J and Cunningham, S (2014) *Sociology and Social Work*, 2nd edn. London: Sage/Learning Matters.

Cunningham, S (2002) Reform or recalcitrance? The Home Office and the regulation of child labour, 1939–1951. *Historical Studies in Industrial Relations*, 13(4), 1–35.

Cunningham, S (2006) 'Demographic time bomb', or 'apocalyptic demography': the great pensions debate, in Lavalette, M and Pratt, A (eds) *Social Policy: A Conceptual and Methodological Introduction*. London: Sage.

Cunningham, S and Lavalette, M (2016) *Schools Out: The Hidden History of Britain's School Student Strikes*. London: Bookmarks.

Curtis Committee (1946) *Report of the Care of Children Committee*, Cmd. 6922. London: HMSO.

D'Ancona, M (2011) If you leave the broken window, the shop gets looted again. *The Telegraph*, 14 August.

Daily Mail (1945) *Our Trust*. 20 March

Daily Mail (2011) *Comment: Reckless immorality that shames Britain*. 10 August.

Davies, C (2010) £200 vasectomy fee to addict 'immoral'. *Guardian*, 19 October.

Dean, H (2004) *Growing Older in the 21st Century*. London: ESRC.

Delebarre, J (2016a) *NEET: Young people Not in Education, Employment or Training*, House of Commons Library Briefing Paper, 21 June. http://researchbriefings.files.parliament.uk/documents/SN06705/SN06705.pdf

Delebarre, J (2016b) *Unemployment by Ethnic Background*, House of Commons Library Briefing Paper, 27 April. 6385. London: HMSO.

Department for Communities and Local Government (2012) *Working with Troubled Families*. https://www.gov.uk/government/uploads/system/uploads/attachment_data/file/66113/121214_Working_with_troubled_families_FINAL_v2.pdf.

Department for Communities and Local Government (2015a) *PM Praises Troubled Families Success*. Press Release, 22 June. https://www.gov.uk/government/news/pm-praises-troubled-families-programme-success.

Department for Communities and Local Government (2015b) *More than 105,000 Troubled Families Turned Around Saving Taxpayers an Estimated £1.2 Billion*. Press Release, 10 March. https://www.gov.uk/government/news/more-than-105000-troubled-families-turned-around-saving-taxpayers-an-estimated-12-billion.

Department for Education (2010) *Government Sets Out New Vision for Ending Child Poverty*. Press release, 21 December. www.education.gov.uk/childrenandyoungpeople/families/childpoverty/a0071184/government-sets-out-new-vi ion-for-ending-child-poverty.

Department for Education (2015) *GSCE and Equivalent Attainment by Pupil Characteristics, 2013 to 2014*. https://www.gov.uk/government/uploads/system/uploads/attachment_data/file/399005/SFR06_2015_Text.pdf.

Department for Education (2016a) *Characteristics of Children in Need, 2014–2015*. https://www.gov.uk/government/uploads/system/uploads/attachment_data/file/469737/SFR41-2015_Text.pdf.

Department for Education (2016b) *Children's Social Work Workforce*. https://www.gov.uk/government/uploads/system/uploads/attachment_data/file/503071/SFR07_2016_Main_Text.pdf.

Department for Education (2016c) *Memorandum to the Education Select Committee's Inquiry into Social Work Reform*. www.parliament.uk/documents/commons-committees/Education/Department-for-Education-memorandum-on-social-work-reform.pdf.

Department for Education (2016d) *Revised GCSE Equivalent Results in England, 2014 to 2015*. https://www.gov.uk/government/uploads/system/uploads/attachment_data/file/494073/SFR01_2016.pdf.

Department for Work and Pensions (2005) *Income Related Benefits: Estimates of Take-up*. London: DfWP.

Department for Work and Pensions (2008) *Fraud and Error in the Benefit System, April 2007 to March 2008*. www.dwp.gov.uk/asd/asd2/fem/fem_apr07_mar08.pdf.

Department for Work and Pensions (2009) *Income Related Benefits: Estimates of Take-up: 2007/08*. http://research.dwp.gov.uk/asd/income_analysis/jun_2009/0708_Publication.pdf.

Department for Work and Pensions (2012) *Income Related Benefits: Estimates of Take-Up in 2009-10*. https://www.gov.uk/government/uploads/system/uploads/attachment_data/file/222914/tkup_first_release_0910.pdf.

Department for Work and Pensions (2013) *The Benefits Cap: Public Perceptions and Pre-implementation Effects*. https://www.gov.uk/government/uploads/system/uploads/attachment_data/file/249005/rrep850.pdf.

Department for Work and Pensions (2015a) *Welfare Reform and Work Bill: Impact Assessment for the Benefit Cap*. www.parliament.uk/documents/impact-assessments/IA15-006.pdf.

Department for Work and Pensions (2015b) *Employment Statistics for Workers Aged 50 and Over*. https://www.gov.uk/government/uploads/system/uploads/attachment_data/file/473821/employment-stats-workers-aged-50-and-over-1984-2015.pdf.

Department for Work and Pensions (2015c) *Fraud and Error in the Benefits System, 2014/15.* https://www.gov.uk/government/uploads/system/uploads/attachment_data/file/473968/fraud-and-error-stats-release-fy-2014-15.pdf.

Department for Work and Pensions (2015d) *Income Related Benefits: Estimates of Take Up, 2013/14.* https://www.gov.uk/government/uploads/system/uploads/attachment_data/file/437501/ir-benefits-take-up-main-report-2013-14.pdf.

Department for Work and Pensions (2016a) *Income-related Benefits: Estimates of Take-up, 2014/15.* https://www.gov.uk/government/uploads/system/uploads/attachment_data/file/535362/ir-benefits-take-up-main-report-2014-15.pdf.

Department for Work and Pensions (2016b) *Income-related Benefits: Estimates of Take-up: Financial Year 2014/15.* https://www.gov.uk/government/statistics/income-related-benefits-estimates-of-take-up-financial-year-201415.

Department for Work and Pensions Select Committee (2009) *DWP's Commissioning Strategy and the Flexible New Deal: Volume 1.* London: HMSO.

Department of Health (2001) *National Service Framework for Older People.* London: HMSO.

Department of Health (2005) *Independence, Well-being and Choice: Our Vision for the Future of Social Care for Adults in England,* Cm 6499. London: HMSO.

Department of Health (2007) *Implementation Plan for Reducing Health Inequalities in Infant Mortality: A Good Practice Guide.* London: Department of Health.

Department of Health (2010) *A Vision for Adult Social Care: Capable Communities and Active Citizens.* London: Department of Health.

Domokos, J (2011) Jobseekers tricked out of benefits to meet staff targets. *Guardian,* 2 April.

Doughty, S (1999) Hostel scheme to help teenage mothers work. *Daily Mail,* 1 February.

Doward, J (2010) Anti-drugs campaigner who pays addicts to be sterilised brings her crusade to the UK. *The Observer,* 20 May.

Drugscope and Adfam (2012) *The Troubled Families Agenda: What Does It Mean?* www.drugwise.org.uk/wp-content/uploads/troubled-families.pdf.

Duncan Smith, I (2014) *A Welfare State Fit for the 21st Century,* Speech, 23 January. https://www.gov.uk/government/speeches/a-welfare-state-fit-for-the-21st-century

Dunning, J (2010) Councils deny social care support to all but the most needs. *Community Care,* 15 September.

Ebrahimi, H and Wilson, H (2012) Treasury committee could grill US companies over tax evasion. *The Telegraph,* 4 November.

Elgot, J (2015) UN to investigate impact of welfare cuts on vulnerable groups. *Guardian,* 29 October.

Engels, F (1845) *The Condition of the Working Class in England.* Frankfurt: Literarische Anstalt.

Esping Anderson, G (1990) *The Three Worlds of Welfare Capitalism.* London: Polity Press.

European Child Safety Alliance (2012) *Child Safety Report Card, 2012.* www.childsafetyeurope. org/publications/info/child-safety-report-cards-europe-summary-2012.pdf.

European Union (2016) *Sweden: Successful Reconciliation of Work and Family Life.* http://europa. eu/epic/countries/sweden/index_en.htm

European Union News (2016) *Emma Urges Social Workers to Join Union to Protect Their Profession.* 1 September. https://www.nexis.com/results/enhdocview.do?docLinkInd=true&ersKey= 23_T24813215659&format=GNBFI&startDocNo=0&resultsUrlKey=0_T24813215661& backKey=20_T24813215662&csi=400456&docNo=14

Eurostat (2016a) *People at Risk of Poverty and Social Exclusion, May.* http://ec.europa.eu/eurostat/ statistics-explained/index.php/People_at_risk_of_poverty_or_social_exclusion.

Eurostat (2016b) *Infant Mortality per 1000 Live Births.* http://ec.europa.eu/eurostat/tgm/table. do?tab=table&init=1&language=en&pcode=tps00027&plugin=1.

Eurostat (2016c) *Real GDP Growth Rate.* http://ec.europa.eu/eurostat/tgm/table.do?tab=table &init=1&language=en&pcode=tec00115&plugin=1.

Eurostat (2016d) *Marriage and Divorce Statistics.* http://ec.europa.eu/eurostat/ statistics-explained/extensions/EurostatPDFGenerator/getfile.php?fi le=193.61.255.87_1470850768_64.pdf.

Eurostat (2016e) *Share of Live Births Outside Marriage.* http://ec.europa.eu/eurostat/tgm/table. do?tab=table&init=1&language=en&pcode=tps00018&plugin=1.

Evans, EJ (1978) *Social Policy 1830–1814: Individualism, Collectivism and the Origins of the Welfare State.* London: Routledge & Kegan Paul.

Farnsworth, K (2015) *The British Corporate Welfare State: Public Provision for Private Businesses.* Sheffield: Sheffield Political Economy Research Institute.

Ferguson, I (2007) Increasing user choice or privatizing risk? The antinomies of personalization. *British Journal of Social Work,* 37(3), 387–403.

Ferguson, I (2008) *Reclaiming Social Work: Challenging Neo-liberalism and Promoting Social Justice.* London: Sage.

Ferguson, I and Lavalette, M (2014) *Adult Social Care.* Bristol: Policy Press.

Ferguson, I and Smith, L (2012) Education for change: student placements in campaigning organisations and social movements in South Africa. *British Journal of Social Work,* 42(5), 974–94.

Ferguson, I and Woodward, R (2009) *Radical Social Work in Practice: Making a Difference.* Bristol: Policy Press.

Ferguson, I, Lavalette, M and Mooney, G (2002) *Rethinking Welfare: A Critical Perspective*. London: Sage.

Ferguson, I, Taylor, I and Watterson, A (2012) Care inspectors must return to Glasgow to investigate centre closures: correspondence. *The Herald*, 18 December

Field, F (1989) *Losing Out: Emergence of Britain's Underclass*. Oxford: Blackwell.

Field, F (2010) *The Foundation Years: Preventing Poor Children Becoming Poor Adults*. London: HM Government.

Fitzgibbon, S, Curry, D and Lea, J (2013) Supervising rioters: the role of probation. *Howard Journal*, 52(5), 445–61.

Flynn, M (2012) *South Gloucestershire Safeguarding Adults Board. Winterbourne View Hospital: A Serious Care Review*. http://hosted.southglos.gov.uk/wv/report.pdf

Forrester, D and Harwin, J (2007) Parental substance misuse and child welfare: outcomes for children two years after referral. *British Journal of Social Work*, 38(8), 1518–35.

Franklin, B (1999) *Social Policy, Media and Misrepresentation*. Florence, KY: Routledge.

Franklin, B (2014) Citizen journalists or cyber bigots? Child abuse, the media and the possibilities for public conversation: the case of Baby P, in Wagg, S and Pilcher, J (ed.) *Thatcher's Grandchildren? Politics and Childhood in the Twenty-first Century*. Basingstoke: Palgrave Macmillan.

Fraser, D (2009) *The Evolution of the British Welfare State*. London: Palgrave: Macmillan.

Furedi, F (2002) *Paranoid Parenting: Why Ignoring the Experts Might Be Best for Your Child*. Chicago: Chicago Review Press.

Furlong, A and Cartmel, F (2007) *Young People and Social Change: New Perspectives*. Maidenhead: Open University Press.

Gardner, A (2014) *Personalisation in Social Work*, 2nd edn. Exeter: Learning Matters.

Garrett, PM (2007) 'Sinbin solutions': the 'pioneer' projects for 'problem families' and the forgetfulness of social policy research. *Critical Social Policy*, 27(2), 203–30.

Garrett, PM (2013) *Children and Families*. Bristol: Policy Press

Gentleman, A (2010) Anger and alarm as Tory minister attacks benefit claimants who have large families. *Guardian*, 8 October.

George, V and Wilding, P (1994) *Welfare and Ideology*. Hemel Hempstead: Harvester Wheatsheaf.

Gilbert, BB (1973) *The Evolution of National Insurance in Britain: The Origins of the British Welfare State*. London: Michael Joseph.

Glasby, J and Littlechild, R (2002) *Social Work and Direct Payments*. Bristol: Policy Press.

Glasby, J and Littlechild, R (2009) *Direct Payments and Personal Budgets: Putting Personalisation into Practice*. Bristol: Policy Press.

Golding, P and Middleton, S (1982) *Images of Welfare: Press and Public Attitudes to Poverty*. Oxford: Martin Roberts.

Goodman, A and Gregg, P (eds) (2010) *Poorer Children's Educational Attainment*. York: Joseph Rowntree Foundation.

Goodman, A, Myck, M and Shephard, A (2003) *Sharing in the Nation's Prosperity? Pensioner Poverty in Britain*. London: Institute for Fiscal Studies.

Gough, I (1979) *The Political Economy of the Welfare State*. London: Macmillan.

Green, D (1999) *An End to Welfare Rights: The Rediscovery of Independence*. London: CIVITAS.

Greenland, C (1986) Inquiries into child abuse and neglect (CAN) deaths in the United Kingdom. *British Journal of Criminology*, 26(2), 164–72.

Gregg, P (2010) *Family Intervention Projects: A Classic Case of Policy Based Evidence*. London: Centre for Crime and Criminal Justice Studies.

Guardian (1945a) Boy killed by neglect and violence. 13 February.

Guardian (1945b) Gough gets six years for manslaughter of boy. 20 March.

Guardian (1946a) The Curtis Report, 16 October.

Guardian (1946b) The children, 20 October.

Guardian/London School of Economics (2012) *Reading the Riots: Investigating England's Summer of Disorder*. http://eprints.lse.ac.uk/46297/1/Reading%20the%20riots%28published%29.pdf.

Hackett, S, Kuronen, M, Matthies A-L and Kresal, B (2003) The motivation, professional development and identity of social work students in four European countries. *European Journal of Social Work*, 6(2), 163–78.

Hall, S (1984) The rise of the representative/interventionist state 1880s–1920s. In McLennan, G, Held, D and Hall, S (eds) *State and Society in Contemporary Britain*. Cambridge: Polity Press.

Hall, S (1998) The great moving nowhere show. *Marxism Today*, November/December, p14.

Hall, S and Jacques, M (1983) *The Politics of Thatcherism*. London: Lawrence & Wishart

Halsey, K and White, R (2008) *Young People, Crime and Public Perceptions: A Review of the Literature*. London: Local Government Association.

Hamilton, S, Tew, J, Szmczynska, P, Clewett, N, Manthorpe, J, Larsen, J and Pinfold, V (2016) Power, choice and control: how do personal budgets affect the experiences of people with mental health problems and their relationships with social workers and other practitioners? *British Journal of Social Work*, 46(3), 719–36.

Harris, J (2004) Consumerism: social development or social delimitation? *International Social Work*, 47(4), 533–42.

Harris, R (1971) A gift horse. In Boyson, R (ed.) *Down with the Poor.* Middlesex: Churchill Press.

Hastings, A, Bailey, N, Bramley, G, Gannon, M and Watkins, D (2015) *The Cost of the Cuts: The Impact on Local Government and Poorer Communities.* York: JRF

Hastings, M (2011) Years of liberal dogma have spawned a generation of amoral, uneducated, unparented, welfare dependent, brutalised youngsters. *Daily Mail,* 10 August.

Hatton, C and Waters, J (2015) Personal health budget holders and family carers: the POET surveys, 2015. *In Control.* www.in-control.org.uk/media/177094/poet%20phb%20sept%20 2015.pdf

Health and Social Care Information Centre (2015) *Learning Disability Census Report, England, 30 September 2015.* http://digital.nhs.uk/catalogue/PUB19428/ld-census-initial-sep15-rep.pdf.

Healthcare Commission and Commission for Social Care Inspection (2006) *Joint Investigation into the Provision of Services for People with Learning Disabilities at Cornwall Partnership NHS Trust.* London: Commission for Healthcare Audit and Inspection. http:www.cqc.org.uk/_db/_ documents/cornwa11_investigation_report.pdf.

Helm, T (2011) Most Britons believe children will have worse lives than their parents – poll. *Guardian,* 3 December.

Helm, T (2012) Demonisation of the poor is taking place . . . horrible things will happen. *Guardian,* 17 November.

Helm, T and Boffey, D (2011) Lib Dems in mutiny over benefit cap. *Observer,* 27 March.

Herden, E, Power, A and Provan, B (2015) *Is Welfare Reform Working? Impacts on Working Age Tenants.* London: LSE. http://sticerd.lse.ac.uk/dps/case/cr/casereport90.pdf.

Heywood, A (1998) *Political Ideologies: An Introduction.* London: Macmillan Press.

Hillyard, P and Watson, S (1996) Postmodern social policy: a contradiction in terms? *Journal of Social Policy,* 2(3), 321–46.

Hitchens, P (2015) Posh tests won't rob your child of a job. *Mail on Sunday,* 21 June.

HM Government (2007) *Putting People First. A Shared Vision and Commitment to the Transformation of Adult Social Care.* London: HMSO.

HM Government (2010) *Building the National Care Service,* Cm 7854. London: HMSO.

HM Government (2014) *Consultation on the Child Poverty Strategy, 2014–17.* London: HMSO.

HM Revenue and Customs (2014) *Child Benefit, Child Tax Credit and Working Tax Credit: Take Up Rates in 2012/13.* https://www.gov.uk/government/uploads/system/uploads/attachment_ data/file/382787/cwtcchb-take-up2012-13_final.pdf.

HM Treasury (2015) *Public Expenditure: Statistical Analysis, 2015,* Cm 9122. London: HMSO.

HM Treasury and Department for Children, Schools and Families (2007) *Aiming High for Young People: A Ten Year Strategy for Positive Experiences.* London: HMSO.

Homeless Link (2012) *Young and Homeless: A Survey of Social Services and Local Authorities, 2011*. www.homeless.org.uk/sites/default/files/site-attachments/Young%20%26%20Homeless%20 Report%202011.pdf.

House of Commons Home Affairs Select Committee (2012) *Policing Large Scale Disorder: The Lessons from the Disturbances of August 2011*, Volume 1. www.publications.parliament.uk/pa/ cm201012/cmselect/cmhaff/1456/1456i.pdf.

House of Commons Library (2009) *Welfare Reform Bill: Social Security Provisions*, Research Paper 09/08. London: HMSO.

House of Commons Public Accounts Committee (2016) *Personal Budgets in Social Care*, HC 74. London: HMSO. www.publications.parliament.uk/pa/cm201617/cmselect/ cmpubacc/74/74.pdf.

House of Commons Public Accounts Select Committee (2015) *Care Services for People with Learning Disabilities and Challenging Behaviour*, HC 973. London: HMSO.

House of Commons Work and Pensions Committee (2009) *Tackling Pensioner Poverty*. London: HMSO.

House of Commons Work and Pensions Committee (2014) *Support for Housing Costs in the Reformed Welfare System*, HC 720. London: HMSO.

House of Commons Work and Pensions Committee (2015) *Welfare to Work*. www.publications. parliament.uk/pa/cm201516/cmselect/cmworpen/363/363.pdf.

House of Lords Select Committee on Economic Affairs (2003) *Aspects of the Economics of an Ageing Population*, HL Paper 179-I. London: HMSO.

House of Lords Select Committee on Public Service and Democratic Change (2013) *Ready for Ageing?* HL Paper 140. London: HMSO.

Humphries, R, Thorlby, R, Holder, H, Hall, P and Charles, A (2016) *Social Care for Older People: Home Truths*. https://www.kingsfund.org.uk/sites/files/kf/field/field_publication_file/ Social_care_older_people_Kings_Fund_Sep_2016.pdf.

Independent Age (2016) *The Over-looked Over-75s. Poverty Amongst the 'Silent Generation' Who Lived Through the Second World Wa*r. https://www.independentage.org/sites/default/ files/2016-05/pensioner-poverty-report_final_website.pdf.

Independent Commission on Youth Crime and Anti-Social Behaviour (2010) *Time for a Fresh Start*. London: Police Foundation.

Individual Budgets Evaluation Network (2008) *Evaluation of the Individual Budgets Pilot Programme*. York: University of York Social Policy Research Unit.

Ioakimidis, V, Santos, CC and Herrero, IM (2014) Reconceptualizing social work in times of crisis: an examination of the cases of Greece, Spain and Portugal. *International Social Work*, 57(4), 285–300.

Ipsos MORI (2006) *Attitudes Towards Teenagers and Crime*. www.ipsos-mori.com/research publications/researcharchive/pol1.aspx?oltemld=287.

Ipsos MORI (2010) *Youth Aspirations in London*. http://ipsos-rsl.com/ DownloadPublication/1374_sri-third-sector-youth-aspirations-in-london-march-2010.pdf.

Ipsos MORI (2015) *How Britain Voted in 2015*. https://www.ipsos-mori.com/ researchpublications/researcharchive/3575/How-Britain-voted-in-2015.aspx.

Ismail, S, Thorlby, R and Holder, H (2014) *Focus on Social Care For Older People: Reductions in Adult Social Services for Older People in England*. London: Health Foundation and Nuffield Trust.

Jarrett, T (2015) *Social Care: How the Postponed Changes to Paying for Care, Including the Cap, Would Have Worked (England)*. House of Commons Library Briefing Paper. http:// researchbriefings.files.parliament.uk/documents/SN07106/SN07106.pdf.

Jeong, JJ, Pepler, DJ, Motz, M, DeMarchi, G and Espinet, S (2015) Readiness for treatment: does it matter for women with substance use problems who are parenting? *Journal of Social Work Practice in the Addictions*, 15(4), 394–417.

Johns, L (2011) Apologists for these thugs should hang their heads in shame. *Daily Mail*, 9 August.

Johnson, P (2011) The long retreat of order. *The Telegraph*, 10 August.

Johnston, J (1909) *The Wastage of Child Life: As Exemplified by Conditions in Lancashire*. London: Fabian Society.

Jones, C (1976) *The Foundations of Social Work Education*, Working Papers in Sociology, No. 11. Durham: University of Durham.

Jones, C (1983) *State Social Work and the Working Class*. London: Routledge.

Jones, C (2005) The neo-liberal assault: voices from the front line of British state social work. In Ferguson, I, Lavalette, M and Whitmore, E (eds) *Globalisation, Global Justice and Social Work*. London: Routledge.

Jones, C (2011) The best and worst of times: reflections on the impact of radicalism on British social work education in the 1970s. In Lavalette, M (ed.) *Radical Social Work Today: Social Work at the Crossroads*. Bristol: Policy Press.

Jones, C and Novak, T (1999) *Poverty, Welfare and the Disciplinary State*. London: Routledge.

Jones, C, Burstrom, B, Martilla, A, Canvin, K and Whitehead, M (2006) Studying social policy and resilience to adversity in different welfare states: Britain and Sweden. *International Journal of Health Services*, 36(3), 425–42.

Jones, C, Ferguson, I, Lavalette, M and Penketh, L (2004) *Social Work and Social Justice: A Manifesto for a New Engaged Practice*. www.socialworkfuture.org/index.php/swan-organisation/ manifesto?84e4966ffb2a94832870f77fe3157220=20f4f975c2a709187cb009e189e08fa1.

Jones, O (2011) *Chavs: The Demonization of the Working Class*. London: Verso.

Jones, O (2013) The Welfare Bill: a government of millionaires just made the poor poorer – and laughed as they did it. *The Independent*, 9 January 2013.

Jones, O (2014a) *The Establishment: And How They Get Away with It*. London: Penguin.

Jones, O (2014b) Who are the real scroungers? *Guardian*, 30 August.

Jones, R (2013) How to privatise child protection in six easy stages. *Guardian*, 20 November.

Jones, R (2014a) Second thoughts: privatising child protection is a radical step. It must not be done under the radar. *Guardian*, 4 June.

Jones, R (2014b) *The story of Baby P: setting the record straight*. Bristol: Policy Press.

Joseph Rowntree Foundation (2013) *Welfare Sanctions and Conditionality in the UK*. https://www.jrf.org.uk/sites/default/files/jrf/migrated/files/Welfare-conditionality-UK-Summary.pdf.

Kawalerowicz, J and Biggs, M (2015) Anarchy in the UK: economic deprivation, social disorganization, and political grievances in the London riot of 2011. *Social Forces*, 94(2), 673–98.

Keep, M, Delebare, J, Keen, R, Rhodes, C and Wilson, W (2015) *Spending Review and Autumn Statement 2015: A Summary*, House of Commons Library Briefing Paper No 7401. http://researchbriefings.files.parliament.uk/documents/CBP-7401/CBP-7401.pdf.

Kelsey, D (2015) Defining the 'sick society': discourses of class and morality in British right-wing newspapers during the 2011 England riots. *Capital and Class*, 39(2), 243–64.

Kishita, N, Fisher, P and Laidlaw, K (2015) *What Are the Attitudes of Different Age Groups Towards Contributing and Benefitting from the Wider Society and How Are These Experienced by Individuals in Those Age Groups?* London: Government Office for Science. https://www.gov.uk/government/uploads/system/uploads/attachment_data/file/454795/gs-15-16-future-ageing-attitudes-psychological-er07.pdf.

Kleeman, J (2010) This woman thinks drug addicts should not be allowed to have children. *Weekend Guardian*, 12 June.

Kotecha, M, Arthur, S and Coutinho, S (2013) *Understanding the Relationship Between Pensioner Poverty and Material Deprivation*, DWP Research Report 827. London: DWP.

Labour Research (2014) At risk: child protection. *Labour Research*, July.

Lakhani, N (2012) Six workers jailed over Winterbourne View abuse. *The Independent*, 27 October.

Laming, Lord (2009) *The Protection of Children in England: A Progress Report*, HC 330. London: HMSO.

Langan, M and Lee, P (1989) *Radical Social Work Today*. London: Unwin Hyman.

Lavalette, M (ed.) (2011) *Radical Social Work Today: Social Work at the Crossroads*. Bristol: Policy Press.

Lavalette, M and Ferguson, I (2009) Social work after 'Baby P'. *International Socialism*, 122, March.

Lawrence, S, Lyons, K, Simpson, G and Huegler, N (2009) *Introducing International Social Work*. Exeter: Learning Matters.

Lawton, A (2009) *Personalisation and Learning Disabilities: A Review of Evidence on Advocacy and Its Practice for People with Learning Disabilities and High Support Needs*. London: SCIE.

Leece, J and Bornat, J (eds) (2006) *Developments in Direct Payments*. Bristol: Policy Press.

Leonard, P (1975) Towards a paradigm for radical practice. In Bailey, R and Brake, M (eds) *Radical Social Work*. London: Edward Arnold.

Levitas, R (2005) *The Inclusive Society: Social Exclusion and New Labour*. London: Macmillan.

Lightowlers, C and Quirk, H (2015) The 2011 riots: prosecutorial zeal and judicial abandon. *British Journal of Criminology*, 55(1), 65–85.

Littlejohn, R (2011) The politics of envy was bound to end up in flames. *The Mail*, 12 August.

Lloyd, CM (1923) Industrial welfare work. *Manchester Guardian*, 17 May.

Local Government Association (2014) *Adult Social Care Funding: 2014 State of the Nation Report*. www.local.gov.uk/documents/10180/5854661/Adult+social+care+funding+2014+state+of+the+nation+report/e32866fa-d512-4e77-9961-8861d2d93238.

Lodge, C, Carnell, E and Coleman, M (2016) *The New Age of Ageing: How Society Needs to Change*. Bristol: Policy Press.

Lourie, J (2001) *Age Equality Commission Bill*, House of Commons Research Paper 01/100. London: HMSO.

Lowe, R (1993) *The Welfare State in Britain Since 1945*. London: Macmillan.

Lymbery, M (2010) A new vision for adult social care? Continuities and change in the care of older people. *Critical Social Policy*, 30(1), 5–26.

Lymbery, M. (2014) Austerity, personalisation and older people: the prospects for creative social work practice in England. *European Journal of Social Work*, 17(3), 367–82.

McGuiness, F (2016) *Poverty in the UK: Statistics*. London: House of Commons Library. http://researchbriefings.files.parliament.uk/documents/SN07096/SN07096.pdf

McKinstry, L (2011) Young offenders are mollycoddled by justice system. *Express*, 11 February.

McLennan, G (1986) *Beliefs and Ideologies*. Maidenhead: Open University Press.

Macnicol, J (1986) The effect of the evacuation of schoolchildren on official attitudes to state intervention. In Smith, HL (ed.) *War and Social Change: British Society and the Second World War*. Manchester: Manchester University Press.

Macnicol, J (1987) In pursuit of the underclass. *Journal of Social Policy*, 16(3), 293–318.

Macnicol, J (2015) *Neoliberalising Old Age*. Cambridge: Cambridge University Press.

McNicoll, A (2016) Minister: We won't privatise child protection or politicize social work. *Community Care*, 7 July. www.communitycare.co.uk/2016/07/07/minister-wont-privatise-child-protection-politicise-social-work/.

Malnick, E (2014) Academics warn of privatisation of care services. *Guardian*, 17 May.

Malthus, TR (1973) *An Essay on the Principle of Population*. London: Dent.

Marmot, M (2010) *Fair Society: Healthy Lives: The Marmot Review*. www.instituteofhealthequity.org/projects/fair-society-healthy-lives-the-marmot-review/fair-society-healthy-lives-full-report.

Marsden, D (1969) *Mothers Alone: Poverty and the Fatherless Family*. London: Penguin.

Marshall, TH (1967) *Social Policy*. London: Hutchinson University Library.

Marsland, D (1996) *Welfare or Welfare State: Contradictions and Dilemmas in Social Policy*. New York: St. Martin's Press.

Marsland, D (2010) *Iconclasts*. Radio 4 broadcast, 28 August.

Marx, K and Engels, F (1969) *Manifesto of the Communist Party*. Moscow: Progress Publishers.

Mason, R and Wintour, P (2013) PM's despair at private school grip on top jobs. *Guardian*, 14 November.

Miliband, R (1973) *The State in Capitalist Society*. London: Quartet.

Miliband, R (1977) *Marxism and Politics*. Oxford: Oxford University Press.

Ministry of Justice (2012) *Statistical Bulletin on the Public Order Disorder of 6th to 9th August 2011, October update*. https://www.gov.uk/government/uploads/system/uploads/attachment_data/file/217807/august-public-disorder-stats-bulletin-241011.pdf.

Mishra, R (1977) *Society and Social Policy: Theoretical Perspectives on Welfare*. London: Macmillan.

Mishra, R (1984) *The Welfare State in Crisis: Social Thought and Social Change*. Brighton: Wheatsheaf.

Moffatt, S and Higgs, P (2007) Charity or entitlement? Generational habits and the welfare state among older people in north-east England. *Social Policy and Administration*, 41(5), 449–64.

Monkton, W (1945) *Report on the Circumstances Which Led to the Boarding out of Dennis and Terence O'Neill*, Cmd 6636. London: HMSO.

Mooney, G (1998) Remoralizing the poor? Gender, class and philanthropy in Victorian Britain. In Lewis, G (ed.) *Forming Nation, Framing Welfare*. London: Routledge.

MORI (2006) *A Comparative Study of Attitudes and Behaviours in the UK, Germany and Sweden*. www.centrica.co.uk/files/pdf/iposos_mori.pdf.

Morris, J (1993) *Independent Lives: Community Care and Disabled People*. Basingstoke: Macmillan.

Morris, J (1997) Care or empowerment? A disability rights perspective. *Social Policy and Administration*, 31(1), 54–60.

Mortimer, J and Green, M (2015) *Briefing: The Health and Care of Older People in England, 2015.* Age UK. http://www.ageuk.org.uk/Documents/EN-GB/For-professionals/Research/Briefing-The_Health_and_Care_of_Older_People_in_England-2015.pdf?dtrk=true

Mullan, P (2000) *The Imaginary Time Bomb: Why an Ageing Population Is Not a Social Problem.* London: Tauris.

Muncie, J (2015) *Youth and Crime*, 4th edn. London: Sage

Munro, E (2011) *The Munro Review of Child Protection: Final Report*, Cm 8062 London: HMSO.

Munro, E and Liquid Personnel (2015) *The Social Work Survey: 2014/15.* London: BASW.

Murray, C (1999) *Charles Murray and the Underclass: The Developing Debate.* London: CIVITAS.

Murray, K (2014) Almost three-quarters feel living standards will fall in old age. *Guardian*, 26 February.

Narey, M (2014) Child protection system backed by Narey. *Children and Young People Now*, 26 May. http://www.cypnow.co.uk/cyp/analysis/1144263/child-protection-competition-backed by narey

National Audit Office (2015a) *Tax Reliefs*, HC 1256. https://www.nao.org.uk/wp-content/uploads/2014/03/Tax-reliefs.pdf.

National Audit Office (2015b) *Outcome-based Payments Schemes: Government's Use of Payment by Results.* https://www.nao.org.uk/wp-content/uploads/2015/06/Outcome-based-payment-schemes-governments-use-of-payment-by-results.pdf.

National Audit Office (2015c) *Care Leavers Transition to Adulthood.* London: NAO. https://www.nao.org.uk/wp-content/uploads/2015/07/Care-leavers-transition-to-adulthood.pdf.

National Audit Office (2016a) *Transforming rehabilitation.* https://www.nao.org.uk/wp-content/uploads/2016/04/Transforming-rehabilitation.pdf

National Audit Office (2016b) *Personalised Commissioning in Adult Social Care.* https://www.nao.org.uk/wp-content/uploads/2016/03/Personalised-commissioning-in-adult-social-care-update.pdf.

National Centre for Independent Living (2011) *We Must Preserve Independent Living.* Press Release, 16 February. www.ncil.org.uk/show.php?contentid=71&categoryid=16.

National Council for Voluntary Organisations (2016) *UK Civil Society Almanac 2016/Volunteer Profiles.* https://data.ncvo.org.uk/a/almanac16/volunteer-profiles-2/#Young_people.

National Health Service (2016) *The NHS Constitution for England.* https://www.gov.uk/government/publications/the-nhs-constitution-for-england/the-nhs-constitution-for-england.

National Pensioners Convention (2009) *Shaping the Future of Care Together: Response to the Green Paper.* London: NPC.

National Pensioners Convention (2011) *Green Paper Pulls the Pensions Ladder Up from Today's Pensioners.* http://npcuk.org/164#_ftn4.

Neal, S (2003) The Scarman Report, the Macphersn Report and the media: how newspapers respond to race centred social policy interventions. *Journal of Social Policy*, 32(1), 55–74.

Newburn, T (2015) The 2011 England riots in historical perspective. *British Journal of Criminology*, 55(1), 39–64

Nordic Social Insurance Portal (2016) *Unemployment Benefits.* www.nordsoc.org/en/Sweden/Unemployment1/.

Norrie, C, Weinstein, J, Jones, R, Hood, R and Bhanbro, S (2014) Early experiences in extending personal budgets in one local authority. *Working With Older People*, 18(4), 176–85.

NSPCC (2016) *It's Time: Campaign Report.* https://www.nspcc.org.uk/globalassets/documents/research-reports/its-time-campaign-report.pdf.

O'Carroll, L (2016) 1.3bn troubled families scheme has had 'no discernible impact'. *Guardian*, 8 August.

O'Hara, M (2015) *Austerity Bites: A Journey to the Sharp End of Cuts in the UK.* Bristol: Policy Press.

OECD (2014) *Children in Families by Employment Status.* www.oecd.org/els/family/LMF_1_1_Children_in_families_by_employment_status_Jul2014.pdf

OECD (2015) *Pensions at a Glance.* Geneva: OECD.

OECD (2016a) *Health at a Glance, 2015.* Paris: OECD. www.keepeek.com/Digital-Asset-Management/oecd/social-issues-migration-health/health-at-a-glance-2015_health_glance-2015-en#page3.

OECD (2016b) *Pensions at a Glance: OECD and G20 Indicators.* www.oecd-ilibrary.org/docserver/download/8115201e.pdf?expires=1475046433&id=id&accname=guest&checksum=C026BDA08B422D2A53F66234F1989E61.

Office for National Statistics (2011) *Labour Market Statistics, October 2011.* webarchive.national archives.gov.uk/20160105160709/http://www.ons.gov.uk/ons/dcp171778_237932.pdf.

Office for National Statistics (2013a) *Estimates of the Very Old.* www.ons.gov.uk/ons/dcp 171778_418037.pdf.

Office for National Statistics (2013b) *One Third of Babies Born in 2013 Are Expected to Live to 100.* www.ons.gov.uk/ons/rel/lifetables/historic-and-projected-data-from-the-period-and-cohort-life-tables/2012-based/sty-babies-living-to-100.html.

Office for National Statistics (2014a) *Teenage Conception Rates Highest in the Most Deprived Areas.* http://webarchive.nationalarchives.gov.uk/20160105160709/http://www.ons.gov.uk/ons/rel/regional-trends/area-based-analysis/conceptions-deprivation-analysis-toolkit/conceptions-deprivation-measures--2009-11.html.

Office for National Statistics (2014b) *Changes in the Older Resident Care Home Population between 2001 and 2011*. http://webarchive.nationalarchives.gov.uk/20160105160709/http://www.ons.gov.uk/ons/dcp171776_373040.pdf.

Office for National Statistics (2015a) *Life Expectancy at Birth*. www.ons.gov.uk/ons/dcp171778_422285.pdf.

Office for National Statistics (2015b) *Life Expectancy at Birth*. www.ons.gov.uk/ons/dcp171778_422285.pdf.

Office for National Statistics (2015c) *Excess Winter Mortality in England and Wales, 2014/15*. www.ons.gov.uk/peoplepopulationandcommunity/birthsdeathsandmarriages/deaths/bulletins/excesswintermortalityinenglandandwales/201415provisionaland201314final/pdf.

Office for National Statistics (2016) *Birth Cohort Tables for Infant Deaths*. https://www.ons.gov.uk/file?uri=/peoplepopulationandcommunity/birthsdeathsandmarriages/deaths/datasets/birthcohorttablesforinfantdeaths/2013/birthcohorttables2013.xls.

Office of the Children's Commissioner (2013) *A Child Rights Assessment of Budget Decision*. https://www.childrenscommissioner.gov.uk/sites/default/files/publications/A_Child_Rights_Impact_Assessment_of_Budget_Decisions.pdf.

Ofsted (2015) *Serious Incident Notifications from Local Authority Children's Services*. https://www.google.co.uk/url?sa=t&rct=j&q=&esrc=s&source=web&cd=2&ved=0ahUKEwjR1YKEp8DNAhXFC8AKHQ55A8IQFggiMAE&url=https%3A%2F%2Fwww.gov.uk%2Fgovernment%2Fuploads%2Fsystem%2Fuploads%2Fattachment_data%2Ffile%2F471759%2FSerious_incident_notifications_from_local_authority_children_s_services_financial_year_ending_March_2015.docx&usg=AFQjCNE-jKfTOEWkTMWGTw6x23UmdedUiA&bvm=bv.125221236,d.ZGg.

Owen, T (2006) *My Home Life: Quality of Life in Care Homes*. London: Help the Aged.

Oxford City Council Welfare Reform Team (2016) *Evaluation of European Social Fund Pilot Project*. https://www.google.co.uk/url?sa=t&rct=j&q=&esrc=s&source=web&cd=9&ved=0ahUKEwje4Kyq9InQAhXsCMAKHSI0B14QFghHMAg&url=https%3A%2F%2Fwww.oxford.gov.uk%2Fdownload%2Fdownloads%2Fid%2F2119%2Fwelfare_reform_european_social_fund_project_evaluation_report.pdf&usg=AFQjCNG7NUCHf9jUsrSmi3lsZVDLrXA0Hg.

Parr, S (2011) Intensive family casework with 'problem families': past and present. *Family Science*, 2(2), 240–9.

Pearson, C (2000) Money talks? Competing discourses in the implementation of direct payments. *Critical Social Policy*, 20(4), 459–77.

Pearson, G (1975) Making social workers: bad promises and good omens. In Bailey, R and Brake, M (eds) *Radical Social Work*. London: Edward Arnold.

Pearson, G (1983) *Hooligan: A History of Respectable Fears*. London: Macmillan.

Phillips, M (2008) Shannon's mother, a crude culture of greed and why we must abolish child benefit. *Daily Mail*, 8 December.

Phillipson, C (1982) *Capitalism and the Construction of Old Age.* London: Macmillan.

Pierson, J (2011) *Understanding Social Work: History and Context.* Maidenhead: Open University Press.

Portes, J (2015) *A Troubling Attitude to Statistics.* Press Release National Institute of Economic and Social Research, 15 March. www.niesr.ac.uk/blog/troubling-attitude-statistics#. V6nGAIWMolJ.

Project Prevention (2010) *Objectives.* www.projectprevention.org/objectives/.

Project Prevention (2016) *Project Prevention in the United Kingdom.* www.projectprevention.org/ united-kingdom/.

Public Health England (2016) *Infant and Perinatal Mortality in the West Midlands.* https://www.gov.uk/government/uploads/system/uploads/attachment_data/file/515800/ InfantMortalityInTheWestMidlandsFinal.pdf.

QAA (2008) *Social Work Benchmarks.* www.qaa.ac.uk/academicinfrastructure/benchmark/ statements/socialwork08.pdf.

QAA (2016) *Subject Benchmark Statement: Social Work: Draft for Consultation.* www.qaa.ac.uk/en/ Publications/Documents/SBS-Social-Work-consultation-16.pdf.

Rawnsley, A (2014) Kenneth Clark: I had a lot of views, but they didn't coincide with No 10's. *Guardian,* 19 July.

Ray, S, Sharp, E and Abrams, D (2006) *Ageism: A Benchmark of Public Attitudes in Britain.* London: Age Concern.

Reed, H and Elson, D (2014) *An Adequate Standard of Living: A Child Rights-based Analysis of Tax and Social Security Policy Changes in the Autumn Statement 2013 and the Budget 2014.* London: Office of the Children's Commissioner.

Reeves, A and de Vries, R (2016) Does media coverage influence public attitudes towards welfare recipients? The impact of the 2011 English riots. *British Journal of Sociology,* 67(2), 281–306.

Respect (2006) *Family Intervention Projects.* London: Respect Agenda.

Riddell, M (2011) The underclass is lashing out at a Britain that has turned its back. *The Telegraph,* 9 August.

Rockett, K (2014) £200m blitz on families that shame Britain. *The Express,* 25 June.

Rogowski, S (2012) Social work with children and families: challenges and possibilities in the neo-liberal world, *British Journal of Social Work,* 45(5), 921–40.

Rogowski, S (2014) Radical/critical social work with young offenders: challenges and possibilities. *Journal of Social Work Practice,* 28(1), 7–21.

Rogowski, S (2015) From child welfare to child protection/safeguarding: a critical practitioner's view of changing conceptions, policies and practice. *Practice,* 27(2), 97–112.

Rogowski, S (2016) *Social Work with Children and Families: Reflections of a Critical Practitioner*. London: Routledge.

Rose, ME (1971) *The English Poor Law: 1780–1930*. Newton Abbot: David & Charles.

Royal Commission on Long-Term Care for the Elderly (1998) *With Respect to Old Age: Long-term Care – Rights and Responsibilities*, Cm 4912-I. London: HMSO.

Roycroft-Davies, C (2011) We must establish order –with the Army if necessary: Editorial. *The Express*, 10 August.

Rutherford, T (2013) *Historical Rates of Social Security Benefits*. House of Commons Library, Standard Note 6762. http://researchbriefings.files.parliament.uk/documents/SN06762/SN06762.pdf.

Rutter, J (2015) *Childcare Costs Survey, 2015*. Family and Childcare Trust. www.familyandchildcaretrust.org/sites/default/files/files/Childcare_cost_survey_2015_Final.pdf.

Samuel, M (2010a) Social care news. *Community Care*, 21 October.

Samuel, M (2010b) The doubts remain. *Community Care*, 20 May.

Scarman, Lord (1981) *The Brixton Disorders, 10–12 April 1981*, Cmnd 8427. London: HMSO.

Scourfield, P (2005) Implementing the Community Care (Direct Payments) Act: will the supply of personal assistants meet the demand and at what price? *Journal of Social Policy*, 34(3), 469–88.

Scourfield, P (2006) Helping older people in residential care remain full citizens. *British Journal of Social Work*, 37(7), 1135–52.

Scourfield, P (2007) Social care and the modern citizen: client, consumer, service user, manager and entrepreneur. *British Journal of Social Work*, 37(1), 107–22.

Shaw, V (2016) One in three millennial graduates 'regret going to university because of debt'. *The Independent*, 10 August.

Shier, ML and Graham, JR (2015) Subjective well-being, social work, and the environment: the impact of the socio-political context of practice on social worker happiness. *Journal of Social Work*, 15(1), 3–23.

Shipman, T (2011) Left-wing cynics blame the Tory cuts for the orgy of violence: MPs and activists line up to make excuses for thugs. *The Mail*, 9 August.

Shoesmith, S (2016) *Learning from Baby P: The Politics of Blame, Fear and Denial*. London: Jessica Kingsley.

Skott-Myhre, HA (2005) Captured by capital: youth work and the loss of revolutionary potential. *Child and Youth Care Forum*, 34(2), 141–57.

Sloan, A and Allison, E (2015) Sharp rise in proportion of black and minority ethnic prisoners. *Guardian*, 24 June.

Smith, M (1946) Unwanted children scandal: the full facts. *Daily Mail*, 16 October.

Smith, R (2008) *Social Work with Young People*. London: Wiley.

Social Mobility and Child Poverty Commission (2014) *Elitist Britain*. https://www.gov.uk/government/uploads/system/uploads/attachment_data/file/347915/Elitist_Britain_-_Final.pdf.

Social Mobility and Child Poverty Commission (2015) *State of the Nation 2015: Social Mobility and Child Poverty in GB*. https://www.gov.uk/government/uploads/system/uploads/attachment_data/file/485926/State_of_the_nation_2015__social_mobility_and_child_poverty_in_Great_Britain.pdf.

Social Work Action Network (2009) *A Radical Campaigning Network within Social Work*. www.socialworkfuture.org/.

Spandler, H (2004) Friend or foe? Towards a critical assessment of direct payments. *Critical Social Policy*, 24(2), 187–209.

Spandler, H and Vick, N (2005) Enabling access to direct payments: an exploration of care coordinators' decision-making practices. *Journal of Mental Health*, 14(2), 145–55.

Sparrow, A (2011a) Ministers hid evidence over benefits cap. *Observer*, 4 July.

Sparrow, A (2011b) Nick Clegg defends government response to London riots. *Guardian*, 8 August.

Spinks, J (2015) Charities highlight lack of action since Winterbourne View. *Learning Disability Practice*, 17(6), 7.

Stainton, T, Boyce, S and Phillips, CJ (2009) Independence pays: a cost and resource analysis of direct payments in two local authorities. *Disability and Society*, 24(2), 161–72.

Starkey, P (1998) The medical officer of health, the social worker , and the problem family. 1943–1968: The case of family service units. *Social History of Medicine*, 11(3), 421–41.

Stevens, J (2015) 500,000 problem families cost us £30 billion a year. *Daily Mail*, 18 August.

Stevens, M, Moriarty, J, Manthorpe, J, Hussein, S, Sharpe, E, Orme, J, Mcyntyre, J, Cavanagh, K, Green-Lister, P and Crisp, BR (2010) Helping others or a rewarding career? Investigating student motivations to train as social workers in England. *Journal of Social Work*, 29(6) 584–5.

Stevenson, L (2015) Are child protection thresholds too high? *Community Care*, 10 September. http://www.communitycare.co.uk/2015/09/10/child-protection-thresholds-high/.

Sweden.se (2016) *Elderly Care in Sweden*. https://sweden.se/society/elderly-care-in-sweden/.

Swinford, S (2011) Punches, slaps and abuse in care home 'campaign of cruelty'. *The Telegraph*, 1 June.

Tawney, RH (1964) *Equality*, 4th edn. London: George Allen & Unwin.

Taylor Gooby, P (1994) Postmodernism and social policy: a great leap backwards? *Journal of Social Policy*, 23(3), 385–404.

Taylor, A (2016) *Youth Unemployment Statistics*, House of Commons Library Briefing Paper, 17 August. http://researchbriefings.files.parliament.uk/documents/SN05871/SN05871.pdf.

Taylor, W (1904) Memorandum for the physical deterioration committee on the state of army recruits. In *Inter-departmental Committee on Physical Deterioration: Volume 1: Report and Appendix*, Cm 2175. London: HMSO, pp956.

Telegraph, The (2012a) Six Winterbourne carers jailed, 27 October.

Telegraph, The (2012b) Winterbourne View: criminal law to hold care owners to account. 10 December.

Thane, P (1996) *Foundations of the Welfare State*. London: Longman.

Thane, P (2000) *Old Age in English History: Past Experiences and Present Issues*. Oxford: Oxford University Press.

Thatcher, M (1983) Speech to Glasgow Chamber of Commerce (bicentenary), 28 January. www.margaretthatcher.org/speeches/displaydocument.asp?docid=105244.

Thompson, EP (1972) *The Making of the English Working Class*. Harmondsworth: Penguin.

Times, The (2008) Poverty and dignity: Editorial. 21 November.

Timmins, N (1996) *The Five Giants: A Biography of the Welfare State*. London: Fontana Press.

Titmuss, RM (1950) *Problems of Social Policy*. London: HMSO/Longmans.

Titmuss, RM (1966) *Essays on the Welfare State*. London: Unwin University Books.

Titmuss, RM (1973) *Commitment to Welfare*. London: George Allen & Unwin.

Townsend, P (1962) The meaning of poverty. *British Journal of Sociology*, 13(3), 210–27.

Townsend, P (1964) *The Last Refuge. A Survey of Residential Institutions and Homes for the Aged in England and Wales*. London: Routledge & Kegan Paul.

Toynbee, P (2008) This frenzy of hatred is a disaster for children at risk. *Guardian*, 18 November.

Trades Union Congress (2013) *Nearly Seven Million Grandparents Provide Regular Childcare*. Press Release, 13 December. https://www.tuc.org.uk/workplace-issues/employment-rights/working-time-holidays/work-life-balance/nearly-seven-million.

Travis, A (2015) Oliver Letwin blocked help for black youth after 1985 riots. *Guardian*, 30 December.

Trussell Trust (2016) *Trussell Trust Foodbank Use Remains at Record High*. https://www.trusselltrust.org/news-and-blog/latest-stats/.

Tunley, M (2011) Counterblast: another case of old wine in new bottles? The Coalition's misguided strategy to reduce benefit fraud. *Howard Journal*, 50(3), 314–17.

Turbett, C (2014) *Doing Radical Social Work*. Basingstoke: Palgrave Macmillan.

UK Children's Commissioners (2015) *Report of the UK's Children's Commissioners: UN Committee on the Rights of the Child: Examination of the Fifth Periodic Report of the United Kingdom of Great Britain and Northern Ireland.* https://www.childrenscommissioner.gov.uk/sites/default/files/publications/UNCRC%20final_0.pdf.

UK Government (2016a) *Unpaid Parental Leave.* https://www.gov.uk/parental-leave/overview

UK Government (2016b) Jobseekers Allowance. https://www.gov.uk/jobseekers-allowance/overview.

UN Committee on the Elimination of Racial Discrimination (2016) *Concluding Observations on the Twenty-first to Twenty-third Periodic Reports of United Kingdom.* Geneva: UN.

UN Committee on the Rights of Persons with Disabilities (2016) *Report of the Committee: UK.* Geneva: UNCRPD.

UN Committee on the Rights of the Child (2016) *Concluding Observations on the Fifth Periodic Report of the United Kingdom of Great Britain and Northern Ireland.* www.google.co.uk/url?sa=t&rct=j&q=&esrc=s&source=web&cd=2&cad=rja&uact=8&ved=0ahUKEwiT39_506DQAhWFbBoKHRXeCQ4QFggjMAE&url=http%3A%2F%2Ftbinternet.ohchr.org%2FTreaties%2FCRC%2FShared%2520Documents%2FGBR%2FCRC_C_GBR_CO_5_24195_E.docx&usg=AFQjCNHi_oqVOrowa05YahWfIGb63AZeVA.

Ungerson, C (1997) Give them the money: is cash the route to empowerment? *Social Policy and Administration,* 31(1), 45–53.

Ungerson, C (2006) Direct payments and the employment relationship: some insights from cross national research. In Leece, J and Bornat, J (eds) *Developments in Direct Payments.* Bristol: Policy Press.

UNICEF (2000) *A League Table of Child Poverty in Rich Nations.* Florence: UNICEF.

UNICEF (2005) *Child Poverty in Rich Countries.* Florence: UNICEF.

UNICEF (2007) *An Overview of Child Well-being in Rich Countries.* Florence: UNICEF.

UNICEF (2013) *Child Well-being in Rich Countries: A Comparative Overview.* Florence: UNICEF.

UNICEF (2016) *Fairness for Children: A League Table of Inequality in Child Well-being in Rich Nations.* Florence: UNICEF.

UNISON (2011) *Private Practices for Social Workers: Big Con Trick,* UNISON Briefing and Advice to Branches. www.unison.org.uk/acrobat/briefing_on_social_workpercent20practices.pdf.

UNISON (2014) *Government Leaves Backdoor Route into Child Protection for Profit,* Press Release, 26 June. https://www.unison.org.uk/news/article/2014/06/government-leaves-backdoor-route-into-child-protection-for-profit-making-companies/.

UNISON (2015) *An Austerity Audit: Coalition Cuts to Local Communities in England since 2010.* https://www.unison.org.uk/content/uploads/2015/05/On-line-Catalogue23139.pdf.

United Nations (2013) *Report of the Special Rapporteur on Adequate Housing as a Component of the Right to an Adequate Standard of Living, and on the Right to Non-discrimination in this Context*. www.ohchr.org/EN/HRBodies/HRC/RegularSessions/Session25/Documents/A_HRC_25_54_Add.2_ENG.DOC.

Utley, T (2014) Clearing a blocked sink at 1am in a beer can strewn kitchen: I don't feel one of the hated elite. *Daly Mail*, 29 August.

Vincent, J (1995) *Inequality and Old Age*. Florence, KY: Routledge.

Vincent, J (1999) *Politics, Power and Old Age*. Buckingham: Open University Press.

Vincent, J (2003) *Old Age*. London: Routledge.

Walker, P (2012) Anti-disabled abuse fuelled by benefits cuts. *Guardian*, 6 February 2012.

Waller, P (1981) Liverpool: why the clue to violence is economic not racial. *The Times*, 7 July, p12

Wanless, D (2006) *Securing Good Care for Older People: Taking a Long Term View*. London: King's Fund.

Warner, J (2013) Social work, class politics and risk in the moral panic over Baby P. *Health, Risk and Society*, 15(3), 217–23.

Warner, J (2014) 'Heads must roll'? Emotional politics, the press and the death of Baby P. *British Journal of Social Work*, 44(6), 1637–53.

Waugh, MJ, Robbins, I, Davies, S and Feigenbaum, J (2007) The long-term impact of war experiences and evacuation on people who were children during World War Two. *Aging and Mental Health*, 11(2), 168–74.

Webb, S (2010) *Dramatic Rise in Pensioners as Baby Boomers Enter Golden Years*. Press Release, 21 September. https://www.gov.uk/government/news/dramatic-rise-in-pensioners-as-baby-boomers-enter-golden-years.

Webster, D (2016) *The DWP's JSA/ESA Sanctions Statistics Release*, 17 February. www.google.co.uk/url?sa=t&rct=j&q=&esrc=s&source=web&cd=1&cad=rja&uact=8&ved=0ahUKEwip-sTV9rvNAhWkA8AKHUmcClIQFgghMAA&url=http%3A%2F%2Fwww.cpag.org.uk%2Fsites%2Fdefault%2Ffiles%2Fuploads%2F16-02%2520Sanctions%2520Stats%2520Briefing%2520-%2520D%2520Webster%2520Feb%25202016.docx&usg=AFQjCNGfvCwvgdtvCweNXX-gqvfJ6PD1Hg

Weinstein, J (2014) *Mental Health*. Bristol: Policy Press.

Welshman, J (1999) The social history of social work: the issue of the problem family, 1940–1970. *British Journal of Social Work*, 29(3), 457–76.

Welshman, J (2010) *Churchill's Children: The Evacuee Experience in Wartime Britain*. Oxford: University Press.

Welshman, J (2013) *Underclass: A History of the Excluded since 1880*, 2nd edn. London: Bloomsbury.

Whelan, R (2001) *Helping the Poor: Friendly Visiting, Dole Charities and Dole Queues*. London: CIVITAS.

Wilding, P (1983) The evolution of social administration. In Bean, P and MacPherson, S (eds) *Approaches to Welfare*. London: Routledge & Kegan Paul.

Wilkinson, R and Pickett, K (2010) *The Spirit Level*. London: Penguin.

Williams, F (1989) *Social Policy: A Critical Introduction*. Cambridge: Polity Press.

Williams, F (1992) Somewhere over the rainbow: universality and diversity in social policy. In Manning, N and Page, R (eds) *Social Policy Review 4*. Canterbury: Social Policy Association.

Wilson, H (1971) *The Labour Government, 1964–1970: A Personal Record*. London: Weidenfield & Nicolson.

Wilson, W (2016) *The Benefits Cap*, House of Commons Library Briefing Paper No. 06294. http://researchbriefings.files.parliament.uk/documents/SN06294/SN06294.pdf.

Wittenburg, R and Hu, B (2015) *Projections of Demand for and Costs of Social Care for Older People and Younger Adults in England, 2015 to 2035*. London: LSE. www.pssru.ac.uk/pdf/DP2900.pdf.

Wolfe, I, MacFarlane, A, Donkin, A, Marmot, M and Viner, R (2014) *Why Children Die: Death in Infants, Children and Young People in the UK, Part A*. www.rcpch.ac.uk/sites/default/files/page/Death%20in%20infants,%20children%20and%20young%20people%20in%20the%20UK.pdf.

Wollard, C (2015) Fury as council plan to shut more learning disability centres. *The Herald*, 19 January.

Women's Group on Public Welfare (1943) *Our Towns: A Close Up*. London: Oxford University Press.

Wootton, B (1959) *Social Science and Social Pathology*. London: George Allen & Unwin.

World Bank (2010) *The World's Top 100 Economies*. http://siteresources.worldbank.org/INTUWM/Resources/WorldsTop100Economies.pdf

World Bank (2016) *Health Expenditure, Total (GDP)*. http://data.worldbank.org/indicator/SH.XPD.TOTL.ZS

World Economic Forum (2015) *The Global Competitiveness Report, 2015–16*. http://reports.weforum.org/global-competitiveness-report-2015-2016/competitiveness-rankings/.

Wright, O (2012) Government powerless to stop large multinational companies like Starbucks and Google paying almost no tax on UK profits. *The Independent*, 5 November.

Wyn, J and White, R (1997) *Rethinking Youth*. London: Sage.

YMCA England (2014) *YMCA England's Response to the Work and Pensions Committee Inquiry into 'Benefit Sanctions Policy Beyond the Oakley Review'*. www.ymca.org.uk/wp-content/uploads/2016/07/Benefit-sanctions-policy-Dec-2014.pdf.

YouGov (2015) *Survey Results: Young People's Behavior.* http://cdn.yougov.com/cumulus_uploads/document/b31iil8e7h/InternalResults_150227_16-24_year_olds_W.pdf.

Young, AF and Ashton, ET (1956) *British Social Work in the Nineteenth Century.* London: Routledge & Kegan Paul.

Younge, G (2011) These riots were political: they were looting, not shoplifting. *Guardian*, 14 August.

Younghusband, E (1978) *Social Work in Britain, 1950–1975: A Follow Up Study.* London: George Allen & Unwin.

Youth Justice Board/Ministry of Justice (2016) *Youth Justice Statistics, 2014/15.* https://www.gov.uk/government/uploads/system/uploads/attachment_data/file/495708/youth-justice-statistics-2014-to-2015.pdf.

Zayed, Y and Harker, R (2015) *Children in Care in England: Statistics*, House of Commons Library Briefing Paper No. 04470. http://researchbriefings.files.parliament.uk/documents/SN04470/SN04470.pdf.

Index